# CONSTITUTIONAL AND ADMINISTRATIVE LAW AND EU LAW

The
University of
Law

# CONSTITUTIONAL AND ADMINISTRATIVE LAW AND EU LAW

## FIFTH EDITION

Trevor Tayleur

This edition published 2025 by
The University of Law
2 Bunhill Row
London EC1Y 8HQ



British Library Cataloguing in Publication Data

A catalogue record for this book is available from the British Library.

ISBN 978 1 80502 257 2

# Preface

This book is part of a series of Study Manuals that have been specially designed to support the reader to achieve the SQE1 Assessment Specification in relation to Functioning Legal Knowledge. Each Study Manual aims to provide the reader with a solid knowledge and understanding of fundamental legal principles and rules, including how those principles and rules might be applied in practice.

This Study Manual covers the Solicitors Regulation Authority's syllabus for the SQE1 assessment for Constitutional and Administrative Law and EU Law in a concise and tightly focused manner. The Manual provides a clear statement of relevant legal rules and a well-defined road map through examinable law and practice. The Manual aims to bring the law and practice to life through the use of example scenarios based on realistic client-based problems and allows the reader to test their knowledge and understanding through single best answer questions that have been modelled on the SRA's sample assessment questions.

For those readers who are students at the University of Law, the Study Manual is used alongside other learning resources and the University's assessment bank to best prepare students not only for the SQE1 assessments, but also for a future life in professional legal practice.

We hope that you find the Study Manual supportive of your preparation for SQE1 and we wish you every success.

The legal principles and rules contained within this Manual are stated as at 1 May 2025.

**Author acknowledgments**
Trevor would like to thank Savvas Michael for reviewing and commenting on the content of chapters and sample questions and Nancy Duffield and Gary Atkinson for their source materials; their input was invaluable. Thanks must also go to David Stott for his editorial support and guidance.

# Contents

# Table of Cases

**R**

# Table of Statutes

# 1 Constitutional Fundamentals and Sources of the Constitution



## SQE1 syllabus

This chapter will enable you to achieve the SQE1 assessment specification in relation to functioning legal knowledge concerned with core constitutional principles, including:

- the role of constitutional conventions; and
- prerogative power: relationship with legislation and constitutional conventions.

Note that for SQE1, candidates are not usually required to recall specific case names or cite statutory or regulatory authorities. Cases are provided for illustrative purposes only.

## Learning outcomes

By the end of this chapter you will be able to understand and apply some fundamental constitutional principles appropriately and effectively, at the level required of a competent newly qualified solicitor in practice, to realistic client-based problems and situations, including the ability to:

- explain the meaning of the word 'constitution' and understand the ways in which a constitution may be classified or described;
- appreciate the key principles upon which the UK constitution is based;
- explain the diverse sources of the UK constitution, including constitutional conventions;
- understand the distinctions between the 'legal' and 'non-legal' sources of the UK constitution; and
- understand the relationship between the royal prerogative and constitutional conventions.

## 1.1 What is a constitution?

Constitutions are used in many types of organisation (for example political parties, clubs and societies) to establish the fundamental rules and principles by which the organisation is governed. A political constitution deals with the entire organisation of a state and how its legal order is established. It will also give effect to the values that society regards as important.

For our purposes, a constitution will usually define a state's fundamental political principles, establish the framework of the government of the state, and guarantee certain rights and freedoms to the citizens. The fundamental political principles of a state will be the key political ideas or doctrines on which the state is based. The framework of government will set out the powers and duties of the executive, legislative and judicial branches of the state (see **1.3.2** below). The rights and freedoms of citizens will be those basic rights and freedoms which it is agreed all citizens of the state should enjoy (for example, the right to free speech, or the right to vote in free elections).

## 1.2 Classifying constitutions

Although we can identify what the basic elements of a constitution are, the constitution of a state may be classified or described in a number of different ways. The 'classification' of a constitution means identifying what the most important features of that particular constitution are. The following paragraphs explain how constitutions can be classified and how the UK constitution is usually classified.

### 1.2.1 Written/unwritten

A state with a written or codified constitution will have its constitution set out in a single document. This document will contain the fundamental laws of the constitution and define the powers of the different branches of state. It may also contain a Bill of Rights setting out the fundamental civil liberties to be enjoyed by citizens of the state.

A state with an unwritten or uncodified constitution will not have its constitution set out in a single authoritative document. Rather the constitution will be made up of a number of different sources, such as statute and case law.

Unlike most countries, the UK has an unwritten constitution in the sense that there is no single authoritative written document that sets out how the government should operate and what the rights of individual citizens are. Rather, the UK constitution is made up of a variety of different sources, which you will examine in detail later in this chapter.

### 1.2.2 Republican/monarchical

A state with a republican constitution will usually have a president (often elected directly or indirectly) as its head of state. A state with a monarchical constitution will have an unelected monarch as head of state (although the monarch's role may be largely ceremonial).

The UK has a monarchical constitution. The head of state is the Monarch, who is unelected and head of state by virtue of their position within the royal family. As you will see later, however, in practice the Monarch exercises little real power. Most of their powers are, by convention, exercised by the government on their behalf.

### 1.2.3 Federal/unitary

A state with a federal constitution will have a division of power between the central government and regional government. A state with a unitary constitution will have a single sovereign legislative body, with power being concentrated at the centre.

The constitution of the UK is unitary. The Parliament at Westminster is the supreme (or sovereign) law-making body, and other law-making bodies within the UK (such as the Scottish Parliament or local authorities) derive their law-making powers from powers they have been given by the Westminster Parliament. However, some commentators argue that, as a result of devolution, the UK constitution now exhibits some quasi-federal characteristics. As further powers are devolved, this argument is likely to take on increasing strength.

### 1.2.4 Rigid/flexible

A state that has a rigid constitution has a constitution that is said to be 'entrenched'. This means that the constitution may be changed only by following a special procedure. Most states with written constitutions tend to be rigid. A state that has a flexible constitution has a constitution that is comparatively easy to change because no special procedures are necessary for the constitution to be amended.

As a result of being unwritten, the UK constitution is flexible. Although from a political point of view it may often be difficult to amend the constitution as some principles attract widespread adherence across the political spectrum, legally it is possible to change the constitution quite easily because there are no lengthy or complex procedures to follow.

### 1.2.5 Formal separation of powers/informal separation of powers

A state that has a formal separation of powers has a clear separation both of functions and of personnel between the executive (ie the government), the legislative (ie the parliament) and the judicial (ie the courts) branches of state. A state that has an informal separation of powers is likely to have a significant degree of overlap in terms of functions and personnel between the executive, the legislative and the judicial branches of state.

The UK constitution has a largely informal separation of powers. Although it is possible to identify the executive, legislative and judicial branches of state, no formal mechanism exists to keep them separate, and there is a degree of overlap between them both in terms of function and personnel. There is little formal separation of powers under the UK constitution because there is no written constitution to strictly separate the membership and functions of each branch of state from other branches of state.

## 1.3 Core constitutional principles

Before you consider the detailed sources of the UK constitution, you need to be familiar with the core principles on which the UK constitution is based. These principles are:

(a) the rule of law;

(b) the separation of powers; and

(c) the sovereignty (or supremacy) of Parliament.

In this section you will briefly consider the rule of law, the separation of powers and the sovereignty of Parliament, but you will study them in more depth in later chapters.

### 1.3.1 The rule of law

You will study this in more detail in **Chapter 4**. Its key elements, though, can be summarised as follows:

- There should be no arbitrary exercise of power by the state or government – all actions of the state or government must be permitted by the law.
- Laws should be made properly, following a set procedure.

- Laws should be clear - laws should be set out clearly and be accessible, and a citizen should be punished only for a clearly defined breach of the law.
- Laws should be certain - laws should not operate retrospectively and a citizen should not be punished for an act that was not a crime at the time they carried out that act.
- There should be equality before the law - all citizens should have equal access to the legal process for the redress of grievances, and the law should treat all persons in the same way (for example, the law should not provide special exemptions or 'get-outs' for government officials).
- The judiciary should be independent and impartial - the courts should be sufficiently independent from the legislature and the executive so that judges can uphold the law without fear of repercussions from the other branches of state.

### 1.3.2 The separation of powers

You will also study this in more detail in **Chapter 4**. Its essence is that there are three branches of government:

(a) the legislature (or parliament) - the body that makes the law. In the UK the legislature (Parliament) comprises the Monarch, the House of Lords and the House of Commons;

(b) the executive (or government) - the body that implements the law. In the UK the executive is made up of the Monarch, the Prime Minister and other government ministers, the civil service, and the members of the police and armed forces; and

(c) the judiciary (or courts) - the body that resolves disputes about the law. The judicial branch of state is made up of the Monarch, all legally qualified judges, and magistrates (non-legally qualified members of the public who deal with some criminal matters).

As a result of the complex way in which modern states work, it is unrealistic for each branch of state to be kept completely separate from the others. Most constitutions have therefore developed the concept of 'checks and balances'. The idea behind this is that each branch of state is kept in check by powers given to the other branches, so that no one branch of state may exert an excessive amount of power or influence. In **Chapter 4** you will consider the extent of the separation of powers in the UK in more depth.

### 1.3.3 The sovereignty of Parliament

You saw in **1.2.3** that the UK has a unitary constitution, with the Westminster Parliament being the supreme law-making body. The doctrine of the supremacy (or sovereignty) of Parliament is central to an understanding of how the UK constitution operates.

Parliamentary sovereignty (or supremacy) is a common law doctrine accepted by the judiciary, under which the courts acknowledge that legislation enacted by Parliament takes precedence over the common law. Basically it means that Parliament can pass any law that it wants to, though you will see in **Chapter 2**, when you consider the principle in more depth, that there may be limitations on its sovereignty.

## 1.4 Sources of the UK constitution

The constitution of the UK is not set out in a single written document. Rather, the UK constitution is unwritten and has a variety of different sources. It is helpful to think of it as being like a jigsaw - it is made up of a variety of different parts, and only when those parts are pieced together can the constitution as a whole be understood.

In this section, you will consider the different sources of the UK constitution. There are four principal sources:

(a) Acts of Parliament;

(b) case law;

(c) the royal prerogative; and

(d) constitutional conventions.

Each source will be considered in turn.

### 1.4.1 Acts of Parliament

Although our constitution is said to be unwritten, many important aspects of it are located in various statutes that Parliament has enacted.

**Magna Carta 1215:** This has symbolic value as the first assertion of the limits on the powers of the Monarch and of the rights of individuals. Magna Carta was extracted from King John by his feudal lords and guaranteed certain rights to 'freemen of the realm', including trial by jury.

Magna Carta embodies the principle that government must be conducted according to the law and with the consent of the governed. It established the principle that no one is above the law and compelled King John to renounce certain rights, respect specified legal procedures and accept that his will could be bound by the law. It also introduced the right to protection from unlawful imprisonment

**Bill of Rights 1689:** This imposed limitations on the powers of the Crown (ie the Monarch) and its relationship with Parliament. The Bill of Rights removed the power of the Monarch arbitrarily to suspend Acts of Parliament and the power of the Monarch to impose taxation without Parliament's consent.

The Bill of Rights also provided that Parliament should meet on a regular basis, elections to Parliament should be free from interference by the Monarch, and 'freedom of speech and debates in proceedings in Parliament ought not to be impeached or questioned in any court or place out of Parliament' (see **Chapter 2**).

**Acts of Union 1706–07:** These united England and Scotland under a single Parliament of Great Britain (the Parliament at Westminster). They also contained provisions to preserve the separate Scottish church and legal system (see **Chapter 2**).

**Parliament Acts 1911 and 1949:** The Parliament Acts altered the relationship between the House of Lords and the House of Commons. These Acts ensured that the will of the elected House of Commons would prevail over that of the unelected House of Lords by enabling legislation to be enacted without the consent of the House of Lords (see **Chapters 2 and 3**).

**Police and Criminal Evidence Act 1984:** This Act is relevant to civil liberties. It provides the police with extensive powers of arrest, search and detention, but also contains important procedural safeguards to ensure that the police do not abuse such powers.

**Public Order Act 1986:** This Act is also relevant to civil liberties. It allows limitations to be placed on the rights of citizens to hold marches and meetings in public places.

**Human Rights Act 1998:** The Human Rights Act 1998 (HRA 1998) incorporates the European Convention on Human Rights (ECHR) into our domestic law. It marks a fundamental change in the protection of human rights by allowing citizens to raise alleged breaches of their human rights before domestic courts (see **Chapters 2 and 9**).

**Acts of devolution** (eg Scotland Act 1998): The Acts of devolution created a devolved system of government in various parts of the UK. Acts establishing a Scottish Parliament, the Senedd Cymru or Welsh Parliament and the Northern Ireland Assembly have decentralised the process of government and given greater autonomy to these parts of the UK (see **Chapter 3**).

**Constitutional Reform Act 2005:** This Act reformed the office of Lord Chancellor, transferring the Lord Chancellor's powers as head of the judiciary to the Lord Chief Justice and permitting the House of Lords to elect its own Speaker. It also provided for the creation of a Supreme Court (to replace the Appellate Committee of the House of Lords) and created a new body (the Judicial Appointments Commission) to oversee the appointment of judges (see **Chapter 4**).

**European Union (Withdrawal) Act 2018 and European Union (Withdrawal Agreement) Act 2020:** These Acts provided for the UK's departure from the European Union ('Brexit'). The European Union (Withdrawal) Act 2018 repealed the European Communities Act 1972 (ECA 1972), which had paved the way for the UK's membership of the European Union. It also ended the supremacy of EU law and introduced into the UK's legal systems the concept of retained EU law/assimilated law (see **Chapter 10**).

Although the above Acts are of great constitutional importance, each was enacted by Parliament in the same way as any other Act of Parliament. No special procedure or majority was required. Similarly, these Acts are not 'entrenched'. In other words, each Act may be repealed by an ordinary Act of Parliament, just as with any other statute. No special procedure is required for its repeal. However, as you will see later, some recent Acts of Parliament, such as the Scotland Act 2016, contain provisions stating that Parliament will not legislate to achieve certain aims without first holding a referendum on the relevant issue.

As a result of having an unwritten constitution, in strictly legal terms, it is easy for Parliament to make significant changes to the constitution. In the absence of a written constitution setting out a 'higher' form of law against which all other legislation may be judged (and also as a result of the development of the doctrine of parliamentary sovereignty), Parliament may enact such legislation as it wishes and our courts cannot strike down such legislation as being unconstitutional. Factors that limit Parliament's ability to change the constitution tend to be more political, economic or social as opposed to strictly legal. You will consider this further in **Chapter 2**.

### 1.4.2 Case law

#### 1.4.2.1 The common law

The common law is an important source of some key principles of our constitution.

(a) Residual freedom

The principle of 'residual freedom' (upon which civil liberties in this country are based) developed through the common law. It means that citizens are free to do or say whatever they wish unless the law (primarily expressed through Acts of Parliament) clearly states that such an action or statement is prohibited.

(b) Actions of the state must have legal authority

It has also been established through the common law that actions taken by state officials (such as police officers) must have a legal basis if they are to be lawful. This again links to the principle of the rule of law and is illustrated by the very significant case of *Entick v Carrington* (1765) 19 St Tr 1030. The Secretary of State issued a general warrant for the arrest and search of Entick, who had allegedly been publishing 'seditious material'. The court found that there was no legal authority that enabled the Secretary of State to issue such general warrants, and so the search was unlawful. The case established the principle that state officials could not act in an arbitrary manner and that the exercise of power by the state had to have clear legal authority.

(c) Legal disputes should be resolved by the judiciary

One of the earliest examples of the common law setting out constitutionally important principles is the *Case of Prohibitions (Prohibitions del Roy)* (1607) 12 Co Rep 63. The case concerned a dispute over land, which the King sought to settle by making a ruling. The court held that the Monarch had no power to decide legal matters by way of arbitrary rulings, and that legal disputes should properly be resolved by the courts. The resolution of legal disputes by the judiciary is another aspect of the rule of law.

(d) Habeas corpus and individual liberty

Although it is now strengthened by statute, the remedy of habeas corpus, whereby an individual who has been detained by the state has the right to have the legality of that detention tested before a court, developed originally through the common law.

(e) Right to a fair hearing

Through the common law, the courts have repeatedly stressed the importance of the right to a fair hearing as a fundamental constitutional principle and an important part of the rule of law. The right to a fair trial is also contained in Art 6 of the ECHR, which now forms part of UK law following the enactment of the HRA 1998.

1.4.2.2 Judicial review of executive actions

In addition to the common law being the source of several important constitutional principles, the courts have also developed the process of 'judicial review'. This is a mechanism that enables the courts to ensure that the Government and other public bodies exercise the powers that they have been granted in the proper way and so do not breach the rule of law. You will consider judicial review in more detail in **Chapters 6 and 7.**

1.4.2.3 The interpretation of statute

In addition to developing important constitutional principles through the common law, the judiciary have also made decisions of constitutional significance when interpreting statute law. A noteworthy example of this is *R (Miller) v Secretary of State for Exiting the European Union* [2017] UKSC 5 (*Miller (No 1)*). In this case, the Supreme Court interpreted the ECA 1972 as preventing the Government from using the royal prerogative (see **1.4.3** below) as the legal basis for the notice of withdrawal from the EU.

### 1.4.3 The royal prerogative

1.4.3.1 Scope of the royal prerogative

The UK Government derives most of its powers from various statutes in which Parliament has given government ministers authority to make decisions or take action in a particular area. In addition, however, some powers that the Government exercises are derived from the royal prerogative.

Dicey defined the royal prerogative as follows: 'the residue of discretionary or arbitrary authority, which at any given time is legally left in the hands of the Crown ... Every act which the government can lawfully do without the authority of an Act of Parliament is done in virtue of this prerogative' (*An Introduction to the Study of the Law of the Constitution*, 1885).

Prerogative powers derive from the common law and are exercised by (or in the name of) the Monarch. The royal prerogative is essentially what remains of the absolute powers that at one time were exercised by the Monarch and that have not been removed by Parliament.

Although there is no definitive list of prerogative powers, the modern extent of the royal prerogative covers the following principal areas:

(a) Foreign affairs:

(i) declarations of war and the deployment of armed forces overseas;

(ii) making treaties; and

(iii) the recognition of foreign states.

(b) Domestic affairs:

   (i) the summoning of Parliament;

   (ii) the appointment and dismissal of the Prime Minister (and other government ministers);

   (iii) the giving of Royal Assent to bills;

   (iv) defence of the realm (ie the deployment of armed forces within the UK);

   (v) the exercise of the prerogatives of pardon and mercy;

   (vi) granting public honours; and

   (vii) the setting up of public bodies to disburse funds made available by Parliament.

Although the Monarch is legally responsible for the exercise of the prerogative powers, most of these powers are by convention exercised by the Prime Minister and other government ministers on the Monarch's behalf.

The ability of the Government to spend money to exercise its prerogative powers does however depend on Parliament's willingness to vote to provide the necessary funds.

You will consider the way in which the Government's exercise of royal prerogative powers may be regulated or controlled by Parliament and the judiciary in **Chapter 4**.

1.4.3.2 The royal prerogative and statute

Acts of Parliament can remove prerogative powers, as the Crown Proceedings Act 1947 shows. This Act abolished the immunity that the Crown previously had in respect of claims against it both in tort and contract. Another more recent example of Parliament removing a prerogative power is the Fixed-term Parliaments Act 2011 (though the Dissolution and Calling of Parliament Act 2022 has now repealed the 2011 Act). The 2011 Act provided for fixed days for polls for parliamentary general elections, and it was envisaged that elections would be held every five years; however, early elections took place in 2017 and 2019. While in force, it removed the power that the Monarch formerly exercised under the royal prerogative to dissolve Parliament at a time of her choosing (by convention, the Monarch would always dissolve Parliament when requested to do so by the Prime Minister).

The position, however, is more complex when an Act does not explicitly override an aspect of the prerogative, but nonetheless covers the same subject matter. In *Attorney General v De Keyser's Royal Hotel* [1920] AC 508, during World War I a hotel was requisitioned by the Government for staff officers. The hotel sought compensation under the Defence Act 1842, which authorised requisitioning and set out a right to compensation. The Government argued it was using the royal prerogative and did not have to pay compensation. The House of Lords stated that the issue depended on the construction of the statute. It might add a statutory power or it might replace (and thus repeal) the prerogative power.

In this case the statute set out limitations and conditions on the exercise of the power of requisitioning. It must have been contrary to the intention of Parliament for a government to avoid these using the royal prerogative. Lord Dunedin stated that 'if the whole ground of something which could be done by the prerogative is covered by the statute, it is the statute that rules'. Lord Atkinson commented that the prerogative had been abridged by statute and so remained in abeyance as long as the statutory power remained in force. This suggests that if the statute were repealed, the prerogative power would revive.

The Court of Appeal reached a contrasting decision in *R v Secretary of State for the Home Department, ex p Northumbria Police Authority* [1989] QB 26. The Home Secretary wanted to supply plastic bullets to local police forces, cutting out the police authorities. He issued circulars to Chief Police Officers inviting them to apply direct for stores if they anticipated any problem with their local police authority. The Northumbria Police Authority argued that, as the Police Act 1964 gave police authorities the power to supply such equipment to police forces, statute conflicted with the prerogative power, so the circulars were unlawful. The court held that under the royal prerogative the Home Secretary had the power to maintain the Queen's Peace and to keep law and order. The court held that the statutory power could co-exist side by side with the prerogative power, as they were not inconsistent. The prerogative would only be curtailed if inconsistent with the statutory powers.

The House of Lords took a similar approach in *R v Secretary of State for the Home Department, ex p Fire Brigades Union* [1995] 2 AC 513 to the one they had taken in the *De Keyser* case. In 1964 the Government had set up a criminal injury compensation scheme under prerogative powers with compensation being assessed on the basis of common law damages. Parliament then passed the Criminal Justice Act 1988, which provided for a new scheme with compensation payable on the same basis. Instead of bringing the Act into force, the Home Secretary introduced under prerogative powers a new tariff-based system which generally provided less compensation. The claimants challenged the legality of the new scheme.

The House of Lords held that the new tariff scheme was unlawful. It was an abuse of the prerogative power to introduce a tariff scheme inconsistent with the statutory scheme approved by Parliament. Statute had restricted the Home Secretary's ability to introduce a prerogative scheme based on inconsistent criteria.

As explained at **1.4.2.3** above, in *Miller (No 1)* the Supreme Court ruled that the ECA 1972 had curtailed the Government's powers with regards to foreign relations. It could not use the prerogative to change domestic law and to nullify rights that Parliament had created by statute. The accepted current position of law is accordingly in line with the principle set out in *De Keyser.*

The Dissolution and Calling of Parliament Act 2022 is an interesting development as it revives the royal prerogative power to dissolve Parliament, as Parliament has legislated to make the prerogative power 'exercisable again' (2022 Act, s 2(1)). While, in line with the principle set out in *De Keyser*, the prerogative power to dissolve Parliament was 'in abeyance' while the Fixed-term Parliaments Act 2011 was in force, it revived upon the repeal of the 2011 Act.

## 1.4.4 Constitutional conventions

Constitutional conventions are a non-legal source of the constitution. Accordingly, the courts will not directly enforce them. Nonetheless, they play a crucial role in the UK constitution and the workings of government.

### 1.4.4.1 Defining a constitutional convention

The sources of the constitution you have considered so far are often said to be its 'legal' sources because they have a clear legal basis. Constitutional conventions are an important 'non-legal' source of the constitution. Marshall and Moodie defined constitutional conventions as: 'rules of constitutional behaviour which are considered to be binding upon those who operate the constitution but which are not enforced by the law courts ... nor by the presiding officers in the House of Commons' (Marshall and Moodie, *Some Problems of the Constitution* (Hutchinson, 1971)).

This definition may be broken down into three parts:

(a) 'rules of constitutional behaviour' – ie how those who perform a role within the constitution should behave;

(b) 'considered to be binding' – ie there should be no deviation from these rules;

(c) 'not enforced' – ie the rules have no legal basis and so will not be enforced by any judicial body.

Constitutional conventions are flexible. As they are 'non-legal', such conventions do not require any particular step or procedure for their creation. Similarly, if a constitutional convention becomes obsolete, it can be dispensed with without any formal steps being taken.

To gain a proper understanding of how the UK constitution works, you need to appreciate the central role played by constitutional conventions. Set out below is a table with some legal rules of the constitution and how in practice their operation is affected by conventions.

**Table 1.1** Legal rules and conventions

| **Legal rule** | | **Convention** |
|---|---|---|
| Royal Assent is required for a bill to become a valid Act of Parliament. The Monarch may refuse to give Royal Assent. | → | The Monarch, on the advice of the Prime Minister, always assents to a bill that has passed through Parliament. |
| The Monarch constitutes part of the executive branch of government. | → | The Monarch acts only on the advice of the Prime Minister and other ministers, and in practice most decisions are taken by the Prime Minister and other ministers themselves. Executive powers are exercised through ministers, who are collectively and individually responsible to Parliament. |
| The Government is the 'Monarch's government', and they can therefore appoint and dismiss its members as they choose. | → | The Monarch must appoint as Prime Minister the person who can command the support of the majority of the House of Commons (nowadays usually an elected party leader successful in a general election). The Monarch must appoint and dismiss ministers on the advice of the Prime Minister, all of whom must be members of the House of Commons or Lords. Most will be members of the Commons. |

1.4.4.2 Important constitutional conventions

Set out below are the most common constitutional conventions in the UK:

(a) The Monarch plays no active role in matters of government, and the legal powers that are vested in the Monarch are exercised on her behalf by the elected government of the day. For example, the Monarch will appoint and dismiss government ministers on the advice of the Prime Minister.

(b) The Monarch, acting on the advice of the Prime Minister, will not refuse Royal Assent to a bill that has been passed by the House of Commons and the House of Lords. If advised by the Prime Minister to assent to a bill, the Monarch will always do so. (Indeed, the last time a Monarch refused Royal Assent was in 1707.)

(c) The Monarch will appoint as Prime Minister the person who is best able to command the confidence of the House of Commons.

(d) All government ministers will be members either of the House of Commons or of the House of Lords, and the Prime Minister (and most other senior government ministers) should be a member of the democratically elected House of Commons rather than the unelected House of Lords. It is now rare for a peer (other than the Leader of the House of Lords) to sit in the cabinet, the appointment in November 2023 of former Prime Minister Lord Cameron as Foreign Secretary providing a departure from the norm.

(e) Individual ministerial responsibility. Government ministers are responsible to Parliament both for the running and proper administration of their respective departments, and also for their personal conduct. There must be no conflict of interest between a minister's public duties and his or her private interests. A minister who breaches this convention should resign. For example, in 1982 the Foreign Secretary, Lord Carrington, resigned following criticism of the administrative failings of his department, which had failed to foresee the Argentine invasion of the Falkland Islands. Ministerial resignations owing to departmental failings are, however, comparatively rare. In contrast, resignations relating to a minister's personal conduct are more frequent. For example, in November 2017 Priti Patel resigned as International Development Secretary after conducting unauthorised meetings with Israeli officials. There is further analysis of this convention at **4.3.4.2** below.

(f) Collective cabinet (or ministerial) responsibility. This constitutional convention has several aspects to it:

  (i) The cabinet is collectively responsible to Parliament for the actions of the Government as a whole, and the Government must retain the confidence of the House of Commons. A government that is defeated on a vote of 'confidence' in the House of Commons must resign (as did the Labour Government when it lost such a vote in 1979).

  (ii) The cabinet must be united in public in support of government policy, and so a cabinet minister must resign if he or she wishes to speak out in public against such policy, as did Robin Cook in 2003, when he wished to voice his opposition to the war in Iraq, and Boris Johnson in July 2018 over Theresa May's Brexit policies.

  (iii) Cabinet discussions must remain secret.

(g) The unelected House of Lords will not reject legislation that gives effect to an important manifesto commitment of the democratically elected Government (the 'Salisbury Convention').

(h) The UK Parliament will normally only legislate on a matter that has been devolved to the Scottish Parliament if the Scottish Parliament has given its consent (the 'Sewel Convention'). Note that this convention was inserted into s 28 of the Scotland Act 1998 by the Scotland Act 2016.

(i) Members of the judiciary do not play an active part in political life.

(j) Ministers and Members of Parliament do not criticise in public individual members of the judiciary.

1.4.4.3 Why have constitutional conventions developed?

Reasons why conventions have developed include:

(a) To limit the wide legal powers of the Monarch without the need for major constitutional upheaval.

It would be unacceptable in a modern democracy for an unelected Monarch to have wide powers, so by convention these powers are now exercised by ministers on the Monarch's behalf. Moreover, if the Monarch were to disregard these conventions (outlined at **1.4.4.2** (a)–(c) above), serious constitutional difficulties would arise. For example, there would be a constitutional crisis were the Monarch ever to refuse Royal Assent to a bill that had passed the Commons and Lords. Further, there would be legislative deadlock if the Monarch failed to appoint as Prime Minister someone who could command the confidence of the House of Commons.

(b) To ensure that the Government is accountable to Parliament for its actions.

Individual ministerial responsibility ensures that government ministers are held to account for their actions and do not abuse their powers. Collective cabinet responsibility ensures that the Government as a whole must retain the confidence of Parliament, and can be held to account by Parliament for its actions.

(c) To maintain the separation of powers between the different branches of state.

The convention that members of the judiciary do not play an active role in politics helps to preserve judicial independence. Similarly, the convention that ministers and MPs do not criticise individual members of the judiciary also helps to preserve this.

#### 1.4.4.4 Constitutional conventions and the courts

As you have seen, constitutional conventions differ from laws because they are non-legal rules and so are not enforceable by the courts. The Supreme Court reaffirmed this in *Miller (No 1)* (above). The Court emphasised that this was because conventions operated in the political sphere alone. It also stated that including reference to the Sewel Convention in statute had not turned it into a legal rule. Thus, despite the fact that triggering Article 50 might breach the Sewel Convention, there would be no legal remedy.

This does not, however, mean that constitutional conventions have no legal significance. In *Carltona Ltd v Commissioners of Works* [1943] 2 All ER 560, the Minister of Works had delegated emergency powers to requisition property to a civil servant. Owners of a factory requisitioned in this way applied for judicial review of the decision, arguing that the minister himself should have taken the decision. The Court of Appeal recognised that under the convention of ministerial responsibility the minister was accountable to Parliament for this decision.

As the *Carltona* case shows, courts will acknowledge the existence of conventions, and conventions may indirectly give rise to legal consequences that the courts will recognise. However, if Parliament passes an Act that breaches a convention, the Act might be unconstitutional, but the courts will not refuse to apply it for that reason.

In December 2010 the Government published for the first time a Ministerial Code setting out the main laws, rules and conventions affecting the conduct and operation of government. Accordingly, many of the conventions described in this chapter have been set out in written form. However, the Ministerial Code is not intended to have any legal effect but instead to provide guidance to ministers and officials.

The Code also provides that ministers who knowingly mislead Parliament will be expected to offer their resignation to the Prime Minister. Whilst this does not explicitly cover the Prime Minister, opposition politicians called on the then Prime Minister, Boris Johnson, to resign over the so-called 'Partygate' affair, arising out of gatherings held at 10 Downing Street, the official residence and the office of the Prime Minister, while Covid-19 lockdown restrictions were in force. They accused Mr Johnson of deliberately misleading Parliament when he assured Parliament that all rules had been followed. After reports emerged that parties had taken place at 10 Downing Street during lockdown, in December 2021 Mr Johnson set up a Cabinet Office inquiry (chaired by Sue Gray, a very senior civil servant) to investigate whether these gatherings breached Covid-19 restrictions.

As the Metropolitan Police started its own investigation in January 2021, Ms Gray delayed releasing her final report until the police had concluded their investigation. Subsequently, the police issued fixed penalty notices for breach of Covid-19 restrictions, including one on Mr Johnson for a gathering taking place on 19 June 2020. Mr Johnson then apologised to Parliament, stating that it had not occurred to him at the time or subsequently that the gathering could amount to a breach of the rules. Ms Gray then issued her report in which she found that whatever 'the initial intent' many of the gatherings breached Covid-19 restrictions and this should not have happened, irrespective of the pressures that existed at the time. She further concluded that there were 'failures of leadership and judgment in No 10 and the Cabinet Office'.

Mr Johnson initially tried to stay in office, but he resigned as Prime Minister in July 2022 after he had claimed that he was unaware of specific complaints of sexual misconduct made against Chris Pincher MP before appointing him as deputy chief whip of the Conservative Party. However, it then transpired that Mr Johnson had previously been briefed about complaints against Mr Pincher. Mass resignations from the Government forced him to step down.

Additionally, in April 2022, Parliament voted to refer to the Commons Select Committee of Privileges the question of whether the Prime Minister knowingly misled Parliament. In its final report issued in June 2023, the Privileges Committee found that Mr Johnson had committed repeated offences with his Partygate denials and had deliberately misled Parliament. The Committee would have recommended his suspension from Parliament for 90 days if he had not already resigned as an MP. Subsequently MPs voted by 354 votes to 7 to approve the report.

### 1.4.5 Other sources of the constitution

In addition to the sources of the constitution outlined at **1.4.1 to 1.4.4** above, there are some additional, comparatively minor sources of the UK constitution. Such sources include the laws and customs (ie the internal rules and procedures) of Parliament and various academic writings on the UK constitution.

## Summary

The UK constitution is unwritten or uncodified. This means that there is no single document that can be labelled 'the Constitution'. Nonetheless, the UK does have a constitution with diverse sources, in particular:

- Statute: These include statutes of constitutional significance such as the HRA 1998 and the European Union (Withdrawal) Act 2018 (EUWA 2018).
- Case law: Judicial decisions have been responsible for many key constitutional principles, such as the requirement for government actions to have legal authority and the right to a fair trial.
- Royal prerogative: This comprises what is left of the Monarch's arbitrary powers, and has been very substantially curtailed by statute.
- Constitutional conventions: These are a non-legal source of the constitution and aid the operation of the UK constitution.

**Figure 1.1** below summarises these sources.

**Figure 1.1** Sources of the UK constitution

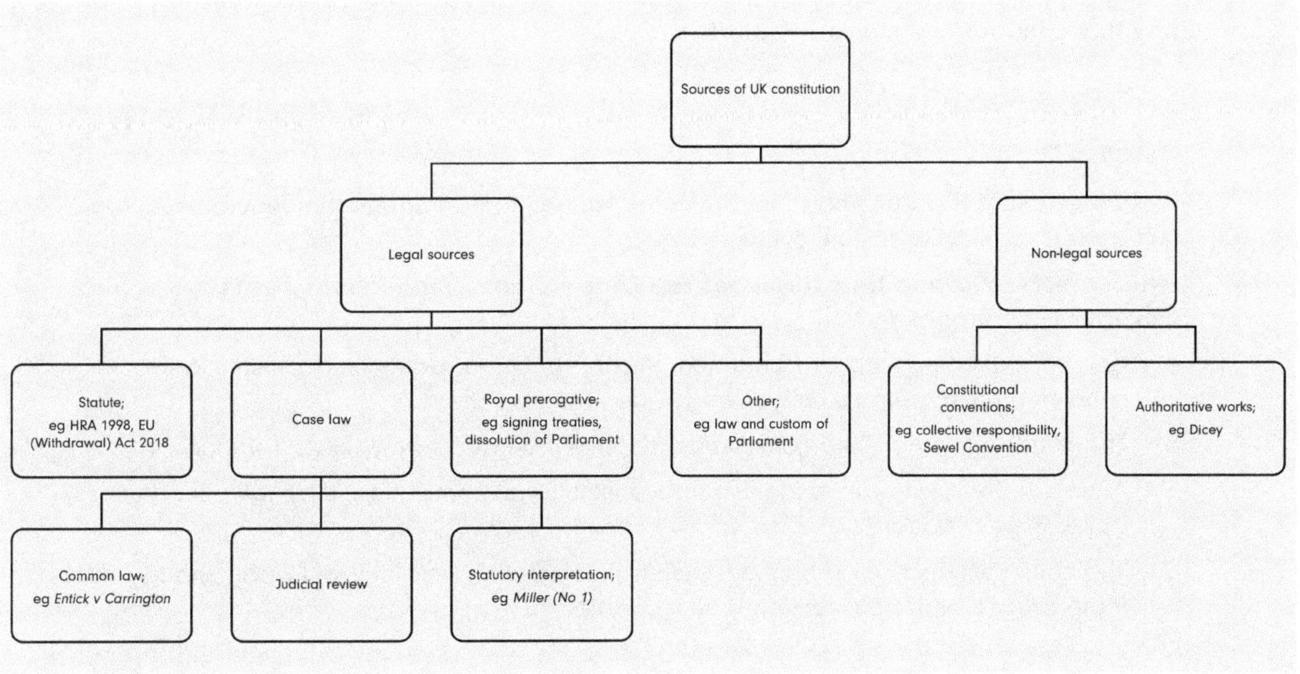

## Sample questions

### Question 1

The Government is considering introducing a compensation scheme for victims of some recent floods.

**Which of the following best describes the options available to the Government in relation to the royal prerogative?**

A In the absence of statutory authority, the Government cannot use prerogative powers.

B By convention the Government should use statutory powers rather than prerogative powers.

C The Government can use prerogative powers to introduce a compensation scheme less generous than an existing statutory scheme.

D In the absence of a statutory scheme, the Government should be able to adopt a non-statutory scheme and raise funds pursuant to its prerogative powers.

E In the absence of a statutory scheme, the Government should be able to adopt a non-statutory scheme pursuant to its prerogative powers, subject to Parliament voting the necessary funds.

### Answer

Option E is correct. The type of scheme proposed in this question is similar to the criminal injuries compensation scheme that was set up using prerogative powers. However, Parliament will need to authorise expenditure, as the Government cannot use the prerogative to authorise expenditure; hence option D is wrong.

Option A is wrong because prerogative powers are by definition non-statutory. In the relatively rare fields where statutory and prerogative powers co-exist, there is no evidence of a convention that the Government should use statutory powers; therefore option B is wrong. Option C is also wrong as the Government cannot use a prerogative power in a way that contradicts a statutory power.

### Question 2

The Government is proposing to introduce legislation in Parliament that would breach a recognised constitutional convention.

**Which of the following best describes the constitutional implications of the Government's proposals?**

A Any legislation passed by Parliament that breaches a recognised constitutional convention risks being struck down by the Supreme Court.

B The courts will ignore the constitutional convention and apply the legislation.

C Although the courts will recognise the constitutional convention, they will nevertheless apply the legislation.

D The courts will recognise the constitutional convention, but they will apply the legislation if the breach of the convention is reasonable.

E It will be illegal for the Government to introduce legislation in Parliament that breaches a recognised constitutional convention.

**Answer**

Option C is correct. Parliament is sovereign and legally can pass any legislation it pleases. The courts will recognise the convention's existence, but this will not stop them applying the legislation.

Option A is wrong because the courts do not have the power to strike down legislation. Option D is wrong as the courts will apply the legislation irrespective of the convention and whether the breach is reasonable or not. Equally, there is no legal limit on the type of legislation that the Government can introduce; hence option E is wrong. On the other hand, the courts will not ignore the convention, so option B is wrong.

**Question 3**

A bill has passed through all stages in Parliament and has been submitted to the Monarch for Royal Assent. The Leader of the Opposition has called on the Monarch to refuse Royal Assent as the bill, on the Government's own admission, breaches international law.

**Will the Monarch refuse Royal Assent?**

A No, because by convention the Monarch always grants Royal Assent to a bill that has been passed by Parliament.

B No, because by law the Monarch must always grant Royal Assent to a bill that has been passed by Parliament.

C Yes, because it is unconstitutional for Parliament to pass a bill that breaches international law.

D Yes, because the bill is invalid due to its breach of international law.

E Yes, because international law is a higher form of law, which the Monarch must obey.

**Answer**

Option A is correct. Indeed, the last time the Monarch refused Royal Assent to a bill was in 1707. Option B is wrong as it is by convention that the Monarch grants Royal Assent; there is no law to that effect. Parliament is sovereign and can pass Acts that breach international law, and there is no precedent for the Monarch to refuse Royal Assent in those circumstances. Hence options D and E are wrong so far as the UK constitution is concerned.

Whilst there might be academic debate whether or not it is 'unconstitutional' for Parliament to breach international law, that will not affect the granting of Royal Assent, so option C is wrong.

# 2 Parliament and Parliamentary Sovereignty



## SQE1 syllabus

This chapter will enable you to achieve the SQE1 assessment specification in relation to functioning legal knowledge concerned with core constitutional principles, including:

- parliament and parliamentary sovereignty;
- parliamentary privilege; and
- powers and procedures for the enactment, implementation and repeal of primary and secondary legislation by Westminster.

Note that for SQE1, candidates are not usually required to recall specific case names or cite statutory or regulatory authorities. Cases are provided for illustrative purposes only.

## Learning outcomes

By the end of this chapter you will be able to understand and apply some fundamental constitutional principles appropriately and effectively, at the level required of a competent newly qualified solicitor in practice, to realistic client-based problems and situations concerned with:

- the role and functions of the UK Parliament;
- the composition of Parliament and the procedure that is followed when legislation is enacted;
- the nature of the relationship between the House of Commons and the House of Lords;
- the doctrine of parliamentary sovereignty;
- the limitations on the operation of parliamentary sovereignty in both a domestic and a European context; and
- parliamentary privilege.

## 2.1 Parliament

Parliament consists of three central elements: the House of Commons, the House of Lords and the Monarch. Of the three elements the House of Commons is the most important. Parliament's main functions may be summarised as:

- Scrutinising the work of the Government
- Passing legislation; ie making new laws
- Debating the key issues of the day
- Approving the funding necessary for the Government to carry out its statutory duties and legislative proposals
- Providing the personnel for Government (since all government ministers are drawn from either the House of Commons or the House of Lords)

It is actually the Government that is responsible for drafting most legislation that is placed before Parliament, and so, when it passes legislation, Parliament's role is that of formal enactment of legislation rather than making the law on its own initiative.

## 2.2 The composition of Parliament

The UK Parliament comprises two separate Houses: the House of Commons, and the House of Lords together with the Monarch. Acts of Parliament must normally be approved by both Houses and also receive Royal Assent.

### 2.2.1 The House of Commons

The House of Commons is a representative body, the membership of which is elected. There are currently 650 Members of Parliament. Members of Parliament are elected by attaining the most votes at a general election in their respective constituencies (the 'first past the post' system).

The Speaker is the chair of the House of Commons. By convention, they carry out their duties impartially (eg ruling on procedural points and controlling debate).

Statute limits the number of holders of ministerial office in the Commons to 95 (House of Commons Disqualification Act 1975, s 2 – see **Chapter 4**).

By convention, the Prime Minister is a member of the House of Commons, as are most other cabinet ministers (see **Chapter 1**).

### 2.2.2 Recall petitions

The Recall of MPs Act 2015 introduced a process whereby an MP can be removed from their seat and for a by-election to follow.

A recall petition may be opened if any one of the following conditions is met:

(i) The MP is convicted of an offence and receives a custodial sentence.

(ii) Following a report from the Committee on Standards, the MP is suspended from the Commons for at least 10 sitting days.

(iii) The MP is convicted of providing false or misleading information for allowances claims.

Once a recall petition has been triggered, the MP will be removed from their seat and a by-election called if at least 10% of registered voters in their constituency sign the petition within six weeks. The recalled MP can stand as a candidate at the by-election.

So far the recall mechanism has been used successfully four times, twice in 2019 and twice in 2023. The prospect of a recall petition may also have contributed to the resignation of a few MPs.

### 2.2.3 The House of Lords

The House of Lords is not elected and is not a representative body. Historically the House of Lords was made up largely of hereditary peers (ie peers entitled to sit in the House of Lords by virtue of their birth). However, the House of Lords Act 1999 enacted the first stage of what the then Labour Government intended to be full-scale reform of the upper House by removing the bulk of hereditary peers from the House. Nonetheless, the Act allowed up to 92 hereditary peers to remain.

Most members of the House of Lords are life peers appointed under the Life Peerages Act 1958. Such peers are appointed by the Monarch on the advice of the Prime Minister (although the Prime Minister will in turn have received suggestions as to whom to appoint from a non-political Appointments Commission, which puts forward prospective peers from a range of different professions, interests and political affiliations).

The current membership of the House of Lords is as follows:

- The Lords Temporal – life peers (currently about 700) created under the Life Peerages Act 1958 and up to 92 hereditary peers.
- The Lords Spiritual (26 senior clergy of the Church of England).

There is a widespread view that the unelected House of Lords in its current form is unsuited to a modern constitutional democracy. Accordingly, following its victory in the July 2024 general election, the Labour Government submitted the House of Lords (Hereditary Peers) Bill to Parliament providing for the abolition of the remaining hereditary peers. Parliament is very likely to pass the Bill.

In addition to abolishing the hereditary peers, the Labour Government is consulting on other reforms such as introducing a mandatory retirement age.

### 2.2.4 The meeting and duration of Parliament

#### 2.2.4.1 Meeting

Under the Meeting of Parliament Act 1694, Parliament must be summoned every three years. By convention, Parliament meets throughout the year, since taxes require annual renewal and political reality, coupled with the volume of work, means that it is in almost permanent operation.

#### 2.2.4.2 Duration

The Parliament Act 1911 limits the maximum life of a Parliament to five years. Historically, however, most Parliaments have not in fact lasted for the full five-year term. Until recently this was because, acting pursuant to the royal prerogative, the Monarch has dissolved Parliament at the request of the Prime Minister, and successive Prime Ministers have tried to seek dissolution at a time when their political parties were popular with the electorate so as to maximise their chances of success in the subsequent general election.

This was changed by the Fixed-term Parliaments Act (FTPA) 2011. This provided for fixed days for polls for parliamentary general elections, and the election held on 7 May 2015 took place pursuant to its provisions. The Act also made provision for the holding of early parliamentary general elections in the event of either a vote of no confidence (unless a new government could be formed) or a vote by at least two-thirds of all MPs in favour of an early election. In April 2017, MPs used this latter provision to vote for a general election which took place 8 June 2017.

In October 2019, following unsuccessful attempts by the Government to obtain the requisite two-thirds majority to trigger a general election, Parliament enacted the Early Parliamentary General Election Act 2019 to circumvent the FTPA in order to pave the way for the December 2019 general election. Only a simple majority of MPs was needed for the Act to pass.

In December 2020 the Government submitted a bill to Parliament providing for the repeal of the FTPA and the revival of the prerogative power to dissolve Parliament. The Dissolution and Calling of Parliament Act 2022 has now repealed the FTPA 2011, so dissolution of Parliament is now once again a royal prerogative power; see **1.4.3.2** above.

2.2.4.3 'Sessions'

Each Parliament is divided into 'sessions'. Parliamentary sessions now usually start in the spring of one year and end in the spring of the next. A session ends when Parliament is 'prorogued' by Royal Decree. Prorogation terminates all business pending at the end of a session. Any public bills that have not passed into law will normally lapse, although it is possible to carry over public bills from one session to the next, subject to agreement.

## 2.3 The legislative process

The legislative procedure for primary legislation differs according to the type of bill passing through its parliamentary stages. As most legislation is in this category, we will concentrate on 'public bills', ie those that apply to the public in general. ('Private' bills in contrast only change the law for an individual or locality.) Unless the Parliament Acts procedure is used (see paragraph **2.3.4** below), a bill must have been approved in the same form by each House before it is presented for Royal Assent.

### 2.3.1 Public bills

Public bills alter the general law (ie the law that concerns the public as a whole). There are two forms of public bill:

(a) Government bills: These bills are bills submitted to Parliament as part of the Government's legislative programme. They are usually listed in the King's Speech at the start of a parliamentary session and are usually public bills. The relevant government department decides on the detailed contents.

(b) Private members' bills: These are bills introduced by MPs or Lords who are not government ministers. Although a very small minority of these ever become law due to lack of parliamentary time, they sometimes create significant publicity regarding an issue so may indirectly influence the Government's legislative proposals.

The table below summarises what happens at each stage of the legislative process.

Except for financial measures, which must be introduced by a minister in the Commons, a bill can generally be introduced in either House first.

Scottish devolution (**Chapter 3** below) also has an impact on parliamentary procedure. The so-called 'West Lothian Question' attracted increasing attention following the referendum on Scottish independence held in September 2014. If some issues (such as education) are devolved to the Scottish Parliament so that English MPs do not discuss them at Westminster, why should Scottish MPs retain a vote at Westminster on corresponding English issues?

In October 2015 the House of Commons approved a change of parliamentary procedure. This added a new stage to the usual procedure, allowing MPs for English constituencies (or English and Welsh constituencies) to vote on issues deemed to affect only England (or only England and Wales), thereby giving these MPs a veto on legislation at committee stage before all MPs from across the United Kingdom vote in the bill's final readings. Parliament, however, abolished this procedure (known as 'English votes for English laws') in July 2021.

### 2.3.2 Private bills

Private bills relate to matters of individual, corporate or local interest, and affect particular persons and/or a particular locality (eg a bill authorising the building of a new railway line or tunnel).

### 2.3.3 The relationship between the House of Commons and the House of Lords

Although a bill must be passed by both Houses of Parliament, the House of Commons is the more important of the two. This is because the members of the House of Commons are directly elected by the people at a general election, and so the House of Commons has more democratic legitimacy than the (currently) unelected House of Lords.

By convention the Prime Minister will sit in the House of Commons. Similarly, most cabinet and junior government ministers will be drawn from the Commons.

**Table 2.1** The legislative process

**First reading**

This stage is purely formal: the title of the bill is read out and it is then printed and published.

↓

**Second reading**

At this stage the main debate takes place in the House of Commons on the general principles of the bill.

↓

**Committee stage**

The bill is usually referred to a general (or public bill) committee, consisting of 16–50 members appointed by the Committee of Selection. There is proportional representation of parties on general committees (ie they reflect the division of the parties within the House).

Important bills (for example, bills of constitutional significance or concerned with authorising government expenditure) or bills that require little discussion because they are uncontroversial and unimportant may be referred to the 'Committee of the Whole House'.

The purpose of the committee stage is to examine the bill in detail. Amendments may be made to its clauses.

↓

**Third reading**

This stage involves the consideration of the bill as amended - normally the debate is brief and only verbal amendments may be made. This is the final opportunity to vote on the bill; often MPs do not.

↓

**Proceedings in the House of Lords**

These do not begin until after the third reading in the Commons. The procedure in the Lords is similar to that outlined above, except that the Committee of the Whole House almost invariably takes the committee stage. When the bill has received its third reading in the Lords, it must be sent back to the Commons if the Lords have made any amendments. Theoretically, the bill can go backwards and forwards an indefinite number of times until the proceedings on it are terminated by prorogation. In practice, however, if the Commons disagrees with Lords' amendments and restores the original wording, the Lords will usually accept it.

↓

**Royal Assent**

Once Royal Assent is received, a bill becomes law and is referred to as an 'Act of Parliament'. The Act may suspend its 'commencement' until some future date, which may be determined by delegated legislation made under the Act.

The House of Lords is often described as being a 'revising chamber'. There is a constitutional convention, the Salisbury Convention, that the House of Lords will not reject a bill giving effect to a major part of the democratically elected Government's manifesto. Rather, the House of Lords will use its considerable expertise to make small changes to legislation with which it disagrees. Amendments are often proposed during proceedings in the Lords and, in a significant number of cases, the Government accepts amendments after a defeat there.

If the House of Lords rejects a bill that has passed the House of Commons, the bill may still eventually become law as a consequence of the provisions of the Parliament Acts of 1911 and 1949; see **2.3.4** below.

### 2.3.4 The Parliament Acts 1911 and 1949

The Lords' role is constrained by the Parliament Acts 1911 and 1949, which ensure that ultimately the will of the Commons may prevail. The Acts permit the Monarch to give Royal Assent to a bill that lacks the consent of the House of Lords, provided that the Speaker has certified that the provisions of the Acts have been complied with. These are as follows:

- 'Money bills' (ie public bills certified by the Speaker as dealing only with national taxation or supply): A money bill passed by the Commons can be presented to the Monarch for assent one month after being sent to the Lords and will become law even though it lacks the consent of the Lords.
- Other public bills: If passed by the Commons and rejected by the Lords in each of two successive sessions, a bill can be sent to the Monarch for her assent. One year must elapse between the second reading in the Commons in the first session, and the third reading there in the second session. Bills seeking to extend the maximum duration of Parliament are excluded.

There had since the passing of the 1949 Act been some academic debate about the validity of that Act and Acts passed under its authority, the Act itself having been passed via the 1911 Act. This debate was settled by the House of Lords (in its judicial capacity prior to the creation of the Supreme Court) in *R (Jackson) v Attorney General* [2005] UKHL 56. It was argued that the 1949 Act was not a valid Act on the grounds that the procedure set out in 1911 Act should not have been used to enact it. The House of Lords rejected this argument and held that the 1949 Act had been properly enacted.

In fact most conflicts between the Lords and Commons are resolved by agreement and application of the usual conventions, rather than by use of the Parliament Acts. They have been used rarely, the only occasions since 1949 being for the War Crimes Act 1991, the European Parliamentary Elections Act 1999, the Sexual Offences (Amendment) Act 2000 and the Hunting Act 2004.

### 2.3.5 Delegated legislation

The provisions of an Act of Parliament often confer upon ministers a power to make delegated or subordinate legislation. Delegated legislation is every exercise of power to legislate that is conferred by or under an Act of Parliament. Delegated legislation may be made by ministers in the form of rules or regulations (often 'statutory instruments'), which supplement the provisions of an Act of Parliament.

Parliament's role is confined to scrutiny of delegated legislation. This is in fact not too different from Parliament's actual role in relation to primary legislation, but there are important distinctions. Neither House of Parliament can amend delegated legislation, and often it can come into effect without either House voting upon it at all. The 'parent' or 'enabling' Act will stipulate the parliamentary procedure to be followed, but the following are the most commonly used procedures:

- Affirmative resolution procedure: The instrument either cannot come into effect, or ceases to have effect, unless one or both Houses passes a resolution approving the instrument.

- Negative resolution procedure: The Government is required to 'annul' the instrument if either House passes a resolution rejecting the instrument within a specified period (usually 40 days) after it is 'laid before Parliament'.

The House is assisted in scrutiny of delegated legislation by the Joint Select Committee on Statutory Instruments (representing both Lords and Commons). Its job is to draw the attention of Parliament to instruments that for various reasons might need to be debated.

## 2.4 The sovereignty (or supremacy) of Parliament

### 2.4.1 Definition of parliamentary sovereignty

You considered the meaning of the doctrine of 'parliamentary sovereignty' (or supremacy) in **Chapter 1**. The classic definition of this term was provided by AV Dicey:

> The principle of parliamentary sovereignty means neither more nor less than this: namely, that Parliament ... has, under the English constitution, the right to make or unmake any law whatever; and, further, that no person or body is recognised by the law ... as having a right to override or set aside the legislation of Parliament.
>
> *An Introduction to the Study of the Law of the Constitution*

Dicey's description may be broken down into three parts:

(a) Parliament is the supreme law-making body and may enact or repeal laws on any subject.

(b) No Parliament may be bound by a predecessor or bind a successor – a particular Act of Parliament cannot be entrenched, or be given a 'higher' status than any other Act.

(c) No other person or body (but particularly a court of law) may question the validity of an Act of Parliament or declare that Act to be unlawful.

### 2.4.2 The development of parliamentary sovereignty

Following the English Civil War during the 1640s and Oliver Cromwell's brief republic, the Stuart Monarchy was restored to the throne in 1660 with the accession of Charles II. When Charles died in 1685, his brother, James II, became king. James was a devout Catholic, and tensions developed between James and a staunchly Protestant Parliament. A number of Parliamentarians opened secret negotiations with William of Orange, the Protestant husband of James's daughter, Mary, with a view to his taking the throne by force. In 1688 William landed with his army in England, but James had already fled to France (the 'Glorious Revolution').

In 1689 William, who was not yet king, summoned a Convention (or meeting) of peers and commoners. The Convention declared itself to be the Parliament of England (it is now known as the 'Convention Parliament') and passed the Bill of Rights, which set out the terms on which the Crown was offered to William and Mary.

The terms of the Bill of Rights altered the balance of power between the Monarch and Parliament in favour of the latter. It removed the powers of the Monarch arbitrarily to suspend Acts of Parliament and to impose taxation without Parliament's consent. The Bill of Rights also provided that Parliament should meet on a regular basis and that elections to Parliament should be free.

In terms of parliamentary sovereignty, the most significant part of the Bill of Rights is article 9, which provided that 'freedom of speech and debates or proceedings in Parliament ought not to be impeached or questioned in any court or place out of Parliament'.

### 2.4.3 The 'Enrolled Act' rule

Although article 9 of the Bill of Rights guaranteed free speech in Parliament, the doctrine of parliamentary sovereignty as defined by Dicey has been developed by the judges through the common law.

The courts have consistently rejected challenges to Acts of Parliament based on alleged irregularities in the procedure by which Parliament passed the relevant Acts. In *Edinburgh & Dalkeith Railway Co v Wauchope* (1842) 8 Cl & F 710 it was claimed that the enactment of a private Act was defective as due notice had not been given to a party affected by its passage. The House of Lords dismissed the claim, Lord Campbell observing:

> All that a court of justice can do is to look to the Parliamentary Roll: if from that it should appear that a bill has passed both Houses and received Royal Assent, no court of justice can enquire into the mode in which it was introduced into Parliament, what was done previously to it being introduced ... or what passed ... during its progress ... through Parliament.

This has become known as the 'Enrolled Act' rule – once an Act of Parliament has been entered onto the Parliamentary roll, the courts will not question the validity of that Act or hold the Act to be void.

In the later case of *Pickin v British* Railways *Board* [1974] AC 765, Lord Reid confirmed that the courts had no power to *disregard* an Act of Parliament, or to investigate proceedings that had taken place in Parliament to determine whether there had been any irregularity of procedure or fraud.

The more recent case of *R (Jackson and others) v HM Attorney General* [2005] UKHL 56 suggests that the courts may, in certain circumstances, be prepared to consider the validity of an Act of Parliament. The case concerned a challenge to the validity of the Hunting Act 2004, which had been enacted pursuant to the Parliament Acts 1911 and 1949. As explained at **2.3.4** above, it was claimed that the 1911 Act could not be used to enact the 1949 Act. If this argument had succeeded, then the Hunting Act would have been invalid as it had been passed using the procedure set out in the 1949 Act. A strict application of the 'Enrolled Act' rule would have precluded the House of Lords from considering the case. However, the House of Lords held that it did have jurisdiction to consider the validity of the Hunting Act as a question of statutory interpretation of the 1911 Act, namely whether the 1911 Act could be used to enact the 1949 Act. It thus concluded that there was no conflict with the 'Enrolled Act' rule.

### 2.4.4 The unlimited legislative competence of Parliament

Parliamentary sovereignty asserts itself through Acts of Parliament (ie statutes), rather than through mere parliamentary resolutions. Dicey's definition of parliamentary sovereignty states that there are no limits on Parliament's legislative powers.

Examples of the unlimited legislative competence of Parliament include:

(a) *Statute may override international law.* In *Cheney v Conn* [1968] 1 All ER 779, a taxpayer challenged an income tax assessment on the ground that part of the tax would be used to finance the manufacture of nuclear weapons, which was contrary to the Geneva Convention, an international treaty to which the UK was a party. The challenge was unsuccessful. The court held that the statute that imposed the tax prevailed over international law.

This aspect of parliamentary sovereignty is of recent relevance as in June 2022 the Government submitted to Parliament the Northern Ireland Protocol Bill which would have overridden certain provisions in the Withdrawal Agreement agreed between the UK and the EU (Agreement on the withdrawal of the United Kingdom of Great Britain and Northern Ireland from the European Union and the European Atomic Energy Community ([2020] OJ L29/7)) (the Withdrawal Agreement) – see also **2.5.3.1** below and **Chapter 10**. The Withdrawal Agreement set out the terms on which the UK left the EU, and includes provisions known as the Northern Ireland Protocol aimed at preventing a hard border on the island of Ireland between Northern Ireland and the Republic of Ireland.

The UK Government believed the Northern Ireland Protocol was causing instability in and economic damage to Northern Ireland and, as the EU has not agreed to change it, it was necessary to override unilaterally some of its provisions. The Government believed that this would not have breached international law as it was acting to safeguard the Belfast or Good Friday Agreement of 1998 which ended three decades of sectarian violence known as 'the Troubles'. On the other hand, much legal opinion took the opposite view. However, even if such legislation had breached international law, Parliament could still have passed it. However, in February 2023, the UK and EU concluded the Windsor Framework, resolving the dispute regarding the Northern Ireland Protocol. The UK Government therefore withdrew the proposed legislation.

(b) *Statute may override constitutional conventions.* The case of *Madzimbamuto v Lardner-Burke* [1969] 1 AC 645 is the authority for this. In 1965, Southern Rhodesia issued a unilateral declaration of independence from Britain. However, the UK Parliament passed the Southern Rhodesia Act 1965, which declared that Southern Rhodesia remained part of the UK's dominion territories. The validity of the Act was challenged on the basis that there was an established constitutional convention that the UK Parliament would not legislate for Southern Rhodesia without the consent of the Rhodesian Government. The challenge was unsuccessful. The House of Lords held that the convention was overridden by the Southern Rhodesia Act.

The Supreme Court confirmed this in *R (Miller) v Secretary of State for Exiting the European Union* [2017] UKSC 5 (*Miller (No 1)*); the Sewel Convention provides that the UK Parliament will not normally legislate for Scotland without the Scottish Parliament's consent; however, the Supreme Court held that it was not legally binding even though it had been codified; see **1.5.4.4** above.

(c) *Statute may alter the constitution.* You have already considered statutes that are of constitutional importance in **Chapter 1**. Some examples of statutes that have altered the constitution include the Acts of Union 1706–07 (which united England and Scotland under a single Parliament), the Parliament Acts and the Human Rights Act 1998 (which incorporated the Convention for the Protection of Human Rights and Fundamental Freedoms (the ECHR) (Rome, 4 November 1950) into the UK legal system.)

(d) *Statute may operate retrospectively.* In *Burmah Oil Co v Lord Advocate* [1965] AC 75, Burmah Oil sought compensation from the British for the destruction of oil installations during World War II (to prevent Japanese forces obtaining control of them). The House of Lords found that the Crown was liable to pay compensation. Parliament then enacted the War Damage Act 1965. This Act applied retrospectively and so removed the right to compensation.

(e) *Statute may abolish or curtail aspects of the royal prerogative.* Some examples of this include:

   (i) the Crown Proceedings Act 1947, which abolished the immunity of the Crown in respect of claims made against it in either tort or contract;

   (ii) the FTPA 2011, which until its repeal removed the power of the Monarch to dissolve Parliament and required Parliament in future to sit for a fixed period of five years before a general election automatically took place (see **2.2.3.2** above);

   (iii) *Miller (No 1),* where the Government argued that it could trigger Article 50 of the Treaty on European Union using its prerogative powers to make or unmake treaties. The majority of the Supreme Court held that the ECA 1972 was inconsistent with the future exercise by government ministers of any prerogative power to withdraw from the EU treaties. The ECA 1972 had given domestic effect to the EU treaties, and EU rights had thereby become enforceable in UK courts. As withdrawal from the EU amounted to a fundamental constitutional change by removing EU law as a source of domestic law, it needed the consent of Parliament. Parliament subsequently passed the European Union (Notification of Withdrawal) Act 2017.

### 2.4.5 Express and implied repeal of statute

You saw in **2.4.1** above that one aspect of parliamentary sovereignty is that no Parliament may be bound by a predecessor or bind a successor. This is given effect through the doctrines of express and implied repeal.

If a later Parliament expressly repeals the contents of an Act made by an earlier Parliament, that earlier Act will no longer be valid. But what happens if a later Parliament passes an Act that contradicts the contents of an Act made by an earlier Parliament but does not expressly repeal that earlier Act? In these circumstances the doctrine of implied repeal will apply.

In *Ellen Street Estates v Minister of Health* [1934] KB 590, the claimant sought to persuade the court to apply compensation provisions contained in the Acquisition of Land (Assessment of Compensation) Act 1919 rather than those contained in the later Housing Acts of 1925 and 1930. The two sets of statutory provisions were inconsistent, but the earlier ones were more favourable.

The 1919 Act stated that any provisions of any other Act 'so far as inconsistent with this Act shall cease to have or shall not have effect'. The claimant argued that this could be construed so as to govern future Acts, and the later Housing Acts contained no express provisions to repeal the 1919 Act.

The Court of Appeal dismissed the claim because it considered that the later Housing Acts impliedly repealed the 1919 Act to the extent of any inconsistency between them. Maugham LJ said in his judgment:

> The legislature cannot, according to our constitution, bind itself as to the form of subsequent legislation, and it is impossible for Parliament to enact that in a subsequent statute dealing with the same subject matter there can be no implied repeal.

In other words, a later Act of Parliament will impliedly repeal the provisions of an earlier Act to the extent of any inconsistency between the two Acts.

---

## 2.5 Limitations on the supremacy of Parliament

### 2.5.1 Domestic limitations

#### 2.5.1.1 The Acts of Union

The United Kingdom was formed following Acts of Union with Scotland in 1706–07 and Ireland in 1801. Some commentators have argued that, as a consequence, Parliament was born 'unfree', because it is limited by the terms of these Acts and cannot legislate so as to override their provisions.

Of particular importance are the Acts of Union 1706–07. These gave effect to a Treaty of Union by which the English and Scottish Parliaments agreed to vest their authority in a new Parliament of Great Britain. The Acts made explicit provision for the preservation of the separate Scottish legal system and the Church of Scotland. Some have argued that, as a result of these provisions, the Acts of Union are in effect a partial written constitution for the UK, by which subsequent Parliaments are bound. Such arguments have become somewhat academic, however, with the return of devolved legislative power to a Scottish Parliament (see **2.5.1.2** below).

Although the matter has never been directly considered by the courts, obiter comments by the Scottish Court of Session in the case of *MacCormick v Lord Advocate* 1953 (Scot) SC 396 suggested that the Westminster Parliament was bound by the terms of the Acts of Union.

#### 2.5.1.2 Devolution

On coming to power in 1997, the Labour Government devolved power to Scotland, Wales and Northern Ireland. You will cover devolution in more depth in **Chapter 3**, so in this chapter we shall simply consider its impact on parliamentary sovereignty.

The Scotland Act 1998 established a Scottish Parliament and Executive. Legislative powers in certain areas (such as health, education and legal affairs) are devolved to the Parliament. Other areas (such as foreign affairs and defence) are reserved to the Westminster Parliament. The Scotland Act 2012 gave additional powers over some aspects of taxation and other areas to the Scottish Parliament. The Scotland Act 2016 amends the Scotland Act 1998 and includes provisions stating that:

(a) the Scottish Parliament and Scottish Government are a permanent part of the constitutional arrangements of the UK;

(b) neither the Scottish Parliament nor Scottish Government may be abolished unless the people of Scotland vote for this in a referendum; and

(c) the UK Parliament will not normally legislate with regard to devolved matters without the consent of the Scottish Parliament (the Sewel Convention).

The Scotland Act 2016 also increased the range of devolved powers, including the power to vary income tax rates and thresholds.

The Government of Wales Act 1998 established a Welsh Assembly, initially without legislative powers. The Wales Act 2017 has changed this, so that devolution in Wales follows a similar format to that in Scotland. The Wales Act 2017 has now devolved power to the Welsh Parliament (now commonly known as the Senedd Cymru) to legislate in those areas that are not reserved to Westminster. The Wales Act 2017 also mirrors the provisions in the Scotland Act 2016 relating to permanency, the need for a referendum and setting out the Sewel Convention.

The Northern Ireland Act 1998 devolved powers to a Northern Ireland Assembly and created a 'power-sharing executive' (which can be – and indeed on occasions has been – suspended under the Act). Following the elections in May 2022, it proved very difficult to form a new executive; eventually a new executive was formed in February 2024 with Sinn Féin's Michelle O'Neill becoming First Minister, the first time that a Nationalist rather than a Unionist has held this post. See further **3.1.3** below. It also contains a provision that Northern Ireland shall not cease to be part of the UK unless the people of Northern Ireland vote for this in a referendum.

The most significant devolution of power has been to Scotland under the terms of the Scotland Act. The Scottish Parliament is not a sovereign legislature in the way that the UK Parliament is as it derives its powers from the Scotland Act, an Act of the UK Parliament. Although its legislation is designated as primary legislation, ie the Scottish Parliament has the power to pass Acts, the Scottish Parliament may legislate only to the extent that it is given power to do so by the UK Parliament under the Scotland Act.

The UK Parliament can also still legislate for Scotland, although the Sewel Convention provides that the UK Parliament 'will not normally legislate with regard to devolved matters without the consent' of the devolved legislatures. As a general rule, in normal circumstances the UK Parliament is unlikely to legislate in devolved areas without the devolved legislature's consent. However, aspects of the European Union (Withdrawal Act) 2018 and the European Union (Withdrawal Agreement) Act 2020 related to devolved matters, even though international relations are reserved to the UK Parliament. The Scottish Parliament, Senedd Cymru and Northern Ireland Assembly refused to give their consent to the bills leading up to the 2018 Act, and the Scottish Parliament also refused consent to the 2020 Act. The UK Parliament nevertheless enacted them.

Whether the UK Parliament can repeal the Scotland Act 1998 is a matter of debate. The Scotland Act 2016 states that the Scottish Parliament and Scottish Government are a permanent part of the constitutional arrangements of the UK, and that neither the Scottish Parliament nor Scottish Government may be abolished unless the people of Scotland vote for this in a referendum. Thus, without such a referendum, it would be difficult for the UK Parliament to do this. Depending on your view of the 'manner and form debate' (which you will consider at **2.5.1.5** below), you may take the view that such difficulties would be political only. Alternatively, you may take the view that the courts would not uphold legislation repealing the Scotland Act 1998 in the absence of a referendum.

2.5.1.3 Acts of independence

During the 20th century, Parliament enacted various Acts granting independence to former colonies of the British Empire. Would it be possible for Parliament to reverse such legislation and resume legislating for former colonies?

In strict legal terms, Parliament could reverse such legislation. But, as with Scottish devolution, both for political and practical reasons it is most unlikely that Parliament would ever consider repealing such legislation. Furthermore, even if Parliament did repeal the Acts of independence and resume legislating for the former colonies, such legislation would be unenforceable.

2.5.1.4 Limits on the doctrine of implied repeal

At **2.4.5** above you considered the doctrine of implied repeal. This holds that an Act of Parliament will impliedly repeal the contents of an Act of an earlier Parliament to the extent of any inconsistency between the two Acts.

It has been suggested, however, that the doctrine of implied repeal may not apply to 'constitutional statutes'. In *Thoburn v Sunderland City Council* [2002] EWHC 195 (Admin), Laws LJ suggested that there are two types of statute, 'ordinary' and 'constitutional'. Statutes that are 'constitutional' are of such significance that the courts would require actual intention from Parliament to change them, not an implied intention.

The test for a constitutional statute is:

(a) the statute must condition the legal relationship between citizen and state in some general, overarching manner; or

(b) the statute must change the scope of fundamental constitutional rights.

Laws LJ said that several key statutes satisfied this test:

> We should recognise a hierarchy of Acts of Parliament: as it were 'ordinary' statutes and 'constitutional' statutes... Examples are the Magna Carta, the bill of Rights 1689 ... the Human Rights Act 1998 ... [and] ... the European Communities Act ... Ordinary statutes may be impliedly repealed. Constitutional statutes may not.

For a constitutional statute to be repealed, there had to be 'express words' or 'words so specific that the inference of an actual determination to effect [the repeal of a constitutional statute] ... was irresistible'.

Clearly, Laws LJ had in mind only a very limited number of statutes as being of sufficient importance to satisfy this test.

Laws LJ's views have subsequently found support in three Supreme Court decisions.

*The first of these Supreme Court decisions is* H v Lord Advocate *[2012] UKSC 24, in which the Supreme Court considered an apparent contradiction between the Extradition Act 2003 and the Scotland Act 1998. The Supreme Court decided that there was no contradiction between the Acts. Nonetheless, Lord Hope, obiter, went on to consider what the position would have been had there been a contradiction between the two Acts.*

*Under the doctrine of implied repeal, the Extradition Act would have prevailed over the Scotland Act. However, Lord Hope rejected this possibility, stating:*

> *It would perhaps have been open to Parliament to override the [relevant] provisions of [the Scotland Act] ... But in my opinion only an express provision to that effect could be held to lead to such a result. This is because of the fundamental constitutional nature of the settlement that was achieved by the Scotland Act.* This in itself must be held to render it incapable of being altered otherwise than by an express enactment. *Its provisions cannot be regarded as vulnerable to alteration by implication from some other enactment in which an*

> *intention to alter the Scotland Act is not set forth expressly on the face of the statute. (emphasis added)*

Whilst Lord Hope was referring to the Scotland Act, there seems no reason to confine his reasoning to that Act. The Scotland Act could not be impliedly repealed because of its 'fundamental constitutional nature'; logically other statutes of a fundamental constitutional nature, ie those described by Laws LJ as 'constitutional statutes', should also be immune to implied repeal.

*The issue of implied repeal was also raised in* R (HS2 Action Alliance Ltd) v Secretary of State for Transport *[2014] UKSC 3. The case concerned a challenge to 'HS2', the proposed high speed rail link between London and northern cities. Opponents of HS2 argued the parliamentary process procedure did not comply with EU Directive 2011/92, which requires public participation in major infrastructure decisions affecting the environment. They argued that the parliamentary process did not provide for effective public participation.*

*The Supreme Court decided that the Directive did not apply, but nonetheless went on to consider in some very interesting obiter dicta what the position would have been had it done so. If it had, the Supreme Court would have been obliged to consider whether the parliamentary procedure complied with the requirements of the Directive. According to Lord Reed, this could have impinged 'upon long-established constitutional principles governing the relationship between Parliament and the courts, as reflected for example in article 9 of the Bill of Rights 1689'. This raised the possibility of conflict between parliamentary privilege as set out in article 9 of the Bill of Rights and EU law, a conflict that Lord Reed affirmed would have to be 'resolved by our courts as an issue arising under the constitutional law of the United Kingdom'.*

*As this case took place during the UK's membership of the EU, the House of Lords accepted the primacy of EU law over national law on the grounds that the ECA 1972 required UK courts to give effect to that principle. However, it is also clear that the Supreme Court thought that there were fundamental principles contained in Acts of Parliament or recognised at common law that will not be overridden even by subsequent constitutional statutes unless there is unequivocal evidence of parliamentary intention to amend or repeal them. On the facts, the Supreme Court held the Directive did not require it to investigate parliamentary procedure. However, if it had done so, the clear tenor of the judgments of the justices is that the Supreme Court would have refused to carry out such an investigation on the basis of article 9 of the Bill of Rights, which prohibits the courts from enquiring into parliamentary procedure. Article 9 of the Bill of Rights would therefore not have been impliedly repealed by the ECA 1972, which would have required such an investigation.*

*In* Miller (No 1) *[2017] UKSC 5, the Supreme Court referred to the 'informative discussion' by Laws LJ in* Thoburn *and concluded that '[t]he 1972 Act accordingly has a constitutional character'.*

#### 2.5.1.5 The 'manner and form' debate

The doctrines of express and implied repeal prevent an earlier Parliament from binding a future Parliament as to the *content* of legislation which that *future* Parliament might enact. But is it possible for an earlier Parliament to bind a future Parliament as to the *procedure* which that future Parliament must follow to enact legislation?

This is known as the 'manner and form' or *entrenchment* theory – can a Parliament bind its successors as to the procedure to be adopted when repealing legislation enacted by that earlier Parliament?

#### Arguments in favour of the 'manner and form' theory

Supporters of the 'manner and form' theory use the Parliament Acts 1911 and 1949 (considered at **2.3.4** above) to support their case. The Parliament Acts made it 'easier' for legislation to be passed because, in certain circumstances, the Acts removed the requirement for legislation to have been approved by the House of Lords.

Supporters of the manner and form theory argue that if Parliament (in enacting the Parliament Acts) could make it 'easier' to legislate, there is no reason why Parliament could not make it 'harder' for a future Parliament to legislate. For example, an earlier Parliament could pass an Act and, within that Act, specify that the Act could be repealed only by a specified majority in Parliament (rather than a simple majority), or that, in addition to a parliamentary vote, repeal could take place only if this was also supported in a referendum. In other words, the Act could be entrenched.

Another argument sometimes raised in support of the manner and form theory is that the rules for identifying an Act of Parliament derive from the common law (ie such rules are 'judge-made'). As an Act of Parliament can override the common law, it is suggested that Parliament can alter the legal rules on which the validity of an Act of Parliament rests.

There are some Commonwealth authorities that suggest that entrenchment of legislation is possible. The case most often cited is *Attorney General for New South Wales v Trethowan* [1932] AC 526. This case concerned an attempt by the Parliament of the Australian state of New South Wales to entrench certain provisions in an Act of Parliament by providing that these provisions could not be repealed unless they were approved in a popular referendum in addition to being approved by the Parliament. When a later Parliament passed a bill repealing the provisions, no referendum was held. The Privy Council held that the repeal of the Act was invalid because a referendum should have taken place.

#### Arguments against the 'manner and form' theory

Those who take issue with the 'manner and form' theory dispute the importance of the *Trethowan* case. First, they argue that, as a Privy Council case, *Trethowan* is persuasive only and not binding on domestic courts. Secondly, they argue that the position of the legislature of New South Wales cannot be seen as analogous to that of the UK Parliament. This is because the UK Parliament is truly 'supreme' (because it was not created by another body), whereas the Parliament of New South Wales is a subordinate legislature in that it was created by an Act of the UK Parliament (the Colonial Laws Validity Act 1865). Indeed, it has been suggested that *Trethowan* supports the argument that parliamentary sovereignty cannot be limited, because the case is an example of a subordinate legislature (ie the Parliament of New South Wales) being kept within the powers granted to it by the supreme UK Parliament.

Some academics who oppose the 'manner and form' theory have argued that the meaning of Parliament was 'fixed' following the constitutional restructuring in 1688 and the enactment of the Bill of Rights in 1689 (see **2.4.2** above). They argue that the meaning of 'Parliament' cannot be altered by an ordinary Act of Parliament, and so no Parliament has the power to redefine this meaning or to place limitations on the way in which a future Parliament may act.

#### Conclusion on the 'manner and form' theory

In conclusion, the position on manner and form is unclear. This was illustrated by the divergent views of two members of the House of Lords in *R (Jackson) v Attorney General* [2005] UKHL 56.

In support of the manner and form theory, Lord Steyn said:

> Parliament could for specific purposes provide for a two-thirds majority in the House of Commons and the House of Lords. This would involve a redefinition of Parliament for a specific purpose. Such redefinition could not be disregarded.

In contrast, Lord Hope said:

> it is a fundamental aspect of the rule of sovereignty that no Parliament can bind its successors. There are no means whereby ... it can entrench an Act of Parliament.

Some provisions in the Scotland Act 2016, the Wales Act 2017 and the Northern Ireland Act 1998 arguably attempt to impose manner and form requirements, in that they require a positive vote in a referendum in addition to an Act of Parliament in some circumstances. The Scotland Act 2016 requires a referendum before either the Scottish Parliament or Scottish Government is abolished (similar provisions are contained in the Wales Act 2017). The Northern Ireland Act 1998 provides that Northern Ireland shall not cease to be part of the UK unless the people vote for this in a poll. It is questionable as to whether domestic courts would uphold legislation that purported to achieve these objectives if approval was not also obtained in a referendum.

#### 2.5.1.6 Henry VIII powers

Legislation that has been introduced by the Government will often contain 'Henry VIII' powers. These powers permit the relevant government minister to amend or even repeal the relevant statute and sometimes other statutes as well by delegated legislation; ie they permit ministers to make changes to Acts of Parliament by delegated legislation. This is said to be contrary to the fundamental principle of the sovereignty of Parliament because it enables ministers - rather than Parliament - to make or change the law. In 2010, the Lord Chief Justice, Lord Judge, expressed concerns relating to Henry VIII powers, cautioning that by 'allowing [such powers] to become a habit, we are [risking] the inevitable consequence of yet further damaging the sovereignty of Parliament'.

#### 2.5.1.7 The rule of law

In *R (Jackson) v Attorney General* [2005] UKHL 56 Lord Steyn considered obiter that parliamentary sovereignty was not absolute and could be limited by the courts in extreme circumstances. Lord Steyn said that the doctrine of parliamentary sovereignty was a 'construct of the common law' (ie principle created by the judges). The judges could therefore qualify the principle in exceptional circumstances to prevent Parliament from legislating in a manner that was contrary to the rule of law. Lord Steyn cited as an example if Parliament enacted legislation to abolish judicial review of executive action or, more generally, if Parliament abolished the role of the courts. In such circumstances he speculated that the courts might be willing to strike down such legislation.

In contrast, Lord Bingham took a more cautious approach, stating:

> The bedrock of the British constitution is, and in 1911 was, the supremacy of the Crown in Parliament ... Then, as now, the Crown in Parliament was unconstrained by any entrenched or codified constitution. It could make or unmake any law it wished. Statutes, formally enacted as Acts of Parliament, properly interpreted, enjoyed the highest legal authority.

Other judges have lent support to the view that the rule of law may trump parliamentary sovereignty in certain circumstances. In *Moohan v Lord Advocate* [2014] UKSC 67, Lord Hodge stated, obiter:

> I do not exclude the possibility that in the very unlikely event that a parliamentary majority abusively sought to entrench its power by a curtailment of the franchise or similar device, the common law, informed by principles of democracy and the rule of law and international norms, would be able to declare such legislation unlawful.

However, he went on to state that 'the existence and extent of such a power is a matter of debate, at least in the context of the doctrine of the sovereignty of the United Kingdom Parliament'.

### 2.5.2 European limitations

The European Union treaties and the ECHR are all international treaties that, according to the UK's dualist' system, required incorporation into domestic law by an Act of the UK Parliament. Incorporation of both EU law and key ECHR rights into domestic law was undoubtedly significant as providing individuals with remedies under the EU treaties and the ECHR in the domestic courts. However, the method of incorporation adopted for each was rather different. We shall now examine each in turn.

### 2.5.3 Membership of the European Union

#### 2.5.3.1 The doctrine of supremacy of European Union law

The legal order of the European Union is based on a number of treaties, the key treaties now being known as the Treaty on European Union ([2008] OJ C115/13) (TEU), the Treaty on the Functioning of the European Union ([2012] OJ C326/01) (TFEU) and the Charter of Fundamental Rights of the European Union ([2000] OJ C364/1). During the UK's membership of the EU, the UK was required to give supremacy to EU law. This led to considerable debate about whether parliamentary sovereignty was compatible with the supremacy of EU law. Although the UK left the EU on 31 January 2020, some understanding of how the UK legal system accommodated the supremacy of EU law is essential to comprehend provisions in the EUWA 2018 regarding retained EU law.

Additionally, the UK and EU negotiated a Withdrawal Agreement setting out the terms of the UK's exit from the EU. The European Union (Withdrawal Agreement) Act 2020 gives supremacy to the Withdrawal Agreement in a very similar manner to which the ECA 1972 gave supremacy to the EU treaties. However, s 38(1) of the 2020 Act, entitled 'Parliamentary sovereignty', recognises that Parliament is sovereign, whilst s 38(2) states that this sovereignty persists notwithstanding any provisions in the 2020 Act giving direct effect to the provisions of the Withdrawal Agreement. Indeed, the Northern Ireland Protocol Bill contained provisions overriding aspects of the Northern Ireland Protocol.

It should also be noted that the Withdrawal Agreement provided for the continued supremacy of EU law during the transition period lasting from the date of the UK's withdrawal until 31 December 2020.

#### 2.5.3.2 Types of EU legislation

The EU treaties comprise the primary source of EU law. They lay down the legal framework of the EU and set out the EU's institutional framework and confer on the EU a wide range of powers in a large number of areas. They also give the EU the power to legislate in a wide range of areas by adopting secondary legislation.

There are four types of EU secondary legislation:

- Regulations: Regulations issued by the EU are directly applicable and automatically binding in all Member States without the need for any further legislation in the Member States.
- Directives: Directives set out objectives to be achieved and oblige Member States to pass domestic legislation themselves to implement those objectives. Directives set a date by which Member States must implement them.
- Decisions: Decisions are directly binding in the same way as regulations, but only on those to whom they are addressed, which may be Member States, companies or individuals.
- Recommendations and opinions: Recommendations and opinions are not binding.

#### 2.5.3.3 Other sources of EU law

(a) *Jurisprudence of the Court of Justice of the European Union*

The Court of Justice of the European Union (CJEU) refers collectively to the European Union's two courts, the Court of Justice (often referred to as the ECJ) and the General Court. The highest court in the EU's judicial hierarchy is the ECJ. Originally the ECJ was the only court, but the General Court (originally the Court of First Instance) was created in 1986 to help with the ECJ's increasing workload.

As EU Law was originally based on civil law legal systems, it does not have a formal system of precedent. Nonetheless, the case law of the CJEU has become a significant source of EU Law. Judgments of the CJEU are binding on the national courts of Member States, and so national courts have applied the CJEU's case law when dealing with questions of EU Law that have arisen in cases that they have been hearing. It is through the CJEU's case law, in particular judgments of the ECJ (the higher of the two courts), that principles such as direct effect and state liability, discussed at **2.5.3.4** and **2.5.3.9** below respectively, have been developed.

Moreover, while the CJEU is not bound by its own previous decisions, it at adheres to the principle of legal certainty and so will not lightly depart from its previous decisions. Accordingly, even in the absence of a formal system of precedent, the CJEU's case law has become a prominent feature of EU Law.

(b) *General principles of EU Law*

The CJEU (mainly through judgments of the ECJ) has in its case law developed general principles of EU Law. Originally, these principles did not explicitly feature in the founding treaties of the original European Economic Community, but the CJEU derived them from the common constitutional traditions of Member States and international treaties to which the Member States were parties, for example the ECHR. Many of these general principles have now found concrete expression in the European Charter of Fundamental Rights.

Examples of general principles include:

- Proportionality: This means that measures taken by Union institutions and Member States when implementing EU Law should be appropriate and necessary for achieving a given aim, and should not go further than is necessary to achieve that aim.
- Equality: This means that when dealing with persons in similar situations, Union institutions and Member States should not treat them differently, unless there is an objective justification for the difference in treatment.
- Fundamental rights, ie internationally recognised human rights.
- Legitimate expectation/legal certainty: This means that, in the absence of overriding concerns of public interest, persons are entitled to assume that EU Law will not be suddenly changed to their disadvantage.

General principles have formed an important source of EU Law, and the CJEU has struck down EU legislation and decisions of the Union institutions for breaching them. Furthermore, national courts have also disapplied national legislation for infringing them.

2.5.3.4 Direct effect

A key principle that gave supremacy to EU law is 'direct effect', which the ECJ first developed in the landmark case of *Van Gend en Loos v Nederlandse Administratie der Belastingen* (Case 26/62) [1963] ECR 1. The claimants had imported a product into the Netherlands from Germany and had been charged a customs duty contrary to what is now Article 30 TFEU. They challenged the duty in the Dutch courts, which referred the case to the ECJ. The ECJ ruled that Article 30 had direct effect and so the claimants could rely on it in the Dutch courts to claim back the customs duty. This was an example of 'vertical' direct effect; ie EU law being enforced against the state or a state body.

Subsequently in *Defrenne v SABENA* (Case 43/75) ECLI:EU:C:1976:56, [1976] ECR 455, the ECJ ruled that Treaty articles could also have horizontal direct effect and be enforced against private bodies. The Belgian airline, SABENA, paid its female cabin crew less than its male cabin crew. Although this was permissible under Belgian law, this breached what is now Article 157 TFEU, which provides that men and women should receive equal pay for equal work or work of equal value. The ECJ held that individuals could rely on the direct effect of

Article 157 against private bodies before their national courts; accordingly, a female member of SABENA's cabin crew was able to claim equal pay.

The ECJ has also ruled that regulations and decisions are capable of both vertical and horizontal direct effect. In contrast, directives can only have vertical direct effect; ie they can only be enforced against the state or emanations of the state. However, in order for a provision of EU law to have direct effect it must be sufficiently clear, precise and unconditional and must not require additional measures, either at national or EU level (the '*Van Gend* criteria'). Furthermore, for a Directive to have direct effect, there is an additional requirement that the time limit for implementation by Member States has expired (*Pubblico Ministero v Ratti* (Case 148/78) EU:C:1979:110, [1979] ECR 1629).

2.5.3.5 The UK's approach

When the UK joined the EU, it signed up to the supremacy of EU law. However, the fact that the UK Government accepts treaty obligations on behalf of the UK does not, however, in itself have any effect on parliamentary sovereignty. Treaties are made by the UK Government alone and do not of themselves change the law. Under the 'dualist' system that operates in the UK, if the Government signs a treaty that requires a change in the law, it is for Parliament to authorise such a change by legislation.

The UK Government signed what is now the TFEU on 22 January 1972, but the Treaty was not incorporated into domestic law until later that year when Parliament enacted the ECA 1972 which came into force on the UK's accession on 1 January 1973.

The principal provisions of the ECA 1972 were as follows:

- Section 2(1): This provided that directly effective rights and obligations arising under EU law should be enforceable in the UK courts.
- Section 2(2): This enabled the UK Government to make delegated legislation to implement EU law (eg directives) within the UK.
- Section 2(4): This required all UK legislation whenever to be adopted (primary and secondary) to 'be construed and have effect' subject to provisions of EU law.
- Section 3(1): This requires UK courts to apply EU law in accordance with principles laid down by the Court of Justice of the European Union (CJEU) (ie decisions of the CJEU were in effect binding).

Accordingly, during the UK's membership of the EU, the ECA 1972 required UK courts to apply EU law in the cases they were hearing. To ensure that the courts of the Member States interpreted EU law correctly, Article 267 TFEU also enables and sometimes requires national courts to refer questions of interpretation of EU law to the Court of Justice (the highest of the two courts which comprise the CJEU and often referred to as the 'ECJ'). During the UK's membership of the EU and the transition period, UK courts often referred questions of EU law to the Court of Justice and then applied the EU's interpretation to the facts of the case they were hearing. The Court of Justice developed many key principles of EU law such as direct effect through Article 267 references from national courts.

2.5.3.6 The effect of ECA 1972, s 2(4)

Section 2(4) of the ECA 1972 had a significant impact on the doctrine of parliamentary sovereignty. It essentially had two limbs. First, it created a rule of construction, by providing that the courts had to read UK legislation in such a way as to make it compliant with EU law. In EU law, this is known as the doctrine of *indirect effect*. If, however, it was not possible for the courts to read UK legislation in such a way, the courts had to give precedence to directly effective EU law and set aside inconsistent national legislation.

2.5.3.7 Indirect effect

The leading case on indirect effect is *Marleasing SA v La Comercial Internacional de Alimentacion* SA (Case C-106/89) [1990] ECR I-4135 in which the ECJ stated that 'in applying national law, whether the provisions in question were adopted before or after the directive, the national court called upon to interpret it [ie national law] is required to do so, as far as possible, in the light of the wording and the purpose of the directive in order to achieve the result pursued by the latter [ie the directive] . . .'.

An example of indirect effect in the UK can be found in *Pickstone v Freemans plc* [1989] AC 66. Female employees brought an equal pay claim against their employer, the catalogue company Freemans. They worked for Freemans as 'warehouse operatives' but were paid less than a male colleague, who was described as a 'warehouse checker operative'. However, their work was of equal value to Freemans as their male colleague's work. Therefore, they argued, the true reason for the difference in pay was sex discrimination. Such discrimination breached Directive 75/117 – the Equal Pay Directive. However, the UK regulations (supposedly implementing the Directive) only provided for equal pay for the same work done by men and women, not for work of equal value.

The House of Lords held that the purpose of the UK regulations had been to give effect to EU law. A strict reading of them failed to achieve this, and so the House of Lords adopted a 'purposive' interpretation in which it departed from the strict literal interpretation of the UK regulations and implied words into the regulations in order to comply with EU law.

#### 2.5.3.8 Conflict between UK law and EU law

Cases such as *Pickstone v Freemans* show that the courts were willing to construe UK legislation in such a way as to make it compliant with EU law, often construing legislation against its strict literal meaning or implying words into statute to achieve the desired result. In some cases, however, it was impossible for the courts to interpret statute in such a way as to comply with EU law because there was a direct conflict between them. This occurred in *R v Secretary of State for Transport, ex p Factortame (No 2)* [1991] AC 603.

The UK passed the Merchant Shipping Act 1988 to prevent fishing in British waters by Spanish fishers who had set up a British company (Factortame Ltd) and registered their boats as British under existing merchant shipping legislation. The Act imposed new conditions for registration, and the Secretary of State made regulations under the Act so that vessels had to re-register. The boats owned by Factortame were refused registration. Factortame challenged the Act on the grounds that it breached EU law on free movement and asked for an interim injunction suspending the operation of the Act. This issue was appealed to the House of Lords. The House of Lords refused the interim injunction, but made an Article 267 reference to the ECJ on whether it was correct to do so.

The ECJ held that the House of Lords should have granted an injunction, as this was necessary to protect the rights of *Factortame* under EU law. Accordingly the House of Lords granted the interim injunction, effectively suspending the operation of an Act of Parliament. The effect of this decision was that the doctrine of implied repeal did not prevent directly effective EU law prevailing over post-1972 Acts of Parliament where there was a conflict between their respective provisions. Where a conflict existed, the provisions of directly effective EU law took precedence by virtue of s 2(4) of the ECA 1972, which had been acknowledged to be a constitutional statute that could not be subject to implied repeal.

The judgment in *Factortame (No 2)* had a profound effect on the doctrine of parliamentary sovereignty. The House of Lords suspended the operation of an Act of Parliament and held that, by virtue of s 2(4), directly effective EU law took precedence over conflicting UK law. However, the reason that the House of Lords did this was because Parliament, by enacting the ECA 1972, had in effect instructed the courts to do so.

Section 18 of the European Union Act 2011 confirmed this approach by clarifying that any 'limits' on sovereignty were imposed only at Parliament's own behest.

#### 2.5.3.9 State liability for non-implementation of EU law

In addition to challenging UK legislation that is incompatible with EU law, an individual who had suffered resulting loss may obtain damages from the Crown, as a result of the decision in *Francovich v Italian Republic* (Joined Cases C-6/90 and 9/90) ECLI:EU:C:1991:428, [1991] ECR I-5357, as considered and developed in later case law. So, for example, if an individual suffered loss because the UK failed to implement a directive, they would have had a right of action under *Francovich* even where they would have been unable to use the directive itself. This might happen where the directive conferred rights against employers (eg to equal treatment in employment) but the individual was employed by a private employer rather than the state. (Directives only have 'vertical' effect, against state bodies.)

The significance of this for parliamentary sovereignty was the UK Government might have been liable to pay damages arising from Parliament's failure to pass legislation giving effect to EU law, or the defective implementation of EU law in an Act of Parliament.

2.5.3.10 Express repeal of the ECA 1972

Although the judgment in *Factortame* made it clear that Parliament could not impliedly repeal EU law, legally there was nothing to prevent Parliament passing an Act which expressly repealed the ECA 1972 or any provision of EU law. Following the 2016 referendum when UK electorate voted to leave the EU, Parliament enacted the EUWA 2018, which repealed the ECA 1972. However, the European Union (Withdrawal Agreement) Act 2020 did keep in force the provisions in ss 2 and 3 of the ECA 1972 providing for the supremacy of EU law until the end of the transition period.

2.5.3.11 Retained EU law/assimilated law

Under the EUWA 2018, all EU law in force at the end of the transition period has been converted into domestic law and labelled 'retained EU law'. Section 5(2) of the EUWA 2018 (as originally enacted) provided that the principle of supremacy of EU law continued to apply to retained EU law, so that if there was a conflict between pre-Brexit domestic law and pre-Brexit directly effective EU law, then the EU law took priority.

The concepts of retained EU law and assimilated law will be covered in more depth in **Chapter 10**. Briefly retained EU law consisted of:

- **EU-derived domestic legislation**: This consisted chiefly of secondary legislation adopted pursuant to s 2(2) of the ECA 1972 to implement EU obligations. The secondary legislation would otherwise have fallen away on the repeal of the ECA 1972. It also included Acts of Parliament enacted to implement EU obligations. Although these Acts would not have fallen away on the repeal of the ECA, it was important to define them as retained EU law to ensure they benefited from its special status.

  Whilst the bulk of EU-derived domestic legislation consisted of secondary legislation, it also included some Acts of Parliament.

  Following the Retained EU Law (Revocation and Reform) Act 2023 (REULA 2023), EU-derived domestic legislation now forms part of assimilated law.

- **Direct EU legislation:** This consisted of EU legislation that applied directly in the UK such as regulations and decisions.

  Following REULA 2023, direct EU legislation forms part of assimilated law and is now known as direct assimilated legislation.

- **Rights etc arising under s 2(1) of the ECA 1972**: This consisted of directly effective EU rights and obligations that did not fall under *either* of the previous two categories. An example given in the explanatory notes accompanying the EUWA 2018 was Article 157 TFEU – equal pay for male and female workers.

  REULA 2023 abolished this category of retained EU law, although it gave the Government a limited power to restate provisions that originally fell within this category.

One important consequence of legislation falling within the scope of retained EU law was that it retained a limited form of supremacy. Whilst the EUWA 2018 terminated the general supremacy of EU law, retained EU law remained supreme over other UK legislation enacted before the end of the transition period until the end of 2023 when REULA 2023 ended its supremacy. For example, suppose an Act of Parliament passed in 2010 conflicted with an earlier piece of retained EU law such as an EU regulation adopted in 2005. Under the doctrine of implied repeal, the 2010 Act would have prevailed over the regulation, but as retained EU law the EU regulation prevailed over the 2010 Act. However, REULA 2023 changed the status of retained EU law, and since 1 January 2024 the 2010 Act will prevail over all EU regulations whenever adopted. However, UK legislation enacted after the end of the transition period always prevailed over retained EU law.

The European Union (Withdrawal Agreement) Act 2020 also gives direct effect to any provisions in the Withdrawal Agreement that meet the criteria for direct effect. **Chapter 10** covers this in more depth.

### 2.5.4 Incorporation of the ECHR into domestic law

The ECHR was written in 1950 and protects rights such as the right to life (Article 2), the right not to be tortured (Article 3), the right to a fair trial (Article 6), the right to a private and family life (Article 8), and freedom of religion, expression and association (Articles 9–11). The UK became a signatory in 1951, but it was only in 1965 that the UK Government recognised the right of individual citizens to petition the European Court of Human Rights (ECtHR) under the Convention. Further, it was not until the enactment of the Human Rights Act that individual citizens could bring a claim for breach of their rights under the ECHR before our domestic courts. Prior to this, domestic courts would not consider a legal claim based on an alleged breach of an individual's human rights. Individuals in the UK could only enforce their ECHR rights by taking their case to the ECtHR in Strasbourg after exhausting all domestic remedies.

### 2.5.5 Method of incorporation

In contrast to the 'strong' method of incorporation of EU law into domestic law, the language used in the HRA 1998 suggests a 'weak' method of incorporation of the ECHR.

The key sections of the HRA 1998 are as follows:

(a) Section 1 (and Schedule 1). Section 1 lists the articles of the Convention incorporated into UK law, with the articles themselves set out in Schedule 1.

(b) Section 2. Although domestic courts must 'take into account' judgments of the ECtHR, they are not bound to follow such judgments. However, in practice domestic courts do normally follow them. Lord Bingham provided an authoritative summary of what s 2 entails for UK courts in *R v Special Adjudicator (Respondent), ex p Ullah* [2004] 2 AC 323:

> While ... case law [of the ECtHR] is not strictly binding ... courts should, in the absence of some special circumstances, follow any clear and constant jurisprudence of the Strasbourg court.

Many commentators argue that Lord Bingham was being overly deferential to the ECtHR. There are signs that UK courts are now more willing to depart from ECtHR case law than previously as can be seen, for example, in the comments of the Supreme Court in *R (Hallam) v Secretary of State for Justice* [2019] UKSC 2 where a majority of justices (5–2) decided to follow domestic precedent even though it possibly conflicted with ECtHR case law, although each judge gave different reasoning for doing so.

(c) Section 3. Primary and secondary legislation must be interpreted in accordance with Convention rights 'so far as it is possible to do so'. This applies to legislation passed both before and after the coming into force of the HRA 1998.

(d) Section 4. Where a court cannot interpret legislation in a manner that makes the legislation compliant with Convention rights, the courts may make a declaration of incompatibility. Such a declaration does not invalidate or affect the operation of the offending Act.

(e) Section 10. Where a declaration of incompatibility has been made under s 4 or a judgment of the ECtHR makes it clear that legislation is incompatible with Convention rights, this section creates a 'fast-track' procedure that the Government may use to amend the relevant legislation, if there are 'compelling reasons' to do so; alternatively it can submit a bill to Parliament for this purpose. The Government is not, however, obliged to amend the offending legislation, and if it decides not to, an aggrieved litigant would have to take their case to the ECtHR to obtain redress.

(f) Section 19. A minister who introduces a government bill into Parliament must, before the second reading of the bill, either make a statement that the provisions in the bill are compatible with Convention rights, or alternatively make a statement to the effect that although they are unable to make a statement of compatibility, the Government nevertheless wishes the House of Commons to proceed with the bill.

This has been described as a 'weak' method of incorporation compared to the ECA 1972. The drafting of the HRA 1998 was designed specifically to preserve the supremacy of Parliament. In its White Paper, *Rights Brought Home: The Human Rights Bill*, the Government said that the Act was 'intended to provide a new basis for judicial interpretation of all legislation, not a basis for striking down any part of it'.

There was a fear that, were a 'strong' method of incorporation chosen, the judiciary would have had the power to strike down Acts of Parliament and deprive such acts of their legal effect.

### 2.5.6 Impact of the Human Rights Act on parliamentary sovereignty

#### 2.5.6.1 Section 3 of the Human Rights Act 1998: principle of construction

Two House of Lords' cases show that the courts have been willing to use s 3 of the HRA 1998 to stretch the meaning of legislation to make such legislation compatible with Convention rights.

In *R v A (No 2)* [2002] 1 AC 45, s 41 of the Youth Justice and Criminal Evidence Act 1999 imposed restrictions on a defendant charged with rape from being permitted to adduce at his trial evidence of his alleged victim's previous sexual history. The House of Lords considered that a strict reading of this section could contravene a defendant's right to a fair trial under Article 6 of the ECHR, because there were circumstances when such evidence might be relevant to the issue of consent. The House of Lords therefore read this section to mean that evidence of a complainant's previous sexual history could not be adduced, provided this did not infringe the defendant's right to a fair trial.

The House of Lords effectively read extra words into the statute. Lord Steyn conceded that this had required the courts to 'adopt an interpretation which may appear linguistically strained'. He also said that s 3 imposed a duty on the courts to 'strive to find a possible interpretation compatible with Convention rights'.

In *Ghaidan v Godin-Mendoza* [2004] 2 AC 557, under relevant housing legislation, the rights to a tenancy of residential premises could be inherited by the tenant's surviving spouse, or by someone living with the tenant at his or her death as the tenant's wife or husband. The issue on appeal was whether this extended to the survivor of a same-sex couple who had been living together and how, therefore, the relevant provisions should be interpreted in the light of Article 8 of the ECHR (the right to respect for private and family life).

The House of Lords held that, when given its ordinary meaning, the housing legislation treated survivors of homosexual partnerships less favourably than survivors of heterosexual partnerships, without any rational or fair ground for such distinction, and this constituted a breach of the surviving partner's rights under Art 8 of the Convention. Accordingly the House of Lords used its power under s 3 of the HRA 1998 to read the housing legislation as extending to same-sex partners. This took the provisions of the legislation much further than their literal meaning. The lead judgment was again given by Lord Steyn:

> Section 3 requires a broad approach concentrating ... in a purposive way on the importance of the fundamental right involved.

Both cases show that the courts have perhaps gone further than Parliament intended when exercising their powers of interpretation under s 3. The only occasions on which the courts will be unable to use their interpretative powers under s 3 to ensure that a statute is compatible with Convention rights is when to do so would be expressly contrary to the wording of the statute.

2.5.6.2 Disapplying s 3 of the Human Rights Act 1998

It appeared that the previous Government had an emerging policy of watering down the effect of s 3 by introducing legislation which disapplied its provisions. Examples are the Illegal Migration Act 2023 and the Safety of Rwanda (Asylum and Immigration) Act 2024 which aimed to deal with challenges facing the UK's asylum process, in particular small boat crossings across the English Channel from France. The aim of these Acts was to facilitate the removal of asylum seekers entering the UK illegally either to their home country or a safe third country such as Rwanda and for their asylum claims to be considered there.

Both Acts disapplied s 3 of the HRA 1998, meaning that courts and public authorities would not be required to interpret provisions of the Acts themselves, nor secondary legislation enacted pursuant to their provisions, compatibly with Convention rights. Additionally, sections in the Victims and Prisoners Act 2024 disapplied s 3 in relation to legislation involving prisoners' release, licences, supervision and recall of offenders.

The aim of disapplying s 3 was to ensure that the courts interpreted and applied specific legislative provisions in the way that Parliament intended, rather than adopting a strained interpretation which departed from the parliamentary intention. In such cases the higher courts would still have the power to issue declarations of incompatibility under s 4.

However, following the change of government after the 2024 general election, on 30 January 2025 the Home Secretary introduced in Parliament the Border Security, Asylum and Immigration Bill which provides for the repeal of the Rwanda Act and much of the Illegal Migration Act. Accordingly, the disapplication provisions in these Acts will be largely of academic interest. Moreover, the provisions in the Victims and Prisoners Act 2024 have not yet come into force, and, as the Labour Government is more favourably disposed th the HRA 1998 than its Conservative predecessor, they may never do so.

2.5.6.3 Section 4 Human Rights Act 1998: declarations of incompatibility

Where the courts are unable to interpret domestic legislation in such a way as to make it compatible with Convention rights, a declaration of incompatibility may be made under s 4 of the HRA 1998. Such a declaration is merely a legal statement that, in the opinion of the court, the relevant legislation contravenes the ECHR. The declaration does not invalidate the legislation, and neither the Government nor Parliament is under any legal obligation to amend it.

However, when the courts have made a declaration of incompatibility there will frequently be considerable political pressure on the Government to amend or repeal the relevant legislation. This occurred following the decision of the House of Lords in *R (Anderson) v Secretary of State for the Home Department* [2002] UKHL 46, [2003] 1 AC 837. This case concerned how long adults convicted of murder should spend in prison for purposes of punishment. At the time of the case, the final decision on this was taken by the Home Secretary in accordance with s 29 of the Crime (Sentences) Act 1997.

It was alleged that the s 29 provision was inconsistent with Article 6 of the ECHR. This was because the imposition of sentence is part of the trial process, and thus should be determined by an independent and impartial tribunal. As a member of the executive, the Home Secretary was not an independent and impartial tribunal. It was not possible to interpret s 29 of the Crime (Sentences) Act 1997 in such a way as to make it compatible with Convention rights, because such an interpretation would have been contrary to the wording of the section:

> Section 3(1) is not available where the suggested interpretation is contrary to express statutory words or is by implication necessarily contradicted by the statute.
>
> (per Lord Steyn)

The House of Lords accordingly made a declaration of incompatibility. The Government subsequently introduced legislation (the Criminal Justice Act 2003) to abolish the Home Secretary's powers to determine the length of sentence in such cases.

The strength of the Government's political obligation to respond to a declaration of incompatibility is illustrated by the Government 's response to the decision of the House of Lords in *A v Secretary of State for the Home Department* [2005] 2 AC 68 (the '*Belmarsh*' case). This involved a challenge to provisions in the Anti-terrorism, Crime and Security Act 2001, which permitted foreign nationals suspected of being involved in terrorist activities (but against whom there was insufficient evidence to bring criminal proceedings) to be detained indefinitely without trial. The House of Lords held that such detention breached the ECHR, and made a declaration of incompatibility in respect of the relevant part of the 2001 Act. Within three months of this decision, the offending legislation was repealed.

The sole example where Parliament has refused to amend incompatible legislation is *Hirst v United Kingdom (No 2)* [2005] ECHR 681, where the ECtHR ruled that a blanket ban on British prisoners exercising the right to vote was contrary to Article 3 of Protocol 1 to the ECHR (the right to free elections). The Scottish Registration Appeal Court in *Smith v Scott* 2007 SC 345 issued a declaration of incompatibility in relation to the ban, but the UK Government and Parliament remain strongly opposed to amending the incompatible UK legislation, and any amendments to UK legislation seem highly unlikely. Instead a compromise was reached, with the Government allowing prisoners who are released on temporary licence or on home detention curfew to vote (this did not require a change in legislation). The Council of Europe in December 2018 accepted that this is sufficient to comply with the ECtHR's judgment.

2.5.6.4 Express repeal of the Human Rights Act 1998

Legally there is nothing to prevent Parliament amending or expressly repealing the HRA 1998. For political reasons, however, it has been thought that Parliament is unlikely to take such a step. By incorporating the ECHR into UK law, the 1998 Act has put in place a number of basic rights for citizens of the UK, and to remove such rights would be politically unpopular.

However, there has been considerable criticism of the operation of the 1998 Act and ECHR by some politicians and sections of the media. Consequently the Conservative Party manifesto for the 2019 general election contained a commitment to 'update [the 1998 Act] to ensure that there is a proper balance between the rights of individuals, our vital national security and effective government'. Accordingly, in December 2020 the previous Conservative Government announced an independent review, the Independent Human Rights Act Review (IHRAR), to examine the framework of the HRA 1998, its operation in practice and whether any changes were required.

The IHRAR reported in December 2021 that the HRA 1998 has been a success and made only modest recommendations for change. The Conservative Government then announced a consultation on reforms to the HRA 1998, and in the Queen's Speech of May 2022 set out proposals for a British Bill of Rights to replace the HRA 1998. These proposals went considerably beyond the IHRAR's recommendations and, according to the Government, aimed to 'restore the balance of power between the legislature and the courts' and 'end the abuse of the human rights framework and restore some common sense to our justice system'. Subsequently, the Government submitted to Parliament the Bill of Rights Bill 2022 which would have repealed and replaced the HRA 1998. There were some similarities between the Bill of Rights Bill and the HRA 1998. In particular, the Bill of Rights Bill would have:

- incorporated the same Convention rights as the HRA 1998;
- required public authorities to act compatibly with Convention rights; and
- given higher courts the power to issue declarations of incompatibility.

There were also some crucial differences, as the Bill would have replaced various provisions of the HRA 1998 with a range of new measures, including:

- introducing a new permission stage, requiring claimants to prove they had suffered significant disadvantage due to a breach of their rights before they can take their claim to court;
- removing the requirement for courts to interpret legislation compatibly with Convention rights;
- removing the requirement for courts to take into account judgments of the ECtHR and instead requiring them to adopt a more literal reading of Convention rights;
- making it harder for offenders to rely on their Convention rights; and
- removing the requirement for ministers introducing bills to Parliament to make a statement regarding the bill's compatibility with Convention rights.

Critics of the Bill of Rights Bill argued that it would have reduced human rights protection in the UK and resulted in more cases against the UK Government being taken to the ECtHR, and in June 2023 the Conservative Government announced that it was not proceeding with the Bill.

## 2.6 Parliamentary privilege

Both Houses of Parliament have a privilege jurisdiction, which is designed to enable them to manage their own proceedings without outside interference. This is part of the law and custom of Parliament. In outline, the main privileges of the House of Commons are as follows:

(a) Freedom of speech

(b) The right to control its own composition and procedures ('exclusive cognisance')

The Committee of Privileges, a Commons select committee, is responsible for considering specific matters relating to privileges referred to it by the House.

### 2.6.1 Freedom of speech

Freedom of speech is based on article 9 of the Bill of Rights 1689, which provides that freedom of speech and debates or proceedings in Parliament 'ought not to be impeached or questioned in any court or place out of Parliament'. The aim of freedom of speech is to enable parliamentarians to carry out their functions without fear of civil proceedings or criminal prosecutions. However, it also applies to parliamentary officials and non-members such as witnesses before a committee of one of the Houses.

A consequence of this privilege is that MPs and Lords have immunity from legal proceedings, leading to concerns that MPs or Lords may abuse this privilege, for example by libelling individuals with impunity. MPs and Lords also have immunity from contempt of court and have sometimes disclosed in debates facts that could not otherwise be lawfully disclosed. For example, in May 2011 Liberal Democrat MP John Hemming named the former Manchester United footballer Ryan Giggs as being involved in an affair notwithstanding an injunction preventing disclosure of his name. In October 2018 Lord Hain, a former cabinet minister, during a debate in the Lords named Sir Philip Green as the businessman accused of sexual harassment and bullying, even though Sir Philip had obtained an interim injunction preventing disclosure of his identity.

Subsequently, Sir Philip brought proceedings before the ECtHR, claiming that the use of parliamentary privilege to disclose his identity despite the existence of the injunction violated his rights under Article 6 (right to a fair trial) and Article 8 (right to respect for private and family life) of the ECHR. The ECtHR ruled that the UK had not violated the ECHR, finding that it should be left to the UK, and the UK Parliament in particular, to decide on whether and to what extent controls might be needed to prevent parliamentarians from disclosing information subject to injunctions. To rule otherwise would be contrary to the principle of the autonomy of Parliament (*Green v United Kingdom*, Application no 22077/19 (ECtHR, 8 April 2025)).

This privilege only covers 'proceedings in Parliament'. Whilst the privilege clearly includes core proceedings such as parliamentary debates, questions in Parliament and committee proceedings, defining its exact extent can be problematic. Erskine May (*Parliamentary Practice*, 25th edn

(London, 2019)) states; 'it has been concluded that an exhaustive definition [of proceedings in Parliament] could not be achieved'. As a general rule, however, privilege encompasses ancillary matters such as words spoken or written and actions taken outside the core proceedings themselves, but which are of necessity connected to those proceedings. Parliament, through its committees, has sometimes attempted to define the scope of privilege. A particularly noteworthy case was that of Duncan Sandys MP. In 1938 he was threatened with prosecution for breaching the Official Secrets Act 1911 when he brought up a matter of national security in a parliamentary question but refused to disclose his source, namely a leak regarding British military preparedness. The Select Committee of Privileges ruled that an MP should not to be threatened with prosecution in this way and that such threats could constitute a breach of privilege.

Although Parliament has asserted its right to define the scope of parliamentary privilege, the Bill of Rights is a statute and so article 9 is subject to interpretation by the courts. In general the courts have interpreted the scope of this privilege widely. In *Church of Scientology v Johnson-Smith* [1972] 1 All ER 37 the claimant was not permitted, in libel proceedings, to prove allegations of malice by relying on statements made by the defendant, an MP, in the House of Commons, as they were absolutely privileged. In contrast, in *Rost v Edwards* [1990] 2 QB 460 the High Court held that the Register of Members' Interests (a records of MPs' financial interests) did not fall within the definition of a proceeding in Parliament, though there has been some debate whether this judgment is correct.

The privilege also extends to official reports of proceedings in Parliament and to committee proceedings. After litigation in the 1830s, Parliament enacted the Parliamentary Papers Act 1840, which makes it clear that papers published by Parliament attract absolute privilege.

There has also been discussion regarding to what extent parliamentary privilege exists for communications between constituents and MPs. In *Rivlin v Bilainkin* (1953) 1 QBD 534 the court held that where there is no connection to proceedings in Parliament, there is no privilege. On the other hand, it is believed that where there is a connection to proceedings in Parliament, privilege will exist.

In addition to the absolute privilege relating to proceedings in Parliament, the courts have held that certain statements and publications are eligible for qualified privilege (ie they are protected from defamations action unless malice can be proved). Accordingly in *Wason v Walter* (1868) LR 4 QB 73 the court held that fair and accurate reports of parliamentary proceedings had qualified privilege.

In *Pepper v Hart* [1993] AC 593 the House of Lords held that where an Act of Parliament is ambiguous or obscure the courts may take into account statements made in Parliament by ministers or other promoters of a bill in construing that legislation. Previously, using Hansard in this way would have been regarded as a breach of parliamentary privilege.

### 2.6.2 The right to control its own composition and procedures – 'exclusive cognisance'

Parliament has sole control over all aspects of its own affairs: to decide for itself what procedures it should adopt, whether any of its procedures have been breached and, if so, what the consequences will be. This has been largely accepted by the courts who will not question the validity of an Act on the basis that correct procedures were not followed (*Pickin v British Railways Board* [1974] AC 765).

Parliament's right to regulate its own affairs includes disciplinary powers over MPs; eg the right to suspend them for misconduct. It also includes the right to punish anyone, including non-members, for contempt of Parliament – any conduct that might substantially prevent or hinder the work of either House. In theory, Parliament may punish contempt by imprisonment, though this has not occurred since the 19th century. More usually, offenders are given reprimands. In December 2018 MPs voted to hold the Government in contempt of Parliament. The Government had refused to release the legal advice given by the Attorney General Geoffrey Cox to the then Prime Minister, Theresa May, regarding an agreement that the UK had reached with the EU, despite Parliament passing a motion demanding that it be made available. After the contempt motion, the Government published the advice. However, there were no further consequences.

### 2.6.3 Recent developments

The issue of MPs' expenses and allowances has attracted significant media attention in recent years as a result of a scandal during 2009 particularly focusing on expenses claims by MPs with second homes in London. As a result, criminal prosecutions were started against a few MPs relating to fraudulent expenses claims. One question the courts had to consider was whether parliamentary privilege precluded their jurisdiction to deal with such issues. In December 2010, in *R v Chaytor (David) and others* [2010] UKSC 52, the Supreme Court held that neither article 9 of the Bill of Rights 1689 nor the House of Commons' right to 'exclusive cognisance' of its own affairs affected the Crown Court's jurisdiction to try MPs on charges of false accounting in relation to their parliamentary expenses claims. The Supreme Court regarded article 9 as principally directed at MPs' freedom of speech and debate in the Houses of Parliament and in parliamentary committees. Examination of MPs' expenses claims by the courts would not according to the Supreme Court adversely affect the core or essential business of Parliament.

The Supreme Court also said that Parliament had never claimed an exclusive right to deal with criminal conduct within the precincts of Parliament, even where it relates to or interferes with parliamentary proceedings.

Largely as a response to the expenses scandal, Parliament enacted the Parliamentary Standards Act 2009 setting up the Independent Parliamentary Standards Authority (IPSA) to independently oversee and regulate MPs' expenses.

---

## Summary

Parliament is one of the key actors in the UK constitution. It is the legislative branch of government, but also performs other vital functions such as scrutinising the Government's policies and also providing the personnel of government.

Most Acts of Parliament are passed by both the House of Commons and the House of Lords. However, the Parliament Acts 1911 and 1949 provide a procedure that enables the Commons to bypass the Lords and submit a bill for Royal Assent without the Lords' consent.

Parliamentary sovereignty is one of the fundamental features of the UK constitution. In theory this means Parliament can pass any law it wants to and no one (including the courts) can challenge an Act of Parliament. However, there are limitations on parliamentary sovereignty - domestic and European.

Domestic limitations include:

- The impact of devolution
- The concept of constitutional statutes that cannot be impliedly repealed
- The 'manner and form' debate
- The rule of law

The European limitations arise from the UK's membership of the EU and the incorporation of the ECHR into UK law. Whilst the UK left the EU on 31 January 2020, an understanding of the impact of EU law in the UK remains essential.

You should also check your understanding of parliamentary sovereignty by considering the summary diagram set out in **Figure 2.1**.

Proceedings in Parliament are absolutely privileged. This is to ensure that parliamentarians can perform their duties without outside interference.

**Figure 2.1** Parliamentary sovereignty

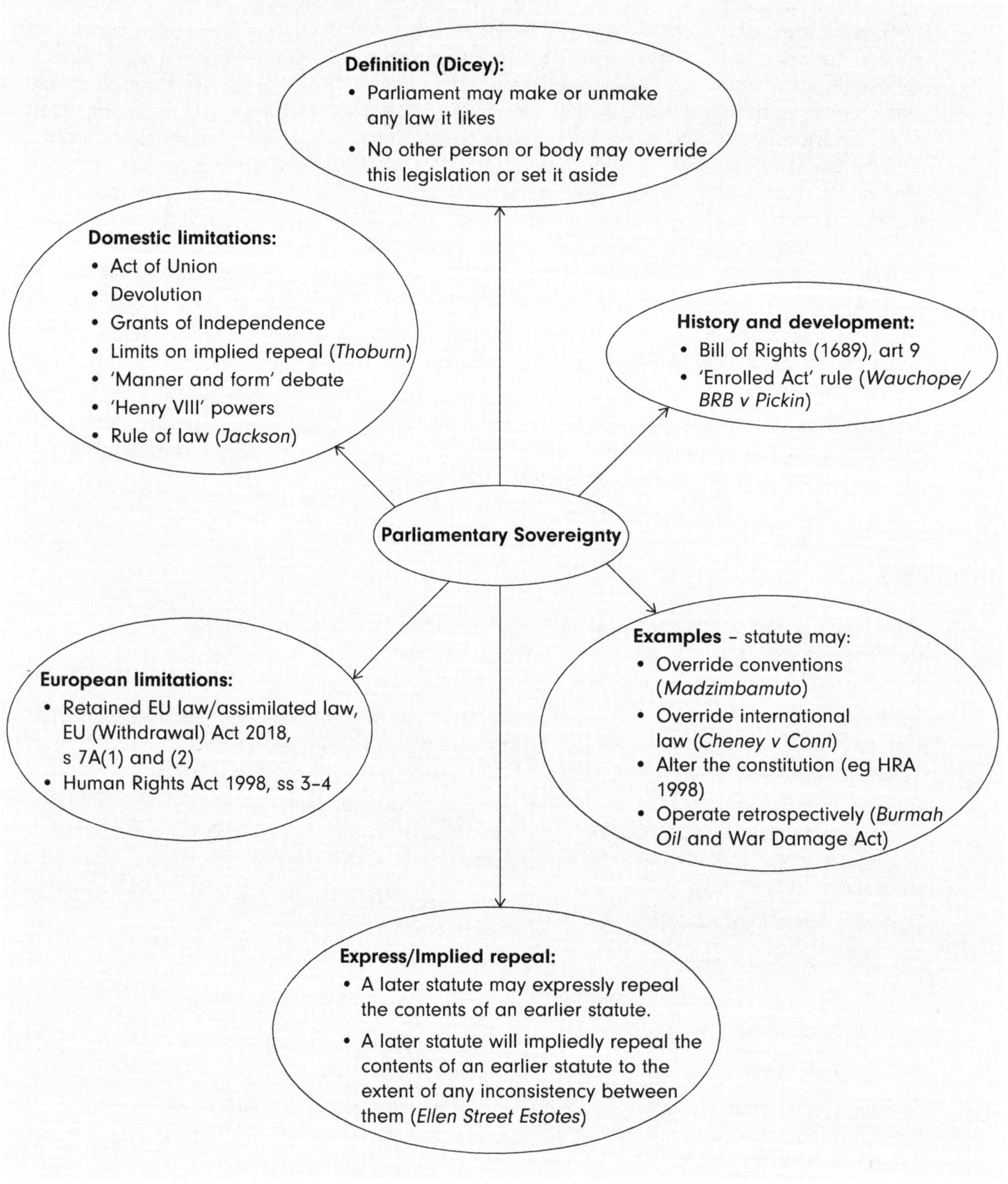

## Sample questions

**Question 1**

Assume that Parliament passed an Act (fictitious) in 2021 giving voting rights to 16- and 17-year-olds in local government elections in England. Following a change of government, Parliament passed another Act in 2024 removing the voting rights of 16- and 17-year-olds. The Act of 2024, however, makes no reference to the Act of 2021. A 16-year-old who has been barred from voting in a local government election wants to challenge in court the loss of her voting rights.

**Will the challenge by the 16-year-old be successful?**

A No, because the Act of 2024 impliedly repealed the inconsistent provisions contained in the Act of 2021.

B No, because the Act of 2024 contained express words making clear the intention to repeal the voting rights of 16- and 17-year-olds.

C Yes, because the Act of 2021 is a constitutional statute and cannot be impliedly repealed.

D Yes, because the Act of 2024 did not expressly repeal the Act of 2021, a constitutional statute.

E Yes, because the Act of 2024 did not refer to the Act of 2021, a constitutional statute.

**Answer**

Option B is correct. The Act of 2021, dealing with the franchise for local elections, is clearly a constitutional statute. In *Thoburn*, Laws LJ stated that constitutional statutes cannot be impliedly repealed, so option A is wrong. However, constitutional statutes may be repealed by express words or words so specific that make Parliament's intention to repeal very clear. The wording of the Act of 2024 removing the voting rights of 16- and 17-year-olds seems very clear.

Whilst option C is correct in stating that constitutional statutes cannot be impliedly repealed, in this instance the words of the Act of 2024 are sufficiently clear to repeal the Act of 2021. Options D and E are wrong due to the clarity of the wording of the Act of 2024.

**Question 2**

The Government is considering introducing a bill that it believes will violate Convention rights.

**Which of the following best describes whether the Government can proceed with the bill?**

A The Government cannot proceed with the bill as the Human Rights Act 1998 precludes the passage of legislation that violates Convention rights.

B The Government cannot proceed with the bill as the Human Rights Act 1998 is a constitutional statute, which cannot be impliedly repealed.

C The Government can proceed with the bill. However, the minister introducing the bill must state that, although they are unable to make a statement of compatibility, the Government nevertheless wishes the House of Commons to proceed with the bill.

D The Government can proceed with the bill. However, the minister introducing the bill must state that the Government wishes the House of Commons to proceed using the procedures set out in the Parliament Acts 1911 and 1949.

E The Government can proceed with the bill. Parliament is sovereign and can expressly or impliedly repeal the Human Rights Act 1998.

**Answer**

The correct answer is C. The Human Rights Act 1998 preserved parliamentary sovereignty as it permits the Government to proceed with a bill that violates Convention rights, subject to the minister responsible for the bill making a statement on the proposed legislation's compatibility with Convention rights. Accordingly option A is wrong as the 1998 Act does not preclude legislation that violates Convention rights. Although the 1998 Act is a constitutional statute, option B is wrong as the doctrine of implied repeal does not prevent Parliament expressly passing legislation violating human rights.

Option D is wrong because the Parliament Acts 1911 and 1949 enable the House of Commons to override the House of Lords when enacting legislation. They have no direct connection with the 1998 Act.

Option E is wrong because the Human Rights Act 1998 has been recognised by the courts as a constitutional statute and so cannot be impliedly repealed.

**Question 3**

An MP makes a speech in a parliamentary debate in which she defames a well-known celebrity. The statement is clearly untrue.

**Which of the following best describes whether the celebrity can sue the MP?**

A The celebrity cannot sue unless the Speaker of the House of Commons certifies that he may proceed.

B The celebrity cannot sue as statements in parliamentary proceedings are absolutely privileged.

C The celebrity can sue because parliamentary privilege does not protect statements that are clearly untrue.

D The celebrity can sue because the MP has abused parliamentary privilege by making an untrue statement.

E The celebrity can sue because the courts have decided that defamation proceedings do not interfere with Parliament's core business.

**Answer**

Option B is correct. MPs are immune from civil and criminal proceedings regarding anything they say in parliamentary proceedings. This is based on article 9 of the Bill of Rights – freedom of speech.

Option A is wrong because the privilege is absolute and the Speaker cannot waive it. Whilst there are concerns that MPs may abuse parliamentary privilege by making defamatory statements, the courts have no jurisdiction even if they do. Options C and D are therefore wrong.

Option E is wrong, as the reasoning in it relates to the criminal prosecution of MPs for false accounting in relation to expenses claims.

# 3 Devolution



## SQE1 syllabus

This chapter will enable you to achieve the SQE1 assessment specification in relation to functioning legal knowledge concerned with core constitutional principles, including:

- the status of the devolved institutions and their relationship with Westminster; and
- powers and procedures for the enactment, implementation and repeal of primary and secondary legislation by Senedd Cymru and Welsh Ministers.

Note that for SQE1, candidates are not usually required to recall specific case names or cite statutory or regulatory authorities. Cases are provided for illustrative purposes only.

## Learning outcomes

By the end of this chapter you will be able to understand and apply some fundamental constitutional principles appropriately and effectively, at the level required of a competent newly qualified solicitor in practice, to realistic client-based problems and situations concerned with:

- the creation of the Scottish Parliament, the Senedd Cymru of Wales (the Welsh Parliament) and the Northern Ireland Assembly;
- the composition of the devolved institutions (legislative and executive);
- the powers of the devolved legislatures;
- the relationship between the devolved institutions and the UK Government and Parliament; and
- the role of the courts regarding devolution issues.

## 3.1 The United Kingdom

The United Kingdom of Great Britain and Northern Ireland consists of four countries: England, Wales, Scotland and Northern Ireland. The union evolved over several centuries in stages.

### 3.1.1 Scotland

Scotland was a separate country with a separate legal system and constitution until the Act of Union 1707. From the accession of James I (VI of Scotland) in 1603 Scotland had shared the same monarch as England and Wales. The effect of the Act of Union (and similar Scottish legislation) was to abolish the separate Parliaments of England and Wales, and Scotland, and to create a single Parliament of Great Britain, with authority over all three countries. In certain key areas, for example the legal system, education and local government, Scotland has remained distinct from England.

### 3.1.2 Wales

Wales was militarily conquered by Edward I, the English King, in 1283 and after that English influence steadily grew. Under Henry VIII, the English Parliament passed the Laws in Wales Acts 1535–1542 (subsequently labelled the Acts of Union) under which Wales was effectively incorporated into England. The Welsh were granted the same rights as the King's subjects in England, and Welsh constituencies were added to the House of Commons. English was declared to be the official language of the law.

Over the centuries that followed there was only limited constitutional recognition of the distinctiveness of Wales, and it was not until 1964 that the UK Government created the cabinet post of Secretary of State for Wales. The Welsh Language Act 1967 permitted the use of the Welsh language in legal proceedings in Wales.

### 3.1.3 Northern Ireland

Although the Crown claimed authority over the whole of Ireland from 1541, Ireland retained its own Parliament until 1800. Before 1800, the Parliament of Great Britain claimed a disputed authority to legislate for Ireland. The issue was resolved by the Act of Union 1800, which united the Kingdoms of Great Britain and Ireland, abolished the Irish Parliament and established the legislative supremacy of the Parliament of Great Britain and Ireland, which had (protestant) Irish representation.

As a result of armed conflict in Ireland the Government of Ireland Act 1920 divided Ireland between six of the counties of Ulster in the north, and the rest of Ireland, the south. The 1920 Act provided for the creation of separate Parliaments for Northern and Southern Ireland with the power to legislate for their respective territories, subject to the exclusion of certain matters that were reserved to the Westminster Parliament.

However, the Southern Ireland Parliament never came into being as in 1922, following the signing of the Anglo-Irish Treaty, the southern counties were given Dominion status (similar to that of Canada for example) making them in effect self-governing as a 'Free State' (the Irish Free State (Constitution) Act 1922). The UK Parliament retained ultimate authority until 1937 when the Irish Government unilaterally adopted an independent constitution. It was not until 1949 that the UK Parliament accepted this loss of supremacy (in the Ireland Act 1949).

From 1922 until 1972 Northern Ireland had its own legislature (the 'Stormont Parliament'). Northern Ireland continued to be represented by MPs in the House of Commons, and Parliament retained supremacy over Northern Ireland. Due to the sectarian violence in Northern Ireland known as 'the Troubles', the UK Government suspended the Stormont Parliament in 1972 and introduced direct rule pursuant to the Northern Ireland (Temporary Provisions) Act 1972. The Northern Ireland Constitution Act 1973 subsequently abolished the Stormont Parliament and replaced it with a Northern Ireland Assembly in an attempt to restore devolved government. However, the Assembly collapsed in 1974 and the Northern Ireland

Act 1974 then made provision for the governing of Northern Ireland. The 1974 Act authorised the dissolution of the Northern Ireland Assembly and transferred its legislative powers to the Queen in Council, ie the UK Government.

In April 1998 the UK Government agreed proposals for constitutional change with the Irish Government and various political parties in Northern Ireland, culminating in the Belfast or Good Friday Agreement which brought an end to the Troubles. The proposals were submitted to the electorate in both Northern Ireland and the Republic of Ireland in May 1998, and approved by referendum. As a result, Parliament passed the Northern Ireland Act (NIA) 1998, which devolved legislative powers to a new Northern Ireland Assembly and created a 'power-sharing executive'. Further details are at **3.5.3** below.

However, in January 2017 the Northern Ireland executive collapsed and was not reconstituted until January 2020. Following the Assembly elections in May 2022, it has not been possible to form a new executive; the executive ministers who held office before the elections remain in post, but only on a caretaker basis.

## 3.2 Devolution

The United Kingdom is a unitary state. Although it comprises four countries, the Westminster Parliament is sovereign and can, in theory at least, pass whatever legislation it likes for all four countries. It is the one principal source of legal power in the UK and has the competence to legislate for the whole of the UK at all levels. This is in contrast to a federal state where the constitution gives powers to different levels of government, the federal government and state governments, as in the USA and Germany. In a federal state the constitution will allocate certain powers to the federal government, usually those relating to foreign policy, defence, immigration, tariffs and responsibility for the country's currency. There will be certain powers that can be exercised concurrently by the federal and state governments, whilst the constitution will allocate other powers such as education and ownership of property exclusively to the states. In a modern state the division of powers between federal and state governments can raise highly complex legal issues, but in simple terms if the federal government passes legislation on a matter exclusively allocated to the states, then the courts can strike that legislation down.

The UK remains a unitary state despite devolution. The UK Parliament has devolved legislative powers in many fields to the Scottish Parliament and Welsh and Northern Ireland assemblies. However, the crucial difference between the UK and a federal state is that the UK Parliament has delegated certain powers to the devolved legislatures and legally could revoke those powers. The UK Parliament remains supreme, and so retains the power to legislate on all devolved matters and to override the devolved legislatures. Whilst overriding the devolved legislatures could have very significant political consequences, it is legally possible for the UK Parliament to do so. Unlike in a federal state, power is not divided between the different levels of government. Instead, the UK Parliament has delegated some of its powers to the devolved legislatures without giving up those powers.

The political and legal impact of devolution has nonetheless been significant. The UK has moved from being a very centralised state with power concentrated in London to one where, in some areas at least, power is dispersed across the four countries.

## 3.3 Scotland

The first attempt at devolution in Scotland occurred in the late 1970s. The Scotland Act 1978 provided for the creation of a devolved assembly, subject to confirmation in a referendum. The Act also required 40% of the eligible electorate to vote in favour of devolution. However, although a majority of those voting supported the creation of the assembly, they represented only 32.9% of the eligible electorate.

Following the election of a new Labour Government in May 1997, the Referendums (Scotland and Wales) Act 1997 paved the way for referendums on devolution in Wales and Scotland, and a substantial majority of Scottish voters supported the creation of a Scottish Parliament. According to s 63A of the Scotland Act 1998 (added by the Scotland Act 2016), the Scottish Parliament and Scottish Government are a permanent part of the constitutional arrangements of the UK; accordingly, neither institution may be abolished unless the people of Scotland vote for this in a referendum.

### 3.3.1 The Scottish Parliament

The Scotland Act 1998 established the Scottish Parliament and Scottish Executive (now Scottish Government). The Scottish Parliament has 129 members, known as Members of the Scottish Parliament (MSPs). Of these, 73 are constituency members and 56 are regional members. Originally the Scottish Parliament's constituencies were the same as those for the Westminster Parliament, but following devolution the number of Scottish Westminster constituencies was reduced to reflect the population of Scotland more accurately. The constituency MSPs are elected using the first past the post system, whilst seven regional members are elected from each of eight Scottish regions. The Scottish Parliament has a Presiding Officer (equivalent to the Speaker) assisted by two or more deputies. In Scottish parliamentary elections, 16- and 17-year-olds are able to vote.

Initially elections for the Scottish Parliament took place every four years, but the Scottish Elections (Reform) Act 2020, an Act of the Scottish Parliament, extended this to five years. An early (extraordinary) election will take place if two-thirds of MSPs vote in favour of it or Parliament does not nominate a First Minister within 28 days of an election due to:

- the First Minister resigning or otherwise ceasing to be First Minister; or
- the First Minister ceasing to be an MSP otherwise than by dissolution of Parliament.

The First Minister must resign if the Government loses a vote of no confidence.

The last election took place on 6 May 2021 and the next one is scheduled for 7 May 2026. If an extraordinary general election takes place, it is in addition to any scheduled ordinary general elections unless taking place less than six months before the due date of an ordinary general election, in which case the ordinary election would be cancelled.

The 1998 Act gave the Scottish Parliament the power to pass primary legislation. Once the Scottish Parliament has passed a bill and it has received Royal Assent, it is known as an Act of the Scottish Parliament. The process for enacting legislation is very similar to that for the Senedd Cymru set out at **3.4.1.3** below.

### 3.3.2 Devolved matters

The 1998 Act devolved to the Scottish Parliament all matters other than reserved matters. This is known as the 'reserved powers' model, in that the Scottish Parliament has the power to legislate on all matters that are not expressly reserved to Westminster. Thus, the Scottish Parliament has the power to legislate over a wide range of matters, including health, education, much of civil and criminal law, and local government. Other functions (including responsibility for the constitution, foreign policy and defence) are retained by the UK Parliament.

Following the election of a Scottish National Party Government in Scotland, a referendum took place in 2014 on whether Scotland should become an independent state and leave the UK. During the campaign, the UK Government promised to devolve further powers to Scotland should Scottish voters decide against independence. As Scottish voters voted against independence, the UK Parliament then devolved further powers on the Scottish Parliament. The Scottish Parliament therefore now has significant tax-raising powers. Since 2015, it has had the power to levy its own Scottish Landfill Tax (a tax on the disposal of waste to landfill) in place of the UK Landfill Tax and a Land and Buildings Transaction Tax in place of the UK's Stamp Duty Land Tax (SDLT). It also intends to levy Air Departure Tax (ADT) to replace Air Passenger Duty, a tax levied on passengers departing from UK airports, but ADT had not, at the time of writing, yet come into force.

Originally, the Scottish Parliament also had the power to raise or cut income tax by 3p in the pound, a power it never used. Since April 2016 the Scottish Parliament has had the power to set a different rate of income tax in Scotland, known as the Scottish Rate of Income Tax (SRIT). Since April 2017 it has had the power to set the tax band thresholds (excluding the personal allowance) as well as the rates. This applies to all non-savings and non-dividend income of Scottish taxpayers. Accordingly, while outside Scotland the additional rate of income tax for income over £125,140 is 45%, the rate in Scotland is 48%.

3.3.2.1 Legislative competence

The Scotland Act 1998 provides that an Act of the Scottish Parliament is not law so far as any of its provisions are outside the legislative competence of the Parliament, and expressly specifies which areas are outside its competence. Provisions outside its legislative competence are those that:

- would form part of the law of any territory other than Scotland;
- relate to reserved matters;
- modify certain enactments, including specified provisions of the Union with Scotland Act 1706 and the Union with England Act 1707 so far as they relate to the freedom of trade, certain specified provisions of the European Communities Act 1972 (until the transition period ended), the European Union (Withdrawal) Act (EUWA) 2018 and the Human Rights Act 1998;
- are incompatible with the ECHR and, until the transition period ended, with European Union law; or
- would remove the Lord Advocate from their position as head of the systems of criminal prosecution and investigation of deaths.

The Scottish Parliament has the power to amend or repeal Acts of the UK Parliament provided the subject-matter falls within its legislative competence. Any such amendment or repeal would, however, only be effective in relation to Scotland.

The minister in charge of a bill must make a statement that, in their view, the provisions of the bill are within the Scottish Parliament's legislative competence. The Presiding Officer must also make a statement on legislative competence, but this differs from that of the minister in charge. Whilst the minister's statement must assert the Parliament's legislative competence, the Presiding Officer's statement may, with reasons, indicate that in their opinion the bill is outside its competence. A statement by the Presiding Officer in such terms does not preclude the bill from proceeding. Neither opinion is, however, conclusive on the Parliament's legislative competence. Therefore, the Advocate General (the UK Government's chief adviser legal adviser on Scots law), the Lord Advocate (see **3.3.3** below) or the Attorney General may refer to the Supreme Court the question whether a bill or any of its provisions are within the Parliament's legislative competence.

The Scotland Act 1998 also provides that where a provision in an Act of the Scottish Parliament could be read as being outside its legislative competence, such a provision is to be read as narrowly as is required for it to be within competence, if such a reading is possible.

### 3.3.3 The Scottish Government

The Scottish Government is headed by the First Minister, currently John Swinney, who is appointed by the Monarch. The First Minister will normally be the leader of the largest party in the Scottish Parliament, currently the Scottish National Party. The Scottish Government will also include:

- ministers and junior ministers appointed by the First Minister with Parliament's agreement and the approval of the Monarch; and

- the Lord Advocate and the Solicitor-General for Scotland (equivalent to the Attorney General and Solicitor-General in the UK Government) recommended by the First Minister with Parliament's agreement but appointed by the Monarch. The cabinet consists of 10 Scottish Ministers. There are also 18 Junior Scottish Ministers.

### 3.3.4 The Sewel Convention

In July 1998, during the passage of the Scotland Act 1998 through the UK Parliament, the UK Government announced that a convention would be established that Westminster would not normally legislate on devolved matters in Scotland without the consent of the Scottish Parliament. This convention has been labelled 'the Sewel Convention' after Lord Sewel, the minister who first announced the policy. The convention was also extended to Wales and Northern Ireland, and was incorporated in a series of memorandums of understanding between the UK Government and the devolved administrations.

There is now statutory recognition of the Sewel Convention, as the Scotland Act 2016 added a provision to the 1998 Act providing that the UK Parliament 'will not normally legislate with regard to devolved matters without the consent of the Scottish Parliament' (s 28(8)). However, this does not affect s 28(7) of the 1998 Act, which provides that the creation of the Scottish Parliament does not affect the power of the UK Parliament to make laws for Scotland. The Sewel Convention does not affect parliamentary sovereignty. The Supreme Court affirmed this in *R (Miller) v Secretary of State for Exiting the European Union* [2017] UKSC 5 (*Miller (No 1)*) by holding that the Sewel Convention, despite its recognition in statute, created no legal obligation on the UK Parliament to seek the consent of the Scottish Parliament before passing legislation to leave the European Union. Whilst the Sewel Convention provides a political constraint on the Westminster Parliament, it is not the role of the courts to police it.

When the UK Parliament wants to legislate on a matter devolved to the Scottish Parliament, it will, pursuant to the Sewel Convention, seek the Scottish Parliament's consent before enacting the legislation in question. The Scottish Parliament will give its consent through Legislative Consent Motions (LCMs). LCMs are often uncontroversial. For example, suppose the UK Parliament is considering legislation extending to Scotland that pertains to both devolved and reserved matters, for example because it deals with technical issues that are sensibly handled on a UK-wide basis. If the Scottish Parliament supports the legislation, it is more convenient for the UK Parliament to deal with it. This avoids the need for two pieces of legislation, an Act of the UK Parliament and an Act of the Scottish Parliament.

Whilst the Scottish Parliament has often been willing to pass LCMs, it has refused to do so regarding much of the legislation regarding the UK's withdrawal from the European Union. For example, it refused consent to the EUWA 2018 and the European Union (Withdrawal Agreement) Act 2020. Indeed, all three devolved legislatures refused consent to the 2020 Act. Nonetheless, the UK Parliament proceeded with their enactment.

## 3.4 Wales

As with Scotland, there was also an abortive attempt at devolution in the late 1970s. Under the then Labour Government, Parliament passed the Wales Act 1978, which provided for the creation of a devolved assembly in Wales if Welsh voters supported it in a referendum. However, in the ensuing Welsh referendum, 80% of the electorate voted against devolution.

Following the election of a new Labour Government in May 1997, in the referendum triggered by the Referendums (Scotland and Wales) Act 1997, there was a very narrow majority in favour of devolution. Parliament then enacted the Government of Wales Act 1998, which established the National Assembly of Wales. The 1998 Act granted the National Assembly the power to pass delegated legislation in certain specified fields. In contrast to the reserved powers model, this was termed a 'conferred powers' model as it limited the competence of the National Assembly to those powers specifically granted to it. Initially there was no distinction between the legislative and executive branches of the National Assembly, but the Government of Wales Act (GWA) 2006 split it into two parts, the National Assembly (the legislature – now the Senedd Cymru) and the Welsh Assembly Government, now simply called the Welsh Government (the executive). Section A1 of the GWA 2006 declares these institutions to be a permanent part of the UK's constitutional arrangements in the same way as their Scottish counterparts. Accordingly, they can only be abolished following a referendum.

### 3.4.1 Senedd Cymru/Welsh Parliament

3.4.1.1 Composition and elections

The Senedd and Elections (Wales) Act 2020, an Act of the National Assembly, provided for the National Assembly to be renamed as Senedd Cymru or the Welsh Parliament, commonly known as the Senedd. Acts of the Assembly are now known as Acts of the Senedd, whilst Assembly Members (AMs) are now known as Members of the Senedd (MSs).

The Senedd has 60 MSs, of which 40 are elected to represent the same Welsh constituencies as are used in elections for the UK Parliament whilst a further 20 are elected to represent the five electoral regions of Wales, based on a system of proportional representation. Those aged 16 and 17 years are now able to vote in Senedd elections. The Senedd Cymru (Members and Elections) Act 2024 increases the number of MSs to 96 with effect from the May 2026 elections due to the increase in the Senedd's responsibilities. It also changes the Senedd's electoral system so that all MSs are elected via closed list proportional representation.

Originally, elections were to be held every four years, but they currently take place every five years with the next election scheduled for 7 May 2026. However, after the 2026 election, the Senedd Cymru (Members and Elections) Act 2024 provides that elections will once again take place every four years. An early (extraordinary) election will be triggered in similar circumstances to those in which one would be triggered in Scotland (see **3.3.1** above). The Labour Party won 30 of the 60 seats in the May 2021 elections and governed Wales with the aid of a co-operation agreement with Plaid Cymru, the Welsh nationalist party, until May 2024 when Plaid Cymru withdrew from the agreement. The Labour Party continues in office even though it is one seat short of an overall majority.

3.4.1.2 Legislative competence

The GWA 2006 also paved the way for the extension of the National Assembly's legislative powers, as it conferred the power on the National Assembly to pass primary legislation, known as Acts of the Assembly (now Acts of the Senedd). The procedure for passing an Act of the Senedd is similar to passing an Act of the UK Parliament, as the Senedd must pass a bill, which becomes an Act when it receives Royal Assent. However, the provisions extending the National Assembly's powers had to be approved by a referendum before they could come into force. A referendum took place in 2011 and the electorate voted in favour of them. The 2011 Act gave the Assembly the power to pass legislation in 21 broad subject areas such as agriculture, education, health, the environment, housing, local government and tourism. There were some exceptions; for example, on health the National Assembly could not legislate on health and human embryology.

Subsequently the Wales Act 2017 changed the devolution settlement by moving to a reserved powers model (see **3.3.2** above). This means that the Senedd has the power to pass legislation on all matters that are not explicitly reserved to the Westminster Parliament, such as defence, foreign affairs and immigration. This is the same model that is used for Scotland and Northern Ireland. Whilst some reserved matters are common to all three devolved legislatures, such as constitutional matters, immigration, defence and foreign affairs, others are not. For example, criminal justice is largely a devolved matter in Scotland and Northern Ireland, but a reserved matter in Wales (though there are discussions under way about devolving criminal justice to the Senedd). The Senedd also has some powers regarding taxation, as in April 2018 two taxes, the Land Transaction Tax (LTT) and Landfill Disposals Tax (LDT) were devolved. The LTT, a tax on property transactions, replaced SDLT in Wales whilst LDT replaced the UK Landfill Tax.

Like the Scottish Parliament, an Act outside the Senedd's legislative competence is not law (GWA 2006, s 108A(1)). Very similar restrictions apply to the Senedd's legislative competence as apply to the Scottish Parliament (GWA 2006, s 108A; also see **3.3.2** above). Thus, the minister introducing a bill to the Senedd and the Presiding Officer (the Senedd's equivalent of the Speaker) must make statements regarding whether the provisions of the bill are within the Senedd's legislative competence. Similarly, the Counsel General (see **3.4.2** below) or the Attorney General may refer the question whether a bill, or any provision of a bill, is within the Senedd's legislative competence to the Supreme Court. Where any provision of an Act of the Senedd could be read in such a way as to be outside or inside the Senedd's legislative competence, it should be interpreted as being inside its competence (GWA 2006, s 154(2)).

3.4.1.3 Legislative procedures

**(a) Government bills**

The Welsh Government sends the bill and related documents to the Senedd, and the bill then undergoes scrutiny. This is usually a four-stage process:

*Stage 1: consideration and agreement of the bill's general principles*

General principles committees examine the bill. MSs then vote on whether it should continue to Stage 2.

*Stage 2: detailed consideration of the bill and any changes by a committee*

MSs can propose amendments. The committee of MSs responsible for the bill's subject-matter considers the amendments and then votes on them.

*Stage 3: detailed consideration of the bill and any changes by the Senedd*

MSs can propose further amendments to the bill. These are then debated in the Senedd and MSs then vote on each of them.

*Report stage: an optional stage to make amendments (if required)*

On completion of Stage 3, the MS in charge of the bill may propose that the Senedd consider amendments at Report Stage. This is an additional amending stage, and may be invoked where MSs have agreed substantial or significant changes at Stage 3.

*Stage 4: a vote by the Senedd to pass the bill's final text.*

The Senedd votes on a motion to pass the final text of the bill. Once the bill is passed, it is normally sent for Royal Assent after about four weeks. The period of four weeks provides a window for the law officers to refer the question of whether the bill is within the Senedd's legislative competence to the Supreme Court; see **3.6.1** below.

**(b) Member bills**

As well as Welsh Government bills, there is an equivalent to the Westminster Parliament's private members' bills (see **2.3.1** above). These are known as member bills and are introduced by individual MSs. Member bills are subject to the same process as other bills.

**(c) Private bills**

It is also possible to introduce private bills which alter the law only as it applies to specific individuals or bodies (rather than the public as a whole); see **2.3.2** above.

**(d) Secondary legislation**

Welsh minsters may also enact secondary legislation where authorised to do so by a parent act. This may be an Act of the Westminster Parliament or an Act of the Senedd Cymru. Similar to the Westminster Parliament, Welsh secondary legislation will usually be subject to either the affirmative procedure or negative procedure; see **2.3.5** above. Under the affirmative procedure, the secondary legislation will not come into effect unless approved by the Senedd. In contrast, secondary legislation subject to the negative procedure will come into force unless MSs object to it within 40 days of a draft being laid before the Senedd.

3.4.1.4 Welsh law

As a result of the devolution process, a significant body of law pertaining only to Wales is coming into being. Although England and Wales remain a single jurisdiction, there are now some calls for Wales to become a separate jurisdiction in its own right, as are Scotland and Northern Ireland. Indeed, s A2 of the GWA 2006 (added by the Wales Act 2017) recognises the existence of Welsh law, although the provisions fall short of recognising Wales as a separate jurisdiction, as Welsh law is described as being part of the law of England and Wales.

### 3.4.2 The Welsh Government

The Welsh Government is headed by the First Minister, currently Eluned Morgan, appointed by the Monarch after having been nominated by the Senedd. The First Minister recommends for appointment, by the Monarch, the Counsel General to the Welsh Government (equivalent to the Attorney General in the UK Government) and appoints up to 12 Welsh ministers and deputy ministers (with the approval of the Monarch) to serve in the cabinet.

### 3.4.3 The Sewel Convention

The Sewel Convention discussed at **3.3.3** above also applies to Wales. The Wales Act 2017 added to the GWA 2006 provisions giving statutory recognition to the Sewel Convention; see now s 107(5) and (6). These are identical to those applying in Scotland.

## 3.5 Northern Ireland

### 3.5.1 The Good Friday Agreement

Following often violent conflict starting in the late 1960s (often described as 'the Troubles'), multi-party negotiations between the British and Irish governments and the main Northern Irish political parties culminated in the 'Good Friday Agreement' (or 'Belfast Agreement') of April 1998. As part of the constitutional settlement for Northern Ireland, the Irish Government agreed to amend the Irish Constitution to recognise that a united Ireland shall be brought about only by peaceful means with the consent of a majority of the people in both Northern Ireland and the Irish Republic. Section 1 of the Northern Ireland Act 1998, which the UK Parliament enacted following the Good Friday Agreement, provides that Northern Ireland shall not cease to be part of the UK without the consent of a majority of the people of Northern Ireland voting in a referendum.

There are three strands to the Good Friday Agreement:

(a) The first strand provides for a democratically elected assembly with a power-sharing executive;

(b) The second is the North/South Ministerial Council, comprising ministers from Northern Ireland and the Irish Republic. It co-operates and develops policies on matters of mutual interest within the island of Ireland in fields such as agriculture, education and the environment.

(c) The third is the British-Irish Council, comprising representatives from the British and Irish governments, the devolved administrations (Northern Ireland, Scotland and Wales), the Isle of Man, Guernsey and Jersey. Its purpose is to promote harmonious and mutually beneficial relationships between the peoples represented in the Council.

### 3.5.2 The Northern Ireland Assembly

The NIA 1998 established the Northern Ireland Assembly, granting it the power to enact primary legislation, known as Acts of the Northern Ireland Assembly. A bill becomes an Act once the Assembly has passed it and it has received Royal Assent. The 1998 Act in essence followed the reserved powers model, although it uses different terminology. It grants the Assembly the competence to legislate over 'transferred matters', but defines transferred matters as all matters except for 'reserved matters' and 'excepted matters'. As with the other devolved legislatures, an Act outside the Assembly's legislative competence is not law (NIA 1998, s 6(1)).

Excepted matters will remain with the UK Government indefinitely and include international relations, defence and immigration. Reserved matters are areas where the Northern Ireland Assembly can legislate with the consent of the Secretary of State and may be devolved in the future. These include firearms and explosives, financial services and pensions regulation, broadcasting, disqualification from Assembly membership, consumer safety and intellectual property. Policing and criminal justice were originally reserved matters but in April 2010 they were devolved and so became transferred matters.

The minister in charge of a bill must make a statement on or before its introduction that in their opinion the bill is within the legislative competence of the Assembly. The Presiding Officer (the Assembly's equivalent to the Speaker) must refer to the Secretary of State any bill that the Presiding Officer considers relates to an excepted or reserved matter.

There is also some entrenched legislation that the Assembly cannot amend, the most significant being the Human Rights Act 1998 and many provisions in the NIA 1998 and, until the transition period ended, the ECA 1972.

Legislation that discriminates against any person or class of person on the ground of religious belief or political opinion is also outside the Assembly's competence (NIA 1998, s 6(2)(e)). Also, where primary legislation is capable of being interpreted as within the Assembly's legislative competence or outside a competence, then it should be interpreted as being within a competence (NIA 1998, s 83(2)).

The Sewel Convention applies to Northern Ireland but, unlike the position in Scotland and Wales, it does not have express statutory recognition.

The Assembly comprises 90 members known as Members of the Legislative Assembly ('MLAs'). Members are elected under the single transferable vote form of proportional representation. Originally, elections were to be held every four years, but they now take place every five years. An early (extraordinary) election will take place if two-thirds of MLAs vote in favour of it or ministerial offices are not filled within the requisite time limit. The next election must take place on or before 6 May 2027.

### 3.5.3 Northern Ireland Executive

Unlike most executives, the Northern Ireland Executive does not consist chiefly of members of the ruling party or parties. Due to the legacy of the Troubles, the Northern Ireland Act 1998 provides for power-sharing between the different communities in Northern Ireland. To ensure balanced community representation, there are three political designations - 'Nationalist', 'Unionist' and 'Other'. Following an Assembly election, the Assembly must appoint a First Minister ('FM'), deputy First Minister ('DFM') and Northern Ireland ministers within 14 days after the first meeting of the Assembly following an election. If it does not appoint them, the Secretary of State must propose a date for another (extraordinary) election, though to stop this happening after the 2017 election the Westminster Parliament passed legislation providing for extensions of the deadline.

The FM is the nominee of the largest political party of the largest political designation, whilst the DFM is the nominee of the largest political party of the next largest political designation. The FM and DFM hold office jointly, so that if one resigns the other ceases to hold office. Despite the different titles, the FM and DFM also have equal status.

Ongoing difficulties with the peace process in Northern Ireland have hindered the practical achievement of devolution. Northern Ireland reverted to the direct control of the relevant Secretary of State for a time during 2000 and 2001, and in fact remained under such control from late 2002 for over four years. However, following a breakthrough in negotiations between the main political parties, the power-sharing executive was restored in 2007. Subsequently, in January 2017 Martin McGuinness of Sinn Féin resigned as DFM in a protest over what has been called the 'Renewable Heat Incentive scandal' and this led to the collapse of the Northern Ireland Executive. It was not until January 2020 that the Northern Irish political parties were able to agree on a new FM and DFM. However, the Democratic Unionist Party (DUP) withdrew from the executive in February 2022 as a protest against the Northern Ireland Protocol; consequently the executive ceased to function.

Elections took place in May 2022 with Sinn Féin emerging as the largest party. This is the first time a Nationalist rather than Unionist party has been the largest. However, the DUP refused to nominate a DFM due to its concerns regarding the Northern Ireland Protocol, and it was only in February 2024 that the DUP agreed to re-enter the executive. Accordingly, Sinn Féin's Michelle O'Neill became Northern Ireland's first nationalist FM, while the DUP's Emma Little-Pengelly became DFM..

The FM and DFM decide the number of ministerial offices, though these cannot exceed 10 without the Secretary of State's consent. Ministers are appointed by the Assembly based on the share of seats held by the political parties, save for the Minister of Justice who is appointed through a cross-community Assembly vote.

## 3.6 The role of the Supreme Court

As explained above, the devolved legislatures only have the competence to pass legislation on devolved matters; they cannot pass legislation on reserved matters. Both the Scotland Act 1998 and Government of Wales Act 1998 provide that whether a provision 'relates to a reserved matter' is to be determined by reference to the purpose of the provision, having regard (amongst other things) to its effect in all the circumstances. There are also other limitations on their competence; for example they cannot pass legislation infringing the ECHR. Although ministers introducing bills in the devolved legislatures and their Presiding Officers have the duty to make statements whether the provisions in bills are within their legislature's competence, it is the courts that actually decide on issues of legislative competence. The Supreme Court plays a particularly significant role in this regard.

There are three ways in which the question whether legislation passed by a devolved legislature is outside its legislative competence can come before the Supreme Court:

- through a reference by a devolved or UK law officer (including the Attorney General for England and Wales) to the Supreme Court. The law officers have the power to refer a bill that the devolved legislature has passed but has not yet received Royal Assent to the Supreme Court for a ruling on whether the bill is within the legislature's competence;
- through an appeal from certain higher courts in England and Wales, Scotland and Northern Ireland; and
- through a reference from certain appellate courts.

### 3.6.1 Referring a bill to the Supreme Court

References to the Supreme Court of a bill that is before a devolved legislature to determine whether the bill is within the legislature's legislative competence are a key aspect of devolution, as they help to determine how far the powers of the devolved legislatures extend. Both the UK Law officers (the Attorney General) and the chief law officers of each of the devolved governments (eg the Lord Advocate in Scotland) have the power to make a reference.

Section 33 of the Scotland Act 1998 gives the law officers the power to refer to the Supreme Court bills that the Scottish Parliament has passed for a ruling on the bill's legislative competence. Section 12 of the GWA 2006 and s 11 of the Northern Ireland Act 1998 contain equivalent procedures.

The case of *Agricultural Sector (Wales) Bill, Reference by the Attorney General for England and Wales* [2014] UKSC 43 provides an example of a reference to the Supreme Court. The bill, which the National Assembly of Wales had passed, aimed to establish a scheme regulating the wages of agricultural workers in Wales. The Attorney General disagreed with the Assembly's view that the bill was within the Assembly's competence, arguing that the bill did not relate to agriculture but to employment and industrial relations, which had not been devolved. The Supreme Court held that the bill's provisions regulating the wages of agricultural workers did 'relate to' agriculture, which was a devolved matter and thus within the Assembly's legislative competence. The Supreme Court stated that the bill's purpose was to regulate agricultural wages so that the agricultural industry in Wales would be supported and protected. It did not matter whether the bill might also be capable of being classified as relating to a matter that had not been devolved, such as employment and industrial relations. The devolution legislation did not require that a provision should only be capable of being characterised as relating to a devolved matter.

The case of *UK Withdrawal from the European Union (Legal Continuity) (Scotland) Bill 2018 – Reference by the Attorney General and Advocate General for Scotland* [2018] UKSC 64 was particularly controversial. The Scottish Parliament passed the UK Withdrawal from the European Union (Legal Continuity) (Scotland) Bill 2018 (the Continuity Bill), aimed at ensuring legal continuity in Scottish law after the UK's exit from the EU. The UK Government's law officers referred the Continuity Bill to the Supreme Court, arguing that its provisions were outside the Scottish Parliament's competence.

The Supreme Court stated that, at the time of the Continuity Bill's passage, most of its provisions were within the Scottish Parliament's legislative competence. However, the UK Parliament subsequently enacted the EUWA 2018, which provided that some of the matters covered by the Continuity Bill should become reserved matters. This resulted in many more provisions of the Continuity Bill being outside the Scottish Parliament's competence.

The cases discussed in this paragraph relate to references of bills that had already been passed by the devolved legislatures. In contrast, the case concerning the Scottish Independence Referendum Bill, *Reference by the Lord Advocate of devolution issues under paragraph 34 of Schedule 6 to the Scotland Act 1998* [2022] UKSC 31, involved a draft bill.

***Scottish Independence Referendum case***

*The Scottish Government wanted to introduce a bill to the Scottish Parliament providing for a referendum on whether Scotland should be an independent country. Unlike the referendum held in 2014, the UK Government refused its consent to the second proposed referendum. The Lord Advocate was unsure whether the bill was within the Scottish Parliament's legislative competence, so could not clear the required ministerial statement that it was; see* ***3.3.2*** *above. The Lord Advocate therefore wanted to refer the question of whether the bill was within the Scottish Parliament's legislative competence to the Supreme Court.*

*The UK Government argued:*

*(i) that the Lord Advocate did not have the power to refer a draft bill to the Supreme Court as the question was purely hypothetical; and*

*(ii) in any event, that the draft bill was outside the Scottish Parliament's legislative competence.*

***Judgment***

*(i) The Supreme Court held that the Lord Advocate did have the requisite power. Paragraph 34 of Sch 6 to the Scotland Act 1998 gave the law officers the power to refer 'devolution issues' to the Supreme Court, and whether the Scottish Parliament had legislative competence to pass the bill in question was a devolution issue*

*as it related to the powers of the Scottish Parliament. Moreover, the issue was not hypothetical as the Scottish Government would submit the bill to the Scottish Parliament should it transpire that the bill fell within its legislative competence.*

*(ii) However, the Supreme Court held that the bill was outside the Scottish Parliament's legislative competence as it related to a reserved matter, namely the Union of the Kingdoms of Scotland and England and/or the Parliament of the United Kingdom. The Scottish Government argued that it did not relate to reserved matters as the result of the referendum would not have been legally binding. However, the Supreme Court stated that, even if a referendum had 'no immediate legal consequences', it would still be 'a political event with important political consequences', and concluded:*

*It is therefore clear that the proposed bill has more than a loose or consequential connection with the reserved matters of the Union of Scotland and England and the sovereignty of the United Kingdom Parliament.*

In the absence of the UK Government's consent, the Scottish Government has been unable to proceed with the proposed referendum.

### 3.6.2 Appeals/references from higher/appellate courts

Significant cases involving devolution issues have also reached the Supreme Court by way of appeals from the superior courts of England and Wales, Scotland and Northern Ireland. Some of these appeals take place under the specific provisions of the Scotland Act 1998, the GWA 2006 and NIA 1998 relating to devolution issues, while others take place in the normal course of legal proceedings. Certain appellate courts can also refer devolution issues to the Supreme Court.

A case involving an appeal was *Imperial Tobacco Ltd v Lord Advocate (Scotland)* [2012] UKSC 61 regarding ss 1 and 9 of the Tobacco and Primary Medical Services (Scotland) Act 2010. Section 1 prohibited the display of tobacco products in a place where tobacco products were offered for sale, whilst s 9 prohibited vending machines for the sale of tobacco products. Imperial Tobacco applied for judicial review of these provisions, arguing that the sections in the 2010 Act related to 'the sale and supply of goods to consumers', which were reserved matters. Imperial Tobacco failed at first instance in the Court of Session and on appeal in the Inner House of the Court of Session, so appealed to the Supreme Court.

The Supreme Court stated that the rules in the Scotland Act 1998 regarding legislative competence must be interpreted in the same way as other rules found in a UK statute. Also, although the 1998 Act was a 'constitutional statute', that could not, in itself, be taken as a guide to its interpretation; it must be interpreted like any other statute. The Supreme Court then went on to reject the appeal after examining the purpose of the 2010 Act. The purpose of s 1 was to render tobacco products less visible to potential consumers and thereby achieve a reduction in sales and thus in smoking. The purpose of s 9 was to make cigarettes less readily available, particularly (but not only) to children and young people, with the aim of reducing smoking. This had no connection with any reserved matter, and so the 2010 Act was within the Scottish Parliament's legislative competence.

The Supreme Court has made it clear that Acts of the devolved legislatures can normally only be challenged on the grounds that they exceed the legislative competence of the legislature, for example by covering a reserved matter or violating the ECHR (*AXA General Insurance v Lord Advocate* [2011] UKSC 46). They cannot be challenged on common law grounds such as irrationality, as it would be inappropriate for the judges to substitute their opinions for the considered views of a democratically elected legislature.

Challenges to legislative competence have also arisen in the context of criminal prosecutions, as in *HM Lord Advocate v Martin* [2010] UKSC 10. The Road Traffic Offenders Act 1988 provided that the maximum sentence that a Scottish sheriff (similar to a magistrate) sitting summarily could impose for the offence of driving while disqualified under the Road Traffic Act 1988 (RTA) was six months' imprisonment or the statutory maximum fine or both. If the offence was prosecuted on indictment (triable before a jury), the maximum sentence was 12 months' imprisonment or a fine or both.

The Scottish Parliament enacted the Criminal Proceedings etc (Reform) (Scotland) Act 2007 increasing the maximum sentence that sheriffs sitting summarily could impose for the offence of driving while disqualified. The aim of the 2007 Act was to reduce pressure on the higher courts.

Two individuals were each sentenced by sheriffs to terms of more than six months' imprisonment for driving while disqualified contrary to the RTA. They both challenged their sentences, claiming that the relevant provisions of the 2007 Act were outside the legislative competence of the Scottish Parliament. After the High Court of Justiciary dismissed their appeals, they appealed to the Supreme Court. The basis of their appeal was that the Scotland Act 1998 defined, under the heading 'Road Transport', the following as reserved matters: 'the Road Traffic Act 1988 and the Road Traffic Offenders Act 1988'.

The Supreme Court by a 3–2 majority rejected the appeal. The change was within the competence of the Scottish Parliament. The purpose of the provisions was to reform summary justice by reducing pressure on the higher courts by reallocating business within the Scottish court system; the jurisdiction of a sheriff was a matter of Scots criminal law, and so did not relate to a reserved matter. It was a simply a change in procedure.

### 3.6.3 Section 35 orders

Section 35 of the Scotland Act 1998 grants the Secretary of State for Scotland the power, in specified circumstances, to prevent legislation enacted by the Scottish Parliament being submitted for royal assent, even if it covers a devolved matter.

In December 2022 the Scottish Parliament passed the Gender Recognition Reform (Scotland) Bill, modifying the Gender Recognition Act 2004 (a UK Act) making it easier for residents of Scotland to obtain a Gender Recognition Certificate (GRC), a document which changes a person's legal sex on their birth certificate. While gender recognition is devolved in Scotland, equal opportunities is a 'reserved matter'. A GRC changes someone's legal sex for the purpose of the Equality Act 2010, and the UK Government has argued that the Bill would adversely affect the Equality Act's application to reserved matters. According to the UK Government, having a different system in Scotland compared to England and Wales could cause confusion, for example in relation to the use of single-sex spaces which the Equality Act permits in certain circumstances. It could also result in an increase in fraudulent applications. The Secretary of State for Scotland therefore issued a s 35 order, effectively vetoing the bill.

In *Scottish Ministers v Advocate General for Scotland* [2023] CSOH 89, the Outer House of the Court of Session rejected the Scottish Government's petition for judicial review of the s 35 order. The case could well reach the Supreme Court.

Section 114 of the Government of Wales Act 2006 contains equivalent provision regarding the Senedd Cymru, but the UK Government has not yet exercised its powers under it.

## 3.7 Relationships between the UK Government and the devolved administrations

The UK Government and the devolved governments agreed a memorandum of understanding in 1999 aimed at co-ordinating the overall relationship between them. The memorandum of understanding created the Joint Ministerial Committee (JMC) that consisted of ministers from the UK and the devolved governments, including in certain circumstances the Prime Minister and the First Ministers. Despite updates to the memorandum of understanding, relations between the UK Government and devolved governments became increasingly strained, as Brexit and the Covid-19 pandemic raised questions about the operation of devolution. Accordingly, a new three-tier intergovernmental relations ('IGR') structure was introduced in January 2022 aimed at improving relations and inter-government cooperation.

The IGR structure now governs the relationship between the UK Government and the devolved governments, and aims to facilitate cooperation and coordination on matters of shared interest.

### 3.7.1 Committee structure

A three-tier committee structure provides for formal multilateral engagement between ministers, which is supplemented by informal interaction at both political and official levels.

3.7.1.1 The Prime Minister and Heads of Devolved Government Council

The Prime Minister and Heads of Devolved Government Council ('the Council') is the top tier of the new structure. Chaired by the Prime Minister, its membership includes the First Ministers of Scotland and Wales, as well as the First and Deputy First Ministers of Northern Ireland. Other ministers are invited as necessary.

The Council considers strategic issues affecting the UK as a whole and provides direction to the wider IGR structure.

3.7.1.2 Interministerial Standing Committee and Finance Interministerial Standing Committee

The middle tier comprises the Interministerial Standing Committee ('IMSC') and the Finance Interministerial Standing Committee ('F:ISC'), with additional time-limited committees possible for specific issues.

IMSC addresses strategic matters beyond individual portfolios and reviews portfolio-level engagement. Its membership varies but always includes ministers responsible for IGR.

F:ISC has a similar strategic role but focuses on fiscal issues, including funding and financial disputes, with finance ministers from the UK and devolved governments as members.

3.7.1.3 Interministerial Groups

Interministerial Groups ('IMGs') are the lowest tier. These are intended to facilitate regular portfolio-level discussion between departmental ministers and cover devolved areas (eg culture) as well as reserved areas that have an impact on devolved matters (eg trade).

### 3.7.2 Other bodies/initiatives

3.7.2.1 The Intergovernmental Secretariat

The Secretariat Provides administrative support for intergovernmental meetings and drafts annual reports on IGR for scrutiny by the four legislatures. Despite being hosted in the Cabinet Office, it is accountable to the Council as a whole, rather than any single government.

3.7.2.2 Common frameworks

Operating in parallel with the IGR structures discussed above, a set of 'common frameworks' have been agreed to facilitate coordination and manage divergence in devolved policy areas that EU law previously covered, eg motor insurance, blood safety, and chemicals and pesticides.

3.7.2.3 The Council of Nations and Regions

The Council of Nations and Regions ('CNR') was set up in 2024 by the Labour Government independently from the IGR framework. Chaired by the Prime Minister, it includes the First Ministers of Scotland and Wales, as well as the First and Deputy First Ministers of Northern Ireland, the Mayor of London, and English metro mayors. Its purpose is to promote collaboration and share best practices on shared challenges. The first meeting, held in Edinburgh in October 2024, focused on attracting inward investment to support economic growth.

### 3.7.3 Dispute Resolution Mechanism

A formal dispute resolution system exists to prevent escalation and to encourage cooperation between governments. Disagreements should be resolved at the portfolio level if possible, with mediation sought before the start of formal procedures. An impartial body must chair the process.

While no disputes have yet been officially resolved through this system, the previous JMC protocol was invoked four times – three over funding allocations and one concerning fishing quotas.

## Summary

The process of devolution in its modern form began in 1998 with the enactment by the UK Parliament of legislation providing for the creation of devolved legislatures and governments in Scotland, Wales and Northern Ireland. Since 1998, the UK Parliament has granted increasing powers to the devolved legislatures – the Scottish Parliament, the Senedd Cymru or Welsh Parliament, and the Northern Ireland Assembly.

Those three legislatures can only pass Acts on devolved matters (or 'transferred' areas in the case of Northern Ireland), with reserved matters (or reserved and excepted in Northern Ireland) remaining with the UK Parliament. The UK Parliament can still legislate in devolved areas, but under the Sewel Convention does 'not normally' do so without the consent of the relevant devolved legislature. **Figure 3.1** below summarises the devolution settlement for each legislature.

In each of the devolved legislatures the minister introducing a bill and the Presiding Officer must make statements regarding whether the provisions of the bill are within the legislature's legislative competence. However, the courts are the final arbiter of whether legislation passed by the devolved legislatures are within their competence.

**Figure 3.1** Devolution models

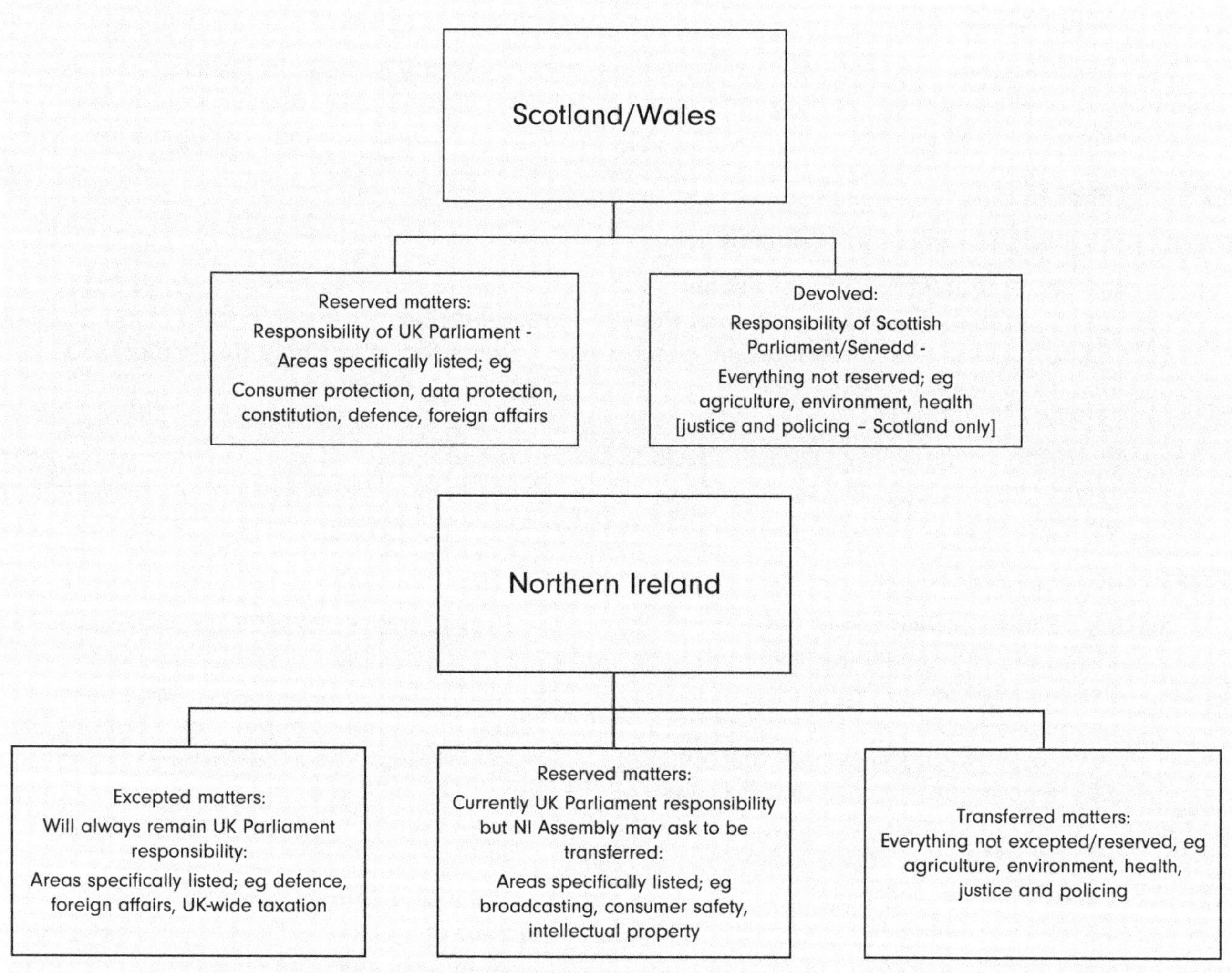

## Sample questions

**Question 1**

The minister in charge of a bill being presented to the Scottish Parliament has asked for advice on whether they can make a statement that the bill is within the Parliament's legislative competence. The minister's main concern is that the bill amends an Act of the UK Parliament.

**Can the minister make a statement that the bill is within the Parliament's legislative competence?**

A No, because the bill amends an Act of the UK Parliament, which is a reserved matter.

B No, because amending Acts of the UK Parliament is explicitly excluded from the Scottish Parliament's legislative competence.

C No, because secondary legislation cannot be used to amend primary legislation.

D Yes, because the Scottish Parliament has full power to amend Acts of the UK Parliament as Acts of the Scottish Parliament are primary legislation.

E Yes, because the Scottish Parliament has power to amend Acts of the UK Parliament unless the subject matter of the bill is outside its legislative competence.

**Answer**

Option E is correct. The Scottish Parliament has power to amend Acts of the UK Parliament so far as they relate to Scotland unless the subject-matter of the bill is outside the legislative competence of the Scottish Parliament.

Option A is wrong as Acts of the UK Parliament are not in themselves reserved matters. The subject matter of some Acts are reserved matters, but the Acts concerned must be specifically listed in the devolution legislation. Option B is wrong. Although there are some protected statutes such as the Human Rights Act 1998, which the Scottish Parliament cannot amend, Acts of the UK Parliament are not in general protected.

Option C is wrong as Acts of the Scottish Parliament are primary legislation. Although the Scottish Parliament is not sovereign in the way that the UK Parliament is, its Acts are still primary legislation. In any event, it is possible for secondary legislation to amend primary legislation. See for example Henry VIII powers discussed in **Chapter 2**.

Option D is wrong as, unlike the UK Parliament, there are limits on the Scottish Parliament's legislative competence.

**Question 2**

The Senedd Cymru, or Welsh Parliament, has passed an Act of the Senedd promoting tourism. The Government of Wales Act 2006 (as amended) does not list tourism as a devolved matter. A business affected by the Act has challenged it by way of judicial review on the grounds that it is outside the Senedd's legislative competence and irrational.

**Which of the following best describes the approach the courts are likely to take to the challenge?**

A The courts will reject the challenge on the basis of the 'Enrolled Act' rule. UK courts will not allow challenges to primary legislation.

B The courts will reject the challenge unless tourism is listed in the 2006 Act as a reserved matter.

C The courts will uphold the challenge as the 2006 Act has not expressly devolved tourism to the Senedd.

D The courts will uphold the challenge if they consider that the Act of the Senedd is irrational.

E The courts will reject the challenge as only the law officers of the UK Government or devolved governments have the standing to challenge Acts of the devolved legislatures.

**Answer**

Option B is correct. The reserved powers model applies to the Senedd. This means that the Senedd has the power to pass legislation on all matters which are not explicitly reserved to the Westminster Parliament. (In fact, tourism is not a reserved matter so the Act will be within the Senedd's legislative competence.)

Option A is wrong because the Enrolled Act rule only applies to Acts of the UK Parliament, which is a sovereign legislature. Option C is wrong, because under the reserved powers model devolved matters are all those matters except for those that are reserved. Originally, the conferred powers model applied in Wales; ie the National Assembly only had powers over the matters expressly devolved to it. However, the reserved powers model now applies to the Senedd.

Option D is wrong as the Supreme Court has stated that Acts of the devolved legislatures cannot be challenged on common law grounds such as irrationality. Option E is wrong as individuals (including businesses) do have the standing to challenge Acts of the devolved legislatures.

**Question 3**

The UK Parliament has passed an Act (fictitious) creating a new criminal offence in England and Wales. The criminal offence relates to a matter that has not been reserved to the UK Parliament. The Senedd Cymru has not passed a legislative consent motion in relation to the Act as it opposed the legislation. A man has been prosecuted for committing the new criminal offence in Wales. The man claims that he has not committed a criminal offence as the Act creating it is unenforceable in Wales.

**Will the courts uphold the man's claim?**

A Yes, because the UK Parliament does not have the competence to legislate on devolved matters.

B Yes, because the Senedd Cymru has not passed a legislative consent motion.

C No, because the UK Parliament has power to pass Acts covering the whole of the UK even if the devolved legislature opposes the legislation.

D No, because the Senedd Cymru lacks competence regarding criminal offences even in relation to devolved matters.

E No, because the Senedd Cymru has not formally vetoed the application of the Act in Wales.

**Answer**

Option C is correct. The Westminster Parliament remains sovereign notwithstanding devolution. It can therefore can pass Acts for the whole of the UK pertaining to devolved matters even in the face of opposition from the devolved legislatures. Although the Sewel Convention provides that the UK Parliament will not normally legislate on a devolved matter without the devolved legislature's consent, it has the competence to do so as the Sewel Convention is not legally enforceable. Accordingly, options A and B are both wrong.

Options D and E are wrong as they give incorrect reasons for why the courts will reject the man's claim. Contrary to what option D states, the Senedd Cymru does have the power to create new offences relating to devolved matters. Option E incorrectly suggests that the Senedd Cymru has a veto over Acts of the UK Parliament; as explained above, the UK Parliament is sovereign.

# 4 Legitimacy, Separation of Powers and the Rule of Law



## SQE1 syllabus

This chapter will enable you to achieve the SQE1 assessment specification in relation to functioning legal knowledge concerned with core constitutional principles, including:

- the separation of powers and the rule of law.

Note that for SQE1, candidates are not usually required to recall specific case names or cite statutory or regulatory authorities. Cases are provided for illustrative purposes only.

## Learning outcomes

By the end of this chapter you will be able to understand and apply some fundamental constitutional principles appropriately and effectively, at the level required of a competent newly qualified solicitor in practice, to realistic client-based problems and situations, including the ability to:

- explain what is meant by the idea of the 'rule of law', using traditional and modern interpretations, and appreciate the importance of this principle;
- appreciate the extent of judicial and statutory recognition of the rule of law;
- describe the doctrine of the separation of powers and explain the reason(s) behind its development;
- understand and analyse the relationship between the executive, legislative and judicial branches of state in the UK; and
- assess the extent to which the UK constitution demonstrates a separation of powers between the different branches of state.

## 4.1 Legitimacy

The rules that determine whether a particular law has been legally enacted require justification. Individuals need to know why they should obey the law of the land, even if at times it may be inconvenient and on occasion disadvantageous to do so. Political power must be derived from a valid source of authority in terms of shared beliefs on the part of society as a whole to command the respect of citizens. In addition, the rules of power must ensure that the people who wield power have the appropriate qualities to do so and that they govern in the general interest. There need to be constraints on the rulers to ensure that they do not abuse their power. To protect society, the rulers should not have untrammelled powers which they can exercise arbitrarily; their conduct should be subject to adjudication by the courts to ensure that they act lawfully.

Events in South Africa during the apartheid era show that it is not enough for correct procedures to be followed in order for laws to be legitimate. The racially discriminatory laws that deprived black South Africans of voting rights, denied them the right to own property in most of the country and enforced rigid segregation were all validly enacted under the South African constitution, which could be traced back to an Act of the Westminster Parliament, the South Africa Act 1909. However, the apartheid system blatantly lacked legitimacy as it resulted in the gross oppression of the black majority by a white minority government.

The rule of law and separation of powers are two key constitutional principles that buttress the legitimacy of the UK's constitution and prevent the arbitrary exercise of power. They help to ensure the legitimacy of the laws to which British citizens and residents are subject.

## 4.2 The rule of law

You briefly considered what is meant by the 'rule of law' in **Chapter 1**. It has a long history going back at least to Magna Carta in 1215, which enshrined the principle that not even the King was above the law. A further noteworthy historical development was the creation of the writ of habeas corpus, an order by the court that a prisoner be brought before it so that it can decide whether their detention is lawful and consequently whether they should be released. The Habeas Corpus Acts 1640 and 1679 codified the procedure to counter the King's practice of detaining prisoners and simply asserting his command was sufficient justification for their detention.

### 4.2.1 The 'traditional' definition of the rule of law

AV Dicey, in his seminal work *An Introduction to the Study of the Law of the Constitution* (1885), said that the rule of law in the context of the UK constitution meant the following three things:

1. 'No man is punishable or can be lawfully made to suffer in body or goods except for a distinct breach of the law established in the ordinary legal manner before the ordinary courts of the land ... It means ... the absolute supremacy ... of regular law as opposed to the influence of arbitrary power'
2. '... no man is above the law ... every man and woman, whatever be his rank or condition, is subject to the ordinary law of the realm and amenable to the jurisdiction of the ordinary tribunals'
3. '... the general principles of the constitution (for example, the right to personal liberty, or the right of public meeting) are with us as a result of judicial decisions ... in particular cases brought before the courts.'

Today, Dicey's account of the rule of law can be seen as dated, particularly because it failed to anticipate modern developments in administrative law (ie the law relating to the control of the exercise of powers by public officials and public bodies - see **Chapters 6** and **7**). However, it is important to consider Dicey's approach because, however dated his interpretation, it has substantially influenced the development of English law. Accordingly, to give Dicey's formulation a more modern slant, the table below attempts to 'translate' his formulation into contemporary language

| Dicey's formulation | Present-day values/ constitutional requirements |
|---|---|
| 1. 'No man is punishable or can be lawfully made to suffer in body or goods except for a distinct breach of the law established in the ordinary legal manner before the ordinary courts of the land ... It means... the absolute supremacy ... of regular law as opposed to the influence of arbitrary power' | This element has a number of connotations:<br>• **Legal certainty**<br>Citizens should be able to rely on laws that are both made and set out clearly. There should be no arbitrary exercise of power, where the Government disregards the law and acts in any manner it sees fit.<br>• **Personal liberty**<br>Citizens should be detained and subject to punishment only if they have broken the law.<br>• **Due process of law**<br>Citizens have a right to fair procedures for determining civil or criminal liability. |
| 2. '... no man is above the law...every man and woman, whatever be his rank or condition, is subject to the ordinary law of the realm and amenable to the jurisdiction of the ordinary tribunals' | This element is concerned with *equality before the law*. This means not only equality between citizens, but also between public officials and citizens. Thus:<br>• Like cases should be treated in like ways; there should be no unjustified discrimination (for example, on the grounds of race or gender).<br>• State officials have no exemption from legal control or accountability as a result of their position, and are subject to the 'ordinary' law of the land (see *Entick v Carrington* in **Chapter 1**).<br>• Members of the executive should not legislate or adjudicate in court cases (this links to the principle of the separation of powers). |
| 3. '... the general principles of the constitution (for example, the right to personal liberty, or the right of public meeting) are with us as a result of judicial decisions ... in particular cases brought before the courts.' | Dicey sees the courts as protectors of individual liberty, thereby developing constitutional principles through 'ordinary' judicial decisions (this links to case law being an important source of constitutional law - see **Chapter 1**). |

Now that we have given a more up-to-date meaning to Dicey's view of the rule of law, you also need to understand why upholding the rule of law is such an important principle of the UK constitution.

### 4.2.2 The importance of the rule of law

Observing the rule of law should ensure that:

(a) the Government is prevented from exercising arbitrary power (because 'regular' law is supreme);

(b) the Government can be held to account for its actions (through the process of judicial review, in which the courts ensure that the Government does not exceed or abuse the powers that it has been granted);

(c) the law is set out clearly for all citizens and is made properly following a set procedure;
(d) the law does not operate retrospectively (ie someone should not be punished for an act that was not a crime at the time he carried out that act, if that act subsequently becomes a crime);
(e) there is equality before the law for all citizens;
(f) there is equal access to the law and the Government or state has no special exemptions or 'get-outs';
(g) citizens have a means of legal redress for their grievances; and
(h) the independence of the judiciary is maintained, thereby preserving the separation of powers and preventing the Government from exercising its powers in an arbitrary way.

### 4.2.3 Modern interpretations of the rule of law

One of the most authoritative modern definitions of the rule of law was provided by Lord Bingham of Cornhill, an eminent British judge who was successively Master of the Rolls, Lord Chief Justice and Senior Law Lord.

Lord Bingham said that the core of the existing principle of the rule of law was as follows: 'all persons and authorities within the state, whether public or private, should be bound by and entitled to the benefit of laws publicly and prospectively promulgated and publicly administered by the courts.'

Lord Bingham broke this definition down into eight sub-rules:

1. The law must be accessible, intelligible, clear and predictable.
2. Questions of legal right and liability should ordinarily be resolved by application of the law and not the exercise of discretion.
3. The laws of the land should apply equally to all, save to the extent that objective differences justify differentiation.
4. The law must afford adequate protection of human rights.
5. Means must be provided for resolving, without excessive cost or delay, civil disputes that the parties cannot resolve themselves.
6. Ministers and public officers must exercise the powers conferred on them reasonably, in good faith, for the purpose for which the powers were conferred and without exceeding the limits of such powers.
7. The adjudicative procedures provided by the state should be fair.
8. The state must comply with its obligations in international law.

In some areas Lord Bingham's definition overlaps with that of Dicey (for example, the idea that laws must be certain and the concept of equality before the law), whilst in other areas Lord Bingham goes a little further (for example, the importance of the protection of human rights and compliance with international law).

### 4.2.4 The contemporary relevance of the rule of law

Although, as we have seen so far in this chapter, the rule of law is a concept open to varying interpretations, it remains fundamental to an understanding of the UK constitution.

#### 4.2.4.1 Judicial and statutory recognition

In recent years, there has been an explicit recognition in both statute and case law of the continuing significance of the rule of law. For example:

- Section 1 of the Constitutional Reform Act 2005 (a statute that you will look at later in this chapter) acknowledges the importance of 'the constitutional principle of the rule of law' although, perhaps because of the difficulties of definition, does not seek to define it.
- In *R (Jackson) v Attorney General* [2005] UKHL 56, Lord Hope spoke of the rule of law enforced by the courts as 'the ultimate controlling factor on which our constitution is based'.

Whilst these examples may seem academic, the courts have also been willing to use the rule of law to justify their judgments.

4.2.4.2 The right to liberty

The case of *A and others v Secretary of State for the Home Department* [2005] 2 AC 68 (often referred to as the '*Belmarsh* case') is a significant case in showing the importance that the judiciary attaches to the rule of law. The case involved a challenge to, amongst other things, provisions in the Anti-terrorism, Crime and Security Act 2001 enacted in the aftermath of the 9/11 terrorist attacks in the USA. The 2001 Act permitted foreign nationals suspected of being involved in terrorist activities (but against whom there was insufficient evidence to bring criminal proceedings) to be detained indefinitely without trial.

The House of Lords held that such provisions breached Article 5 (right to liberty and security) and Article 14 (protection from discrimination) of the ECHR in so far as it permitted the detention of suspected terrorists in a way that discriminated against them on the ground of nationality, since there were British suspected terrorists who could not be detained under the 2001 Act. The House of Lords issued a declaration of incompatibility pursuant to s 4 of the HRA 1998 regarding the offending provisions in the 2001 Act.

This case emphasises the significance of the rule of law, Lord Nicholls stating that 'indefinite imprisonment without charge or trial is anathema in any country which observes the rule of law .... Wholly exceptional circumstances must exist before this extreme step can be justified'.

The burden on the Government to justify imprisonment without charge was therefore a very heavy one, which it could not discharge.

4.2.4.3 The right to a fair hearing

The right to a fair trial is a fundamental aspect of the rule of law and the courts have been keen to uphold the principle, as shown by the decision of the House of Lords in *R (Anderson) v Secretary of State for the Home Department* [2002] UKHL 46, [2003] 1 AC 837. This case involved an offender who had been convicted of murder and had been given a mandatory life sentence. A mandatory life sentence is accompanied by a tariff, a minimum term that the prisoner must serve before they may be considered for release on licence. At the time of the case, although the trial judge recommended the tariff, s 29 of the Crime (Sentences) Act 1997 gave the Home Secretary the power to set it. In *Anderson* the Home Secretary increased the tariff beyond that recommended by the trial judge. The claimant challenged the increase in tariff, arguing the Home Secretary's power was a breach of Article 6(1) (the right to a fair trial) of the ECHR via the HRA 1998.

In his speech, Lord Steyn stated that 'the proposition that a decision to punish an offender by ordering him to serve a period of imprisonment may only be made by a court of law ... is a principal feature of the rule of law on which our unwritten constitution is based'. Parliament had overridden this principle by enacting s 29 of the 1997 Act but had also, through enacting the Human Rights Act 1998, given the courts the power to decide upon the compatibility of s 29 with Article 6(1) of the ECHR. Accordingly, the House of Lords issued a declaration of incompatibility regarding s 29. Parliament subsequently removed the power to set the tariff from the Home Secretary.

As well as illustrating the significance of the rule of law, this case also shows how the Human Rights Act enables the courts to uphold the principle.

### 4.2.4.4 Access to justice

The Supreme Court's decision in *R (UNISON) v Lord Chancellor* [2017] UKSC 51 also shows the continuing significance of the rule of law in its jurisprudence. The Lord Chancellor had adopted the Employment Tribunals and the Employment Appeal Tribunal Fees Order 2013, SI 2013/1893 ('the Fees Order') relating to proceedings in employment tribunals and the Employment Appeal Tribunal. Prior to the Fees Order, claimants were able to bring proceedings in an employment tribunal and appeal to the Employment Appeal Tribunal without paying any fees. The trade union, UNISON, challenged the Fees Order by way of judicial review on various grounds, including their effect on access to justice. The Supreme Court held that the Fees Order was unlawful.

Lord Reed emphasised the link between access to justice and the rule of law, stating that the constitutional right of access to the courts is inherent in the rule of law: it is needed to ensure that the courts are able to apply and enforce the laws created by Parliament and also the common law created by the courts themselves. To enable the courts to perform that role, people must in principle have unimpeded access to them.

The Supreme Court held that in order for the fees to be lawful, they had to be set at a level that everyone can afford, taking into account the availability of full or partial remission. Even if the fees were affordable, they might still prevent access to justice if they rendered it futile or irrational to bring a claim. This might include situations where the fee was excessive in comparison to the amount at stake or the remedy sought was not financial (such as the right to written particulars of employment), which had the effect of preventing a sensible person, with no guarantee of fee reimbursement and success, from pursuing a claim. Accordingly, the Fees Order was unlawful as it effectively prevented access to justice.

### 4.2.4.5 Equality before the law

The case of *M v Home Office* [1993] UKHL 5 also illustrates the fundamental nature of the rule of law. M, a citizen of Zaire, had applied for political asylum in the UK, but his application was refused and he was informed that he would be deported. He applied to the High Court for judicial review of the refusal and the High Court judge asked for M's deportation to be delayed while he considered the case. However, M was already on a plane from London to Paris on his way to Zaire. When the judge was told about the situation, he made an interim order for M's return to the UK. Home Office officials arranged for M's return, but the Home Secretary cancelled those arrangements, believing he had acted legally in ordering M's deportation and that the judge did not have the legal power to make an interim order against a minister of the Crown.

In subsequent contempt proceedings lodged on behalf of M, the judge held that the Crown Proceedings Act 1947 preserved the Crown's immunity from injunction. On appeal, the Court of Appeal held that the Home Secretary was in contempt. On his appeal, the House of Lords held that injunctions were available against officers of the Crown and that the Home Secretary was in contempt of court in ignoring them, rejecting his argument that contempt and injunctions did not apply to the Crown. However, there had been a genuine misunderstanding on the Home Secretary's part and although he was in contempt of court, no penalty other than the finding of contempt was imposed.

In his speech Lord Templeman criticised 'the argument that there is no power to enforce the law by injunction or contempt proceedings against a minister in his official capacity' as it would 'establish the proposition that the executive obey the law as a matter of grace and not as a matter of necessity, a proposition which would reverse the result of the Civil War'.

Lord Woolf stated in his speech that 'the object of the exercise is not so much to punish an individual as to vindicate the rule of law by a finding of contempt'.

The notion of equality before the law and the rule of law were clearly central to the judgment of the House of Lords. The UK constitution does not grant special privileges or immunities to officers of the state.

4.2.4.6 The limits of the rule of law

There is a potential tension between parliamentary sovereignty and the rule of law. In theory Parliament can pass any Act it chooses, no matter how arbitrary or oppressive. Indeed, there have been obiter comments by prominent judges suggesting that that the courts might strike down legislation that is contrary to the rule of law, such as abolishing judicial review; see **2.5.1.6**. The examples given in these obiter comments have been extreme, and the courts have generally acknowledged parliamentary sovereignty by following the 'principle of legality', which Lord Steyn expounded authoritatively in *R v Secretary of State for the Home Dept, ex p Simms* [1999] UKHL 33. Lord Steyn affirmed parliamentary sovereignty by stating that Parliament can, if it chooses to do so, legislate contrary to fundamental principles of human rights. However, he continued that the principle of legality requires Parliament to squarely confront what it is doing and accept the political cost. Fundamental rights cannot be overridden by general or ambiguous words. This assumption can be displaced only by 'clear and specific provision to the contrary'.

However, there are limits to the extent to which the courts will uphold the rule of law. In *R (Corner House Research and Another) v Director of Serious Fraud Office* [2008] UKHL 60, the Director of the Serious Fraud Office decided to halt an investigation into the alleged corruption of a company engaged in arms trading with Saudi Arabia following a threat by Saudi Arabia to end co-operation in counter-terrorism initiatives if the investigation continued. Ministers advised the Director that if the investigation continued those threats would be carried out with grave consequences both for the arms trade and for the safety of British citizens and service personnel. The Court of Appeal held the decision was unlawful, constituting a breach of the rule of law. On appeal, the House of Lords accepted that the Director's decision had been taken with extreme reluctance, and that he had acted lawfully in deciding that the public interest in pursuing an important investigation into alleged bribery was outweighed by the public interest in protecting the lives of British citizens.

Nonetheless, it is clear that the rule of law is a doctrine that forms a key element of part of the UK constitution. There is near universal acceptance that laws should be enacted properly and that they should be clear. Laws should not be applied arbitrarily, no one is above the law and that no one may be punished other than in accordance with the law. Some definitions of the rule of law also have regard to the content of the law, including the extent to which the law upholds human rights; accordingly, any analysis of the extent to which a state complies with the rule of law should not be limited to formal aspects. Although there may be some debate at the margins, it is evident that the rule of law is integral to the UK constitution.

## 4.3 The separation of powers

The separation of powers is closely linked to the rule of law. An independent judiciary is an essential element of the rule of law and the separation of powers helps to secure judicial independence. Similarly, checks on the Government's actions help to prevent the arbitrary exercise of power.

### 4.3.1 Development of the doctrine

Although there is no formal separation of powers within the UK, this doctrine is acknowledged as one of the principles that underpin the constitution of the UK. You may remember from **Chapter 1** that the doctrine of the separation of powers identifies three branches of state:

- the legislature (or parliament), which makes the law;
- the executive (or government), which implements or administers the law; and
- the judiciary (or courts), which resolves disputes about the law.

The doctrine holds that, as each branch of state has a different role to play within the constitution, there should be no overlap between the branches, either in terms of their functions or in terms of their personnel. If such an overlap were to exist, this would represent an unhealthy concentration of power, which could lead to arbitrary or oppressive government.

The doctrine also holds that, as each branch of state cannot in reality operate in isolation from the other branches, there should be a system of 'checks and balances' in place so that one branch can be kept 'in check' by the other branches, resulting in a 'balance of power' between the different branches.

Hilaire Barnett has summed up the doctrine as follows:

> The essence of the doctrine is that there should be, ideally, a clear demarcation of personnel and functions between the legislature, executive and judiciary in order that none should have excessive power, and that there should be in place a system of checks and balances between institutions.
>
> Hilaire Barnett, *Constitutional and Administrative Law*, 15th edn (Routledge, 2023)

### 4.3.2 The United States of America – the 'Model'

The constitution of the United States of America is based firmly on preserving a separation of powers between the different branches of state. One of the aims of the framers of the US constitution was to avoid the dominance of the executive, which they perceived to be one of the problems with the UK constitution.

For example, the executive branch of state in the USA is made up of the President, the Vice President, the members of the President's cabinet, and the various government departments and agencies. The executive is under a constitutional duty to ensure that 'the laws be faithfully executed'. Members of the executive cannot also be members of Congress, which means that there is no overlap in personnel between the executive and legislative branches of state. Neither the President nor his advisers may sit in Congress (the legislative branch) or take part in Congressional votes and debates. This is in stark contrast to the UK where there is considerable overlap between the executive and legislature.

Another stark contrast with the UK relates to the judiciary. The judicial branch of state is made up of the various federal courts, but particularly the Supreme Court. The Supreme Court's function is to settle disputes arising under the law and constitution of the USA. The Supreme Court may strike down either actions of the executive or legislation enacted by Congress if such actions or legislation are unconstitutional. In the case of *Marbury v Madison* 5 U.S. (1 Cranch) 137 (1803), the Supreme Court affirmed the doctrine of judicial review, establishing the courts' authority to declare unconstitutional acts of the legislative or executive branches of state. This means that the US Supreme Court, unlike UK courts, has the power to strike down statutes.

The three branches of government – legislative, executive and judicial – are co-equal and so are intended to act as check and balance on each other. However, critics of President Trump have accused him of executive overreach and of usurping the powers of the other branches in the early months of his second term as President starting in January 2025.

### 4.3.3 Separation of powers in the UK constitution?

Unlike in the USA, there is no formal separation of powers under the UK constitution. The standard rationale for this is that, unlike in the USA, there has been no formal 'break' in the constitutional history of the UK. In the USA, the constitution was written in 1787, shortly after the end of the War of Independence from Great Britain. One of the key objectives of the 'founding fathers' who prepared the constitution was to write a document that would ensure the separation of powers between the executive, legislative and judicial branches of state, thereby preventing the exercise of tyrannical and arbitrary government by the executive (which they saw as the weakness of the British constitution).

The absence of a 'break' in the constitutional history of the UK means that our constitution has developed on an ad hoc basis and remains unwritten or uncodified. As a result of having an unwritten constitution, no formal system or arrangement has been put in place to ensure that the separation of powers is maintained. Instead, a partial separation of powers between the three branches of state exists, together with a largely informal system of checks and balances.

Although there is no formal separation of powers within the UK constitution, you saw in **Chapter 1** that it is possible to identify the persons or bodies that make up the branches of state in the UK, as illustrated in **Figure 4.1** below.

**Figure 4.1** Branches of central government

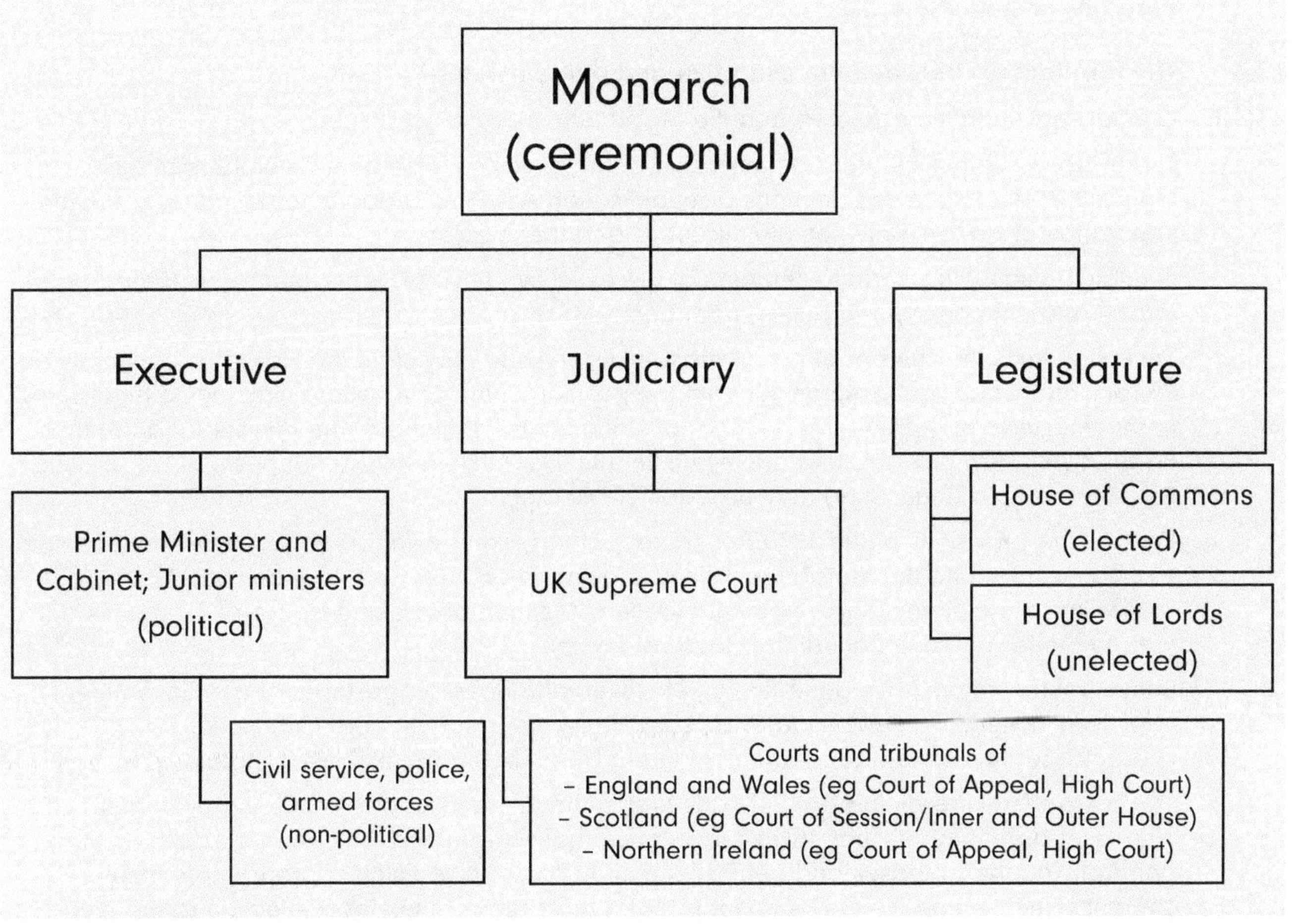


The *executive* branch of state is made up of the Monarch, the Prime Minister and other government ministers, the civil service, and the members of the police and armed forces. You may come across the terms 'central government' and 'the Crown' in connection with the executive. Central government comprises the Monarch, government ministers and members of the civil service. The Crown is the central government plus members of the police and the armed forces.

The *legislative* branch of state is made up of the Monarch, the House of Lords and the House of Commons.

The *judicial* branch of state is made up of the Monarch, all legally qualified judges, and magistrates.

Although the Monarch is part of all three branches of state, their role is largely ceremonial. The Government is legally 'His Majesty's Government', although in reality government ministers are appointed by the Prime Minister and, by convention, most of the Monarch's legal powers are exercised by the Government on their behalf. You considered some examples of this in **Chapter 1**.

The Monarch is part of the legislature because they must give Royal Assent before a bill that has passed through Parliament becomes an Act of Parliament. Although legally the Monarch may refuse to give Royal Assent to a bill, by convention they will always give this (see **Chapter 1**).

The Monarch is also head of the judiciary. Judges are the 'King's judges' and the courts are the 'King's courts'. That is why criminal cases are always cited: '*R v* ...' – '*R*' stands for '*Rex*' (or '*Regina*') or the Crown. The Monarch does not, however, exercise any judicial power.

In the rest of this chapter you will consider the degree of separation and overlap between the branches of state in the UK.

### 4.3.4 The relationship between the executive and the legislature

#### 4.3.4.1 Overlap between the executive and the legislature

There are statutory limitations on members of the executive also being members of the legislature. The House of Commons Disqualification Act 1975 supports to a limited extent the separation of powers between the executive and the legislature.

Section 1 disqualifies certain members of the executive (civil servants, members of the armed forces, and members of the police) from being MPs.

Section 2 limits the number of government ministers who may sit in the House of Commons to 95 (although you might contrast this with the position in the USA, where virtually no members of the executive may also be a member of Congress). Additionally, the Ministerial and other Salaries Act 1975 provides that the maximum number of paid ministerial posts is 109, of whom 21 (plus the Lord Chancellor) may be Cabinet Ministers.

Despite the provisions of the 1975 Act, there is clearly some overlap between the membership of the executive and the legislature, because government ministers can also be MPs (by convention the majority of government ministers are members of the House of Commons and the remainder are members of the House of Lords).

Some commentators have gone further, however, and have suggested that the Government effectively controls Parliament. In 1976, Lord Hailsham, a former Lord Chancellor, characterised the system of government in the UK as being an 'elective dictatorship'.

The phrase 'elective dictatorship' means that, although the people elect the Government whenever a general election takes place, once that Government has been elected it can generally act as it pleases and get Parliament to enact its legislative programme in full. The only limitation on the Government is that it must submit itself for re-election at the next general election. Lord Hailsham was suggesting that Parliament does not really play a role in debating or considering legislation proposed by the Government, but merely 'rubber stamps' the Government's legislative plans.

Lord Hailsham described the UK system of government as operating in this way because:

1. Our current 'first past the post' electoral system means that normally most MPs in the House of Commons will be members of the political party that forms the Government. (Although this is the usual position and now pertains following the December 2019 general election, following the general election in May 2010 no single party obtained sufficient seats to form an overall majority. As a result, the UK had a coalition government comprising the Conservative and Liberal Democrat parties between 2010 and May 2015. Similarly, no party gained an overall majority in the June 2017 general election. The Conservative Party obtained the largest number of seats and entered a confidence and supply agreement with the Democratic Unionist Party. This gave it a slim overall majority,

but it only applied to votes on the King's speech; the budget; legislation relating to Brexit and national security.)

2. The Government therefore has an in-built majority in the House of Commons, particularly given that most members of the Government (including the Prime Minister and other cabinet ministers) are also MPs.
3. The Government has significant control over the parliamentary timetable, and most of Parliament's time is devoted to the Government's legislative programme.
4. Most of the bills considered by Parliament are introduced by government ministers, and the overwhelming majority of these bills will be passed by Parliament because the majority of MPs represent the governing party.
5. The constitutional convention that the Government will resign if defeated in the House of Commons on a confidence vote or a major part of its legislative programme means that governments are able to persuade their backbench MPs to support government legislation, even if those MPs are reluctant to do so. While the Fixed-term Parliaments Act 2011 was in force, its provisions had a similar effect but, following its repeal, the pre-2011 convention applies once again. The Prime Minister is also expected to resign if they no longer have the confidence of the House and an alternative Government does have the confidence.
6. Huge pressure is placed on MPs from the governing party to support bills introduced by the Government through the government whips.
7. Although Parliament enacts primary legislation, many laws take the form of delegated or subordinate legislation. This is legislation made by government ministers under powers delegated by Parliament and there are only limited opportunities for Parliament to scrutinise such legislation.
8. Acts of Parliament legislation will often contain what are referred to as 'Henry VIII' powers (so called after the 1539 Statute of Proclamations, in which King Henry VIII gave his own declarations the same force as legislation enacted by Parliament). Such powers enable the Government to amend or repeal primary legislation by way of delegated legislation, without reference back to Parliament. The Retained EU Law (Reform and Revocation) Act 2023 has given the Government extensive Henry VIII powers to amend or repeal retained EU law/assimilated law.
9. Although the Government will not necessarily have a majority of the peers in the House of Lords, the House of Lords is weak in comparison to the House of Commons and is unable to keep the Government 'in check'. There is a constitutional convention, the Salisbury Convention, that the House of Lords will not reject a bill giving effect to a significant manifesto commitment of the democratically elected Government. In addition, the Parliament Acts of 1911 and 1949 limit the power of the House of Lords to reject a bill that has been passed by the House of Commons (see **2.2.3.2**).

There have been rule of law and separation of powers concerns regarding the Coronavirus Act 2020 and secondary legislation enforcing the lockdown to prevent the spread of the COVID-19 virus. Whilst most commentators have accepted the need for emergency legislation to deal with the pandemic, some have thought that there has been inadequate parliamentary scrutiny of the measures that the Government has taken.

#### 4.3.4.2 Parliamentary scrutiny of the executive

As the previous section shows, there is a significant degree of overlap between the executive and the legislature in the UK. Further, although it is Parliament that enacts legislation, Parliament is effectively legitimising legislative proposals that have been put forward by the Government. Nevertheless, Parliament still has a role to play in scrutinising the Government and holding it to account for its actions. The following are examples of some checks and balances that enable Parliament to fulfil this role.

- *Questions.* Time is set aside each day for MPs to put oral questions to ministers, and MPs may also ask written questions. The Prime Minister answers questions for 30 minutes each Wednesday.
- *Debates.* The 'standing orders' of the House of Commons provide for 'emergency debates' on matters that need urgent consideration. The Speaker decides whether the matter should be debated. 'Standing orders' also allocate time to the official Opposition in which it may initiate debates. All government bills are debated by Parliament at their second reading (see **Chapter 2**). The 'standing orders' also allow for brief debates to take place on topical issues of regional, national or international importance.
- *General committees* (including public bill committees). All government bills are referred to a public bill committee of MPs after the main principles of the bill have been debated. The purpose of the committee is to review the detailed clauses of the bill and make such amendments as are necessary. Additional general committees exist to discuss matters in specific areas, for example the Scottish Grand Committee, the Welsh Grand Committee, the Northern Ireland Grand Committee, committees on delegated legislation and European documents.
- *Select committees.* These committees are appointed for the life of a Parliament to examine the 'expenditure, administration and policy' of the main government departments. There are select committees for both Houses of Parliament. There is a Commons select committee for each government department, and also some that cross departmental boundaries, eg the Public Accounts and Environmental Audit Committees. Only backbench MPs serve on the Commons committees. The Government has a majority on each, but the chairman may be a member of the Opposition. The Commons committees report to the House of Commons and it is for the House to consider any necessary action. Select committees will often question government ministers (including the Prime Minister).

  The House of Lords Select Committees do not shadow the work of government departments, but investigate specialist subjects, benefiting from the Lords' expertise. 'Permanent' House of Lords Select Committees include the Communications and Digital Committee, the Constitution Committee and the Environment and Climate Change Committee.
- *Parliamentary and Health Service Ombudsman ('the Ombudsman').* The Ombudsman combines two functions, the Parliamentary Commissioner for Administration (PCA) and Health Service Commissioner for England. The Ombudsman is appointed by the Crown, and in their capacity as PCA their main function is to investigate the complaints of persons who have suffered injustice in consequence of 'maladministration' by government departments in exercise of their administrative functions. However, the Ombudsman's decisions are not binding on government ministers.
- *MPs may reject government bills.* In normal times it is rare for a government bill to suffer a defeat in the House of Commons. Nevertheless, this does occasionally happen, for example in March 2016 when the Government was defeated in its plan to extend Sunday opening hours.

  The period between the June 2017 and December 2019 general elections during which there was a Conservative Party minority government was, however, highly unusual. The Government suffered a large number of defeats during this period, in particular relating to its Brexit policies. Indeed, Parliament passed two Acts, the European Union (Withdrawal) Act 2019 and the European Union (Withdrawal) (No 2) Act 2019 despite government opposition. MPs opposed to the Government's policies on the UK's withdrawal from the EU voted to suspend the normal standing orders giving priority to government business. These Acts required the Government in certain circumstances to seek limited extensions to the UK's membership of the EU to prevent the UK from leaving without a withdrawal agreement in place.

In addition to the formal mechanisms by which Parliament holds the Government to account for its actions, the constitutional conventions of individual ministerial responsibility and collective cabinet responsibility (which you considered in **Chapter 1**) also play an important role here. Legally, government ministers are not accountable to Parliament for their decisions or actions. However, through the operation of these conventions, accountability exists.

Under the convention of *individual ministerial responsibility*, ministers are responsible to Parliament both for the running and proper administration of their respective departments and also for their personal conduct. There must be no conflict of interest between a minister's public duties and his or her private interests. A minister who breaches this convention should resign. Examples of ministers resigning following a breach of this convention include:

- In 1982, the Foreign Secretary and two junior ministers resigned over allegations that the Foreign Office should have foreseen the Argentine invasion of the Falklands Islands and planned accordingly.
- In 2004, David Blunkett resigned as Home Secretary after he had an affair with a married woman and then had her nanny's visa application fast-tracked. In 2005 he resigned as Work and Pensions Secretary, following allegations concerning financial interests about which he had failed to make proper disclosure.
- In 2017 Priti Patel resigned as Secretary for State for International Development following unauthorised meetings with Israeli government officials about which she had misled the Foreign Secretary and Prime Minister.
- In 2018 Amber Rudd resigned as Home Secretary in connection with the Windrush deportation scandal. She had misled MPs over whether the Home Office had targets for removing illegal immigrants.
- In 2024 Louise Haigh stepped down as Transport Secretary after it transpired that in 2013 she had pleaded guilty to a criminal offence regarding incorrectly reporting a work mobile phone as stolen.
- There has also been considerable debate regarding whether the Prime Minister, Boris Johnson, breached this convention in his conduct regarding the 'Partygate' affair. Ultimately, in June 2023, the House of Commons Privileges Committee found that Mr Johnson had deliberately misled Parliament over parties at 10 Downing Street. Mr Johnson resigned as an MP before a parliamentary vote on the report, but MPs voted on 19 June 2023 by 354 votes to seven to accept it.

The convention of *collective cabinet responsibility* provides that the cabinet is collectively responsible to Parliament for the actions of the Government as a whole, and the Government must retain the confidence of the House of Commons.

This convention also holds that ministers must resign if they wish to speak out in public against government policy. An example of this occurred in 2003, when both Robin Cook and Clare Short resigned as cabinet ministers in order to voice in public their opposition to the war in Iraq. Further examples are the resignation of Baroness Warsi as Foreign Office Minister in 2014 in protest at government policy on Gaza, Iain Duncan Smith's resignation as the Secretary of State for Work and Pensions in 2016 in protest at the Government's proposed cuts to disability benefits and Anneliese Dodds' resignation in 2025 as International Development Minister over cuts to overseas aid to fund an increase in defence spending. There were 36 ministerial resignations between June 2018 and May 2019, most relating to Theresa May's Brexit policies. They included David Davis and Dominic Raab, who had both been Secretaries of State for Exiting the EU, and Boris Johnson who was the Foreign Secretary at the time. Five cabinet ministers and 25 junior ministers resigned from the Government in July 2022 as they could no longer support Mr Johnson continuing as Prime Minister, a major factor in precipitating his resignation.

Note that it is open to the Prime Minister to suspend the operation of the convention of collective cabinet responsibility, as David Cameron did in the run up to the EU referendum in June 2016.

4.3.4.3 Parliament and the royal prerogative

There are some areas of government activity over which Parliament has historically been unable to exercise effective scrutiny. These are predominantly powers that the Government exercises under the royal prerogative, and include matters of national security, the defence of the realm and the deployment of the armed forces (there is, for example, no legal requirement for the Government to obtain parliamentary approval before sending troops into action). You will see later in this chapter that these are also areas where the powers of the courts to review actions taken by the Government are limited, because the courts consider such areas to be 'non-justiciable' (ie not areas in which the courts should properly become involved).

However, there are indications that Parliament is taking on a greater role in these areas. For example, in 2003 the Government obtained parliamentary approval before sending troops to Iraq. Also in 2013 the Government recalled Parliament to vote and debate possible military action in Syria. Following a 'No' vote in the Commons, the Prime Minister acknowledged that the Government would not become involved in military action in Syria. Subsequently, in September 2014, the Government sought and obtained parliamentary approval for air strikes against Isis targets in Iraq, but not in Syria.

In contrast, in 2011 the Government only sought approval for the deployment of forces in Libya retrospectively, three days after the start of British participation, whilst the deployment of British military personnel in Mali in 2013 was not the subject of a parliamentary debate or vote.

Overall, though, it appears that there is a new convention that, before the Government commits troops to military operations, the House of Commons should have an opportunity to debate the issue. Indeed, the Cabinet Manual states:

> In 2011, the Government acknowledged that a convention had developed in Parliament that before troops were committed the House of Commons should have an opportunity to debate the matter and said that it proposed to observe that Convention except where there was an emergency and such action would not be appropriate.

The (then) Prime Minister repeated this commitment in relation to Libya in Parliament in March 2016.

Like many constitutional conventions, however, the exact scope of this new convention is unclear. In April 2018 the Prime Minister, Theresa May, authorised a military airstrike against Syria without seeking prior parliamentary approval. She stated that this was due to the situation being an emergency. However, the decision not to seek prior approval was controversial, and some argued that the Prime Minister had acted in breach of the convention.

There are also legislative restrictions on the exercise of the royal prerogative. In particular the Constitutional Reform and Governance Act 2010 put parliamentary scrutiny of treaty ratification by the Government on a statutory basis, giving legal effect to any resolution of the House of Commons or Lords that a treaty should not be ratified. According to the explanatory notes to the Act:

> should the House of Commons take the view that the Government should not proceed to ratify a treaty, it can resolve against ratification and thus make it unlawful for the Government to ratify the treaty. The House of Lords will not be able to prevent the Government from ratifying a treaty, but if they resolve against ratification the Government will have to produce a further explanatory statement explaining its belief that the agreement should be ratified.

Whilst treaty ratification remains a prerogative power, the House of Commons can prevent the Government from exercising it. However, treaties are subject to the 'negative resolution procedure', which means that no debate or vote is required prior to ratification. Indeed, no debates have taken place in the House of Commons under the provisions in the 2010 Act since it was passed.

## 4.4 The relationship between the executive and the judiciary

### 4.4.1 The importance of judicial independence

The importance of judicial independence from the executive is recognised in s 3 of the Constitutional Reform Act 2005, which provides that the Government is under a duty to uphold the independence of the judiciary and that individual ministers should not seek to influence particular decisions through any special access to the judiciary. In 2017 the Lord Chief Justice criticised the Lord Chancellor for failing in her duty under s 3 following the criticism of the judiciary in the press after the High Court's decision in *R (Miller) v Secretary of State for Exiting the European Union* [2017] UKSC 5 (*Miller (No 1)*) (the 'Brexit case'). Various sections of the press had decried the judges, the *Daily Mail* claiming that they were the 'enemies of the people'.

### 4.4.2 Judicial independence from the executive

In the UK, judicial independence from the executive is secured in a number of ways

(a) *Appointment.* Judicial appointments are now dealt with by the Judicial Appointments Commission, which is politically impartial and free from executive control.

(b) *Tenure.* Security of tenure (ie job security) was given to judges of the senior courts historically by the Act of Settlement 1701, although the modern basis of the law is the Senior Courts Act 1981 and, in the case of the Justices of the Supreme Court, the Constitutional Reform Act 2005. Senior judges hold office 'during good behaviour', and may be dismissed by the Monarch only following a vote of both Houses of Parliament. Judges cannot be dismissed merely because they give a judgment with which the Government disagrees.

(c) *Salary.* Judicial salaries are determined by an independent body (the Senior Salaries Review Board) and are paid from the Consolidated Fund. Under the Consolidated Fund legislation, certain expenditure is authorised in permanent form and does not therefore require annual approval. This means that payment of judicial salaries is insulated from executive and parliamentary control (the salaries of judges appointed to the Supreme Court are determined by the Lord Chancellor but will be charged on the Consolidated Fund, making them effectively immune from political interference).

(d) *Immunity from civil action.* Judges, particularly in the higher courts, have wide-ranging immunity from claims in tort in respect of their judicial actions. In other words, an unsuccessful litigant cannot sue a judge for making an error when carrying out their duties.

(e) *Constitutional conventions.* By convention, members of the executive do not criticise judicial decisions, and members of the judiciary do not engage in party political activity.

(f) *The 'sub-judice' rule.* Under this rule, Parliament (and therefore government ministers) refrains from discussing matters currently being heard or waiting to be heard by the courts.

(g) *Contempt of court laws.* Common law contempt of court and statutory contempt under the Contempt of Court Act 1981 ensure that there is no outside interference with the administration of justice. This prevents government ministers commenting prejudicially outside proceedings in Parliament on cases before the courts, while the sub-judice rule applies to proceedings in Parliament.

### 4.4.3 The Constitutional Reform Act 2005

One of the reasons for this Act being passed was the perception that there was too much of an overlap between the executive and the judicial branches of state, particularly in relation to the office of the Lord Chancellor and some of the quasi-judicial functions government ministers undertook. Hence in 2005 Parliament took steps to remedy the position.

#### 4.4.3.1 Role of the Lord Chancellor

Prior to 2005, the Lord Chancellor was a member of both the executive and the judiciary. As a government minister, the Lord Chancellor was a political appointee with a seat in the cabinet. However, they were also the head of the judiciary of England and Wales, with responsibility for the appointment of senior members of the judiciary. The Lord Chancellor was also entitled to sit as a Law Lord. It was considered that this dual role of the Lord Chancellor created the impression that the executive had too much influence over the judiciary.

There were also concerns about the lack of transparency in the appointment of the judiciary. Judicial appointments depended on a consultation process, or so-called 'secret soundings', following which the Lord Chancellor approached prospective judges regarding their appointment. Critics of the system pointed out that this led to a judiciary that was comprised predominantly of white men who were privately and Oxbridge educated.

To address these concerns, the Constitutional Reform Act 2005 introduced the following reforms:

(a) *Role of Lord Chancellor.* The Lord Chancellor's role as head of the judiciary was transferred to the Lord Chief Justice (now also known as the 'President of the Courts of England and Wales'). The Lord Chief Justice has overall responsibility for the training, guidance and deployment of judges, and for representing the views of the judiciary to Parliament, the Lord Chancellor and other ministers. The Lord Chief Justice has the right to make written representations to Parliament on important matters relating to the judiciary or the administration of justice. The Lord Chancellor remains a member of the cabinet (although this role has now been combined with that of Secretary of State for Justice).

(b) *Creation of the Judicial Appointments Commission.* The Judicial Appointments Commission (JAC) is an independent body that has been created to ensure that the appointment of judges in England and Wales occurs solely on merit and is not influenced by political considerations. Prior to the Act being passed, the appointment of the judiciary was solely in the hands of the executive and was conducted on the basis of 'secret soundings'. Similar bodies exist in Scotland and Northern Ireland.

The system for appointing judges operates as follows:

(a) The Prime Minister (after receiving a recommendation from the Lord Chancellor) must advise the Monarch on filling any vacancy for the Lord Chief Justice, the Master of the Rolls, Lord Justices of Appeal, the President of the Family Division and of the King's Bench Division, and High Court judges. The Lord Chancellor must consult the Lord Chief Justice before making his or her recommendation, and will normally ask the JAC to convene a 'selection panel' to select a candidate for such recommendation. Similar procedures apply to appointments as circuit judges, recorders, district judges and magistrates.

(b) Appointments to fill vacancies in the Supreme Court are made by the Monarch on the advice of the Prime Minister, who will in turn have received a recommendation from the Lord Chancellor. A 'selection commission' consisting of the President of the Supreme Court, a senior UK judge nominated by the President of the Supreme Court, and one member from each of the three judicial appointments bodies will select candidates for such recommendation.

(c) The system that has been introduced places primary responsibility for judicial appointments on independent bodies, thus minimising any perception of improper political involvement in the appointment of judges.

(d) The Act also requires that selection be based solely on merit. Nonetheless, where there are two or more candidates of equal merit, a candidate may be selected for a post in order to increase judicial diversity.

The Constitutional Reform Act 2005 also created the Supreme Court to replace the Judicial Committee of the House of Lords. You will consider this below when you examine the relationship between the legislature and the judiciary.

#### 4.4.3.2 The judicial functions of the executive

One of the reasons behind the enactment of the Constitutional Reform Act 2005 was to enhance the separation of powers between the executive and judiciary. Nonetheless, it remains the case that members of the executive sometimes perform quasi-judicial functions. The impact of Article 6 of the ECHR has been to reduce these functions in some areas (eg the removal of the Home Secretary's power to determine the length of tariff for prisoners given a life sentence following the *Anderson* case). Members of the executive do, however, continue to perform quasi-judicial functions in some areas. Compulsory purchase orders (CPOs) provide an example of this. It is sometimes necessary for land to be made the subject of a CPO if it is required for a particular purpose (eg the building of a new motorway). The decision as to which land is to be purchased is a quasi-judicial decision, but will be taken by the relevant government minister.

Nonetheless, although members of the executive are acting in a quasi-judicial capacity, any decisions they make will be susceptible to judicial review (see below). If such decisions are unlawful, irrational or breach any relevant procedural requirements, the courts can quash them.

#### 4.4.3.3 How the judiciary holds the executive to account

One consequence of the UK having an unwritten constitution is that the judiciary does not have the power to declare actions of the executive (or legislation enacted by Parliament) to be unconstitutional. There is no 'higher law' against which all other actions or pieces of legislation may be judged. However, through the process of judicial review, the judiciary is able to ensure that the executive does not exceed or abuse the powers it has been granted, and that any decisions the executive is required to make are made using the correct procedure.

The executive derives its power from two sources: statute and the royal prerogative. If Parliament has granted statutory powers to the executive (for example, giving a particular power to a government minister), through the mechanism of judicial review the courts can ensure that those powers are exercised in accordance with the purpose of the statute and are not exceeded or abused. Again through the mechanism of judicial review, the courts can determine the extent of the royal prerogative and, in most cases, can review the exercise of prerogative powers (see below) to ensure that they have been exercised in an appropriate manner.

When the courts judicially review the actions of the executive, they are examining only the legality of a decision or action, not its merits. The courts' function is to ensure that the executive has acted within its powers and has acted using the correct procedures. This is important in preserving the separation of powers between the executive and judiciary. Were the judiciary to examine the merits of a decision, it would usurp the role of the executive.

#### 4.4.3.4 Judicial control of the exercise of royal prerogative powers

You may remember from **Chapter 1** that the royal prerogative is what remains of the absolute powers that at one time were exercised by the Monarch, which have not been removed by Parliament. By convention, such powers are today exercised by the Government on the Monarch's behalf.

Historically, the courts have been willing to adjudicate upon the extent of the royal prerogative, but only fairly recently have they been prepared to consider how it is exercised.

**Extent of the royal prerogative**

The judiciary is responsible for deciding the extent of the royal prerogative (in other words, whether a prerogative power exists or not). Through case law, the courts have established that new prerogative powers cannot be created or the scope of existing powers extended. See, for example, the *Case of Proclamations* (1611) 12 Co Rep 74. The King had the power to make royal proclamations that had the force of statute. The powers were intended for use in times of emergency and were subject to a number of qualifications, but the King used them, amongst other things, to prohibit the construction of new houses in London. The Commons sought the opinion of Chief Justice Coke and four fellow judges as to the legality of the proclamations. In his judgment, Chief Justice Coke held that 'the King hath no power but that which the law of the land allows him' (ie the King could not create new prerogative powers for himself).

In the more recent case of *BBC v Johns* [1965] Ch 3, the BBC claimed that the Crown had a prerogative power to regulate broadcasting, which manifested itself in the BBC's Royal Charter. As such, it argued that it was entitled to rely upon the Crown's exemption from income tax (ie a widening of the Crown exemption). This argument was rejected, the court holding that the Crown could not extend the scope of the existing prerogative.

The Supreme Court's judgment in *R (Miller) v The Prime Minister, Cherry v Advocate General for Scotland* [2019] UKSC 41 (*Miller (No 2)/Cherry*) shows that the courts are willing to take a wide approach in analysing the extent of prerogative powers. The case concerned the legality of the Prime Minister's advice to the Queen to prorogue Parliament for five weeks from 10 September 2019 to 14 October 2019, a period that would occupy a large portion of the time available ahead of the UK's withdrawal from the EU, which was then scheduled for 31 October 2019, an event that would bring about a fundamental change to the UK constitution.

The Supreme Court classified the case as being about the extent of the prerogative power rather than the manner of its exercise, stating that the power to prorogue was limited by the constitutional principles with which it would otherwise conflict. The relevant constitutional principles in this case were parliamentary sovereignty and parliamentary accountability. The exercise of the power was unlawful as, without reasonable justification, it frustrated or prevented Parliament's ability to carry out its constitutional functions. The prorogation took place in exceptional circumstances and prevented Parliament from exercising its constitutional functions for five out of the eight weeks leading up to the date on which the UK was due to leave the EU; Parliament would have no voice in the withdrawal process at a very critical period. The Government failed to put forward any justification for taking action with such extreme consequences. The advice to the Queen was therefore unlawful and hence the prorogation was void.

**Exercise of the royal prerogative**

Although the courts can decide the extent of the royal prerogative, their power to review the exercise of prerogative powers is more limited.

In *Blackburn v Attorney General* [1971] 2 All ER 1380, Blackburn sought a declaration that the Government, by signing the Treaty of Rome (now the Treaty on the Functioning of the European Union), would unlawfully surrender part of Parliament's sovereignty. The court held that it had the power to determine whether a prerogative power existed but, once it had determined the existence of the power, it had no right to review the exercise of the power. The power to sign an international treaty was part of the royal prerogative and the exercise of that power was immune from judicial review.

In *CCSU v Minister for Civil Service* [1984] UKHL 9, the Council of Civil Service Unions asked the courts to review the decision of the Minister for the Civil Service to prohibit staff at GCHQ from being members of a trade union without first consulting with the relevant trade union. On the particular facts of the case, the House of Lords held that the minister's decision had been prompted by concerns about national security and the minister had been entitled to act as she did; the Government was better placed to judge what was in the interests of national security than the courts.

The case is more important, however, for what it said generally about the power of the courts to review the *exercise* of royal prerogative powers by the executive. Retreating from the decision in *Blackburn*, their Lordships held that the exercise of prerogative powers was not automatically immune from the judicial review process. In his speech, Lord Roskill said that any power exercised by the executive, whether the source of that power was from statute or the royal prerogative, was capable of being judicially reviewed. The only exception to this was if the power being exercised was not 'justiciable' (ie not an appropriate area for the involvement of the courts).

Lord Roskill identified the following royal prerogative powers as being 'non-justiciable':

- Making international treaties
- Control of the armed forces
- Defence of the realm
- The dissolution of Parliament (following the repeal of the Fixed-term Parliaments Act 2011, the power to dissolve Parliament is once again a prerogative power) (see **Chapter 1**)
- The prerogative of mercy
- Granting public honours

The courts have subsequently reduced Lord Roskill's list by judicially reviewing the exercise of some of those prerogative powers that Lord Roskill considered to be non-justiciable. The courts have, for example, reviewed the exercise of the prerogative of mercy by the Home Secretary (*R v Secretary of State for the Home Department, ex p Bentley* [1993] 4 All ER 442). Nonetheless, there are still some royal prerogative powers that remain non-justiciable and therefore beyond the scope of the courts.

These are areas of 'high politics' (such as the conduct of foreign relations), and the areas of national security and defence of the realm. An example is the prerogative power to make international treaties, the exercise of which the Supreme Court confirmed in *R (Miller) v Secretary of State for Exiting the European Union* [2017] UKSC 5 (*Miller (No 1)*) is not subject to judicial review.

The courts are reluctant to become involved in these areas for two reasons. First, these are areas that are often highly political in nature, and members of the judiciary are concerned that reviewing the actions of the executive in these areas will lead to their becoming politicised and potentially losing their independence. The accountability of the executive in these areas is better secured through the electorate at a general election than through the courts. Secondly, these are areas where the executive is deemed to have greater technical knowledge and expertise than the judiciary.

One consequence of the courts' refusal to review the exercise of prerogative powers in certain areas is that this leaves some of the executive's powers effectively beyond the scrutiny of both the legislature and the judiciary. Some of the areas that the courts deem to be non-justiciable (particularly matters of defence and national security) are the same areas in which Parliament's ability to hold the executive to account is limited (see **4.3.4.3** above).

### 4.4.4 The relationship between the legislature and the judiciary

#### 4.4.4.1 Keeping the legislature and judiciary separate

You have already seen that various statutory and other methods are in place to ensure that the executive and judiciary are kept apart. Similarly, there are statutory and other methods for ensuring some degree of separation between the legislature and judiciary. These include:

(a) *House of* Commons *(Disqualification) Act 1975*. Under s 1 of this Act, holders of judicial office are disqualified from membership of the House of Commons.

(b) *Impact of convention.* There is a constitutional convention that Members of Parliament will not make a criticism of a particular judge, and a further convention that members of the judiciary will not become involved in political activities.

(c) *The 'sub-judice' rule.* Under this rule, Parliament will refrain from discussing details of cases before the courts or waiting to come before the courts.

(d) *Bill of Rights 1689, art 9.* This article guaranteed freedom of speech in Parliament by stating that Members of Parliament cannot be made subject to legal sanction by the courts for comments made in Parliament. Comments made by members of either House of Parliament are protected by 'parliamentary privilege'. This means that Lords and MPs enjoy immunity from any criminal or civil proceedings arising out of any statements made by them within Parliament.

4.4.4.2 Areas of overlap between the legislature and judiciary

Prior to the enactment of the Constitutional Reform Act 2005, there were two significant areas of overlap between the legislature and the judiciary.

First, the Appellate Committee of the House of Lords (the highest court in the country) was part of Parliament. The 'Law Lords' were physically based in the Houses of Parliament and, as peers, were entitled to take part in votes and debates in the chamber of the House of Lords.

Secondly, the Lord Chancellor was the Speaker of the House of Lords, in addition to being both the head of the judiciary and a Law Lord (and also a member of the Government).

The Constitutional Reform Act 2005 removed these areas of overlap. The Act created a new Supreme Court for the United Kingdom, consisting of 12 Justices of the Supreme Court. The Supreme Court replaced the 'Law Lords', whose official title was the Appellate Committee of the House of Lords and who heard cases at the Palace of Westminster where Parliament is located.

The Supreme Court opened in 2009 and has its own building away from Parliament. The existing Law Lords at the time of the opening became the first Justices of the Supreme Court. These Lords retained their peerages but did not sit in the House of Lords. However, new Justices of the Supreme Court do not receive a peerage (although in December 2010 the Queen signed a warrant that every Supreme Court Justice should be styled as Lord or Lady).

In addition to the creation of the Supreme Court, the Lord Chancellor is no longer Speaker of the House of Lords. The Lord Speaker is now directly elected by members of the House of Lords.

4.4.4.3 The judiciary's legislative function

Many constitutional commentators have suggested that, in interpreting statute and developing the common law, the judiciary performs a legislative function.

Various theories exist concerning the 'legislative function' of the judiciary. An early theory that developed (the 'declaratory theory') held that judges do not in any sense make the law. All judges do in deciding cases that come before them is to declare what the law - as enacted by Parliament - actually is. This theory is today unrealistic.

Many commentators have argued the opposite, claiming that judges play a significant role in making the law (the 'legislative theory'). Those who support this theory argue that a significant amount of our law is judge-made (ie the common law) and that, in addition to developing the common law, judges also play an important role when interpreting statute.

Although the legislative theory is more persuasive, there are limits on judicial law-making. The theory of 'judicial restraint' holds that the judges should be reluctant to develop the common law either in areas that Parliament intends to consider, or in areas where Parliament has already decided not to legislate because it is satisfied with the current state of the law.

The common law doctrine of the sovereignty of Parliament represents a self-imposed limitation by the judiciary on its powers, with the judiciary accepting that statute takes precedence over the common law. Thus if the courts develop the law in a direction that Parliament dislikes, Parliament may legislate to overturn the common law.

An example of this occurred in 1965. In *Burmah Oil Company v Lord Advocate* [1965] AC 75, the House of Lords awarded compensation to Burmah Oil for financial losses sustained during World War II. Fearing that this would lead to a flood of similar claims, Parliament enacted the War Damage Act 1965, which overruled the House of Lords' decision and provided that compensation was not payable.

4.4.4.4 Judicial powers in relation to primary legislation

The judiciary is unable to prevent Parliament from legislating in any given area. As you have already seen, as a result of the UK having an unwritten constitution (and also the development of the doctrine of the supremacy of Parliament), the judiciary does not have the power to declare an Act of Parliament to be unconstitutional or to strike down such an Act. The UK has no written constitution to provide a 'higher' authority against which all other legislation can be judged.

However, as you saw in **Chapter 2,** during the UK's membership of the EU and also until the end of the transition period following the UK's exit, the courts had the power to suspend legislation that was incompatible with EU law. Following the end of the transition period, a limited form of supremacy of EU law remains. The courts probably have the power to suspend legislation enacted before the end of the transition period that conflicts with retained EU law. Additionally, the European Union (Withdrawal Agreement) Act 2020 also appears to give the Withdrawal Agreement supremacy over UK law. The most likely outcome of this is that if, in future, Parliament passed a statute inconsistent with the Withdrawal Agreement, the courts would disapply the statute in favour of the agreement unless Parliament explicitly instructed them to give priority to the UK Act of Parliament. Indeed, as explained at **2.4.4** above, the Government submitted to Parliament the Northern Ireland Protocol Bill overriding the Northern Ireland Protocol, a key aspect of the Withdrawal Agreement. However, in February 2023, the UK and EU concluded the Windsor Framework, resolving the dispute regarding the Northern Ireland Protocol. The UK Government therefore withdrew the proposed legislation. See **Chapter 10** for further details of retained EU law and the Withdrawal Agreement and for possible changes to the status of retained EU law.

The courts also have the powers under s 4 of the HRA 1998 to declare that an Act of Parliament is incompatible with the ECHR (see **Chapter 2**). Whilst this does not invalidate the relevant statute, it does impose enormous pressure on the Government to amend the offending piece of legislation.

In addition, in *R (Jackson and others) v HM Attorney General* [2005] UKHL 56, obiter comments from the House of Lords suggested that some of their Lordships would be prepared to strike down legislation that infringed the rule of law.

4.4.4.5 The politicisation of the judiciary

**(a) Controversial issues**

As you have seen, a number of statutory and other provisions are in place to ensure that the independence and political neutrality of the judiciary is maintained. In recent years, however, concerns have been expressed over the danger that the judiciary is at risk of becoming politicised.

In recent years, senior members of the judiciary have been appointed to chair public inquiries. These inquiries have often involved issues that are politically sensitive. An example was Lord Hutton's inquiry in 2003 into the death of the government weapons inspector Dr David Kelly. Lord Hutton's subsequent exoneration of the Government from any blame led to allegations that his report was a 'whitewash' and that he had been biased in favour of the Government. Such allegations damage the independence and impartiality of the judiciary.

More recently the Leveson Inquiry, a public inquiry chaired by Leveson LJ into the culture, practices and ethics of the British press, has caused considerable controversy. Its final report, published in November 2012, contained recommendations for press regulation that many newspapers vehemently opposed. The current Grenfell Tower Inquiry – the public inquiry into the fire at Grenfell Tower on the night of 14 June 2017, which caused 72 deaths – has also proved controversial. It is chaired by Sir Martin Moore-Bick, a retired Lord Justice of Appeal,

The implementation of the HRA 1998 and the incorporation of the ECHR into our legal system has, on occasion, resulted in the courts having to decide cases with a significant 'political' element, particularly when the courts are attempting to balance civil liberties and the rights of the individual against the Government's concern about national security and the ongoing terrorist threat. By making such judgments, judges have been drawn into controversial political issues.

There have also been a number of occasions on which both government ministers and backbench MPs have breached the constitutional convention that politicians should not engage in criticism of individual members of the judiciary. Such criticisms have been particularly common in relation to perceived leniency in the sentencing of criminal offenders, and also in relation to a number of judgments in which the courts have declared that some aspects of anti-terror legislation contravene the provisions of the HRA 1998.

More recently, there have been several judgments concerning the rights of individuals, which have brought criticism from politicians. Examples include a ruling from the European Court of Human Rights that the blanket ban on prisoners being entitled to vote was in breach of the ECHR, and a Supreme Court ruling that convicted sex offenders should be permitted (in certain circumstances) to challenge their names being entered for life on the 'Sex Offenders Register'.

The judgments relating to the UK's exit from the EU, *Miller (No 1)* and *Miller (No 2)/Cherry* discussed at **4.4.1** and **4.4.3.4** above respectively, also caused intense controversy. Following the High Court judgment in *Miller* [2016] EWHC 2768 (Admin) the tabloid press attacked the judges in the case with the *Daily Mail* denouncing them as 'enemies of the people'. Lord Neuberger, then President of the Supreme Court, criticised as inadequate the responses of politicians, including the Lord Chancellor, to these virulent attacks. He said that 'some of what was said was undermining the rule of law'.

In February 2025, the Lady Chief Justice, Baroness Carr, criticised the Prime Minister, Sir Keir Starmer, and the Leader of the Opposition, Kemi Badenoch, over comments made the previous week at Prime Minister's Questions. Both Sir Keir and Mrs Badenoch attacked a tribunal's decision purportedly allowing a Palestinian family to come to Britain via the Ukrainian refugee programme, although an analysis of the judgment shows its decision was not based on the Ukrainian scheme. Sir Keir stated that the decision was 'completely wrong' and that the Home Secretary was working to close the 'loophole' in the scheme.

In response Baroness Carr expressed that she had been 'deeply troubled' by the comments which were 'unacceptable'. She added, 'It is for the government visibly to respect and protect the independence of the judiciary. Where parties, including the government, disagree with their findings, they should do so through the appellate process.'

A Government spokesperson replied: 'The Prime Minister has made clear that it is for Parliament to make the laws and for the Government to decide policy.'

There does seem to be some disagreement between the Government and judiciary regarding the precise scope of this convention.

In the Queen's Speech of May 2022, the previous Conservative Government stated that it wanted to 'restore the balance of power between the legislature and the courts by introducing a Bill of Rights'. Although the Conservative Government subsequently dropped its proposals for a British Bill of Rights, this suggests that the Conservative Government was deeply unhappy about court decisions such as those in *Miller (No 1)* and *Miller (No 2)/Cherry*. Critics of these decisions argue that the courts are trespassing into political realms and usurping the functions of government, thereby damaging settled constitutional arrangements. Conversely, supporters of these decisions argue that they uphold the core principles of parliamentary sovereignty and government accountability to Parliament, and that the problematic relationship is the one between the executive and legislature; the main causes for concern are the executive's growing arbitrary power and Parliament's diminishing capacity to hold ministers to account.

### (b) Parliament and the judiciary

(i) The Safety of Rwanda (Asylum and Immigration) Act 2024

The Safety of Rwanda (Asylum and Immigration) Act 2024 ('the Rwanda Act') was a very controversial Act enacted under the previous Conservative Government to facilitate the removal of certain asylum seekers to Rwanda. In *R (AAA (Syria)) v Secretary of State for the Home Department* [2023] UKSC 42, the Supreme Court ruled that Government policy to remove asylum seekers to Rwanda was unlawful due to serious concerns regarding the country's safety. Sending asylum seekers there would have breached their rights under international treaties, including the ECHR; accordingly, the Government would have been unable to send people to Rwanda without breaching its duty in s 6 of the HRA 1998 not to act incompatibly with Convention rights.

As part of the UK Government's response to address the Supreme Court's concerns regarding Rwanda's safety, Parliament enacted the Rwanda Act to make the removal arrangements lawful. A key purpose of the Act was to give effect to 'the judgement of Parliament that the Republic of Rwanda is a safe country'.

Significant provisions in the Rwanda Act included:

- Designation of Rwanda as a safe country: All decision-makers, including immigration officers and courts, were required conclusively to treat Rwanda as a safe country for asylum and immigration purposes. This designation aimed to prevent legal challenges using the argument that Rwanda was unsafe.
- Disapplication of HRA 1998: Specific provisions of the HRA 1998, including s 3, were disapplied in relation to decisions concerning the removal of individuals to Rwanda. The intention was to ensure that Convention rights could not be invoked to prevent the Government from sending people to Rwanda.
- Limitations on legal challenges: A limited scope of review existed where there was 'compelling evidence' that the individual circumstances of a person meant there was a real risk of harm to that person in Rwanda, but there was an express prohibition of review on the grounds that Rwanda was unsafe in general.

Bodies such as the Law Society, the Bar Council and the Bingham Centre for Human Rights criticised the Rwanda Act on separation of powers and rule of law grounds. While it was perfectly acceptable for the Government to respond to a Supreme Court judgment by asking Parliament to pass legislation changing the law, the Rwanda Act required courts to treat as a fact something that might not be a fact, namely that Rwanda was a safe country even if there were overwhelming evidence to the contrary. The way the Rwanda Act sought to preclude judicial scrutiny of decisions to remove people to Rwanda contravened the separation of powers, as judicial scrutiny of government decisions is a vital check and balance. The Rwanda Act also risked breaching the Government's obligations under international law.

Conversely, supporters of the Act such as Policy Exchange argued that Parliament was entitled to legislate based on its own understanding of the relevant facts and its evaluation of their significance. Assessing Rwanda's safety was a political, not judicial, issue and so not a matter for the courts.

The Border Security, Asylum and Immigration Bill will repeal the Rwanda Act, but it remains an interesting example of the interaction between the three branches of government in the UK.

(ii) The Post Office (Horizon System) Offences Act 2024

The Post Office (Horizon System) Offences Act 2024 has also raised rule of law and separation of powers concerns. It was enacted to address the wrongful convictions of over 900 sub-postmasters for crimes such as theft and false accounting due to faults in the Post Office's Horizon IT system. The Act provided for the automatic quashing of these convictions.

Some commentators argued that the Post Office Act infringed upon the separation of powers because Parliament was usurping the proper role of the courts by enacting legislation to overturn criminal convictions. Instead, the Government should have introduced a fast-track scheme enabling the courts to overturn the convictions. However, while the Government acknowledged that using legislation was an unprecedented and wholly exceptional legal solution to a miscarriage of justice of unparalleled scale and impact, it argued that it did not set a constitutional precedent.

---

## Summary

- In this chapter, you have looked at what is meant by the idea of the rule of law by examining first Dicey's views on this subject and then Lord Bingham's more modern version.
- You have also considered the meaning and historical development of the theory of the separation of powers.
- You have examined the relationship between the different branches of state in the UK by considering the degree of overlap and separation between these branches. You have done this in the context of the following relationships:
    - Executive/legislature
    - Executive/judiciary
    - Legislature/judiciary
- You have observed that in the UK separation of powers is achieved by a combination of constitutional conventions and statute, in particular the Constitutional Reform Act 2005.
- You have begun to assess the extent to which the UK constitution demonstrates an effective separation of powers. There is considerable overlap between the executive and legislature, but a substantial degree of separation between the judiciary and the other branches of government.
- You should also check your understanding by considering the summary diagram in **Figure 4.2**.

**Figure 4.2** Separation of powers in the UK

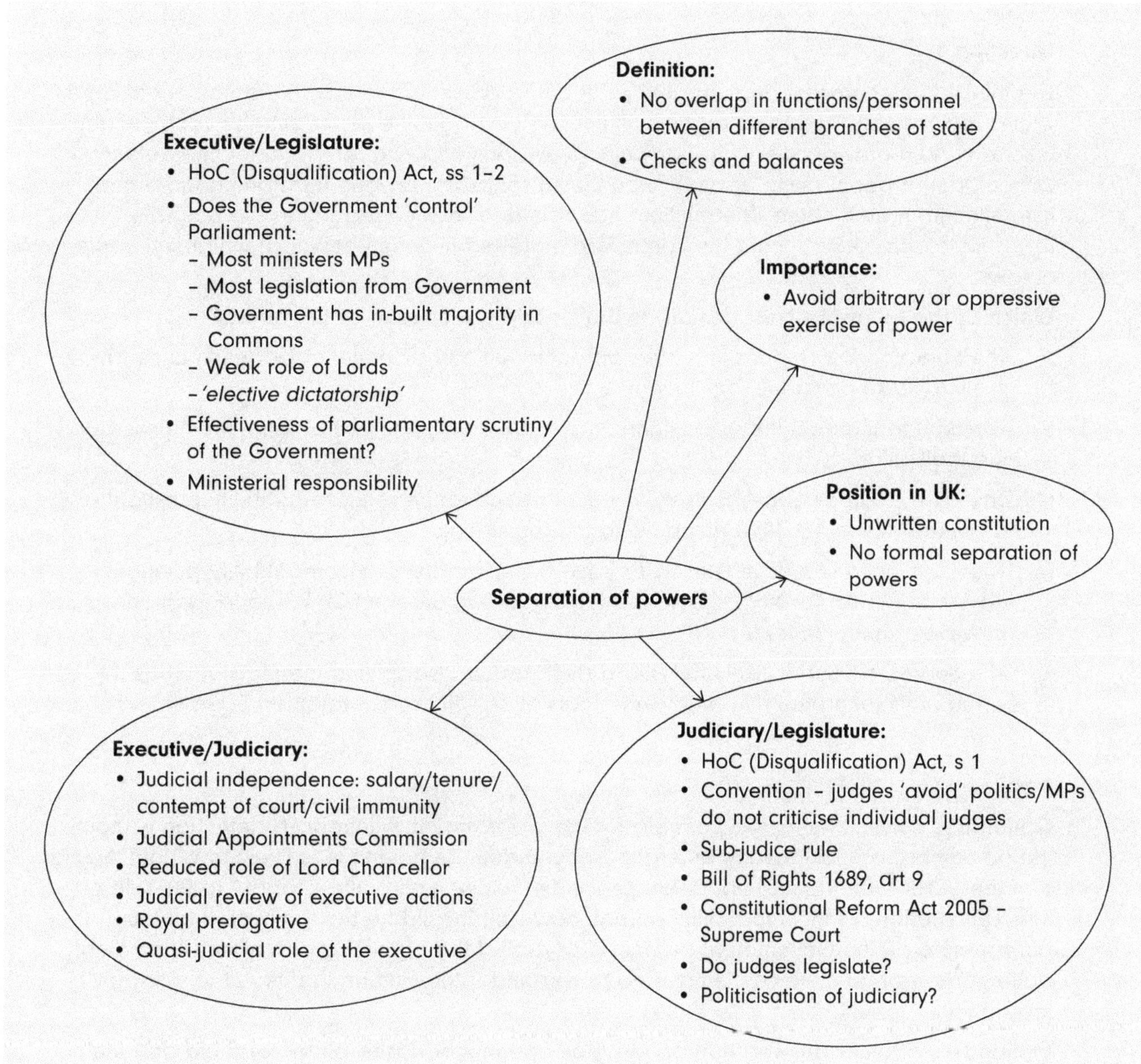

## Sample questions

**Question 1**

The minister in charge of an emergency bill being presented to the UK Parliament to deal with a major public health emergency is concerned about the approach the courts might take to certain provisions in it, in particular provisions allowing for the indefinite detention without trial of people who disobey provisions prohibiting anyone from being more than five miles from their home. The minister has asked for advice regarding the possible response of the courts should the courts find that the bill (when enacted) violates the rule of law.

**Which of the following best describes the possible response of the courts?**

A The Supreme Court, adopting the approach outlined by eminent judges in case law, is likely to strike down the legislation.

B Pursuant to the doctrine of parliamentary sovereignty, the courts will nonetheless apply the legislation.

C The High Court or above is likely to issue a declaration of incompatibility pursuant to s 4 Human Rights Act 1998 disapplying the legislation.

D The High Court or above is likely to issue a declaration of incompatibility pursuant to s 4 Human Rights Act 1998 should the legislation violate the ECHR. The legislation will, however, remain in force.

E The Supreme Court is likely to issue a declaration disapplying the legislation as, by virtue of violating the rule of law, the legislation will breach retained EU law.

**Answer**

Option D is correct. It may be possible for the Government to introduce detention without trial to combat a public health emergency, but indefinite detention is likely to violate Article 5 of the ECHR - the right to liberty and security - as well as being contrary to the rule of law. Declarations of incompatibility do not, however, invalidate the legislation although they put pressure on the Government to amend or repeal the offending provisions. Accordingly, option C is wrong as the courts have no power under the Human Rights Act to disapply legislation.

Option D is a better answer than option A as option A is based on obiter dicta and the Supreme Court has never actually struck down legislation in this way. UK courts have disapplied statutes for infringing EU law during the UK's membership of the EU, but not for infringing the rule of law. Option D is also a better answer than option B. Whilst the courts are likely to apply the legislation due to parliamentary sovereignty, it is highly probable that they would issue a declaration of incompatibility.

Option E is wrong as retained EU law only has limited supremacy over Acts of Parliament enacted before the end of the transition period. Moreover, there is unlikely to be any retained EU law with which the legislation in this question would conflict.

**Question 2**

The Government is considering whether to launch air strikes on a suspected terrorist base in an overseas country. It believes the terrorists concerned pose a direct and imminent threat to the UK. The Government has asked the Attorney General for advice as to whether parliamentary approval is required for the air strikes.

**Which of the following best describes whether parliamentary approval is required?**

A Although it is probable that a convention has recently emerged that the Government should obtain parliamentary approval before taking military action, where an emergency exists the Government need not obtain prior approval.

B The decision whether or not to take military action involves the exercise of a prerogative power and parliamentary approval is unnecessary as the Government is best placed to judge the defence needs of the country.

C Although it is a statutory requirement that the Government should obtain parliamentary approval before taking military action, where an emergency exists the statute dispenses with the need for prior approval.

D It is probable that a convention has recently emerged that the Government should obtain parliamentary approval before taking military action, so the Government must obtain prior approval.

E It is a statutory requirement that the Government should obtain parliamentary approval before taking military action, so the Government must obtain prior approval.

**Answer**

Option A is correct. The Cabinet Manual states that the Government has acknowledged that a convention has developed that the House of Commons should have an opportunity to debate the matter before military action is taken, except where an emergency exists and such action would not be appropriate. Option A is a better answer than option B because the reason parliamentary approval is not needed in the instant case is the existence of an emergency. Option D is wrong because it ignores the possibility of dispensing with the need for parliamentary approval where it would not be appropriate, as in the instant case.

Options C and E are wrong because taking military action is a prerogative power, not a statutory one.

**Question 3**

The UK and South Africa are proposing to enter a treaty relating to the safeguarding of intellectual property rights and data protection. The UK Government proposes to ratify it using the royal prerogative. Some British businesses, relying on expert economic analysis, believe the treaty will be highly damaging to their interests and will give an unfair advantage to South African businesses. They would therefore like to challenge the treaty in the UK courts.

**Can the businesses bring a successful action challenging the treaty?**

A Yes, because the courts are willing to rule on the extent of prerogative powers and it is doubtful whether the UK Government can enter into treaties using prerogative powers.

B Yes, because the courts are willing to rule on how the Government exercises its prerogative powers and on the facts the treaty seems unreasonable.

C No, because traditionally UK courts have refused to rule upon the extent of prerogative powers and how they are exercised.

D No, because traditionally UK courts have refused to rule upon how prerogative powers are exercised.

E No, because UK courts regard certain prerogative powers as non-justiciable and so refuse to review how they are exercised.

**Answer**

Option E is correct. Historically UK courts have been reluctant to review the exercise of prerogative powers, but their approach shifted in the *CCSU* case and they are now willing to review the exercise of some prerogative powers. Whilst option D reflects the traditional approach of the UK courts, option E is a better answer as the courts no longer follow that approach. However, the courts regard treaty-making as a political issue for the Government to decide upon (*Blackburn v Attorney General*) and so is not subject to review by the courts. Option B is therefore wrong because the courts will not interfere even if the treaty is unreasonable.

Option C is wrong because the courts have for centuries been willing to rule on the extent of prerogative powers. Option A is wrong as treaty-making is a prerogative power.

# 5 Public Order Law



## SQE1 syllabus

This chapter will enable you to achieve the SQE1 assessment specification in relation to functioning legal knowledge concerned with police powers to control protests, including:

- processions;
- assemblies; and
- breach of the peace.

Note that for SQE1, candidates are not usually required to recall specific case names or cite statutory or regulatory authorities. Cases are provided for illustrative purposes only.

## Learning outcomes

By the end of this chapter you will be able to understand and apply some fundamental constitutional principles appropriately and effectively, at the level required of a competent newly qualified solicitor in practice, to realistic client-based problems and situations, including the ability to:

- understand and apply the powers of the police to control processions under the Public Order Act 1986 (POA 1986);
- understand and apply the powers of the police to control assemblies under POA 1986;
- identify when a breach of the peace occurs; and
- analyse the powers of the police to deal with a breach of the peace in the context pf processions and assemblies.

## 5.1 Approach of English law to public order

Historically, protection of individual rights and freedoms under the UK constitution was based on the principle of residual or 'negative' freedom developed at common law, ie that citizens are free to do as they wish unless the law clearly states that such conduct is prohibited. Nonetheless, English judges have traditionally acknowledged that a 'right' to protest exists. For example, in *Hubbard v Pitt* [1976] 1 QB 142, Lord Denning affirmed:

> the right to demonstrate and the right to protest on matters of public concern. These are rights which it is in the public interest that individuals should possess; and, indeed, that they should exercise without impediment so long as no wrongful act is done. It is often the only means by which grievances can be brought to the knowledge of those in authority, at any rate with such impact as to gain remedy.

Although the concept of residual freedoms remains an important principle, the Human Rights Act 1998 has had a considerable impact in this area as there is now positive protection of individual rights and freedoms in the UK, not merely residual freedom. The Human Rights Act 1998 incorporated the key rights and freedoms in the ECHR into domestic law as 'Convention rights', and consequently there has been a significant shift under the UK constitution from residual freedom to the positive protection of individual rights and freedoms.

The key provisions of the ECHR in the context of public order are Article 10 - freedom of expression - and especially Article 11 - freedom of assembly and association. Article 11(1) gives a right of peaceful assembly and the separate right of freedom of association. These rights are regarded worldwide as fundamental rights in a democratic society and the courts construe them widely. However, they are subject to qualifications. The state can restrict freedom of assembly if the restrictions are:

- prescribed by law; and
- necessary in a democratic society;
  - in the interests of national security or public safety;
  - for the prevention of disorder or crime;
  - for the protection of health or morals; or
  - for the protection of the rights and freedoms of others.

This chapter focuses very much on the POA 1986. Prior to its enactment in 1986, there were numerous statutory and common law offences concerning public order. Following a period of public disorder that included inner-city riots in 1981 and the miners' strike of 1984–85, which involved violent clashes between miners and the police, the POA 1986 was introduced in reaction to the perceived need to give the police greater powers and to clarify the law.

The basic approach of English law is that processions and meetings are prima facie lawful unless they amount to crimes or torts. As processions are regarded as a reasonable use of a public highway, they are lawful unless disorder or violence breaks out, in which case the possibility arises that the participants may be charged with a public order or other criminal offence. If property is damaged, the participants could in theory face a tort action as well as criminal proceedings.

Protest marches through the streets of a town or city will normally be legal as long as they keep moving. However, if the marchers stop and hold an assembly or meeting, the position alters. For example, meetings on a public highway may amount to wilful obstruction of a highway contrary to s 137 of the Highways Act 1980, which makes it an offence for a person, without lawful authority or excuse, in any way to wilfully obstruct the free passage along a highway. However, in examining 'lawful excuse', courts need to decide if an activity causing an obstruction is itself lawful and whether it is reasonable. In the case of protests, they must take into consideration Articles 10 and 11 of the ECHR and protesters have sometimes been acquitted where the courts considered that the protesters acted reasonably. See also the discussion at **5.3.4** below.

As processions and meetings are prima facie lawful, the police usually need specific powers if they are to control them. The POA 1986 gives them significant powers to deal with potential disruption to society and threats of violence. This chapter concentrates on preventative measures – the power to impose conditions on or ban public processions and public meetings. Additionally, the POA 1986 created a number of public order offences to replace the mainly common law offences that had existed. These offences range from riot (s 1) with a maximum sentence of 12 years' imprisonment to threatening, abusive or insulting behaviour (s 5) with a fine of £1,000 as a maximum sentence. These offences are outside the scope of this manual.

As well as having statutory powers, the police also retain common law powers to prevent breaches of the peace. These sometimes supplement the statutory powers.

## 5.2 Processions

### 5.2.1 Advance notice

Section 11(1) of the POA 1986 requires any person organising a 'public procession' for any of the purposes in s 11(1)(a), (b) and (c) to give the police at least six clear days' notice of the date, time and route of the proposed procession. The purposes set out in these sub-sections are:

(a) to demonstrate support for or opposition to the views or actions of any person or body of persons;

(b) to publicise a cause or campaign; or

(c) to mark or commemorate an event.

Football supporters on their way to watching a match or schoolchildren being led from their school to a local library are therefore outside the notice requirements.

Section 16 defines 'public procession' as 'a procession in a public place' and defines 'public place' as any highway or any other place that the public may lawfully access on payment or otherwise. Public place therefore includes not only places such as public squares, parks and beaches but also privately owned places, such as football grounds and theatres, that the public can access on purchasing a ticket. Accordingly, the definition of public procession would, for example, cover a march into a theatre to protest about a play being performed there.

Section 11(4) requires the organisers to deliver the notice to a police station in the police area where the procession will start.

The purpose of the notice provisions is to enable the police to plan and give directions to avoid public disorder or other disruption.

### 5.2.2 Qualifications and exemptions

Not all processions are caught by the requirement to give notice. It does not apply to funeral processions nor to customary or commonly held processions in a given police area (s 11(2)), as in the latter case the police should be aware that it is a regular occurrence. Thus it would not be necessary to give notice of an annual Remembrance Day or Diwali parade.

*Kay v Commissioner of Police of the Metropolis* [2008] UKHL 69 is a significant case on this topic. It concerned mass cycle rides ('Critical Mass') that had taken place in central London on the last Friday of each month since 1994 for 12 years without any central organisation and any route being pre-planned. The police required the cyclists to give notice under s 11, and one of the cyclists challenged this requirement by way of judicial review. The House of Lords held that Critical Mass was 'commonly or customarily' held even though it did not follow a predetermined route but varied on each occasion. It was therefore exempt from the notice requirement.

There is an also exception for occasions when it is not reasonably practicable to give notice. This would cover an impromptu reaction to some news such as the sudden announcement of a factory closure or unexpected military action by a government.

### 5.2.3 Offences

There are two offences under s 11. The organisers are guilty of the first offence if they do not give the required notice (s 11(7)(a)). They are guilty of the second offence if the processions differ from what the notice specified (s 11(7)(b)). It is a defence to the first offence if the organiser did not know, and did not have any reason to suspect, that s 11 had not been complied with (s 11(8)). It is a defence to the second offence if the departure from the details in the notice arose from circumstances beyond the organiser's control or from something done with the agreement of the police or by their direction (s 11(9)). In both cases the burden of proof is on the defendant on the balance of probabilities to prove that the defence exists.

On conviction the organisers are liable to a fine not exceeding level 3 on the standard scale, currently £1,000.

Failure to provide notice results in the organisers committing an offence, but does not render the protest/procession unlawful. Only the organisers commit an offence. It does not make the participation in such a procession a criminal offence. The procession itself is lawful.

### 5.2.4 Imposing conditions on public processions

Under s 12 of the POA 1986, the police have powers to impose conditions upon public processions, provided that a senior police officer reasonably believes that:

- the march will result in serious public disorder, serious damage to property, or serious disruption to the life of the community (s 12(1)(a)); or
- the purpose of the organisers is to intimidate others with a view to compelling them not to do something that they have a right to do, or to do something that they have a right not to do (s 12(1)(b)).

Intimidation in s 12(1)(b) means more than being a nuisance or causing discomfort, as the reference in the sub-section to 'compelling' suggests. In *Police v Reid* [1987] Crim LR 702, anti-apartheid demonstrators outside South Africa House, where a reception was being held, shouted at guests as they arrived. The demonstrators raised their arms and waved their fingers at the guests as they arrived, chanting 'Apartheid murderers, get out of Britain' and 'You are a dying breed'. The Chief Inspector in charge decided that this was intimidatory and sought to impose a condition on the demonstrators requiring them to move away, relying on s 14(1) of the POA 1986 (see **5.3** below). (Although the case concerned s 14, the court's analysis of intimidation is equally applicable to s 12.) The defendant ignored the condition and was arrested and charged with failing to comply with it. The court held that the condition was ultra vires as the Chief Inspector had applied the wrong test. He defined intimidation as 'putting people in fear or discomfort' and had thereby incorrectly equated intimidation with discomfort. The demonstrators would have needed an intention to compel the guests not to go into the reception for their activities to amount to intimidation.

Section 73 of the Police, Crime, Sentencing and Courts Act 2022, enacted under the previous Conservative Government, amended s 12 of the POA 1986 with effect from 28 June 2022 to broaden the circumstances in which the police can impose conditions on protests to include where noise may cause a significant impact on those in the vicinity or serious disruption to the activities of an organisation. The 2022 Act defines serious disruption to the activities of an organisation as including where it may result in persons connected with the organisation not being reasonably able, for a prolonged period, to carry out their activities within the vicinity of a protest. The 2022 Act has also given the Home Secretary the power to make regulations further defining the meaning of serious disruption.

While the previous Conservative Government was in office, the Home Secretary exercised these powers by adopting the Public Order Act 1986 (Serious Disruption to the Life of the Community) Regulations 2023 (SI 2023/655) ('the 2023 Regulations') which have made some significant changes to the POA 1986.

The 2023 Regulations aim to assist the policing of protests, such as those carried out by Insulate Britain and Just Stop Oil. They amend both ss 12 and 14 of the POA 1986 by enabling the police to intervene in a wider range of circumstances.

Significantly, the 2023 Regulations reduce the threshold for 'serious disruption' by defining it as a disruption that causes 'more than minor' hindrance to day-to-day activities for other people, including in particular the making of a journey (POA 1986, s 12(2A) and s 14(2A)). However, in *R (Liberty) v Secretary of State for the Home Department* [2024] EWHC 1181 (Admin), the Divisional Court held that the 2023 Regulations were unlawful on two grounds. Firstly, the Home Secretary had exceeded her powers by defining 'serious disruption' as any disruption which was 'more than minor'. Using the ordinary and natural meaning of the words, the court held that 'more than minor' did not fall within the ordinary and natural meaning of 'serious'. Secondly, the Home Secretary had acted in a procedurally unfair manner by only consulting law enforcement agencies before adopting the Regulations, and not groups who might be adversely affected by them. Nevertheless, the 2023 Regulations remain in force pending the outcome of an appeal by the Home Secretary.

Other changes made in ss 12(2A) and 14(2A) include requiring the police to consider in deciding whether to impose conditions:

- all relevant disruption, that is disruption that may result from the assembly, or that may occur regardless of whether the assembly or procession is held (including in particular normal traffic congestion); and
- the cumulative impact of concurrent and repeated processions or assemblies in the same area.

Additionally, the 2023 Regulations define the term 'community' to mean any group of persons affected by the procession or assembly and not only people who live or work in the vicinity of a given procession or assembly.

Further, the Crime and Policing Bill currently before Parliament will make it easier for police to impose conditions on protests that might disrupt worshippers trying to attend places of worship such as churches, mosques and synagogues. Specifically the police will have the power to impose conditions on a protest if they have a reasonable belief that the protest may result in the intimidation of those seeking to access places of worship.

The conditions that the senior police officer may impose are those that appear to be necessary to prevent such disorder, damage, disruption or intimidation. This includes conditions prescribing the route or prohibiting the march from entering a particular public place.

Under s 12(2) the identity of the 'senior police officer' with the power to impose conditions depends on the circumstances. For conditions imposed during the procession, it is the most senior police officer present at the scene (s 12(2)(a)) and they may be given verbally. For conditions imposed in advance it is the chief officer of police – the Chief Constable of the relevant police force or the Commissioner of Police of the Metropolis or for the City of London (s 12(2)(b)). When given before the event, they must be provided in writing. Additionally, the chief officer of police must provide sufficient reasons so that, firstly, the demonstrators can understand why the conditions have been imposed and, secondly, a court can assess whether the belief that the procession may result in the consequences listed above (serious disruption etc) is reasonable (*R (Brehony) v Chief Constable of Greater Manchester Police* [2005] EWHC 640 (Admin) – a case on s 14 below applied by analogy to s 12).

When imposing conditions, the police also need to consider the impact of Article 11 ECHR. Any conditions they impose must be proportionate.

### 5.2.5 Offences under s 12

Section 12 of the POA 1986, as amended by the Police, Crime, Sentencing and Courts Act 2022, creates the offences and imposes the possible sanctions set out below:

- s 12(4): Organising a public procession and failing to comply with a condition imposed under s 12(1) where the person concerned knows or ought to know that the condition has been imposed.

  Possible sanctions: Imprisonment not exceeding 51 weeks or a fine not exceeding level 4 on the standard scale (currently £2,500) or both (s 12(8)).

- s 12(5): Taking part in a public procession and failing to comply with a condition imposed under s 12(1) where the person concerned knows or ought to know that the condition has been imposed.

  Possible sanctions: Fine not exceeding level 3 on the standard scale (currently £1,000) (s 12(9)).

- s 12(6): Inciting a participant in a public procession to commit an offence under s 12(5).

  Possible sanctions: Imprisonment for a term not exceeding 51 weeks or a fine not exceeding level 4 on the standard scale (s 12(10)).

Organisers and participants have a defence if they can show that their failure to comply with the conditions was due to circumstances beyond their control, for example that an organiser had become too ill to change the route or that a participant was unwillingly swept along by the crowd. The burden of proof is on the defendant to prove the defence on the balance of probabilities. It is also a defence to prove the conditions are invalid, as in *Police v Reid*.

An issue considered by the courts is whether a person convicted of an offence under s 12 can argue that such a conviction would be a disproportionate interference with their Convention rights. In *Re Abortion Services (Safe Access Zones) (Northern Ireland) Bill* [2022] UKSC 32, the Supreme Court stated that for certain protest-related offences the ingredients of the offence itself strike the proportionality balance. These offences include the offences under s 14 of the POA 1986, and the court's reasoning would apply by analogy to offences under s 12. This means that, provided the condition imposed is lawful (ie the officer holds the necessary belief and had reasonable grounds to do so), the court does not have to check that a conviction would be proportionate on the facts of each individual case.

### 5.2.6 The power to prohibit processions

Section 13(1) of the POA 1986 provides that a chief officer of police can apply for a prohibition order in respect of public processions if they reasonably believe, because of particular circumstances existing in any locality, that the powers in s 12 are insufficient to prevent a risk of serious public disorder (s 13(1)).

The chief officer of police applies to the local authority, which then makes an order with the Home Secretary's consent. Local authorities have no power of their own to seek a ban; the initiative must come from the police.

In London the procedure is different, as s 13(1) does not apply to London. The Commissioner of Police for the City of London or the Commissioner of Police of the Metropolis makes the order for the same reasons as apply outside London, with the Home Secretary's consent (s 13(4)).

The order can be for any period not exceeding three months. The order may ban all processions or processions of a particular class, such as political marches. However, there is no power to ban a specific individual procession. The order must be in writing (s 13(5)).

It is possible to challenge a ban by way of judicial review, as occurred in *Kent v Metropolitan Police Commissioner* (1981) (*The Times,* 15 May). The case concerned equivalent provisions in the Public Order Act 1936 but its reasoning is likely to apply to the POA 1986. Monsignor

Bruce Kent, as General Secretary of the Campaign for Nuclear Disarmament (CND), challenged an order banning all processions in the metropolitan district (covering an area of 786 square miles) for 28 days, other than traditional May Day celebrations and those of a religious character. He argued that the order was ultra vires because it applied to all processions over a large area and was far too wide in its scope. The Metropolitan Police Commissioner adduced evidence of serious public disorder largely due to National Front and anti-National Front demonstrations. He stated that all processions, however peaceful in intent, were potential targets for extremists.

The Court of Appeal upheld the banning order. The claimant had failed to show that the Metropolitan Police Commissioner had no reasonable grounds for making the banning order, although one Lord Justice did think the reasons were 'meagre'. This shows that the courts are reluctant to quash what are essentially operational decisions. The decision in this case had been taken in a context where there had been significant outbreaks of violence in various parts of London. The Court of Appeal suggested that CND should have applied for a relaxation of the order, which is possible under s 13(5).

The power to prohibit processions has not been used frequently. The overwhelming majority of bans have been imposed in relation to proposed marches by the National Front and more recently by the English Defence League.

### 5.2.7 Offences under s 13

Section 13 of the POA 1986 creates the offences and imposes possible sanctions set out below. They are similar to those that s 12 creates:

- s 13(7): Organising a public procession knowing that it is prohibited under s 13.

  Possible sanctions: Imprisonment not exceeding three months or a fine not exceeding level 4 on the standard scale or both (s 13(11)).
- s 13(8): Taking part in a public procession knowing that it is prohibited under s 13.

  Possible sanctions: Fine not exceeding level 3 on the standard scale (s 13(12)).
- s 13(9): Inciting a participant to take part in a public procession that is prohibited under s 13.

Possible sanctions: Imprisonment for a term not exceeding three months or a fine not exceeding level 4 on the standard scale s 13(13).

## 5.3 Meetings

Before the POA 1986 there were no statutory powers to control the holding of public meetings as opposed to processions. Including the power to control meetings in the POA 1986 was a response to concerns that static protests could cause public order problems. The Government was particularly anxious about the impact of mass picketing in industrial disputes such as the miners' strike of 1984/5, although picketing is also covered in trade union legislation.

### 5.3.1 Meetings: permission sometimes required

Whilst the general rule is that there is no requirement to obtain permission to hold a meeting, it would be wrong to assume that it is possible to hold a meeting in any public space such as a public square or park. Local or private Acts of Parliament or byelaws may lay down a requirement for permission. For example, the Trafalgar Square Byelaws 2012 require anyone wanting to use Trafalgar Square for a meeting to obtain permission from the Greater London Authority. Similarly, the Royal Parks and Other Open Spaces Regulations 1997 make it necessary to seek permission to use a Royal Park such as Hyde Park.

A meeting on private land obviously requires the permission of the owner, otherwise the owner can claim damages for trespass or apply to the courts for an injunction. The police could help to eject any trespassers at the request of the owner, for example if there is a breach of the peace, but they have no independent powers unless there is a breach of the peace or crimes such as criminal damage are being committed.

The general rule remains, though, that the police have no power to ban assemblies, as the power to impose conditions was regarded as being sufficient. The Criminal Justice and Public Order Act 1994 has, however, granted a power to ban 'trespassory assemblies' on limited grounds (see **5.3.4** below).

### 5.3.2 Imposing conditions on public assemblies

Under s 14 POA 1986, a senior police officer can impose conditions on any public assembly if they reasonably believe that it may result in serious public disorder, serious damage to property or serious disruption to the life of the community, or that the purpose of the organisers is the intimidation of others. These are the same criteria that are employed in s 12 for imposing conditions on processions. However, there is no requirement for the organisers of a public assembly to give advance notice. Section 74 of the Police, Crime, Sentencing and Courts Act 2022 has added to s 14 the same provisions regarding noise and disruption that s 73 of the 2022 Act added to s 12.

A public assembly is an assembly comprising two or more persons in a public place that is wholly or partly open to the air (POA 1986, s 16, as amended by the Anti-social Behaviour Act 2003, which reduced the number required from 20 to two). This is a very wide definition. For example, it would include a crowd listening to a brass band playing in a park bandstand or gathered together in the garden of a pub, as well as those attending a political meeting. Unlike s 12, the purpose of the assembly is irrelevant.

The conditions that the senior police officer may impose are those which appear to the senior officer as necessary to prevent such disorder, damage, disruption or intimidation. The definition of senior police officer is the same as for s 12.

Prior to the coming into force of s 73 and s 74 of the 2022 Act, there was a difference between s 12 and s 14 regarding the conditions that the police could impose, as the conditions that the police could impose under s 14 were not as extensive as under s 12. However, this difference no longer exists, and under both s 12 and s 14 the police may impose any condition that appears necessary (subject to their reasonableness and proportionality). In both cases, any conditions that the police impose in advance must be in writing and give adequate reasons, whilst conditions imposed during a procession or assembly may be given verbally.

Whilst there is no power under s 14 to ban public assemblies, the police may be able in effect to order participants to disperse. The chief officer of police on the scene may impose conditions limiting the duration of the meeting, so if necessary the police could impose a condition limiting the maximum duration to five minutes from giving the notice of the condition. However, any condition imposing a maximum duration must be proportionate.

Section 79 of the 2022 Act has extended the police powers to give directions so that they can now impose conditions on one-person protests, now set out in s 14ZA of the POA 1986. The police can give directions to one-person protests where the noise created may cause a significant impact on those in the vicinity or serious disruption to the activities of an organisation. The senior police officer may give such directions as appear necessary to prevent such disruption or impact.

### 5.3.3 Offences under s 14

Section 14 of the POA 1986 creates the offences and imposes possible sanctions set out below. They are also similar to those that s 12 and s 13 create:

- s 14(4): Organising a public assembly and failing to comply with a condition imposed under s 14(1) where the person concerned knows or ought to know that the condition has been imposed.

  Possible sanctions: Imprisonment not exceeding 51 weeks or a fine not exceeding level 4 on the standard scale or both (s 14(8)).
- s 14(5): Taking part in a public assembly and failing to comply with a condition imposed under s 14(1) where the person concerned knows or ought to know that the condition has been imposed.

  Possible sanctions: Fine not exceeding level 3 on the standard scale (s 12(9)).
- s 14(6): Inciting a participant in a public procession to commit an offence under s 14(5).

  Possible sanctions: Imprisonment for a term not exceeding 51 weeks or a fine not exceeding level 4 on the standard scale (s 12(10)).

Organisers and participants have a defence if they can show that their failure to comply with the conditions was due to circumstances beyond their control. The burden of proof is on the defendant to establish the defence.

It is also a defence to prove the conditions are invalid, as in *Police v Reid*. Although an assembly can consist of as few as two people, until the amendments made in 2022 to the POA 1986 it was considered doubtful whether an assembly of two people could cause serious public disorder or serious disruption to the life of the community. Where the police impose conditions on a very small gathering, they might find it problematic to argue that those conditions were proportionate. However, the power introduced in 2022 to impose conditions on protests based on the noise they create may make it easier for the police to impose conditions on small assemblies.

*R (Brehony) v Chief Constable of Greater Manchester* (above) provides an interesting example of the application of the principle of proportionality. Saturday demonstrations had been taking place regularly for four years outside Marks & Spencer in the centre of Manchester, protesting against the company's support for the Israeli Government and also calling for a boycott of Marks & Spencer's stores. A counter-demonstration in support of Israel had also been taking place outside the same store for some months. In November 2004, the Chief Constable issued a notice under s 14 requiring the demonstration to move to the nearby Peace Gardens over the Christmas shopping period (29 November to 3 January) due to the serious disruption that would otherwise occur when the number of visitors to the city centre would treble.

The judge refused the organiser's judicial review application, because the conditions were not unreasonable and were proportionate. The test for proportionality was whether the Chief Constable's legitimate objective of preventing serious disruption could have been achieved by means that interfered less with the claimant's rights. Given the limited and temporary nature of the restrictions, they did not.

### 5.3.4 Trespassory assemblies

It was not until that the enactment of the Criminal Justice and Public Order Act 1994 (CJPOA 1994) that the police were given the power to apply for meetings to be banned. The CJPOA 1994 added s 14A to the POA 1986, which introduced the power to ban trespassory assemblies, defined in s 14A(1) as 'an assembly ... to be held ... at a place or on land to which the public has no right of access or only a limited right of access'.

According to s 14A(9), 'assembly means an assembly of 20 or more persons' and land means 'land in the open air'. These definitions are narrower than those applying to the s 14 power to impose conditions in the following ways:

- Under s 14, an assembly need only comprise two people, whilst under s 14A at least 20 people are required.
- The section 14A power only applies to land entirely in the open air, whilst s 14 land applies to land that is just partly in the open air.

- The section 14A power applies only to land to which the public has *no or only a limited right of access*. Accordingly, the s 14A power (unlike the s 14 power) does not cover assemblies on common land to which the public has an unlimited right of access.

The criteria for banning a trespassory assembly are also narrower than those for imposing conditions. The chief officer of police must reasonably believe that it is intended to hold a trespassory assembly:

- without the permission of the occupier or outside the terms of any permission or right of access; and
- which may result in serious disruption to the life of the community or significant damage to the land, building or monument which is of historical, archaeological or scientific importance.

The chief officer may then apply to the local authority for an order prohibiting for a specified period the holding of all trespassory assemblies in the district or part of it. There are, however, strict time and geographical limits on the scope of the order. It must not last for more than four days and must not apply to an area greater than that represented by a circle of five miles' radius from a specified centre. The local authority must also obtain the Home Secretary's consent for the making of such an order.

In London the Police Commissioner for the Metropolis or the Commissioner of the City of London Police may make such an order with the consent of the Secretary of State.

The POA 1986 as amended by the CJPOA 1994 creates the following offences:

- s 14B(1): Organising an assembly knowing it to be prohibited.

  Possible sanctions: Imprisonment not exceeding three months or a fine not exceeding level 4 on the standard scale or both s 14B(5).
- s 14B(2): Taking part in assembly if the participant knows it is prohibited.

  Possible sanctions: Fine not exceeding level 3 on the standard scale (s 14B(6)).
- s 14B(3): Incitement to organise or participate in an assembly if the person knows it is prohibited.

Possible sanctions: Imprisonment for a term not exceeding three months or a fine not exceeding level 4 on the standard scale s 14B(7).

It is important to note, though, a notice prohibiting trespassory assemblies does not constitute an absolute ban on all assemblies on that land. Such a notice only prohibits assemblies to the extent those taking part in it are trespassing on the land. This point has been particularly pertinent in relation to public roads, ie highways, as an assembly on a highway is only trespassory if the participants go outside their right of access. *DPP v Jones* [1999] UKHL 5 is a leading case on this. Salisbury District Council had made an order prohibiting certain trespassory assemblies within a radius of four miles from Stonehenge. Two protesters were arrested while participating in a peaceful, non-obstructive demonstration of 21 people on a highway near Stonehenge. The High Court held that the magistrates had correctly convicted them under s 14B(2), holding that the public's right to use the highway was restricted to passing and repassing and any activities ancillary or incidental to that right, and that a public assembly was not incidental to the right of passage.

The Lords ruled by a 3–2 majority that the defendants had not committed an offence. A public highway was a public place that the public might enjoy for any reasonable purpose, provided the activity in question did not involve a public or private nuisance and did not unreasonably obstruct the highway. Accordingly, the power to ban trespassory assemblies is not as far-reaching as it might seem at first sight.

Additionally, s 14C gives a constable in uniform who reasonably believes that a person is on their way to a trespassory assembly the power to stop that person and direct them not to proceed in the direction of the assembly. It is an offence to ignore such a direction punishable by a level 3 fine (currently £1,000).

## 5.4 The common law: breach of the peace

The police also have common law powers to prevent a breach of the peace. The police can use these powers in many contexts, and their use to control assemblies remains relevant despite the extensive statutory powers granted by the POA 1986.

The authoritative definition of breach of the peace is that set out in by the Court of Appeal in *R v Howell* [1982] QB 416: 'there is a breach of the peace whenever harm is actually done or likely to be done to a person or in his presence to his property or a person is in fear of being so harmed through an assault, an affray, a riot, unlawful assembly or other disturbance.'

A breach of the peace is not a criminal offence, but triggers various police powers to take action to prevent the breach. At common law the police have a power of arrest not only if a breach of the peace has occurred but also to prevent one from occurring. They also have powers to take steps falling short of arrest such as requiring people breaching the peace or threatening do so to move way. Likewise, the police can attend and disperse a gathering if they reasonably fear a breach of the peace. Section 17(6) of the Police and Criminal Evidence Act 1984 preserves the common law powers of entry without a warrant to prevent a breach of the peace.

The case of *Duncan v Jones* [1936] 1 KB 218 shows how the police can use their common law powers to prevent a public meeting. The appellant was about to address a meeting of about 30 people taking place in a road to protest against the Incitement to Disaffection Bill. There was evidence that previous meetings the appellant had addressed at that location had led to disturbances. A policeman ordered the appellant not to hold the meeting, but she persisted in trying to hold it and obstructed the police officer when he tried to stop her doing so. No breach of the peace actually occurred but the Divisional Court upheld the appellant's conviction of wilfully obstructing the officer in the execution of his duty. The fact that the officer reasonably apprehended a breach of the peace justified the finding that he was acting in the execution of his duty. The police had the power to prevent a demonstration on a public highway where there was any fear of a breach of the peace.

The police's use of common law powers has sometimes proved controversial. The police do not need to wait until actual violence occurs before they exercise such powers and can take preventative action to prevent gatherings that could result in a breach of the peace. However, the circumstances in which they can take preventative action against demonstrators have proved contentious, as demonstrated by the case of *Moss v McLachlin* [1985] IRLR 76.

During the miners' strike of 1984–85, the police stopped a convoy of up to 80 striking miners at a junction on the M1 about 1.5 and 5 miles from four collieries at which miners were still working. The striking miners were intending to picket those collieries. The police feared a breach of the peace as violent confrontations were likely to take place if the striking miners continued to their destination. Accordingly, to prevent a breach of the police, the police instructed the miners not to proceed towards the collieries. Some of the miners tried to push past the police cordon, and were arrested and subsequently convicted by magistrates of obstructing a police officer in the execution of his duty.

On appeal the Divisional Court upheld the convictions. There had been numerous violent confrontations during the course of the strike and so the police had acted lawfully. The police had a duty to prevent a reasonably apprehended breach of the peace. The possibility of a breach of the peace in close proximity both in place and time was real and immediate and not remote.

However, under the impact of the Human Rights Act 1998 and Articles 10 and 11 of the ECHR, the approach of the courts has shifted. In *R (Laporte) v Chief Constable of Gloucester* [2006] UKHL 55 a group of about 120 anti-Iraq War campaigners were travelling to a demonstration outside RAF Fairford when their coaches were stopped by the police who then escorted them the 90 miles back to London without permitting breaks for relief or refreshment. The claimant argued her Article 10 right to freedom of expression and Article 11 right to freedom of peaceful assembly had been violated. The Court of Appeal held that it was lawful for the police to prevent demonstrators joining the demonstration if they reasonably apprehended a breach of the peace, stating that the requirement that the breach should be 'imminent' in a strict sense did not apply to actions short of arrest. On further appeal, the House of Lords held that:

1. The police were purporting to use powers to prevent a reasonably apprehended breach of the peace. However, these powers are only available when a breach is 'imminent'. On the facts, the police did not believe that a breach of the peace was imminent.
2. The House of Lords rejected the distinction made by the Court of Appeal between powers of arrest and other powers to prevent a breach of the peace (eg the power to disperse a meeting). In all cases the breach of the peace must be 'imminent'.

Although the House of Lords distinguished *Laporte* from *Moss v McLachlan*, the reasoning in *Laporte* very much relies on the ECHR principle of proportionality. Even if intervention had been permissible, the police would have been unable to show that their actions had constituted a proportionate restriction of Convention rights. Their intervention had been premature. As extensive precautions had been put in place at RAF Fairford to handle the protests, it had been unreasonable to assume that the protesters on the coaches would have become involved in violent protest upon arrival. The police could have taken less drastic action such as allowing everyone to continue to the airbase and arresting anyone who subsequently acted, or threatened to act, violently. The police's conduct was indiscriminate, failing to distinguish between the majority of protesters who had peaceful intent and the small minority who actually threatened violence.

However, the decision of the House of Lords in *Austin v Commissioner of the Police of the Metropolis* [2009] UKHL 5 shows the police can in limited circumstances take drastic action to prevent a breach of the peace, even if it adversely impacts innocent bystanders. This case concerned demonstrators who had been confined within a police cordon at Oxford Circus for several hours (a practice sometimes described as 'kettling') following May Day protests against globalisation and capitalism, which previously had resulted in serious disorder. On this occasion as well some of the protesters had threatened violence.

The House of Lords held that those caught in the police cordon did not suffer a violation of their right to liberty guaranteed by Article 5 of the ECHR, even though some innocent bystanders were caught up in it. Crowd control measures adopted by the police in order to prevent a breach of the peace would not breach Article 5 provided they were not arbitrary but were employed in good faith and were proportionate. In this case, the police intended to maintain the cordon only so long as was reasonably necessary to achieve a controlled dispersal in an unusually difficult exercise in crowd control; accordingly there was no arbitrary deprivation of liberty. There was accordingly only a restriction on movement, which did not engage Article 5.

Subsequently, in *Austin & Others v The United Kingdom* [2012] ECHR 459 the European Court of Human Rights ruled in favour of the UK, stating that the police measures were the least intrusive possible on the facts and there was no obvious point at which the restriction on movement turned into a deprivation of liberty.

The common law powers relating to breach of the peace do give the police considerable discretion in relation to demonstrations and assemblies. However, case law does show that the police need to show their conduct is a proportionate response to the situation they are facing to ensure that they do not violate Convention rights.

---

## Summary

- In this chapter, you have looked at police powers to control public processions and public assemblies.
- Under s 11 POA 1986, organisers of a public procession must, subject to certain exceptions, give the police six clear days' advance notice of their plans. The flowchart in **Figure 5.1** shows the circumstances in which the organisers should give notice.

**Figure 5.1** Section 11 of the Public Order Act 1986: requirement to give notice

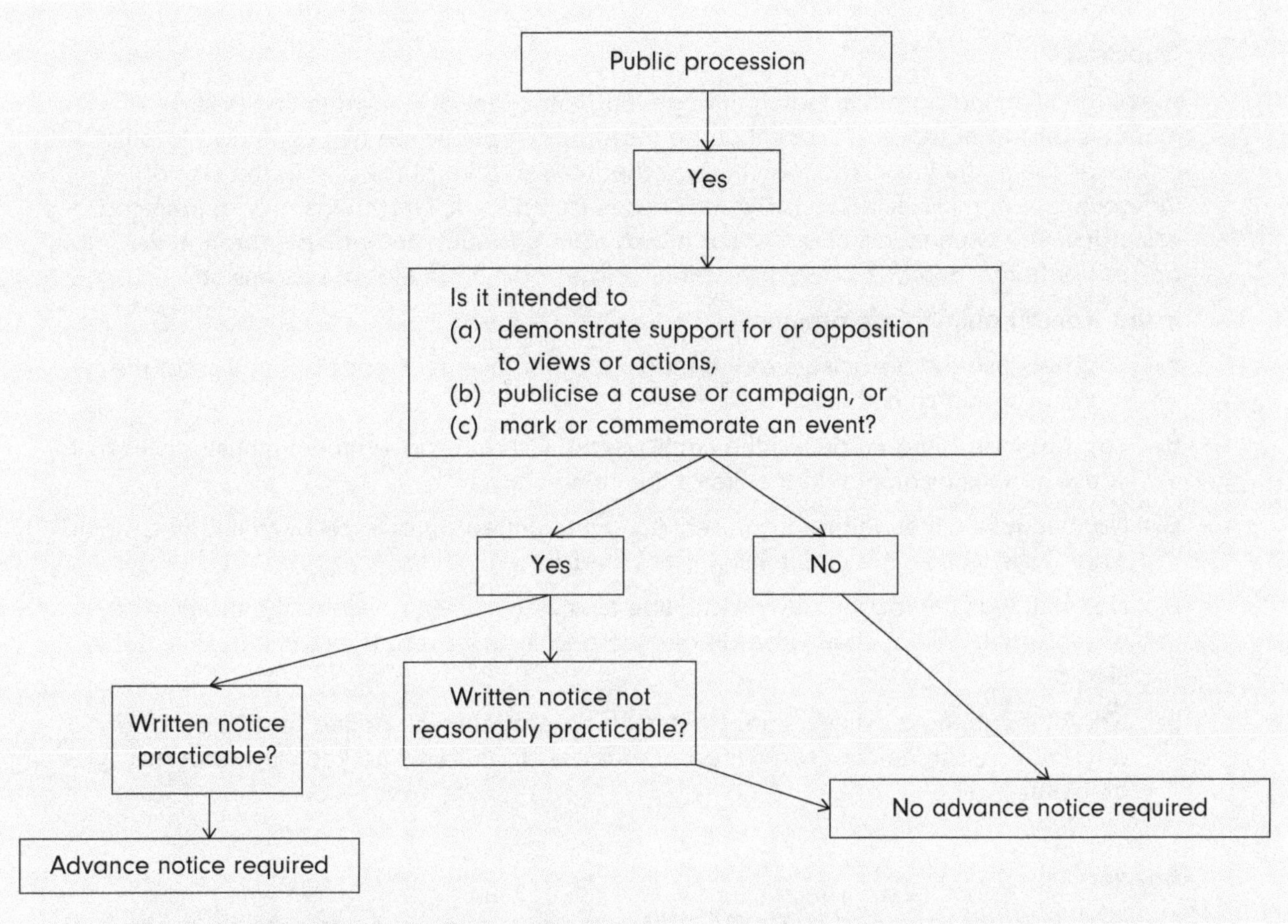


- Under s 12 POA 1986, the police have the power to impose conditions on public processions if necessary to prevent serious adverse consequences to the community or intimidation. The police can impose conditions in advance of the procession or during it.
- Under s 13 POA 1986, the chief officer of police may apply to the local authority to prohibit a public procession if necessary to prevent serious adverse consequences to the community or intimidation. The local authority must obtain the Home Secretary's consent to make the order. The procedure in London is slightly different.
- Under s 14 POA 1986, the police have the power to impose conditions on public assemblies if necessary to prevent serious adverse consequences to the community or intimidation. The police can impose conditions in advance of the assembly or during it.
- Under s 14A POA 1986 the chief officer of police may apply to the local authority to prohibit a trespassory assembly to prevent serious disruption to the life of the community or significant damage to land, buildings or monuments of particular importance. The prohibition can only last for a maximum of four days and can only cover an area represented by a circle with a radius of no more than five miles from a specified centre.

## Sample questions

### Question 1

A woman is taking part in a march through the high street of a town in England. The march is protesting against plans that the Government published two days ago to build a new prison in the town. The march was scheduled to take place during the visit of the government minister responsible for prisons to the town, which was only announced yesterday. The woman learnt about the march from a leaflet that was put through the letter box of her home. She has been arrested for taking part in an illegal procession.

**Is the woman guilty of an offence?**

A Yes, because the organisers of the march did not give six clear days' notice of the march. The march is therefore illegal.

B Yes, because a march during the controversial visit of a government minister is likely to cause serious disruption to the life of the community.

C No, because although the organisers have committed an offence by failing to give six clear days' notice, the march itself is not illegal.

D No. As it was not reasonably practicable to give advance notice of the march, the organisers have not committed an offence and in any event the march itself is not illegal.

E No. Although the organisers have committed an offence by failing to give six clear days' notice, she has not committed an offence as she had no knowledge of this omission.

### Answer

Option D is correct. Under s 11(1) POA 1986 organisers of a public procession (march) must give the police six clear days' notice if it is for any of the purposes specified in the section. Protesting against a new prison comes within these purposes. However, if it is not reasonably practicable to give any advance notice of the procession, there is no duty to give the notice. Here, the march seems to be an immediate response to the announcement of the new prison and coincides with the visit of the responsible government minister. If the organisers had given six clear days' notice, they would have missed the minister's visit. Option D is thus a better answer than option C, as option C sets out what the position would have been had the duty to give notice applied. Option E is wrong as the marches remain legal even when the organisers should have given notice; the knowledge of the marchers whether notice has been given is irrelevant.

Option A is wrong because, as stated above, the march remains legal even if a notice should have been given. As regards option B, whilst the prospect of serious disruption to the life of the community may give the police grounds for imposing conditions on the march, it does not render the march itself illegal.

### Question 2

A group of about 100 demonstrators have gathered in a square outside a town hall protesting against a local authority's cuts to library services. The time is nearly 17.00 when many of the local authority's workers will be leaving the town hall and some of them normally walk through the square on their way home. Most of the demonstrators are chanting slogans such as 'Save our libraries' and 'Down with the council', but there has been no violence. A police sergeant, supervised by her inspector, are the only police at the scene.

The inspector orders the demonstrators to disperse in the next 15 minutes to ensure that the workers can go home without any trouble.

**Which of the following best describes whether the inspector's order is lawful?**

A As the senior police officer is present, she can impose a condition requiring the protesters to disperse as the demonstrators' behaviour will clearly intimidate the local authority's workers.

B She has common law powers to order the demonstrators to disperse as she has reasonable grounds for believing that a breach of the peace will occur.

C Although the inspector is the senior police officer present, she cannot impose conditions on the protest as she does not have reasonable grounds for believing that the demonstrators' behaviour will intimidate the local authority's workers.

D The inspector does not have any common law powers to order the demonstrators to disperse, even though she has reasonable grounds for believing that a breach of the peace will occur.

E Although the inspector does have common law powers, they only empower her to arrest the demonstrators and not to order them to disperse.

**Answer**

Option C is correct. As the senior police officer present at the scene, the inspector does have the power under s 14(1) POA 1986 if she reasonably believes that the assembly will result in serious public disorder, serious damage to property, or serious disruption to the life of the community, or the purpose of the organisers is to intimidate others with a view to compelling them not to do something that they have a right to do, or to do something that they have a right not to. However, based on *Police v Reid*, it seems unlikely that the organisers have intimidatory purpose, and the protest seems unlikely to lead to serious disruption. Moreover, the noise levels seem unlikely to have a significant impact on those in the vicinity or cause serious disruption to the activities of an organisation. While the 2023 Regulations have lowered the threshold for serious disruption, it still seems unlikely that it would have been reached on these facts. For that reason option A is wrong.

The police do have common law powers to prevent a breach of the peace that can be used to disperse meetings, so option D is wrong. However, option B is wrong because on the facts there are no grounds for apprehending a breach of the peace as defined in *R v Howell*, as the conduct of protesters seems unlikely to result in violence. Option E is wrong because the common law powers to prevent a breach of the peace are not limited to arrest, but can include a direction to disperse.

**Question 3**

A local authority has issued a notice prohibiting trespassory assemblies within the vicinity of a well-known landmark. A group of about 25 protesters have, with the permission of the farmer who owns the land, gathered on farm land within the area covered by the notice and within the time frame specified in it. The farmer said they could remain on the land as long as they did not camp on it. The police arrested the protesters for taking part in a trespassory assembly after they put up tents on it.

**Which of the following best describes whether the protesters are guilty of an offence relating to trespassory assemblies?**

A They are guilty because they have taken part in an assembly in the area covered by the notice.

B They are guilty because they have taken part in an assembly on private land in the area covered by the notice.

C They are guilty because they put up tents, breaking the terms of the permission given by the farmer.

D They are not guilty because the farmer gave them permission to be on the land, so they are not trespassers.

E They are not guilty because the farmer gave them permission to be on the land, and they have not threatened to breach the peace.

**Answer**

Option C is correct. Under s 14A the local authority has the power, with the Home Secretary's consent, to prohibit an assembly likely to be held without the permission of the occupier of the land or to conduct itself in such a way as to exceed the limits of any permission granted by the occupier. As long as the protesters remain within the limits of the farmer's permission, the assembly is not trespassory. However, once they put up tents they have exceeded the limits of the permission. Options A and B are wrong as they define the type of land covered by a prohibition notice too widely.

Options D and E are wrong because the protesters have exceeded the limits of the farmer's permission.

# 6 The Grounds of Judicial Review



## SQE1 syllabus

This chapter will enable you to achieve the SQE1 assessment specification in relation to functioning legal knowledge concerned with core constitutional and administrative law principles, including:

- the nature, process and limits of judicial review;
- the supervisory nature of judicial review;
- decisions which may be challenged by judicial review; and
- grounds for judicial review:
  - illegality;
  - irrationality;
  - procedural impropriety; and
  - legitimate expectation.

Note that for SQE1, candidates are not usually required to recall specific case names or cite statutory or regulatory authorities. Cases are provided for illustrative purposes only.

## Learning outcomes

By the end of this chapter you will be able to apply relevant core legal principles and rules appropriately and effectively, at the level of a competent newly qualified solicitor in practice, to realistic client-based and ethical problems and situations, including the ability to:

- identify and apply the grounds under which judicial review claims may be brought;
- identify the ways in which a public body may act illegally;

- apply the concept of irrationality;
- apply the principles of procedural fairness (ie the rules of natural justice: the right to a fair hearing and the rule against bias) and legitimate expectation;
- identify the consequences of breaching a procedural requirement contained in an 'enabling' Act of Parliament; and
- analyse the availability of both the substantive and the procedural grounds of review, and identify their likely chances of success.

## 6.1 Introduction to judicial review and the grounds of claim

This chapter starts with an overview of the overlap with constitutional principles and the grounds of claim. It will then consider in detail each of the grounds:

- illegality
- irrationality
- procedural impropriety.

The chapter will then conclude by looking at the consequences of breaches and how to analyse the availability of grounds and chances of success with some sample questions.

In this chapter you will begin your study of judicial review, and the diagram in **Figure 6.1** is a 'road map' to assist you. The topics you are studying in this chapter are set out under the heading '2. If so, what are C's likely grounds of challenge?', in boxes highlighted in bold.

**Figure 6.1** Judicial review: an overview

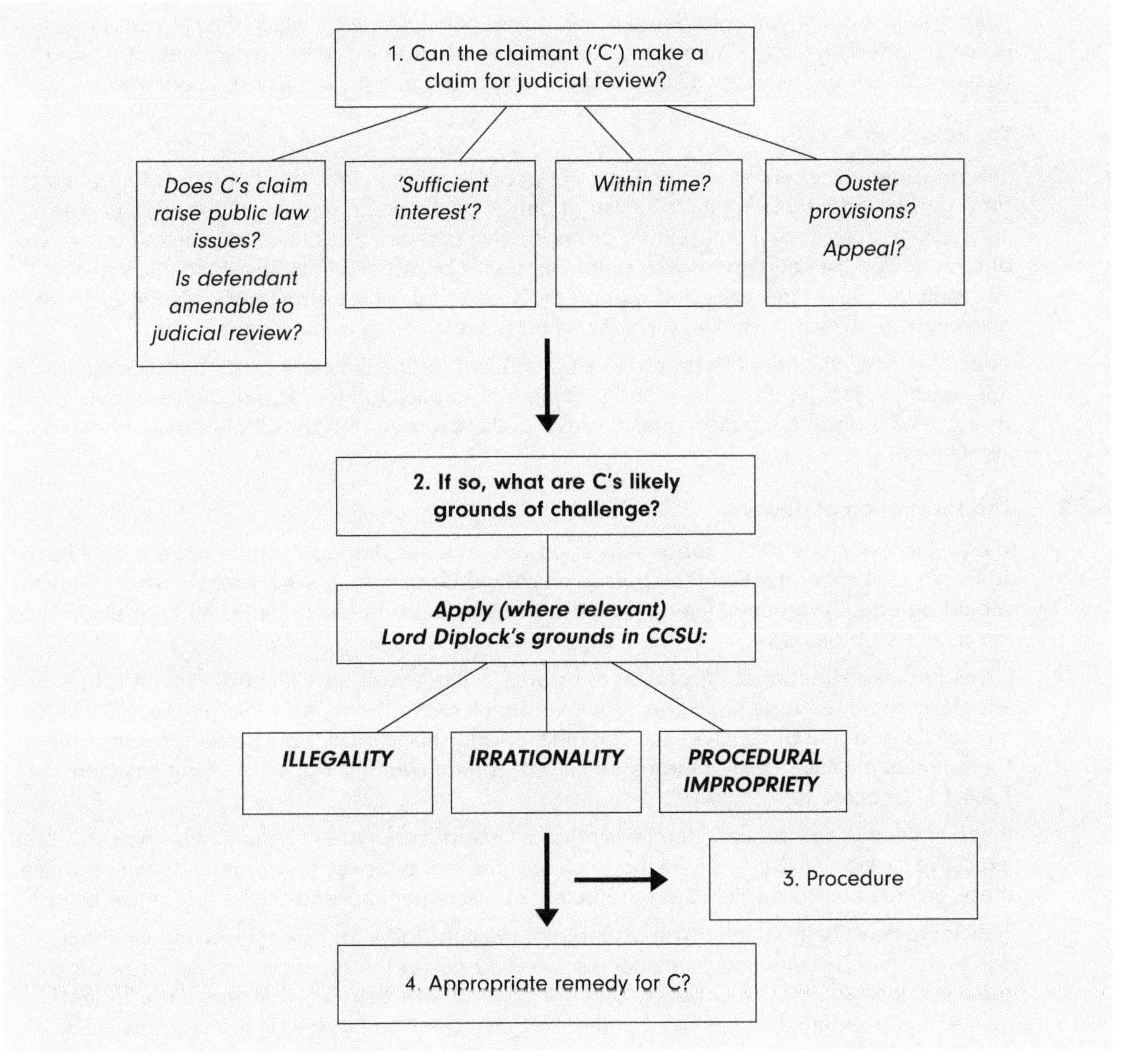


## 6.2 What is judicial review?

Judicial review is the mechanism by which the courts ensure that public bodies act within the powers that they have been granted and do not exceed or abuse those powers.

A court that judicially reviews the actions of a public body is *not* concerned with the merits of that body's decision. Judicial review involves the courts making sure that public bodies make decisions in the 'right way'. If the court became concerned with the merits of the decision, this would encroach on the role of the legislative or executive branches of state, and would contravene the doctrine of the separation of powers (see **6.3.2** below).

## 6.3 Judicial review and fundamental principles of the UK constitution

In **Chapters 2** and **4** you considered a number of principles upon which the UK constitution is based including parliamentary sovereignty, the rule of law and the separation of powers. Outlined below are ways in which judicial review and these principles are interlinked.

### 6.3.1 The rule of law

This principle is concerned with government according to the law. In other words, there must be a proper legal basis for the exercise of power by the state over the citizen, and power must not be exercised in an arbitrary or oppressive manner. If disputes arise from the exercise of such power, the courts provide a potential means of redress. They are concerned to see that statutory duties are complied with properly and that, where statute permits the exercise of discretion by a decision-maker, such discretion is exercised in a fair manner.

Judicial review can therefore be seen as an example of the judiciary fulfilling its traditional role, ensuring that justice is done and that the law applies to members of the executive just as much as it does to the individual. It prevents the exercise of power that does not have a lawful basis.

### 6.3.2 The separation of powers

The political doctrine of the separation of powers requires that each of the three branches of state are kept separate, that their personnel should be unique to each branch, and that they should be equal in terms of the power each branch wields in comparison with that enjoyed by the other two branches.

Given the lack of a formal separation of powers in the 'unwritten' UK constitution, it is therefore important that the courts provide a counter-balance to the prominence of the executive within the constitution and a dispute-resolution mechanism. This is particularly important when the Government exercises such a large measure of control over the House of Commons (see **4.3.4.1** in Chapter 4).

In the judicial review process, the legislative branch passes policy-implementing powers to the executive branch, whilst the judicial branch ensures that the executive branch does not abuse those powers but stays within the parameters of discretion imposed by the legislative branch.

Judicial review can be seen as an example of the separation of powers working smoothly. The legislature decides how much decision-making power the executive should be given, the executive then exercises that power, and the judiciary oversees the executive's use of that power. It is a system that ensures that the executive does no more than the legislature has allowed it to do.

There is another way in which judicial review may be linked to the idea of the separation of powers. In judicially reviewing actions or decisions of the executive, the courts are concerned only that such steps have been exercised in the correct way and using the correct procedure. The courts are not concerned with the merits of any decision. If the courts were to address the merits of a decision, this would trespass on the role of the executive.

### 6.3.3 Parliamentary sovereignty

The common law doctrine of parliamentary sovereignty provides that Parliament can pass any statute it wishes and such law cannot then be overridden or set aside.

Judicial review does not conflict with this doctrine, because review is available only in respect of secondary legislation. The courts do not normally question primary legislation, which would clearly breach parliamentary sovereignty. During the UK's membership of the EU the principle of supremacy of EU law applied, but the EUWA 2018 largely terminated this principle at the end of the transition period.

In addition, when a court judicially reviews the action or decision of a public body, that body will normally have been acting under powers granted to it by Parliament. The court will examine whether the body has acted in accordance with the powers granted to it by Parliament, or whether it has exceeded or abused those powers. In this way, the court will be upholding parliamentary sovereignty by ensuring that public bodies act as Parliament intended.

Another way of understanding the relationship between judicial review and the basic constitutional principles you considered in **Chapters 2** and **4** is to consider the diagram in **Figure 6.2**.

**Figure 6.2** Judicial review and constitutional principles

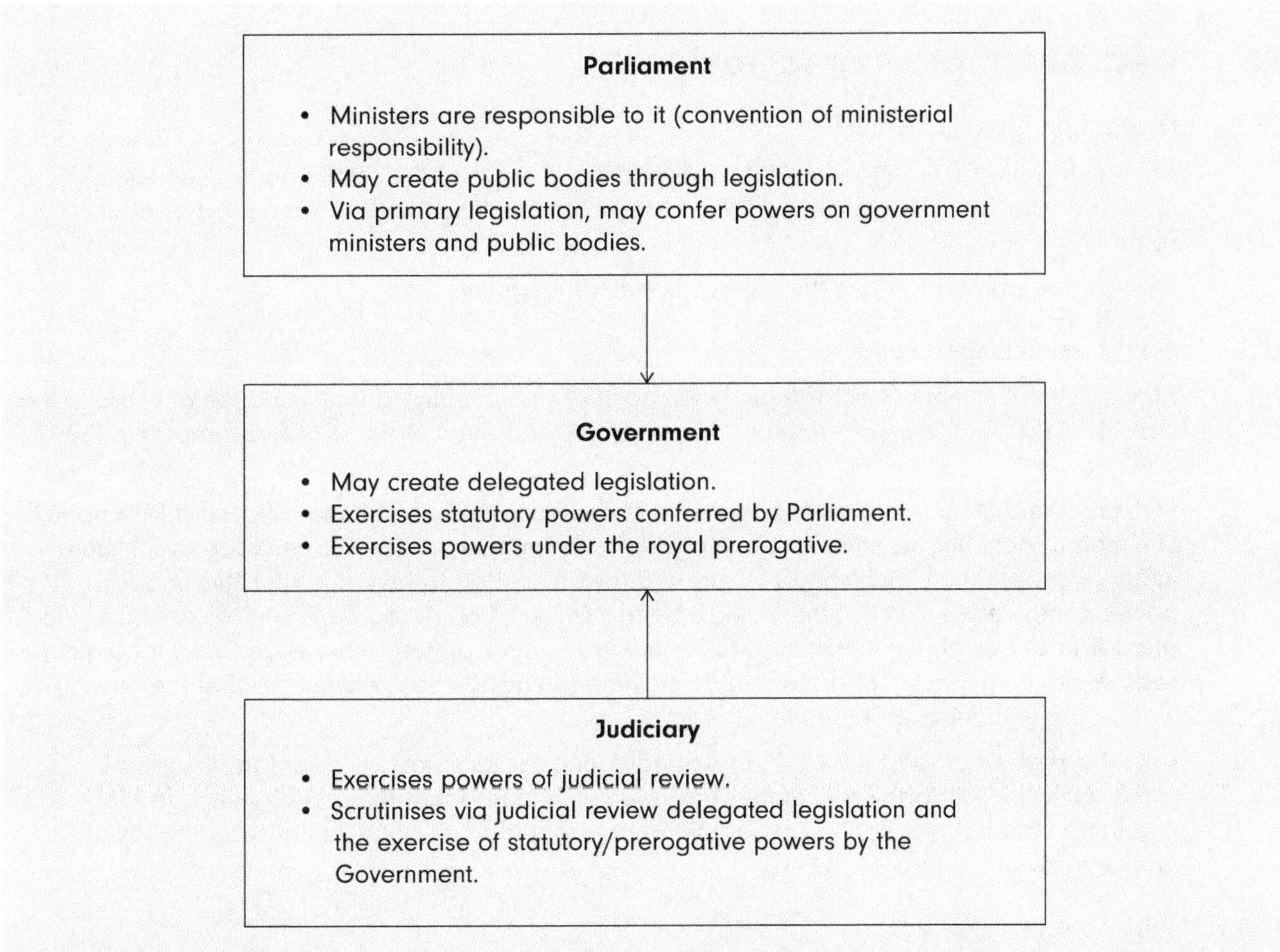


## 6.4 Identifying the grounds of review

Lord Diplock, in *CCSU v Minister for Civil Service* [1984] UKHL 9, identified three grounds of domestic judicial review. These grounds are:

(a) illegality;

(b) irrationality; and

(c) procedural impropriety.

Illegality and irrationality are referred to as the substantive grounds of review. This is because they focus on the 'substance' of the decision under review.

Procedural impropriety focuses instead on the procedure followed in arriving at the decision under review.

In addition to these three domestic grounds, judicial review claims can also be made under two further 'European' grounds:

(a) breach of the ECHR; and

(b) breach of retained EU law.

Breach of the ECHR will be considered as a ground of judicial review claim in **Chapter 9.**

Breach of retained EU law will not be considered in detail in this manual. In practice it is nonetheless important, and lawyers ignore it at their peril.

## 6.5 Illegality as grounds for review

### 6.5.1 How might illegality occur?

An action is illegal or ultra vires if it is beyond the powers of the public body in question either because the powers claimed do not exist, or because they are exceeded or abused in some way.

We will now consider in turn the various heads of illegality.

#### 6.5.1.1 Acting without legal authority

Public authorities cannot act without legal authority, as confirmed by the House of Lords in the case of *R v Richmond-upon-Thames LBC, ex p McCarthy and Stone (Developments) Ltd* [1992] 2 AC 48.

McCarthy and Stone were developers who consulted with the planning officers of Richmond LBC before deciding whether to make a planning application. They were charged for the informal consultation. Richmond LBC argued it was entitled to levy a fee for this under a power contained in s 111 of the Local Government Act 1972 to do 'anything incidental to the discharge of any of [its] functions'. McCarthy and Stone applied to the High Court for judicial review, claiming that s 111 did not allow Richmond LBC to charge a fee, so that the council was acting without legal authority.

Both the High Court and the Court of Appeal found for Richmond LBC, but the House of Lords found for McCarthy and Stone. The Law Lords stated that the charges imposed for providing informal pre-application planning advice were ultra vires because of the lack of a relevant power.

#### 6.5.1.2 The rule against delegation

**The rule**

There is a general rule that decision-making powers, once given by Parliament, cannot then be further delegated, or 'sub-delegated'. This rule was confirmed in the case of *Vine v National Dock Labour Board* [1957] AC 488.

In this case, the Dock Workers (Regulation of Employment) Order 1947 gave local dock labour boards the power to take disciplinary action against dock workers. A complaint was made against Vine, alleging that he had regularly reported late for work. The relevant local dock labour board appointed a committee to deal with the complaint. After hearing evidence, the committee terminated Vine's employment. The House of Lords held that the decision to dismiss Vine was void because the duty of the local board could not be delegated to a separate committee. Lord Somervell commented:

> There are ... many administrative duties which cannot be delegated. Appointment to an office or position is plainly an administrative act. If under a statute a duty to appoint is placed on the holder of an office, whether under the Crown or not, he would, normally, have no authority to delegate.

**Exceptions to the rule against delegation**

There are two important exceptions to the general rule against delegation, namely the '*Carltona* principle' and s 101 of the Local Government Act 1972.

(a) The '*Carltona* principle'

In the case of *Carltona v Commissioners of Works* [1943] 2 All ER 560, the relevant legislation specified that the power to requisition factories during World War II was exercisable by the Minister of Works and Planning. A factory owner whose factory had been requisitioned argued that the requisition was invalid because the order had not in fact been signed by the minister, but by a civil servant within the Ministry.

In the judgment Lord Greene MR confirmed that government ministers sub-delegating decision-making powers to civil servants in their departments provides an exception to the general rule against delegation. He stated that, under the convention of individual ministerial responsibility (which you considered in **Chapter 4**), government ministers are ultimately responsible to Parliament for their departments, so there is an expectation that they act through their civil servants in taking even major decisions.

(b) Local Government Act 1972, s 101

Under s 101 of the Local Government Act 1972, local authorities may delegate decision-making powers to committees, sub-committees or to individual officers, provided they make a *formal resolution so to do.*

6.5.1.3 'Fettering' of discretion

As a general principle, if Parliament provides a public body with a discretionary power, the courts will not permit that body to restrict or 'fetter' such discretion.

'Fettering' of discretion may occur in two ways:

(a) acting under the dictation of another; or

(b) applying a general policy as to the exercise of discretion in too strict a manner.

We shall look at each of these further below.

**Acting under the dictation of another**

Public authorities cannot act under the dictation of another person or body. In the case of *Lavender & Sons Ltd v Minister of Housing and Local Government* [1970] 1 WLR 1231 Lavender & Sons were refused planning permission to extract sand and gravel from high-grade agricultural land. The letter containing the minister's decision stated that he would not grant permission for mineral extraction 'unless the Minister of Agriculture is not opposed to [mineral] working' and that as, in the present case, the agricultural objection had not been waived, he had decided not to grant permission. Lavender & Sons sought judicial review of the rejection of their appeal.

The court found for Lavender & Sons, stating that although the minister was entitled to formulate a general policy, this decision had not been based on a general policy but on another minister's objection. The Minister of Housing and Local Government had fettered his discretion by not opening his mind to Lavender & Sons' application.

**Applying a general policy as to the exercise of discretion in too strict a manner**

Sometimes Parliament requires public authorities to exercise powers in large numbers of similar cases. For example, local authorities have to decide numerous planning applications. Fairness requires that like cases should be decided in like ways, and so public authorities may formulate their own policies to help them take consistent decisions but this should not be undertaken in such a way as to 'fetter discretion'.

In the case of *British Oxygen v Minister of Technology* [1971] AC 610, the Ministry of Technology formulated a general policy relating to the awarding of grants in respect of capital expenditure, but only for items costing at least £25. British Oxygen had spent over £4 million investing in oxygen cylinders, but each cylinder only cost £20. Therefore, under strict application of the policy, British Oxygen's grant application was rejected as each item cost only £20.

The House of Lords held that the Ministry of Technology did have the right to formulate its own general policy, but only provided the policy did not preclude the Ministry from considering individual cases. If the policy had been applied over-rigidly, the minister would effectively have tied his own hands, preventing him from considering each case on its merits. Lord Reid stated that anyone who has a statutory discretion must not shut his ears to an application and *must be always willing to listen to anyone with something new to say*. Nonetheless, on the facts the House of Lords held that the Ministry had acted properly.

6.5.1.4 Using powers for an improper or unauthorised purpose

Public authorities will be acting illegally if they use their powers for an improper or unauthorised purpose. In the case of *Congreve v Home Office* [1976] 1 QB 629, the Government announced that the price of a TV licence would soon go up from £12 to £18. Congreve was one of over 20,000 people who took out a new TV licence before the old one expired, so as to avoid paying the extra cost. The Home Office wrote to those who had purchased their licence before the new charge came into effect demanding the payment of the extra cost, failing which their licences would be revoked. Congreve sought judicial review of the threatened revocation.

The Court of Appeal found for Congreve, stating that the Home Office had no authority to revoke the licences. The purpose of revoking the licence was simply to raise revenue, in a way not provided for by Parliament. The Court of Appeal added that this would represent a misuse of the power conferred on the Government by Parliament.

6.5.1.5 Dual purposes

What happens in situations where a public authority arrives at a decision based on more than one consideration, one of which is relevant to the purpose of the power it is exercising, the other of which is irrelevant?

Over a century ago, the House of Lords established the 'primary purpose' test in the case of *Westminster Corporation v LNWR* [1905] AC 426. The London and Northern Western Railway Company (LNWR) sought judicial review of the Westminster Corporation's decision, under public health legislation, to build underground lavatories at Whitehall. The lavatories could be accessed from either side of the street, effectively creating a subway, thereby making it easier for people to trespass on the LNWR's land. The LNWR argued that the main reason behind the Corporation's decision to build the toilets had not been to provide conveniences but, rather, to build a subway, which the legislation had not authorised.

The House of Lords found in favour of the Westminster Corporation, deciding that the primary object of the Corporation was the construction of the conveniences with the requisite and proper means of approach thereto and exit therefrom. Their Lordships held that where there are dual purposes behind a decision, provided the permitted/authorised purpose is the 'primary' purpose, then the decision is not ultra vires and should stand.

In *R v Inner London Education Authority, ex p Westminster City Council* [1986] 1 WLR 28 the court used a different formulation. The Inner London Education Authority (ILEA) had statutory power to 'arrange for the publication within [its] area information on matters relating to local government'. ILEA mounted a publicity campaign costing £651,000 concerning the Government's proposals for rate-capping, which would limit the amount it could raise in local taxation and thus spend on education. Westminster City Council sought a declaration that this was unlawful.

The High Court held that ILEA had sought to achieve two purposes:

(i) Giving information about rate-capping and its results; this was an authorised purpose.

(ii) Persuading the public to support ILEA's views on rate-capping; this was not an authorised purpose.

The test that the High Court applied when there were two purposes, one authorised and one unauthorised, was as follows: 'Was the authority pursuing an unauthorised purpose, which *materially influenced* the making of its decision?'

The High Court considered that the unauthorised purpose was one of the purposes, if not the major purpose, of the decision to launch the campaign. The unauthorised purpose had therefore materially influenced the making of the decision and therefore the decision was unlawful, because ILEA had taken into account an irrelevant consideration.

Although the High Court thought that the 'material influence' test was consistent with the 'primary purpose' test in the 1905 case, the two tests are not easy to reconcile.

6.5.1.6 Taking account of irrelevant considerations or failing to take account of relevant considerations

A public authority must both disregard irrelevant considerations and take into account relevant considerations when exercising its powers. The case of *Roberts v Hopwood* [1925] AC 578 is authority for both requirements, despite the outmoded language used by the Law Lords.

Poplar Borough Council had exercised its power under statute to pay its employees such wages 'as it saw fit'. It set a generous minimum wage and applied the minimum to female workers in the same way as it did to male workers. The District Auditor ordered that the council make good the financial losses caused by paying its employees so generously. The council sought judicial review of the District Auditor's order.

The House of Lords found for the District Auditor, first because the council had taken account of irrelevant considerations, namely, 'socialist philanthropy' and 'feminist ambition', and, secondly, because the council had also disregarded relevant considerations, namely the wage levels in the labour market and the burden that would be placed on the ratepayers as a consequence of its decision.

It need not always be the case that a public authority both takes into account an irrelevant consideration and fails to take into account a relevant consideration. It may simply do one or the other as the case of *Padfield v Minister of Agriculture* [1968] AC 997, a leading case on taking into account irrelevant considerations, shows.

The Agricultural Marketing Act 1958 gave the Minister of Agriculture the discretionary power to order an investigation by a committee into complaints made by farmers about the conduct of the Milk Distribution Board, a public body set up to regulate the distribution of milk products. A number of farmers made a complaint to the minister, alleging that the Board had fixed milk prices in a way that was prejudicial to their interests. The minister refused to order an investigation, stating that if the complaint were upheld he would be expected to give effect to the committee's recommendations.

The House of Lords held the minister had taken into account an irrelevant consideration in deciding not to exercise his discretion to order an investigation. The potential political embarrassment to the minister was not a matter the minister ought to have taken into account when refusing to consider the complaint.

The example exercise that follows will help you to apply the principle of illegality to a set of facts.

### ***Example***

*Assume that the Public Transport Act 2016 ('the Act') (fictitious) empowers local authorities to give financial assistance in the form of grant aid to organisations involved in operating any form of public transport. The aim of the Act is to encourage the use of public transport to get people to work.*

*Greenborough District Council (GDC) has created a policy as to how it will deal with applications for grant aid. The policy provides, amongst other things, that applications from minibus operators should not be considered as there is no evidence that such vehicles are regularly used in travel to and from work, and exhaust emissions from minibuses are harmful to the environment.*

*Tariq has operated a minibus company for the past five years. He has recently secured contracts with two large employers in the area to provide transport for their workforce. His application for a grant has been refused without consideration, on the basis of GDC's policy.*

*Joanna is a taxi cab licence holder and has applied for a grant to expand her business into operating minibuses. Her application was also refused. The decision was made by GDC's Transport Sub-Committee.*

*Consider whether Tariq and/or Joanna can challenge the decisions of GDC in respect of their applications for grant aid.*

***Answer***

*Before reviewing the answers, consider whether the policy itself is lawful and whether Tariq or Joanna could rely on the following categories of illegality:*

- *Fettering of discretion*
- *Taking into account irrelevant considerations*
- *Improper purpose*
- *Wrongful delegation*

***Policy***

*The statute has created a discretion in respect of the award of grant aid to organisations. Any discretion must be exercised reasonably in accordance with the aims of the statute (you will look at the requirement of reasonableness later). GDC has created a policy as to how applications for grant aid should be processed. There is no objection in principle to the formulation of such a policy by a public authority, provided the policy itself is consistent with the statute. Furthermore, any policy must not be applied in an overly rigid manner so as to fetter GDC's discretion (discussed below).*

***Irrelevant considerations/improper purpose***

*In this particular case, Tariq can first argue that the policy itself is not consistent with the statutory purpose. The policy seeks to prevent applications from minibus operators because, amongst other things, exhaust emissions are harmful to the environment. The environmental issue is not clearly a purpose the legislation was aimed at achieving, and therefore GDC has taken into account an* irrelevant consideration *(*Padfield v Minister of Agriculture *[1968] AC 997). Putting this another way, if GDC has tried to use the statute to* *further environmental objectives, it is using the statute for an improper purpose (*Congreve v Home Office *[1976] 1 QB 629).*

*This could, alternatively, be a case of mixed motives, whereby GDC has in fact achieved two objectives, one of which is authorised (preventing use of private minibuses) and one of which is not (promoting ecological issues). If the primary purpose is lawful then obtaining an incidental advantage may not invalidate the exercise of the power (*Westminster Corporation v LNWR *[1905] AC 426), but much will depend on what the primary purpose was here. Furthermore, in more recent case law, the courts have considered whether the unauthorised purpose 'materially influenced' the decision (*R v ILEA, ex p Westminster City Council *[1986] 1 WLR 28). Tariq would need to establish that the ecological issues materially influenced GDC's formulation of its policy.*

***Fettering of discretion***

*Even if the policy itself is lawful, Tariq could argue that it has been over-rigidly applied in his particular case. Although he operates minibuses, he should be treated as an exception to it, having secured contracts from two employers in the area to transport their workers (*British Oxygen v Minister of Technology *[1971] AC 610).*

***Wrongful delegation***

*Joanna can only raise the fact that the decision was taken by the Transport Sub-Committee. However, under s 101 of the Local Government Act 1972, councils are allowed to delegate their decision-making to council committees or sub-committees. If the GDC has formally delegated its functions in this case, Joanna would not have any grounds of review.*

***Conclusion***

*GDC is entitled to formulate a general policy to guide it in its exercise of its discretionary powers. However, the policy must be lawful. In this case, it seems GDC's policy is unlawful as GDC, through pursuing environmental objectives not envisaged by the empowering statute, has taken into account an irrelevant consideration and is pursuing an improper purpose, which has materially influenced its decision.*

*Even if the policy were lawful, GDC has fettered its discretion by applying its policy over-rigidly. It should have considered Tariq's evidence regarding his contracts.*

*Tariq therefore has a very good chance in succeeding in a judicial review claim.*

*In contrast, Joanna is unlikely to succeed, as GDC has probably delegated the decision-making power lawfully.*

6.5.1.7 Errors of law/errors of fact

**Errors of law**

Errors of law that affect a decision will always be amenable to judicial review, as confirmed in the case of *Anisminic Ltd v Foreign Compensation Commission* [1969] 2 AC 147.

The Foreign Compensation Commission (FCC) had statutory responsibility for deciding on claims for compensation made by UK companies that had suffered losses as a result of war damage overseas. Under the relevant legislation, the owners of damaged property and their 'successors in title' had to be UK subjects. Anisminic was a UK company that, as a result of the Suez Crisis in 1956, had been forced to sell property it owned in Egypt to an Egyptian business for less than its market value. Anisminic applied to the FCC for compensation.

The FCC rejected the claim on the basis that Anisminic had sold its property to a non-UK business. The House of Lords held that, as a matter of law, a purchaser was not a successor in title. A majority of their Lordships held that such an error of law made the FCC's decision not just wrong but outside of its jurisdiction. An error of law will always therefore be amenable to judicial review.

### Errors of fact

Public authorities dealing with the same issues on a daily basis develop expertise in assessing facts, and it would overload the courts if they had to decide all the factual disputes that arise from executive decisions. So the courts are more reluctant to allow judicial review for errors of fact than errors of law. Some errors of fact are, however, amenable to judicial review.

(a) 'Jurisdictional' errors of fact

Alleged 'jurisdictional' errors of fact are reviewable by the courts, as confirmed in the case of *R v Secretary of State for the Home Department, ex p Khawaja* [1984] AC 74. The Immigration Act 1971 allowed the Home Secretary to order the removal from the UK of 'illegal entrants'. The Home Secretary made such an order in respect of a Mr Khera. Khera's lawyer sought judicial review of the order on the grounds that the Home Secretary had got a central fact wrong, in that Khera had not, as the Home Secretary had thought, tried to hide his entry into the UK, and he was therefore not an illegal entrant.

The House of Lords decided that the matter was amenable to judicial review and found for Khera. Their Lordships stated that decisions based on alleged errors of fact that go to the root of a public authority's capacity to act (ie 'jurisdictional' or 'precedent' facts) are reviewable. This was such an error of fact, since the Home Secretary would not have been able to rely on the Act if Khera genuinely had been legally in the UK.

(b) Other errors of fact

'Non-jurisdictional' errors of fact are not usually amenable to judicial review. The courts will defer to the decision of the decision-maker designated by statute.

The example exercises that follow will help you to distinguish between error of law and fact.

***Examples***

*(a) A local authority has a statutory power to buy land compulsorily unless it is residential land, including parks and gardens. The authority makes a compulsory purchase order in respect of some farmland. The owner asserts that the land is in fact part of a park. Is this an error or law or of fact, and, if the latter, is it 'jurisdictional'?*

***Answer***

*Whether farmland is part of a park and therefore 'residential land' depends on evidence and is therefore a question of fact. Assuming that the local authority has made an error, its decision can be challenged on the basis that it has made a 'jurisdictional' error of fact. Under the statute, the local authority did not have the jurisdiction to make a compulsory purchase order if the land was in fact part of a park. This is a 'precedent fact' relevant to the exercise of the power (R v Secretary of State for the Home Department, ex p Khawaja).*

*(b) A statutory tribunal has power to fix rents for unfurnished lettings. The relevant statute provides that a letting is furnished if a substantial part of the rent is attributable to the use of furniture. The tribunal fixes the rent of a flat in one case where the landlord has provided a threadbare carpet and a broken settee. The landlord objects on the grounds that the flat is furnished. Is this an error or law or of fact, and, if the latter, is it 'jurisdictional'?*

***Answer***

*The decision will only be reviewed by the court if there is a 'jurisdictional' error of fact, as in example (a) above. The issue here is whether the provision of a carpet and a settee means that the property is in fact furnished. This depends on the evidence, and therefore, if an error has been made, it is an error of fact. Under the statute, the tribunal had no power to deal with a furnished letting, so the error would be jurisdictional.*

## 6.6 Irrationality

Successful challenges under the irrationality ground of review require proof of a very high degree of unreasonableness. This is possibly due to concerns on the part of the judiciary that ruling on irrationality will open the courts up to accusations of judging the merits of a decision rather than whether the decision was arrived at lawfully.

As the courts have used different tests over the years, we need to consider how the test for irrationality has developed.

### 6.6.1 The '*Wednesbury* Principle'

The concept of irrationality hails from the landmark case of *Associated Provincial Picture Houses Ltd v Wednesbury Corporation* [1948] 1 KB 223. The owners of a cinema were granted a licence by a local authority to show films on Sundays, but only on condition that no under-15s were admitted (whether with an adult or not). The owners challenged the decision on the grounds that the condition was unreasonable.

The test for unreasonableness laid down by Lord Greene MR was whether, *having regard to relevant considerations only, the decision-maker came to a conclusion so unreasonable that no reasonable authority could ever have come to it.* In this instance, the Court of Appeal found for the authority (on the basis that it had made no error of law and its policy was not 'manifestly unreasonable'), but the importance of the case is the test that it established.

Before the test was further developed in 1984, irrationality was more commonly referred to as the '*Wednesbury* principle', or '*Wednesbury* unreasonableness'.

### 6.6.2 Developments post-*Wednesbury*

The *Wednesbury* test stood unaltered until *CCSU v Minister for Civil Service* [1984] UKHL 9, in which Lord Diplock stated that, to be irrational, a decision needed to be *so outrageous in its defiance of logic, or of accepted moral standards, that no sensible person could have arrived at it.*

Although irrationality can be hard to establish, it is not impossible. Public authorities may still fail the test, as happened in the case of *Wheeler v Leicester City Council* [1985] AC 1054. Leicester City Council opposed sporting links with South Africa, which at the time was ruled by a white minority government that imposed oppressive apartheid policies on its population. Three players from Leicester, one of the top rugby clubs in the country, were selected by England to tour South Africa. The club said that it condemned apartheid, but it was up to the players to decide whether they should go on the tour with the national side. The players concerned did travel to South Africa, and the council decided to ban the club from using a council-owned recreation ground.

The club's application for judicial review succeeded. According to the House of Lords, the club could not be punished because it had done nothing wrong; it was not illegal for the players to take part in the England rugby tour of South Africa. By using its powers to punish someone who had acted legally, the council had misused them and so had acted unlawfully and *Wednesbury* unreasonably. However, as is often the case, the House of Lords also justified the decision on the alternative ground of procedural unfairness.

A more recent example of the application of the test for irrationality is the case *of R (DSD and others) v Parole Board* [2018] EWHC 694 (Admin). This case involved a challenge to the decision of the Parole Board to release John Worboys, the 'Black Cab Rapist', on parole. The court held that it was irrational for the Parole Board not to undertake further inquiry into the circumstances of his re-offending. Worboys admitted to only 12 sexual offences, whereas the information given to the Parole Board indicated his involvement in over 80 offences. This potentially undermined his credibility and reliability – key issues relating to the release decision.

The example exercise that follows will give you an opportunity to apply the various tests for irrationality, as well as considering aspects of illegality.

**Example**

*Assume that, to combat traffic congestion in urban areas, Parliament passed the Parking Restrictions Act 2008 ('the Act') (fictitious), giving local authorities power to ban parking of cars 'in such areas as they think fit'.*

*Herbert lives near a busy main road in the centre of Redton. He has received a letter from the 'Transport Officer' of Redton Borough Council stating that he is no longer allowed to park his car on his driveway.*

*Consider whether Herbert can challenge this decision on grounds of irrationality. Could any other ground(s) of challenge be relevant?*

***Answer***

***Irrationality***

*Although there is a statutory power to ban parking of cars 'in such areas as [Redton Borough Council] think[s] fit', the aim of the legislation was to combat traffic congestion in urban areas. Herbert will argue that banning him from parking on his own driveway is not a rational exercise of that power.*

*Applying the* Wednesbury *principle from* Associated Provincial Picture Houses Ltd v Wednesbury Corporation *[1948] 1 KB 223, the court must ask itself if it is a decision that no reasonable local authority could have arrived at and, bearing in mind Lord Diplock's terminology in* CCSU v Minister for Civil Service *[1984] UKHL 9, if it could be regarded as 'outrageous in its defiance of logic'.*

***Other grounds of challenge?***

1. Delegation. *On the face of it, the exercise of the power by the officer breaches the rule against delegation. However, s 101 of the Local Government Act 1972 allows powers given to local authorities to be exercised by officers on their behalf.*
2. Unauthorised purpose. *As noted above, the power was conferred by Parliament to combat traffic congestion. Preventing Herbert from parking on his driveway does not seem to be part of that purpose (*Congreve v Home Office *[1976] 1 QB 629).*

## 6.7 The procedural grounds of judicial review

Procedural grounds of review differ from the substantive grounds in that they focus not on the decision itself, but instead on the *procedure* followed in arriving at the decision under review.

The next example exercise will enable you to distinguish between 'substantive' and 'procedural' grounds of challenge.

**Example**

*Assume that a statute sets up a tribunal to determine appeals from welfare benefit claimants who have had their claims rejected.*

*Which of the following complaints would be procedural and which substantive? Why should claimants be able to use procedural grounds of challenge?*

*(a) Claimant A says that the tribunal has made findings about his private life that he had no chance to contest before the tribunal.*

*(b) Claimant A also says that the findings about his private life are wrong.*

*(c) Claimant B says that she has not been told by the tribunal why her appeal was refused.*

*(d) Claimant C says that a member of the tribunal deciding his case is a neighbour with whom he has quarrelled in the past.*

***Answer***

*All the above complaints are procedural apart from (b). What they have in common is that they are about the steps leading to and the circumstances surrounding the tribunal's decision, rather than the decision itself.*

Procedures should be open to challenge because the claimant needs to know that their case was handled fairly, quite apart from whether the decision affecting them was right or wrong.

Many procedural requirements, on which a decision's validity depends, are found in the statutes that confer the decision-making powers. To breach such requirements is said to be 'procedurally ultra vires'.

Other requirements are derived from the common law rules of natural justice or, as it is now widely known, the doctrine of 'procedural fairness'. We shall examine the common law procedural requirements first.

### 6.7.1 Procedural fairness – the rules of natural justice

The development of the rules of natural justice has led to some controversy. They are common law rules, meaning that they were created by the judiciary, an unelected body. The legal doctrine of parliamentary sovereignty requires that it should be the legislature, rather than the judiciary, that makes law. The rules of natural justice have, however, become an accepted part of administrative law. In the case of *Fairmount Investments Ltd v Secretary of State for the Environment* [1976] 1 WLR 1255, Lord Russell stated that:

> It is to be implied, unless the contrary appears, that Parliament does not authorise by the statute the exercise of powers in breach of the rules of natural justice and that Parliament does ... require compliance with those principles.

There are two rules of natural justice:

(a) the rule against bias (which provides that a decision-maker should have no personal interest in the outcome of his decision); and

(b) the right to a fair hearing.

#### 6.7.1.1 The rule against bias

The application of the rule against bias depends on whether the interest the decision-maker has in the outcome of the decision is 'direct' or 'indirect'.

This distinction is important because, where the interest is direct, the court is normally obliged automatically to 'quash' the decision as bias on the part of the decision-maker is presumed.

#### 6.7.1.2 Direct Interests

In *Dimes v Grand Junction Canal Proprietors* (1852) 10 ER 301, the House of Lords established that an interest that may lead to financial gain falls into the direct interest category.

In that case, the Lord Chancellor at the time, Lord Cottenham, awarded various injunctions to Grand Junction Canal Proprietors in their ongoing litigated dispute with Mr Dimes. Dimes then discovered that Lord Cottenham had, for 10 years, held significant shares in Grand Junction Canal Proprietors. Dimes therefore appealed to the House of Lords against the injunction orders. The House of Lords found for Dimes, stating that Lord Cottenham should have been disqualified from hearing the case because he had a direct interest in the outcome.

In *R v Bow Street Metropolitan Stipendiary Magistrate and Others, ex p Pinochet Ugarte (No 2)* [2000] 1 AC 119, the House of Lords added a new element to this principle. General Augusto Pinochet was indicted for human rights violations committed in his native country while he was the head of the military dictatorship that ruled Chile between 1973 and 1990. He was indicted by a Spanish magistrate on 10 October 1998 and arrested in London six days later pursuant to an international arrest warrant. Initially, he was successful in challenging his arrest in the courts, with the Lord Chief Justice, Lord Bingham, ruling that he was 'entitled to immunity as a former sovereign from the ... English courts'.

The House of Lords disagreed in *R v Bow Street Metropolitan Stipendiary Magistrate and Others, ex p Pinochet Ugarte (No 1)* [2000] 1 AC 61. In November 1998 the Law Lords ruled by a majority of three to two that state immunity applied only to acts that international law recognised as being amongst the functions of a head of state, and this did not include torture or hostage taking. Lord Hoffmann was one of the judges giving the majority decision, but it subsequently became apparent that he had been an unpaid director and chairman of Amnesty International Charity Ltd (AICL) since 1990. AICL was wholly controlled by Amnesty International, which had been allowed to intervene in the appeal. Pinochet sought to have the decision set aside on this basis, arguing that Lord Hoffmann had an interest that disqualified him from taking part in the case.

Lord Browne-Wilkinson classified the case as one in which the decision-maker is a judge in his own cause. Previously this category had been confined to cases of direct financial or proprietary interest in the case. Lord Browne-Wilkinson decided that the category should be extended to cases of non-pecuniary interest, where the decision-maker is involved in promoting the same cause as a party to the case.

The Law Lords in the *Pinochet (No 2)* case thought that the public could not have complete faith that bias had played no part in the original decision because Lord Hoffmann had an apparently direct interest, albeit one from which he did not stand to benefit financially, which should have disqualified him from sitting on the panel. The decision was therefore overturned.

#### 6.7.1.3 Indirect interests

So when does an interest fall short of amounting to a direct interest and amount instead to an indirect interest? An example might be where it is a relative of the decision-maker who has the interest.

In such cases, the reviewing court cannot simply quash the decision automatically; it has to investigate the relationship between the indirect interest and the decision, and decide whether the decision should be quashed on the basis of apparent bias. The case of *Porter v Magill* [2002] 2 AC 357 is a leading case on this topic.

This case concerned Dame Shirley Porter, the Conservative leader of Westminster City Council. As the 1990 local authority elections approached, she offered council house tenants the opportunity to buy their homes. She was accused of deliberately targeting tenants in marginal wards to try to increase her prospects of re-election.

Magill was the auditor who investigated claims that this was an abuse of power by Dame Shirley. Before the very lengthy investigation was complete, Magill called a press conference, at which he said initial results of the investigation suggested strongly that Dame Shirley would be found guilty of abuse of power. Dame Shirley was eventually found guilty and ordered to pay a large fine.

However, Dame Shirley challenged the finding on the ground that it breached the common law rule against bias. She argued that Magill had, through having stated at the press conference that all the signs were that she would be found guilty, put irresistible pressure on himself to ensure that the final verdict would indeed be that she was guilty, so as not to lose face.

The House of Lords agreed that it had been unwise of Magill to call a premature press conference, but disagreed that there was any evidence of bias. The Law Lords were nonetheless satisfied that Magill had not unwittingly created for himself an indirect interest in the outcome of the investigation.

The House of Lords said that the following test should be applied in cases of indirect bias: *would a fair-minded and informed observer conclude that there had been a real possibility of bias?* The court does not ask whether the decision was in fact affected by the bias of the decision-maker, but how the decision would appear to the observer.

Another case that illustrates this rule is *R v Pintori* [2007] EWCA Crim 170. The appellant was convicted of possessing a Class A drug after several police officers had raided his flat. Following the trial, it became apparent that one of the jurors was a civilian working for the police who knew some of the officers involved in the raid reasonably well. The appellant appealed against his conviction on the ground that there was a real possibility that the juror and therefore the jury as a whole was biased against him.

The Court of Appeal allowed the appeal, holding that the appellant did not have a fair trial because the fact that the juror knew the officers would, of itself, have led the fair-minded and informed observer to conclude that there was a real possibility of bias on her part. Such a person would have concluded that the juror was disposed to find the appellant guilty simply because she knew the officers, had worked with them, and therefore wanted (consciously or unconsciously) to support them in the prosecution. Although the deliberations of a jury are secret, the fair-minded and informed observer would also have concluded that there was a real possibility that the juror had influenced her fellow jurors, leading to the conclusion that there had been a 'real possibility' of bias.

### 6.7.1.4 The right to a fair hearing

The right to a fair hearing is the second common law rule of natural justice. In *Board of Education v Rice* [1911] AC 179, Lord Loreburn stated that there is a duty on decision-makers to act in good faith and listen fairly to both sides.

The right to a fair hearing is *flexible and depends on the context of each individual case.*

**Fairness and the claimant's interest**

What precisely is required to be done in order to achieve 'fairness' will depend partly upon the nature of the claimant's interest.

A key determining factor applied by the courts in deciding whether a hearing has been fair is the question of how much the claimant had to lose (ie the nature of the claimant's interest).

In *McInnes v Onslow-Fane* [1978] 1 WLR 1520, Megarry V-C established three categories of claimant, depending on the nature of their interest:

(a) *Forfeiture cases*: cases where the claimant had the most to lose, such as their livelihood or job. These involve the claimant having been deprived of something they previously enjoyed. Such claimants are entitled to expect a lot more from their hearing for it to be considered to amount to a fair hearing.

(b) *Legitimate expectation cases*: cases where it was legitimate for the claimant to expect that an established practice would continue, when seeking the renewal or confirmation of some licence, membership or office that they have held previously. This category also includes those seeking renewal of some form of payment (such as state benefits).

(c) *Application cases*: cases where the claimant is the first-time applicant who merely seeks a licence, membership or office that they have not held previously. Such claimants are entitled to expect a lot less from their hearing for it to be considered to amount to a fair hearing.

In the next example exercise you will consider into which category a potential claimant falls.

### *Example*

*Under the Factory Safety Act 2021 (fictitious), the Factory Approval Board ('the Board') is given the power to regulate matters of health and safety in factories. Any person wishing to open a new factory must apply to the Board for a licence. All existing factory owners must apply to the Board for a licence to continue operating.*

*The Board publishes a circular that states that, in order to ensure the health and safety of workers, it will grant a licence to someone wishing to open a new factory only if that person can show that health and safety training will be provided to all those who are to work at the factory.*

1. *Terence applies to the Board for a licence to open a new factory to manufacture industrial lathes. Terence has never previously operated any factory premises.*
2. *Charlotte has operated a factory making garden ornaments for 10 years. When she applies for a licence to continue operating her factory, she is informed by the Board that her factory is to shut forthwith.*
3. *Paul applies to the Board for a licence to open a new factory that will manufacture computer components. As part of his application, Paul supplied the Board with details of an agreement he has reached with a company that will provide all his prospective employees with two weeks' worth of health and safety training.*

*Identify whether Terence, Charlotte and Paul respectively fall into the category of forfeiture, legitimate expectation, or mere applicant.*

***Answer***

1. *Terence is a mere applicant. He is seeking a licence that he has not held previously.*
2. *Charlotte's case is one of forfeiture. She is being deprived of something (ie the right to use her factory) that she already has.*
3. *Paul has a legitimate expectation that his application will be granted. It is legitimate for him to expect to receive a licence to operate his factory because he appears to meet the criteria set out in the Board's circular.*

#### Forfeiture cases

For an example of a *forfeiture case*, consider *Ridge v Baldwin* [1964] AC 40. Ridge was the Chief Constable of Sussex. Together with some more junior officers, Ridge was accused of conspiracy to obstruct the course of justice. The other officers were found guilty but Ridge was acquitted. Despite his acquittal, the trial judge criticised Ridge for not having set a good example to the junior officers. Ridge was dismissed the following day, apparently on the strength of the judge's comments. He was given no warning and was not told of the case against him. Ridge applied for judicial review of the decision to dismiss him on grounds of procedural unfairness.

The House of Lords held that the outcome of the decision was of special importance in this case, since Ridge stood to lose (or 'forfeit') his pension rights as well as his livelihood. Consequently, he was entitled at the very least to know the case against him. The Law Lords declared the decision to dismiss Ridge unlawful.

#### Legitimate expectation cases

The express promise, or existence of a regular working practice, might give rise to two different types of legitimate expectation:

(1) *procedural* legitimate expectation in which a decision-maker has failed to follow a normal procedure; and

(2) *substantive* legitimate expectation where the decision-maker has led someone to believe that he or she will receive a benefit.

Here, we will examine the first of these: procedural legitimate expectation. *R v Liverpool Corporation, ex p Liverpool Taxi Fleet Operators* [1972] 2 QB 299 provides an example of a procedural legitimate expectation case. 300 existing Liverpool taxi licence holders were given a written assurance by Liverpool City Council that they would first be consulted if the council decided to grant any new licences to more taxi drivers. However, the council then passed a resolution to grant more licences without consulting existing taxi drivers, who challenged the decision on grounds of a broken written promise.

The Court of Appeal held that it had been legitimate for the existing taxi drivers to expect the council to honour its written undertaking. The council was not at liberty to disregard its promise.

What if a procedural policy, such as internal guidance within a government department, has not been published publicly and therefore the claimant has no knowledge of it? In *Mandalia v Home Secretary* [2015] UKSC 59 the Supreme Court held that the public body should apply that policy unless it had a good reason not to do so. It stated that this principle ensured that cases would be dealt with fairly and consistently. Such a principle was related to legitimate expectation but was 'freestanding'.

**Application cases**

For an example of an *application case*, see *McInnes v Onslow-Fane* [1978] 1 WLR 1520.

McInnes made six applications to the Boxing Board of Control for a licence to manage boxers. On each occasion his application was refused, with no oral hearing being granted and no reasons being given. McInnes applied for judicial review on the basis that he had not received a fair hearing.

The court found for the Boxing Board as McInnes was a mere first-time applicant. All that natural justice therefore required of the Board was that it should act honestly and without bias.

Another example of an application case is *R v Gaming Board, ex p Benaim and Khaida* [1970] 2 QB 417. Applications to magistrates for gaming licences could be made only once potential applicants had obtained a certificate of consent from the Gaming Board. The Board refused to grant such a certificate to Benaim and Khaida. The Board gave them an opportunity to make representations and disclosed information that had led them to doubt the applicants' suitability, referring to criteria laid down by statute. Benaim and Khaida sought judicial review of the Board's decision.

The Court of Appeal found in favour of the Board. The Board was under a duty, even with first-time applicants, to give applicants a sufficient indication of the objections against them to enable them to answer those objections. However, it had done this. It had no further duty to give reasons for its decisions.

You have a chance to consider into which of the three categories the claimant falls in the next example exercise.

***Example***

*George, a taxi driver licensed by Blackton District Council, has just had his licence revoked. He has been told that this is 'on account of your inappropriate conduct', but has not been given any further details or granted a hearing.*

*Consider whether George can make a claim for judicial review of the council's decision.*

***Answer***

*The decision affects George's ability to continue to work as a taxi driver, so this is a forfeiture case. This means that George will be entitled to expect more, including the right to an oral hearing, for the hearing to be considered fair.*

> *The common law right to a fair hearing in any case requires that he should have been given notice of the case against him and an opportunity to refute any evidence brought against him prior to any decision being taken to revoke his licence (*Ridge v Baldwin *[1964] AC 40).*

**Does the right to a fair hearing always apply?**

The 'right to a fair hearing' may not apply in certain situations, for example if a decision that has been made is merely 'preliminary'.

For example, in the case of *Lewis v Heffer* [1978] 1 WLR 1061, there had been a struggle for power in the local branch of the Labour Party in Newham North-East. The struggle became so intense that the national party intervened through the National Executive Committee, suspending all officers and committees of the local party and taking over control itself. The Committee gave the disputing members no opportunity to be heard before suspension. The suspended officers sought judicial review of the decision to suspend them.

The Court of Appeal held that the officers had not yet been dismissed, merely suspended. Since the investigation was only at a preliminary stage, and the final decision had not yet been made, the officers did not have the right to seek judicial review.

**Content of the fair hearing rule**

What does the right to a fair hearing include? This depends largely on whether it is a forfeiture, legitimate expectation or mere application case.

The case of *Fairmount Investments Ltd v Secretary of State for the Environment* [1976] 1 WLR 1255 is a good example of a forfeiture case and illustrates how natural justice requires that claimants in such cases should *know the case against them and have the right to reply at each stage of the decision-making process.*

The facts of the case were as follows. Fairmount requested reasons for the receipt of a compulsory purchase order as part of the Government's slum clearance programme. An inspector who later visited the site said the decision to make the CPO had been based on a factor (defective foundations) that had not come to light prior to his visit. Fairmount therefore sought judicial review on the ground that the decision was made before they had had a chance to reply.

The House of Lords found for Fairmount on the ground that natural justice requires that individuals should know the case against them and have the opportunity to respond at each stage of the decision-making process. Viscount Dilhorne stated that it had been on account of his belief as to the inadequacy of the foundations, along with other defects, that the inspector ruled out rehabilitation. The inspector had attached great weight to a factor that formed no part of the council's case, which Fairmount had not been given notice of and with which it had been given no opportunity of dealing.

In legitimate expectation cases, the nature of a fair hearing depends very much on the expectation that the decision-maker created. For example, in *ex p Liverpool Taxi Fleet Operators* it should have first consulted with the existing taxi drivers before issuing new licences.

In mere application cases, *McInnes v Onslow-Fane* shows that as a general rule applicants are merely entitled to have their cases heard honestly and without bias. However, in *ex p Benaim Khaida*, as the refusal of the licence cast doubt on their good character, the applicants were entitled to know the gist of the case against them.

**The right to reasons**

Does the right to a fair hearing include the right to receive reasons for a decision?

As you have just seen, the right to know the case against you is a standard requirement of a fair hearing. However, the law has not yet accepted that public authorities also have a general duty to give reasons for their decisions. In the case *R (Hasan) v Secretary of State for Trade and Industry* [2008] EWCA Civ 1311, the High Court held that the law did not recognise a general duty to give reasons for an administrative decision. However, exceptions do exist.

One exception is when a decision is taken which, in the absence of reasons, looks 'aberrant' (ie completely wrong). For example, in *R v Civil Service Appeal Board, ex p Cunningham* [1991] IRLR 297, Cunningham was dismissed, unfairly in his opinion, from the prison service, whose members had no right to claim unfair dismissal. Cunningham's only option was to apply to the Civil Service Appeal Board for compensation. The usual award in circumstances where, as here, dismissal was considered unfair was around £15,000, but Cunningham was awarded only £6,500. He therefore sought judicial review of the Board's decision to award him such a small amount.

The Court of Appeal ruled that natural justice requires that a decision-maker should give reasons for a decision where fairness requires that a claimant should have an effective right to challenge a decision that looks wrong; where, in the words of Lord Donaldson MR, the decision 'cries out for explanation'. This inexplicably low award amounted to such a case.

In *R v Secretary of State for the Home Department, ex p Doody* [1994] 1 AC 531, the applicants were convicted of murder and received mandatory sentences of life imprisonment. The Parole Board could only consider applications for a parole once the prisoner had served a minimum period of imprisonment. This period, known as the tariff, was set by the Home Secretary following recommendations by the trial judge. In the cases involving the appellants, the Home Secretary decided not to follow recommendations of the trial judges and set longer tariffs. The applicants were not consulted but they were told the tariffs they would have to serve before a review of their sentences. The applicants claimed that the Home Secretary had acted unlawfully by failing to give reasons for his decisions

The House of Lords expressly accepted that there is no general duty to give reasons for an administrative decision. However, such a duty may in appropriate circumstances be implied. In this case, the length of the tariff was of crucial importance to the prisoners. To give effect to the fundamental considerations of procedural fairness, it was necessary to ensure, firstly, that every life prisoner should have the opportunity to make written representations as to the appropriate minimum period in their case and, secondly, those representations should be informed by a full knowledge of any relevant judicial recommendations and comments. This meant that, although the Home Secretary was not obliged to adopt the judicial view of the tariff, if he departed from it he had to give reasons for doing so. Moreover, since the Home Secretary's decision was susceptible to judicial review, it would only be possible to mount an effective attack on it if his reasoning was known.

In the case of *Higher Education Funding Council, ex parte Institute of Dental Surgery* [1994] 1 WLR 242, the court provided guidance on when decision-makers should give reasons. The Higher Education Funding Council awarded research grants to institutions, according to the quality of their research, based on the results of a research assessment exercise it conducted. The council gave the Institute of Dental Surgery a low rating, resulting in a reduction of £270,000 in the amount granted. The council gave no reasons as to why it had reduced the Institute's rating. The Institute applied for judicial review.

Sedley J confirmed that there was no general duty to give reasons, but there were classes of case where fairness required the giving of reasons:

- where the legal subject matter is particularly important, for example, personal liberty;
- where the decision appears aberrant. The giving of reasons will then enable the recipient to know whether the aberration is, in the legal sense, real (and so challengeable) or apparent.

However, as the instant case involved no more than the informed exercise of academic judgment and there was nothing inexplicable about the decision itself, fairness did not require the giving of reasons.

**Right to an oral hearing and cross-examination of witnesses**

Does the right to a fair hearing give parties the right to a full oral hearing? No, not in every case, although, as already mentioned, a claimant in a 'forfeiture case' is entitled to expect far more of a hearing for it to be considered to amount to a fair hearing, and this might include a full oral hearing.

Every claimant, however, regardless of the category of case, is entitled to a hearing that is *fair and reasonable* in all the circumstances. Authority for this point is the case of *Lloyd v McMahon* [1987] AC 625.

The facts of the case were as follows. Prior to the council tax, the Government raised money by imposing 'rates' (a local tax similar to council tax) on local residents. The District Auditor (DA) twice warned Liverpool city councillors that they were in danger of missing the deadline imposed by the Government for setting their rates. When the councillors did then miss the deadline, the DA fined them just over £100,000. Although the DA did not offer councillors a full oral hearing, he did provide detailed reasons for the fine and offered to consider written appeals. The councillors nonetheless sought judicial review of the decision and lack of oral hearing.

The House of Lords found for the DA. The councillors had been warned twice and had not requested an oral hearing. The DA had therefore acted fairly in not offering them one, and the councillors had not been prejudiced by not having been granted an oral hearing.

Lord Bridge stated that:

> what the requirements of fairness demand ... depends on the character of the decision-making body, the kind of decision it has to make and the statutory or other framework in which it operates.

In other words, what fairness requires will depend on the particular circumstances of each case, but every claimant, regardless of the category of case, is entitled to a hearing that is fair and reasonable in all the circumstances.

Another significant case regarding fairness and the cross-examination of witnesses is *R v Hull Prison Board of Visitors, ex p St Germain (No 2)* [1979] 1 WLR 1401. The case arose out of a prison riot, which took place in 1976, and the serious damage that occurred as a consequence. The prisoners were charged with disciplinary offences under the Prison Act 1952 and were brought before the prison's board of visitors. The prisoners subsequently argued that they had not been given a proper opportunity to present their cases as they had not been allowed to call witnesses. Furthermore, the board had acted on statements made during the hearing by the governor, which were based on reports by prison officers who had not given oral evidence.

Lane LJ accepted that, generally, there would be a discretion as to whether cross-examination should be permitted, but if fairness in the circumstances required it, cross-examination should be permitted. Here it was required to enable the prisoners to contest hearsay evidence.

**The making of delegated legislation**

The rules of natural justice do not apply where the decision-maker has a legislative rather than a judicial function, as confirmed in the case of *Bates v Lord Hailsham* [1972] 1 WLR 1373.

Under s 56 of the Solicitors Act 1957, a committee was empowered to make orders (a type of delegated legislation) relating to the payment of solicitors. Using these powers, the committee published a draft order bringing in changes to the way solicitors were paid for conveyancing work. On behalf of the committee and as required by s 56 of the Solicitors Act 1957, Lord Hailsham, the Lord Chancellor, sent a draft of the order to the Law Society allowing a month's consultation period before the proposal would be finalised. The Law Society published the proposal in the *Law Society Gazette*.

Bates was a solicitor who was also a member of the British Legal Association (BLA). The BLA asked Lord Hailsham, the Lord Chancellor, to extend the one-month consultation period to three months. Lord Hailsham refused the BLA's request. Bates sought judicial review of the refusal to extend the consultation period and sought an injunction against the proposed order becoming finalised.

The court found for Lord Hailsham on the grounds that the committee's function was legislative rather than judicial, and so the rules of natural justice did not apply.

The reason why the rules of natural justice do not apply to legislative functions is that delegated legislation usually affects the public or a section of the public as a whole, rather than having a separate effect on each individual's rights. Fairness could not require that each member of the public should be heard before legislation is made.

## 6.8 Procedural ultra vires

### 6.8.1 'Mandatory' or 'directory' requirements

Having considered the common law procedural requirements placed upon decision-makers by the rules of natural justice, we now turn to the statutory procedural requirements sometimes placed upon decision-makers by the wording of the 'enabling' Acts of Parliament that give them their powers.

Such statutory procedural requirements have historically been classified as being either 'mandatory' or 'directory'. The distinction is important, because failure to comply with a mandatory requirement rendered the decision invalid on grounds of procedural ultra vires, but failure to comply with a directory requirement did not.

*Bradbury v London Borough of Enfield* [1967] 1 WLR 1311 provides an example of a mandatory procedural requirement. Section 13 of the Education Act 1944 required local education authorities to give notice to the public if they closed down existing schools, opened new schools, or changed the nature of a school. The borough had failed to provide the required notice to the public when it carried out a major reform of local schools. It tried to justify its failure to give notice on the grounds that, had it done so, educational chaos would have ensued. Eight ratepayers nonetheless sought judicial review of the borough's failure to provide notice.

The Court of Appeal found in favour of the eight ratepayers. In other words, the Court considered non-compliance with s 13 in this case to have been a breach of a mandatory requirement, rather than a breach of a merely directory requirement.

Conversely, the case of *Coney v Choyce* [1975] 1 All ER 979 provides an example of a directory procedural requirement. There, the North Nottinghamshire Local Education Authority announced plans for two Roman Catholic schools to become comprehensive schools.

Section 13(3) of the 1944 Act specifically required that notice should be given to the public in a local newspaper, in some conspicuous places, and at or near the main entrance of the school concerned. The Authority did comply with the first two notice requirements but not with the third.

The changes meant that parents of pupils over 13 years of age might have to travel much further to deliver their children to school. Three hundred parents therefore petitioned the Secretary of State for Education against the planned changes, but the changes went ahead regardless. The parents therefore sought judicial review of the Authority's failure to comply in full with the notice requirements.

The court found in favour of the Authority. In other words, the court considered non-compliance with s 13 in this case to have been breach of a merely directory requirement, rather than breach of a mandatory requirement.

How does the court decide whether a procedural requirement is mandatory or directory?

One of the factors the court will take into account is the wording of the statute itself. However, given that both of the above cases turned on the same section of the Education Act, this is clearly not the only factor they consider.

A closer inspection of any distinguishing facts between the two cases illustrates what other factors the courts take into account.

In *Bradbury*, the London Borough of Enfield had failed to give any notice at all. It had made no effort to comply with any of the notice requirements contained in s 13. The Court of Appeal decided that the borough had thereby substantially prejudiced claimants, who were significantly affected by the major reforms. The Court found that the requirements of the Act were an important procedural safeguard for those likely to be affected by the school closures.

By contrast, in *Coney* the North Nottinghamshire Local Education Authority had placed notices both in the local newspaper and in some conspicuous places. It had even placed notices around the schools, but had simply not done so at or near the main entrances. The court decided the Authority had not thereby substantially prejudiced claimants, who, the court felt, had every prospect of seeing one of the many notices, despite their absence from the school entrances.

A comparison of these two cases, then, shows that whether or not a claimant is *substantially prejudiced by non-compliance with an important procedural safeguard* is a factor for the courts to take into account in determining whether a statutory requirement is mandatory or merely directory.

### 6.8.2 Subsequent developments

In *R v Soneji* [2006] 1 AC 340, Lord Steyn suggested that, rather than trying to make a rigid distinction between mandatory and directory requirements, courts should instead consider the consequences of non-compliance with a statutory procedure. Lord Steyn held that the correct procedure for the court to adopt was to put itself in the position of those who had enacted the legislation – would Parliament have intended the consequence of non-compliance with the relevant statutory requirement to be the invalidity of the decision that had been taken?

In the same case, Lord Carswell suggested that the distinction between mandatory and directory requirements remained a useful starting point, but ultimately the question for the court was whether it had been the intention of Parliament that failure to comply with the procedural requirement would render the decision unlawful.

## 6.9 Legitimate expectations

As you have seen (at **6.7.1.4**), an express promise or existence of a regular working practice may give rise to two different types of legitimate expectation: procedural and substantive. Having already considered procedural legitimate expectation, we will concentrate here on substantive legitimate expectation.

A substantive legitimate expectation may occur where the decision-maker has led someone to believe that they will receive a benefit. The leading case in this area is *R v North and East Devon Health Authority, ex p Coughlan* [2001] QB 213. The claimant, having been injured in a road accident, was severely disabled. She consented to be moved to a new care facility, Mardon House, on the basis that she had been assured by the health authority that this would be her home for life. However, a few years later, the authority decided to close Mardon House on the basis that it was too expensive to run. Lord Woolf LCJ analysed the court's role when dealing with legitimate expectation cases. He stated that there are at least three possible outcomes:

(a) The court may decide that the public authority is only required to bear in mind its previous policy or other representation. It must give this the weight it thinks right, but no more, before deciding whether to change course. Here the court is confined to reviewing the decision on *Wednesbury*, that is irrationality, grounds. It will only be in exceptional cases that irrationality will be found. An example where the decision-maker was found to be irrational was *R v IRC, ex p Unilever plc* [1996] STC 681. The company claimed for loss relief, a type of tax allowance. In this case the loss relief that the company claimed was technically time-barred as the company applied for the relief after the official deadline. However, the Inland Revenue had always accepted such claims by the company in the past. The court held that, on the basis of the Revenue's past practice, refusal to grant the relief would be irrational.

(b) The court may decide that the promise or practice induces a legitimate expectation of, for example, being consulted before a particular decision is taken. This is the 'procedural legitimate expectation', which you considered at **6.7.1.4**.

(c) The court may decide that the promise or practice has induced a legitimate expectation of a substantive benefit and that to frustrate the expectation is so unfair that it would amount to an abuse of power. In these cases, the court will have the task of weighing the requirements of fairness to the individual against any overriding public interest relied on by the public body for its change of policy.

Mrs Coughlan's case fell into the third category. She had received both oral and written assurances from the health authority that she could live at Mardon House for as long as she chose to do so. She had interpreted this to mean for the remainder of her life. The court had to consider the 'compelling reasons' put forward by the health authority for closure of Mrs Coughlan's home, ie that Mardon House had become 'a prohibitively expensive white elephant'. The court decided that Mrs Coughlan did have a substantive legitimate expectation to remain in Mardon House for the remainder of her life. This expectation had arisen in her mind as a result of words and actions of the local authority, which had not properly weighed all the considerations before making its decision. There was no overriding public interest to justify the breach of her legitimate expectation. The decision to close Mardon House was therefore quashed.

The danger exists that in requiring a decision-maker to honour a substantive legitimate expectation, the courts are usurping the role of the decision-maker. However, in *R (Niazi) v Secretary of State for the Home Department* [2008] EWCA Civ 755, Laws LJ stressed that a substantive legitimate expectation (Lord Woolf's third category) would only arise where the public body concerned had made a specific undertaking, directed at a particular individual or group, that the relevant policy would be continued. Such undertakings are likely to be directed at a small class of people. Laws LJ stressed that the type of legitimate expectation found in *Coughlan* was likely to be exceptional. Public bodies will not normally be legally bound to maintain a policy that they have reasonably decided to change. In addition, the consequences of requiring the authority to keep to its promise in *Coughlan* were financial only – and as the group of people was small, the impact on public finances would not be severe.

Legitimate expectation is rather difficult to classify under the traditional judicial review grounds, and it would appear to span all three of Lord Diplock's 'domestic' grounds in the *CCSU* case. In the first of Lord Woolf's categories, a claimant's ground of challenge would appear to be irrationality, in the second procedural impropriety, and in the third 'abuse of power', a type of illegality. Some academics argue that legitimate expectation constitutes a new ground of review. However, so far the courts seem to have squeezed it into the traditional categories.

## Summary

By studying this chapter, you should have gained an understanding of what judicial review can achieve, how a claim can be established by reference to grounds of challenge, and an understanding of the difference between substantive and procedural grounds. This will provide a basis for you to go on in the next chapter to explore in detail how a claim for judicial review is made.

- *Illegality* is a ground for challenge. The main categories of illegality are:
    - **Acting without legal authority (ultra vires):** The decision-maker exceeds the powers given by statute (*ex p McCarthy and Stone*).
    - **Error of law:** the decision-maker misunderstands its powers (*Anisminic*).
    - **Jurisdictional error of fact:** the decision-maker makes a mistake as to a fact that must be in place to trigger the use of the power (*ex p Khawaja* [1984] AC 74).
    - **Policy:** a decision-maker is allowed to formulate a policy on which to base decisions for the purpose of administrative expediency (*British Oxygen*) but it must properly reflect the statutory powers given to the decision-maker.
    - **Fettering discretion by applying a policy too rigidly:** a decision-maker must not close its ears to an applicant who has something new to say (*British Oxygen*).
    - **Fettering discretion by acting under the dictation of another:** a decision-maker must not allow another person to make the decision for it (*Lavender & Son*).
    - **Improper or unauthorised purpose:**: the decision-maker must use its powers for the correct purpose (*ILEA*).
    - **Dual purpose:** the decision-maker should not use its powers to cover two or more different purposes, if one or more of those purposes was unlawful and materially influenced the decision. If, on the other hand, the authorised purpose was the dominant purpose, then the decision will stand (*ILEA*).
    - **Considerations:** a decision-maker must not take irrelevant considerations into account when making its decision and must not ignore relevant considerations (*Roberts v Hopwood*; *Padfield*).
- *Irrationality* is a ground for challenge where a decision is 'so unreasonable' that 'no reasonable authority could ever have come to it' (*Associated Provincial Picture Houses v Wednesbury Corporation*) or 'so outrageous' in its defiance of logic that 'no sensible person' could have reached it (*CCSU*). Whilst the threshold for irrationality is high, cases such as *Wheeler v Leicester City Council* show it can be reached.
- *Procedural impropriety* is a ground for challenge based on the way in which a decision has been reached ('procedure'). **Figure 6.3** illustrates the categories of procedural impropriety.

**Figure 6.3** Procedural impropriety

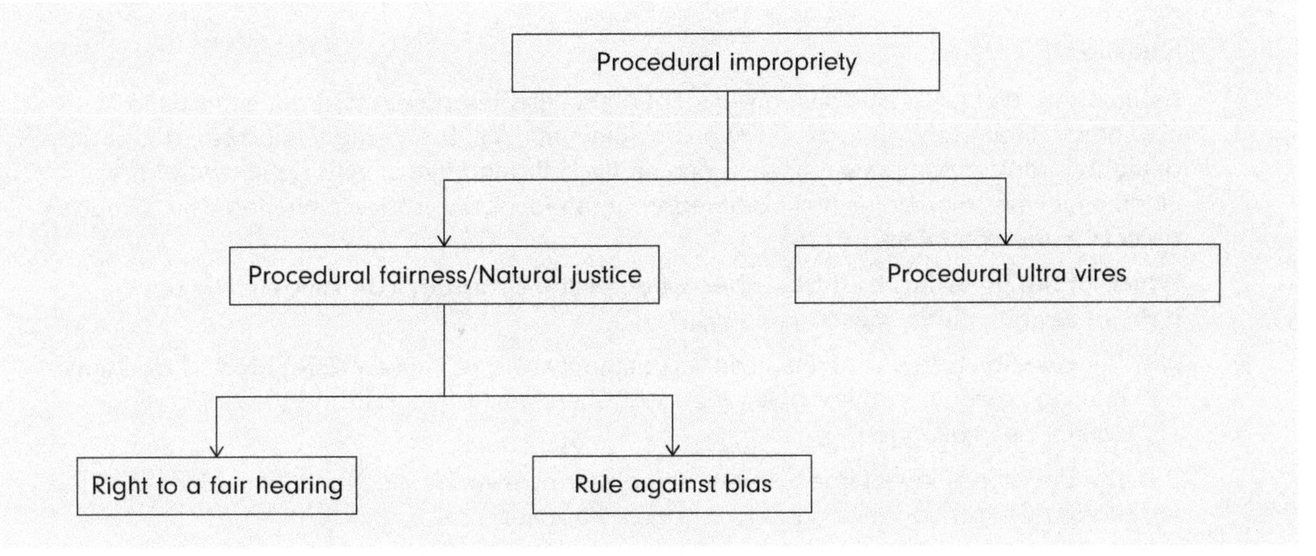


- The two common law rules of procedural fairness, or natural justice, are:
  - **The right to fair hearing:** the rules of natural justice demand that a hearing should be fair in all the circumstances (*Ridge v Baldwin*), although what constitutes a fair hearing depends on factors such as the nature of the interest of a party adversely affected by a decision (*McInnes v Onslow-Fane*).
  - **The rule against bias:** an individual has the right to a fair and independent tribunal, so they can challenge decisions where the decision-maker is biased or appears to be biased. There are two categories of bias:
    - Direct interest: the decision-maker should not judge in their own cause. If they receive a pecuniary advantage as result of their decision, it will automatically be void (*Dimes v Grand Junction Canal Co.*). The same principle applies if they have a shared commitment or belief with one of the parties in the case (*ex p Pinochet Ugarte (No 2)*).
    - Indirect interest: the test is whether a fair-minded and informed observer would conclude that there was a real possibility of bias (*Porter v Magill*).
- The final category of procedural impropriety is:
  - **Breach of statutory procedural requirements**, or procedural ultra vires: according to *R v Soneji*, whether a procedure set within a statute should be followed depends on Parliament's intention in the face of its breach.
- A legitimate expectation, either procedural or substantive, can arise as a result of a promise made by a decision-maker. The promise should be honoured unless public interest prevails (*ex p Coughlan*).

## Sample questions

**Question 1**

Assume that a statute (fictitious) gives local authorities the power to grant licences to cinemas in their area 'on such conditions as they think fit'. Exercising this power, a local authority grants a company a licence on condition that no film should be shown at its cinemas unless approval is first obtained from the local Churches Committee. The company objects to this condition.

**Which of the following best describes whether the company can successfully seek judicial review of this licence condition?**

A The decision is lawful as the licensing authority had effectively delegated its decision-making power to another body, the local Churches Committee and the delegation cannot be challenged.

B The decision is lawful because the delegation was made to a local committee and the statutory exception relating to local bodies applies.

C There is illegality as the delegation to a religious body (the local Churches Committee) was in breach of the rule against delegation.

D There is illegality as the licensing authority had delegated its decision-making power to another body, which was neither a civil servant nor a local authority committee or officer.

E There is illegality as the licensing authority, by delegating its decision-making power to another body, was pursuing an unreasonable purpose.

**Answer**

Option D is correct. The facts are similar to that of *Vine v National Dock Labour Board.* The licensing authority had delegated its powers in breach of the rule against delegation and neither the civil servant nor local authority committee exemption applied because the decision was delegated to a local Churches Committee. Option D is a better answer than option C as the reason the rule against delegation was breached had nothing to do with the nature of the Churches Committee. Option D is also a better answer than option E; on the facts the licensing authority's purpose is not known, but in any event even if its purpose had been legitimate it would have breached the rule against delegation.

Option A is wrong, as there is a clear breach of the rule against delegation. Option B is wrong as the statutory exception it refers to applies only to committees, sub-committees and officers of local authorities, not to local bodies in general.

**Question 2**

Assume that a statute (fictitious) gives power to the Secretary of State to assess claims for property damage arising out of terrorist bomb attacks and to award financial compensation based on the damage suffered. The Act permits a maximum award of £100,000 to be made.

A charity that provides temporary accommodation for the homeless had its premises destroyed in a bomb attack. It applied to the Secretary of State for compensation of £100,000 to go towards the cost of rebuilding, estimated at £150,000. It was awarded compensation of only £5,000. No reasons were given by the Secretary of State for the size of the award. Before applying for compensation, the charity consulted the Secretary of

State's department and was sent a copy of a departmental circular, which states 'when awarding compensation, a full award will normally be given to charitable organisations providing care for disadvantaged groups'.

**Which of the following best describes the grounds on which the charity should seek judicial review of the amount of the award?**

A The charity's claim is likely to fail as it is a mere applicant and the Secretary of State's only duty is to act honestly and without bias. On the facts provided, there is no evidence of dishonesty or bias.

B The charity's claim is likely to fail. The Secretary of State is under no duty to give reasons and, in the absence of reasons, the charity cannot prove the Secretary of State has acted illegally or irrationally.

C The charity's claim is likely to succeed. By failing to award £100,000 compensation, the Secretary of State has breached a mandatory procedural requirement.

D The charity's claim is likely to succeed. The statement in the circular is likely to create a substantive legitimate expectation that its application will be successful and it will be an abuse of power to frustrate that expectation.

E The charity's claim is likely to succeed. In the absence of reasons, the decision is likely to be held to be irrational.

**Answer**

Option E is correct. The charity will most likely be able to bring a claim based on irrationality. Whilst there may also be procedural impropriety, neither option C nor option D correctly summarises the position.

The charity is entitled to a fair hearing. On the face of it, it is a first-time applicant for compensation (*McInnes v Onslow-Fane*), which may impact on what is expected of the decision-maker in order to achieve fairness. However, the charity will argue that the statement in the circular has created a substantive legitimate expectation that its application will be successful.

It is then necessary to analyse whether this case falls within the first or third of Lord Woolf's categories in *Coughlan*. It is likely to fall within the first category as it involves the payment of money rather than a basic need such as healthcare. The charity would therefore have to rely on irrationality. As no reasons have been given for reducing the award of compensation from £100,000 to £5,000, the charity has a strong argument that the *Wednesbury* threshold of irrationality has been reached. Option E is therefore correct and a better answer than option D. Option B is also clearly wrong as the absence of reasons is likely to lead to a finding of irrationality.

Although there is no general requirement for ministers to give reasons for their decisions, the courts may require this if the decision appears wrong. Here, they may require reasons to enable the charity to ascertain whether the minister took all relevant circumstances into account in reaching his decision (*ex p Cunningham*). In this case, the size of the award may appear unjustifiably low, and if so, the decision could be quashed for the failure to give reasons. However, this duty arises from the common law rules of procedural fairness, and do not arise from statute; hence option C is wrong. Option A is wrong as the circular has created a legitimate expectation that the charity will receive a full grant.

**Question 3**

Assume that a statute (fictitious) gives local authorities the power to order the closure of market stalls in a public market if the trader has repeatedly sold goods that are not of a satisfactory quality. The statute provides that the operator of any stall that is to be the subject of a closure order shall be given seven days' notice of the order, and shall also be given the right to make representations against the closure. Using its power, the local authority has sent a notice to a trader ordering the closure of his stall after seven days. The local authority has stated that due to the poor quality of the goods the trader sells, there is no point in him making representations.

**Which of the following best describes whether the trader could seek judicial review of the closure notice?**

A The trader's claim is likely to fail. Due to the seriousness of the matter, the local authority was entitled to dispense with the requirement to allow the trader to make representations.

B The trader's claim is likely to fail. The requirement to allow the trader to make representations is merely a guidance as to good practice and its breach does not render the closure notice invalid.

C The trader's claim is likely to fail. The requirement to allow the trader to make representations is merely a directory procedural requirement and its breach does not render the closure notice invalid.

D The trader's claim is likely to succeed. The requirement to allow the trader to make representations is a mandatory procedural requirement as Parliament probably intended its breach to invalidate the closure notice.

E The trader's claim is likely to succeed. The local authority has acted without legal authority in ordering the closure of the stall without allowing the trader to make representations.

**Answer**

Option D is correct. The issue is whether the local authority has failed to comply with a mandatory procedural requirement or a directory one. Non-compliance with the former renders a decision invalid on grounds of procedural ultra vires, whereas failure to comply with a directory requirement does not. An important factor that the court will take into account is the wording of the statute itself. According to the facts, the statute provides that local authorities 'shall' allow operators of stalls to make representations; this points towards a mandatory obligation to consult. However, the language used is not conclusive.

Case law also shows that where a claimant is substantially prejudiced by non-compliance with an important procedural safeguard, the courts are likely to rule a statutory requirement is mandatory. Another question is whether Parliament would have intended the consequence of non-compliance with the relevant statutory requirement to be the invalidity of the decision. This seems likely, as closure of the stall will deprive the trader of his livelihood. Accordingly, options C and B are wrong for suggesting the requirement is merely directory or guidance as to good practice respectively.

Option A is wrong as, in the absence of statutory authority, the seriousness of the matter does not dispense with the need to observe procedural requirements.

Option E is wrong as the local authority did have the legal authority to order the closure of the stall, provided it followed the correct procedure. Acting without legal authority (one of the headings under illegality) arises when a decision-maker does not have the power at all to take a given decision, no matter how properly it tried to act.

# 7 Judicial Review – Procedure and Remedies



## SQE1 syllabus

This chapter will enable you to achieve the SQE1 assessment specification in relation to functioning legal knowledge concerned with core administrative law principles, including:

- judicial review:
  - remedies;
  - decisions that may be challenged;
  - standing; and
  - time limits.

Note that for SQE1, candidates are not usually required to recall specific case names or cite statutory or regulatory authorities. Cases are provided for illustrative purposes only.

## Learning outcomes

By the end of this chapter you will be able to apply relevant core legal principles and rules appropriately and effectively, at the level of a competent newly qualified solicitor in practice, to realistic client-based and ethical problems and situations in the following areas, including the ability to:

- explain the principle of 'procedural exclusivity';
- assess whether a decision-maker is one against whom judicial review claims may be brought;
- assess whether the claimant is likely to be deemed to have sufficient interest to bring a judicial review claim;
- assess whether attempts by Parliament to oust the judiciary from participating in a judicial review claim are likely to succeed;
- assess whether a court is likely to permit a judicial claim which is brought neither promptly nor without undue delay; and
- consider what remedies a successful claimant is likely to be granted.

## 7.1 Introduction to procedure and remedies

Judicial review procedure is governed by primary legislation (s 31 of the Senior Courts Act 1981) and by rules of court contained in Part 54 of the Civil Procedure Rules (CPR). In this chapter, you will study the procedure required to obtain judicial review and the remedies available.

Set out in **Figure 7.1** is the overview diagram, to which you were introduced in **Chapter 6**. As before, the topics you are studying are in boxes highlighted in bold.

**Figure 7.1** Judicial review: an overview

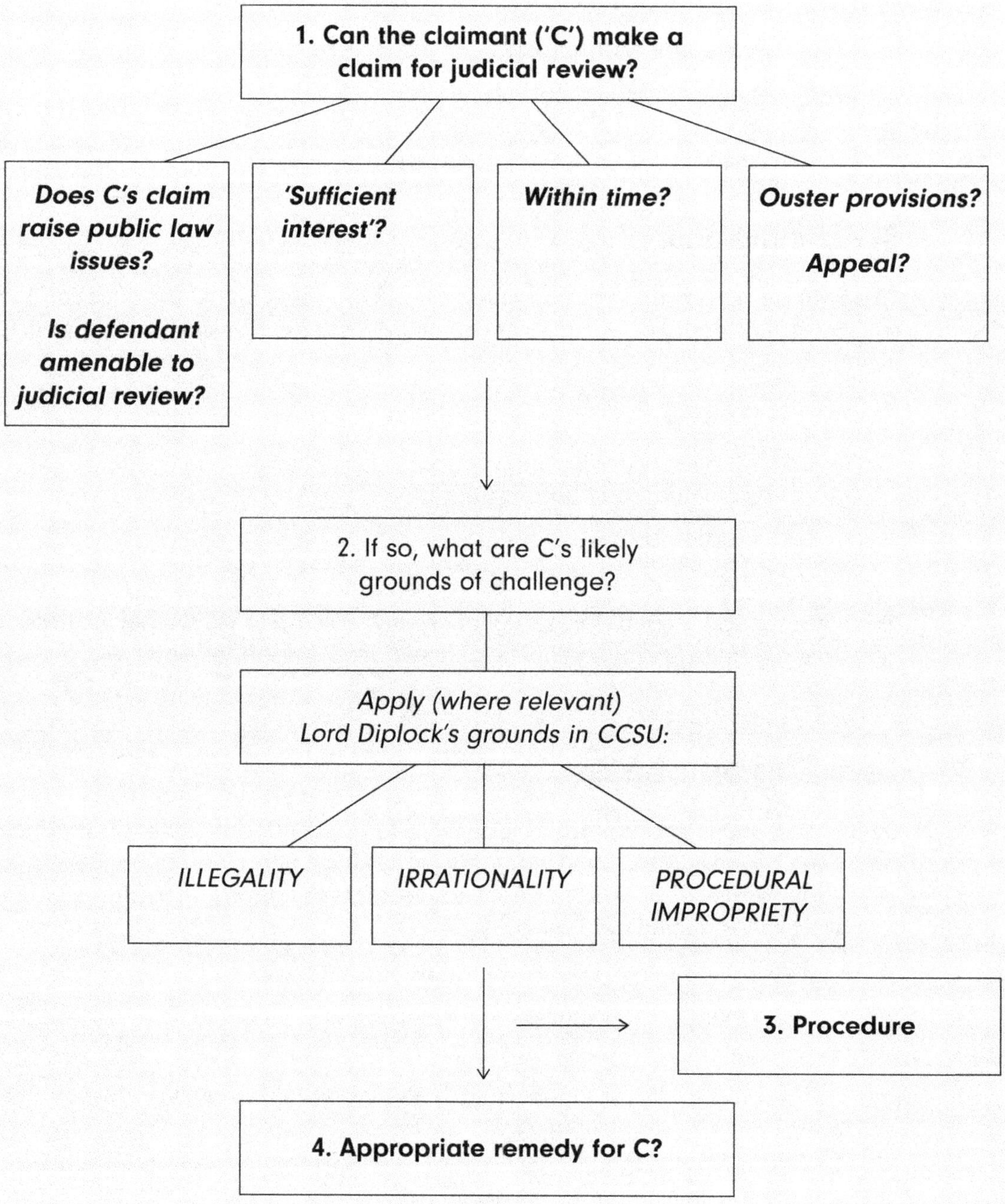

## 7.2 Is judicial review the appropriate procedure to use?

The example exercise that follows will highlight for you the issues that you will address in detail in this section.

***Example***

*Consider which of the following claims you would expect to be brought by way of judicial review proceedings:*

1. *A private care home has told an elderly woman that it is terminating her care contract and will remove her from the home. She wishes to challenge the decision.*
2. *Your client has been given negligent advice by a council planning officer, leading him to spend money on a planning application that has failed. He wishes to recover compensation.*
3. *You act for an electricity company that has been told that the Government is revising its national power strategy in favour of nuclear power sources. The company feels that it was not properly consulted.*

***Answer***

*Only claim 3 would be brought via judicial review proceedings, as it involves a challenge to a public body (the Government) on public law grounds (fair hearing).*

*Claim 1 involves a challenge to a private body (the care home) on private law grounds (breach of contract).*

*Claim 2 involves a claim against a public body (the local authority) but on private law grounds (claim in tort for negligent misstatement).*

### 7.2.1 Public law v private law – the principle of 'procedural exclusivity'

We first need to consider when judicial review is the appropriate procedure to use.

The principle of procedural exclusivity requires that, in a 'public law case', the judicial review procedure *should normally* be followed, rather than the ordinary private law procedure.

In *O'Reilly v Mackman* [1983] 2 AC 2370, the claimants were four prisoners who were charged with, and found guilty of, disciplinary offences by the board of visitors to the prison. They were seeking a declaration that the disciplinary decisions affecting them were void, but by means of a private law action rather than via an application for judicial review.

In his speech Lord Diplock said that the claimants were not complaining about a breach of their private rights because their private right to personal liberty had been taken away by the sentence of the court. They were complaining that they should be entitled to remission of sentence, but this was a matter of discretion rather than right.

Lord Diplock said that the prisoners had a legitimate expectation, based on past practice, that good behaviour would earn remission. This gave them a sufficient interest to challenge the board's decision, using public law grounds of challenge. So they could have brought a judicial review claim.

The House of Lords found for the board of visitors as the claimants had brought the wrong type of claim. The Law Lords stated that it would, as a general rule, be contrary to public policy and an abuse of process of court to allow a claimant to seek to enforce public law rights by way of an ordinary action rather than by judicial review.

Lord Diplock gave the following reasons for using judicial review:

(a) By using private law procedures the claimants were 'evading the safeguards' imposed in the public interest against 'groundless, unmeritorious or tardy' attacks on the validity of decisions (eg the permission and delay rules that affect an application for judicial review - see **7.5** below).

(b) The judicial review procedure had been reformed in 1978 to remove the defects of the old procedures.

### 7.2.2 Cases involving both a public law and a private law element

An exception to the 'procedural exclusivity' principle is where a case involves both private and public law.

This was so in *Roy v Kensington Family Practitioner Committee* [1992] AC 624. Dr Roy, a GP, argued that he was entitled, under NHS regulations, to be paid the 'full rate' on the fee scale provided by the Kensington Family Practitioner Committee. Such a rate was available to any GP where the Committee was satisfied that he or she was devoting a substantial amount of his or her time to general practice.

The Committee believed that Dr Roy did not satisfy this criterion and so paid him 20% less than the 'full rate'. This was a public law decision, challengeable via judicial review. Dr Roy sued the Committee for the balance, alleging breach of contract and pursuing ordinary private law procedure. The Committee argued that he should have sought judicial review and that his private law claim should therefore be dismissed.

The House of Lords found that where a claim is based on a mixture of private rights and public law grounds, the public law element may be raised in private law proceedings.

However, it remains the case that exclusively public law issues must be determined in judicial review proceedings, and exclusively private law issues must be determined in ordinary private law proceedings.

Examples of the most common types of public law cases include challenges to the making of a compulsory purchase order over land, challenges to the grant (or refusal) of a licence permitting a particular type of activity to be carried out, and challenges to the refusal of discretionary financial grants.

A public law issue may also be raised as a defence in private law proceedings, through the principle of 'collateral challenge', as illustrated in the cases of *Wandsworth London Borough Council v Winder* [1985] AC 461 and *Boddington v British Transport Police* [1998] 2 WLR 639.

In *Wandsworth v Winder* the Council had increased council rents substantially and sued a council tenant who had refused to pay the increase. The defendant claimed, as a public law defence, that the increase in rent was *ultra vires*. The Council argued that he should have used judicial review.

The House of Lords confirmed that a defence alleging the invalidity of a public law decision may be raised either in private law proceedings or through judicial review. In this case, the public law issue is said to arise 'collaterally' in the private law proceedings.

In *Boddington* the House of Lords extended the concept of collateral challenge to criminal cases. Mr Boddington had been prosecuted for smoking on a train in breach of a byelaw. His defence was that the byelaw itself was unlawful. Although he failed to establish this, the House of Lords found that a defendant to a criminal charge may normally use a public law issue as a defence.

The Court of Appeal also addressed the public law/private law dichotomy in *R (Shashikanth) v NHS Litigation Authority* [2024] EWCA Civ 1477. A GP had a dispute with an NHS clinical commissioning group ('CCG'). The contract between the GP and the CCG was a non-NHS contract which created contractual rights and liabilities. A dispute arose and the GP exercised his right under the contract to refer the dispute to the Secretary of State to be determined by an adjudicator. The adjudicator found against the GP, and the GP challenged their decision by way of judicial review.

The Court of Appeal stated that the adjudicator had acquired jurisdiction under statute and the procedure for determining the dispute was also regulated by statute. This gave rise to a presumption that this was a public law function amenable to judicial review. Although the adjudicator was determining issues involving private law, those rights arose in a statutory context. The reality of the situation was that the statutory disputes process in relation to this contract did involve a public function and thus judicial review was available.

The next example exercise will enable you to consolidate your understanding of this area.

***Example***

(a) *Aruna is a self-employed accountant who provided some accountancy services to the Constantia District Council. The Council has refused to pay her bill, arguing that it is too high.*

*How should Aruna proceed?*

(b) *A group of protesters is being sued for trespassing on common land in contravention of a local authority byelaw. The protesters claim that the byelaw is* ultra vires *and therefore that they were not trespassing.*

*Will the protesters be able to assert their claim that the byelaw is* ultra vires *as a defence against the claim for trespass?*

*Would your answer differ if the protesters were instead being privately prosecuted for criminal trespass?*

***Answer***

*This activity aims to demonstrate the principle of procedural exclusivity (*O'Reilly v Mackman*). Here, Aruna has a private law (contractual) relationship with the Constantia District Council.*

*She needs to proceed by way of a private law claim for damages, not by way of judicial review.*

*By way of exception to the general principle in* O'Reilly v Mackman*, the protesters should be able to challenge the validity of the byelaw as part of their defence to what appears to be a civil claim for trespass (rather than a criminal prosecution) as they are raising a public law defence to private law proceedings (*Wandsworth LBC v Winder*).*

*If the protesters were defending a private prosecution for criminal trespass, they could still raise the invalidity of the byelaw as a defence, but the appropriate authority for this is* Boddington v British Transport Police.

## 7.3 Identity of the decision-maker

Claimants can seek judicial review only of decisions made by *public* bodies. Decisions of private bodies must be challenged under private law proceedings.

Lloyd LJ established a two-part test to determine what constitutes a public body in the case of *R v Panel on Takeovers, ex p Datafin plc* [1987] QB 815.

The first part of the test is the *source of power* test. Under this, if the body making a decision has been set up under statute or under delegated legislation, or derives its power under a reviewable prerogative power, then it is a public body.

If this part of the test is *not* satisfied then the court goes on to apply the second part, the *nature of power* test. Under this, if the body making the decision is exercising public law functions, it may still be a public body.

The next example exercise *will* enable you to check your understanding of this area.

***Example***

*Under the Advertising Regulation Act 2017 (fictitious) the Advertising Conduct Commission (ACC) is established to regulate the advertising industry. Under the Act, a business wanting to set up a new advertising agency must obtain a licence from the ACC.*

*Is the ACC amenable to judicial review?*

***Answer***

*The ACC was created by statute, namely, the Advertising Regulation Act 2017. It therefore satisfies the first element of the two-part test, ie the source of power test, established in* R v Panel on Takeovers, ex p Datafin plc. *Consequently, it is a public rather than a private body and, as such, is amenable to judicial review.*

An interesting case on amenability is *R (Tortoise Media Ltd) v Conservative and Unionist Party* [2023] EWHC 3088 (Admin). In this case the High Court held that the Conservative Party was not performing a public function when it chose a new leader, mid-parliamentary term. The party was not appointing a new Prime Minister since this was something which could only be done by the monarch.

## 7.4. Standing in claims for judicial review

### 7.4.1 The requirement of 'sufficient interest'

The courts will deem a claimant to have standing to bring a judicial review claim only if he has 'sufficient interest in the matter to which a claim relates', as required by s 31(3) of the Senior Courts Act 1981. This will not present a problem if a claimant is personally affected by a decision, but may be an issue if the claimant has no personal interest. The leading case on this issue is *R v Inland Revenue Commissioners, ex p The National Federation of Self-Employed and Small Businesses Ltd* [1982] AC 617. For many years casual workers employed by Fleet Street newspapers had avoided paying tax by using false names. The Inland Revenue granted them an amnesty and agreed not to pursue the workers for arrears of tax provided they paid tax in the future. The National Federation of Self-Employed and Small Businesses applied for judicial review of this arrangement, claiming that it was unlawful. The Revenue argued that the Federation lacked sufficient interest to have standing.

As explained at **7.7** below, judicial review is a two-stage process. The House of Lords explained that the purpose of the first stage, the permission stage, was to weed out weak and frivolous claims. It was therefore correct at this stage to hold that the Federation did have standing, as its claim was not obviously unmeritorious. However, the issue of standing could not be separated from the merits of the case. At the second stage, the substantive hearing where the facts and legal issues would be considered in depth, the court should re-examine the claimant's standing with regard to the merits of the claim and the claimant's relationship to the merits. As the Federation had been unable to prove any wrongdoing on the part of the Revenue, it did not have sufficient interest because in general one taxpayer has no legitimate interest in the affairs of another.

However, if the Federation had shown serious wrongdoing on the part of the Revenue, then it is likely that it would have been granted standing. Accordingly, the question of standing is closely linked to the merits of the case; the courts are unlikely to reject a valid judicial review claim simply on the grounds of a lack of standing.

Although the Federation failed to establish the requisite standing, it is clear from the judgment that in principle pressure groups may in the right circumstances have standing, and even perhaps a single 'public-spirited individual'. So, when will pressure groups have standing to bring a judicial review claim?

### 7.4.2 Pressure groups and judicial review proceedings

The case of *R v Secretary of State for Foreign Affairs, ex p World Development Movement Limited* [1994] EWHC Admin 1 provided guidance on the factors that courts take into account when deciding whether a pressure group has sufficient interest to bring a claim for judicial review.

In the early 1990s, the Foreign Secretary granted aid to Malaysia towards the building of a hydro-electric power station at the Pergau Dam. He granted the aid under s 1(1) of the

Overseas Development and Co-operation Act 1980, which required that any donations were 'for the purposes of promoting the development or maintaining the economy of a country'.

The World Development Movement Ltd (WDM) was a pressure group, which argued that the Foreign Secretary had known that the Pergau Dam project was economically unsound, and that money was really a payment for the supply of arms by the UK to Malaysia.

The WDM sought judicial review of the granting of the aid. The Foreign Secretary argued that WDM, as a pressure group, lacked standing to seek judicial review.

The Divisional Court found for WDM, and set out the five relevant factors a court should consider in deciding whether a pressure group has standing to bring a judicial review claim.

The five factors are:

1. the need to uphold the rule of law;
2. the importance of the issue raised;
3. the likely absence of any other responsible challenger;
4. the nature of the alleged breach of duty; and
5. the role of the pressure group.

The court emphasised the fifth factor as being particularly relevant to pressure groups, pointing out WDM's expertise and prominence in promoting and protecting aid to developing nations.

Sometimes a number of people who are personally affected by a decision may form a grouping to oppose that decision (for example, a group of local residents who join together to oppose the building of a nuclear power station in their area). Such a grouping would *not* ordinarily need to satisfy the factors set out in *ex p World Development* since each individual member of the group would be personally affected by the decision, and would therefore have sufficient standing under s 31(3).

In recent years the courts have appeared to adopt a liberal approach to standing, but there are indications of a possible tightening as shown by *R (Good Law Project and Runnymede Trust) v Prime Minister and Secretary of State for Health & Social Care* [2022] EWHC 298 (Admin). The Good Law Project (GLP) is a non-profit campaign organisation with a mission to achieve change through the law, while Runnymede is a race equality think tank. They challenged some senior healthcare appointments that the Government made in the early days of the Covid-19 pandemic on the grounds that the appointment process was (i) indirectly discriminatory, (ii) breached the public sector equality duty (PSED) requiring public bodies to eliminate unlawful discrimination and advance equality of opportunity, and (iii) was procedurally unfair and breached the rule against bias.

The High Court held that Runnymede had standing regarding the second issue, the alleged breach of the PSED, as it was an organisation whose specific aims included promoting racial equality, but it did not in relation to the other two issues as Employment Tribunals were the appropriate forum for the claims in question. However, the GLP did not have standing at all due to its broad remit, and moreover Runnymede was a better placed challenger regarding the alleged breach of the PSED.

There have been suggestions following this judgment that public bodies should be more willing to challenge the standing of claimants than they are presently.

The next example exercise will enable you to apply the requirement that a claimant has 'sufficient interest' to be entitled to bring judicial review proceedings.

***Example***

*You will recall from the previous example that, under the Advertising Regulation Act 2017 (fictitious) (as above), a business wanting to set up a new advertising agency must obtain a licence from the ACC. The ACC has granted a licence to Abstotic Marketing Ltd ('Abstotic').*

*The UK Consumer Forum ('the Forum'), a well-known pressure group that campaigns for better standards in the advertising industry, objects to the grant of the licence as one of Abstotic's major shareholders and its chief executive have both recently been convicted and fined substantially under legislation prohibiting misleading advertisements.*

*Does the Forum have standing to bring a judicial review claim?*

***Answer***

*The courts will deem a claimant to have sufficient standing to bring a judicial review claim only if they have 'sufficient interest in the matter to which a claim relates', as required by s 31(3) of the Senior Courts Act 1981.*

*The statute contains no definition of 'sufficient interest'. Instead the courts apply factors developed through case law. In the Forum's case, the courts will apply the five factors set out* ex p World Development. *On the basis of these factors the courts are likely to consider that the Forum has 'sufficient interest' in the decision to grant Abstotic a licence to apply for judicial review, even if the courts do scrutinise the standing of claimants more rigorously.*

---

## 7.5 Making a claim for judicial review

### 7.5.1 The Administrative Court

Judicial review is dealt with by the Administrative Court, a specialist court within the High Court.

### 7.5.2 Time limits

7.5.2.1 What is the rule?

Claimants seeking judicial review must start their claims within the given time limits.

Section 31(6) of the Senior Courts Act 1981 allows a court to refuse a claim where it feels there has been 'undue delay'. In addition, CPR, r 54.5 requires that a claim form must be filed promptly, and in any case within a *maximum* of three months after the ground to make the claim first arose. With effect from 1 July 2013, amendments to r 54.5 reduced the standard time limit for cases within the 'planning acts' to six weeks from the date of the decision. The 'planning acts' are defined within s 336 of the Town and Country Planning Act 1990, and this reduced time limit will only apply to planning decisions that come within this definition. The 2013 amendments also reduced the time limit for public procurement cases (ie those where a public authority acquires supplies or services) to 30 days.

Rule 54.5(3) emphasises that the time limits in the rule are without prejudice to any statutory provision that shortens the time limit for making a claim for judicial review, a point we shall re-visit when considering ouster clauses in **7.6** below.

It is important to appreciate that this is far from saying that every claimant will have the full standard time limit to bring a claim. Three months is the maximum time a court will allow; less in planning and public procurement cases. In *Finn-Kelcey v Milton Keynes Borough Council and MK Windfarm Ltd* [2008] EWCA Civ 1067, the appellant appealed against the refusal by the Administrative Court to grant him permission to apply for judicial review of the grant of planning permission for a wind farm. The appellant was a local landowner who objected to the construction of the wind farm. He issued an application for judicial review just within the three-month period under CPR, r 54.5(1) (note that this case pre-dated the reduction in time limits for planning cases).

The appeal was dismissed. The Court of Appeal held that the appellant had been aware of the decision of the local authority's planning committee to grant permission as soon as that decision had been made, and there was therefore no reason for delaying issuing proceedings until the end of the three-month period. The application had not been made promptly.

*R (British Gas) v Secretary of State for Energy Security and Net Zero* [2023] EWHC 737 (Admin) provides another example of where applications were not made promptly, even though made within three months of the decisions in question. This case concerned the transfer of one retail energy supplier (Bulb) to another (Octopus). Three other energy suppliers, including British Gas, sought to challenge the the Secretary of State's decisions approving the transfer. Their applications were made between three weeks and one month from the relevant decisions. The Court of Appeal refused permission for judicial review on the basis that the applicants had delayed too long as they had known of the grounds for judicial review shortly after the decisions had been made. The court pointed out that, in the financial field, a delay of even a few days can be detrimental to the interests of third parties and to good administration and that the applicants were aware of the urgency of the situation.

7.5.2.2 Can the courts extend the time limit?

The courts do reserve a discretion to extend the time limit, but only for a good reason. For example, in *R v Stratford-upon-Avon DC, ex p Jackson* [1985] 1 WLR 1319, the claimant applied for leave to seek judicial review of the granting of the planning permission for a supermarket eight months after it was granted. She gave three reasons for the delay in applying for leave to submit her claim form. They were:

(a) she had had to await the outcome of her request to have the Secretary of State for the Environment 'call the matter in' for his consideration;

(b) she had encountered difficulties in obtaining legal aid; and

(c) she had also encountered difficulties in obtaining permission from the copyright holders for use of the plans and drawings, which she wished to use in her application for judicial review.

The Court of Appeal allowed her an extension on the grounds that, although her application had not been made promptly or even within three months (the time limit that then applied), these were good reasons for the delay.

However, a court is not *obliged* to allow time extensions, as was seen in *Hardy v Pembrokeshire CC* [2006] EWCA Civ 240. The Court stated that whilst the importance of public safety issues *is* capable of justifying a grant of permission where there has been delay, it remained for the judge to conclude whether the merits of allowing a claim outweighed the undue delay and prejudice that would be caused by granting the permission.

Note also that in *R (Kigen) v Secretary of State for the Home Department* [2015] EWCA Civ 1286 the Court stated that, due to changes that had occurred since the decision in *ex p Jackson*, it was no longer appropriate to treat delay in obtaining legal aid as a complete answer to a failure to comply with procedural requirements. However, it may still be a factor that can be taken into account.

Finally, in *R v Dairy Produce Quota Tribunal, ex p Caswell* [1990] 2 All ER 434, the court stated that, even if permission was granted and the case proceeded to a full hearing, a remedy could be refused if the application had been made outside the three-month time limit.

The next example exercise will enable you to check your understanding of time limits in judicial review.

***Example***

*Under the Advertising Regulation Act 2017 (fictitious) (as above), a business wanting to set up a new advertising agency must obtain a licence from the ACC.*

*Adgreen Ltd made an application to the ACC for a licence, which was rejected. At the time of the rejection, none of the directors of Adgreen Ltd knew of the existence and availability of judicial review. Six months later, one of the directors discovered that it was possible to ask the High Court to review decisions by public bodies such as the ACC.*

*Is it too late for Adgreen Ltd now to bring a claim for judicial review?*

***Answer***

*A claimant for judicial review must make its claim promptly and without undue delay. At the very latest, the claim must be made within three months of the date on which the decision being challenged was made. It is entirely within the court's discretion to decide that a period of less than three months is insufficiently prompt.*

*However, the court also has a discretion to extend the maximum time period beyond three months where it is satisfied that the claim form was submitted late for a very good reason (*ex p Jackson *(above)). In the case of Adgreen Ltd, though, it is unlikely that the court would consider ignorance of the availability of judicial review to be a very good reason. If leave were granted, the delay might result in refusal of a remedy (*R v Dairy Produce Quota Tribunal, ex p Caswell *[1990] 2 All ER 434).*

---

## 7.6 Exclusion of the courts' judicial review jurisdiction

### 7.6.1 Ouster clauses

A further potential pitfall for a judicial review claimant is the presence of an ouster clause in the 'enabling' Act of Parliament which grants the public body the power to make decisions in the first place.

Ouster clauses are inserted by Parliament into such Acts where it wishes to exclude any right of challenge once a decision has been made by a public body.

### 7.6.2 Full ouster clauses

A full ouster clause is one which purports to allow no right of challenge at all, and which attempts to exclude the courts from playing any role in review of the decision.

An example of a case with a full ouster clause is *Anisminic Ltd v Foreign Compensation Commission* [1969] 2 AC 147, which you considered in **Chapter 6**. You may recall that, in this case, the House of Lords held that the Foreign Compensation Commission had made an error of law in deciding that a purchaser of business property amounted to a 'successor in title'.

The House of Lords was prepared to consider this case even though the statute that created the FCC contained a provision stating that any decision made by the FCC 'shall not be called into question in any court of law'. The House of Lords stated if a public body steps outside its permitted area, its decisions are not covered by an ouster clause because invalid decisions are not in fact decisions at all, but 'nullities'. Ouster clauses therefore only protect valid decisions from judicial review.

The rationale of their Lordships in *Anisminic* was that, whenever a body created by statute had misunderstood the law that regulated its decision-making powers, any decision based on such a misunderstanding had to be ultra vires and a 'nullity'. Parliament, in enacting the statute that gave the body its powers, could not have intended decisions that were legally incorrect to be immune from challenge, and therefore any ouster clause would be ineffective in protecting such decisions.

The judgment of the House of Lords in *Anisminic* means that full ouster clauses will not protect decisions that were never legally valid, and it is up to the court to review a decision to decide whether it is legally valid or invalid.

In the recent case of *R (Privacy International) v Investigatory Powers Tribunal* [2019] UKSC 22, Lord Carnwath, who gave the lead judgment, stated that the courts' treatment of ouster clauses was 'a natural application of the constitutional principle of the rule of law'. The Supreme Court accepted that it may be possible to exclude judicial review by the use of very clear and explicit words. However, to date, no legislation has been passed containing a full ouster clause with sufficiently 'clear and explicit words' to be upheld by the courts.

### 7.6.3 Partial ouster clauses

A partial ouster clause provides some opportunity for a decision to be challenged by way of judicial review. The case of *R v Secretary of State for the Environment, ex p Ostler* [1977] QB 122 shows that the courts are more amenable to partial ousters than to full ones. In May 1974, the Secretary of State confirmed a compulsory purchase order, or CPO, as he was authorised to do under the Highways Act 1959, over land near Ostler's house. The Act included a statutory time limit of six weeks for anyone to challenge such an order. Only 19 months later, in December 1975, did Ostler apply for judicial review of the CPO. He argued that his delay in objecting had been due to a belief that the scheme would not affect his premises.

The clause that imposed the time limit for bringing a claim stated that an aggrieved person had the right to challenge the validity of a compulsory purchase order within six weeks from the date of its publication. Subject to that right, the Act further provided that that the order 'shall not ... be questioned in any legal proceedings whatever ...'.

This is a partial ouster clause rather than a full ouster clause because it does allow a challenge, but only if made within six weeks. It simply shortened the time period from that usually allowed to bring a judicial review claim.

The Court of Appeal upheld the validity of the partial ouster clause. Ostler should have applied to the High Court within six weeks of the date of the publication of the notice of confirmation. The court had no jurisdiction to entertain an application made outside such time limit, whatever the claimant's grounds. Moreover, unlike situations where the time limits set out in CPR, r 54.5 apply, the courts have no discretion to grant an extension even if there are good reasons for the delay (*Smith v East Elloe Rural District Council* [1956] AC 736). There has been some academic debate about whether the courts would uphold an unreasonably short time limit, but there is no direct authority on this point.

In *R (Privacy International) v Investigatory Powers Tribunal* [2019] UKSC 22 Lord Carnwath stated that, in the cases on ouster clauses, the courts have tried to find an appropriate balance between the statutory context and the inferred intention of the legislature on the one hand, and the rule of law on the other. He went on to state that 'there is no difficulty in holding that the six-week time limit [in planning cases] provides a proportionate balance between effective judicial review, and the need for certainty to enable such decisions to be acted on with confidence'.

*R (LA (Albania)) v Upper Tribunal* [2023] EWCA Civ 1337 provides an example where the Court of Appeal upheld a partial ouster clause. This case concerned s 11A of the Tribunals, Courts and Enforcement Act 2007 (inserted by s 2 of the Judicial Review and Courts Act 2022). This section prevents judicial review of a decision of the Upper Tribunal to refuse permission to appeal from a decision of the First-Tier Tribunal save in very limited situations. These include that the Upper Tribunal acted in bad faith or 'in such a procedurally defective way as amounts to a fundamental breach of the principles of natural justice'. The Court of Appeal held that the partial ouster clause in s 11A was clear and effectively excluded judicial review in the circumstances of the case, as none of the argued grounds matched any of the exceptions.

### 7.6.4 Other statutory remedies

The provision of an adequate statutory remedy for an aggrieved party, such as a right of appeal, may impliedly oust the courts' judicial review jurisdiction.

This can be seen in the case of *R v Epping and Harlow Commissioners, ex p Goldstraw* [1983] 3 All ER 257.

Goldstraw considered his estimated income tax assessments had been too high, so he appealed under the Taxes Management Act (TMA) 1970, but failed to attend or be represented at the hearing on 11 November 1980. The Inland Revenue Commissioners (IRC) informed him that they had confirmed his tax assessments in his absence. The TMA 1970 gave Goldstraw 30 days to appeal, but he did not make his appeal for almost three months. The

IRC refused to consider his appeal application, so Goldstraw sought leave of the court to apply for judicial review.

The Court of Appeal held that where a claimant had failed to make a proper use of an appropriate statutory procedure for obtaining a remedy, the court would not generally exercise its discretion to allow an application for judicial review.

However, the alternative remedy must be a suitable one. In *Re McAleenon* [2024] UKSC 31, the appellant (Ms McAleenon) lived near a landfill site. She claimed that she and her family had been made ill by the noxious fumes coming from the site. She brought judicial review proceedings against the relevant local authority and the Environment Agency for failing to comply with their statutory duties and accordingly breaching her rights under Article 8 of the ECHR. The defendants argued that Ms McAleenon should have pursued alternative remedies such as a private prosecution or claim for nuisance against the owners of the site.

The Supreme Court reiterated that judicial review is a remedy of last resort and that, where Parliament had enacted a statutory scheme for appeal, then a claimant should normally appeal rather than apply for judicial review. However, in this case, there was no statutory right of appeal. Ms McAleenon's objective in bringing her claim was to compel the defendants to carry out their public law duties as regulators. Neither a private prosecution nor a claim for nuisance against the owners of the site could be regarded as a suitable alternative remedy. These other types of action would neither address the issue nor give a remedy in relation to it.

## 7.7 Procedure for bringing a judicial review claim

### 7.7.1 Outline of procedure

Before starting proceedings the claimant should follow the Pre-Action Protocol for Judicial Review. This involves sending a letter before claim to the decision-maker to give the latter 14 days to reconsider its decision and, if possible, to avoid unnecessary legal proceedings. If the decision-maker's response satisfies the claimant, that ends the matter. If not, the claimant should start formal proceedings. Courts will take into account any failure to follow the Protocol when awarding costs. The claimant does not, however, have to follow it where the matter is urgent or where a time limit of less than three months applies.

Bringing a judicial review claim is a two-stage procedure. The first stage is known as the permission stage, the second the substantive hearing. The detailed rules regarding what the parties must do at each stage are contained in CPR, Part 54.

### 7.7.2 Stage 1: the permission stage

It is at the permission stage that the court considers whether the claimant has standing and whether the claim was begun in sufficient time. Primarily, however, the purpose of this stage is to allow the courts to save time by weeding out hopeless claims before they reach the second stage. Under s 31(3C) of the Senior Courts Act 1981 (inserted by the Criminal Justice and Courts Act 2015) the court must not grant permission to apply for judicial review where the improper conduct complained of would be highly likely not to have resulted in a substantially different outcome for the claimant. The court may, however, disregard this requirement for reasons of exceptional public interest.

### 7.7.3 Stage 2: the hearing of the claim for judicial review

The substantive hearing is before a judge in the Administrative Court. The hearing is usually confined to arguments on points of law, as the facts will rarely be in issue. Following the hearing, the judge will give his or her ruling.

The diagram in **Figure 7.2** summarises the procedure.

**Figure 7.2** Outline of procedure for judicial review

*The claimant issues a claim form in the Administrative Court*

The claim form must:

- state that the claimant is requesting permission to proceed with a claim for judicial review and the remedy/remedies sought;
- state, or be accompanied by a detailed statement of, the claimant's grounds for making the claim, the facts relied on and the supporting evidence.

↓

*The claim form is 'served' on the defendant (and any other interested party)*

Note: if the judicial review proceedings are contested, the defendant should respond to the claim form, indicating the grounds for contesting the claim.

↓

*The court will then decide whether to grant permission to the claimant to proceed with the claim*

Permission will not be granted if the claimant cannot demonstrate a 'sufficient interest' in the claim; if the claimant has been guilty of unjustified delay; or if the conduct complained of would be highly likely not to have resulted in a substantially different outcome for the claimant.

Permission decisions will often be made 'on the papers' (ie without hearing the parties).

↓

*If permission is granted, the defendant (and any other interested party) will file its evidence. The court will now proceed to 'Stage 2', the substantive hearing of the claim for which it will fix a date.*

## 7.8 Remedies in judicial review

Judicial review remedies are discretionary, so a claimant may be able to show that a decision-maker has acted improperly but the court may nonetheless decide not to grant a remedy. Under s 31(2A) of the Senior Courts Act 1981 (inserted by the Criminal Justice and Courts Act 2015) the court must refuse a remedy if it appears to the court to be highly likely that the outcome to the claimant would not have been substantially different if the conduct complained of had not occurred. The court may, however, disregard this requirement for reasons of exceptional public interest.

### 7.8.1 Public law remedies – the 'prerogative orders'

Prerogative orders are the main court orders that a judicial review claimant can seek; they comprise:

(a) Quashing order

(b) Prohibiting order

(c) Mandatory order

Prerogative orders are available against public bodies only.

#### 7.8.1.1 Quashing order

A quashing order 'quashes' a decision that the court has found to be unlawful (ie it deprives the decision of legal effect). The original decision is thereby nullified. However, the court does not usually substitute its own decision but remits it to the decision-maker who must reconsider the decision in light of the court's judgment. The decision-maker may reach the same decision again. However, this time the decision-maker is more likely to reach a lawful decision as it will now have the benefit of the judgment of the court.

The Judicial Review and Courts Act 2022 (which came into force on 28 April 2022) gives the courts powers to award suspended and prospective-only quashing orders. A court therefore now has the power to suspend, until a specified date, the effect of an order quashing a decision. This gives the decision-maker time to put right the identified unlawful act. If it does not do so by the deadline, the quashing order will become effective. A court may also specify that a quashing order will only have prospective effect. This means that the quashing order will only render the decision void from the time of the judgment onwards. It would not invalidate any past decisions.

The court must take into account factors such as the nature and circumstances of the relevant defect, the interests or expectations of persons who would benefit from the quashing of the decision in question, and the interests or expectations of persons who have relied on it. It remains to be seen how much use the courts will make of their new powers. The explanatory notes accompanying the original Bill give the following example of when a suspended quashing order might be appropriate:

> The court finds a decision by a public body to create a regime for issuing certain licenses [sic] to be invalid. This does not prevent the court from issuing a quashing order which is suspended for 30 days on condition that no new licenses are issued. This means that licenses issued already would be treated as valid for the 30 days. A person who had been issued a license would need to prepare for that license to be invalid, but could continue to rely on it for the 30 days. The public body would also have time to put in place transitional arrangements, set up a new licensing regime, or take any other action considered necessary.

*R (ECPAT UK) v Kent CC* [2023] EWHC 2199 (Admin) provides an example of a suspended quashing order. The case concerned amongst other issues issues the Kent Protocol, an agreement between Kent County Council and the Home Office concerning unaccompanied children arriving in the UK, often in small boats, and claiming asylum. The Protocol set a cap on the number of unaccompanied children that the county council would accept into its care. However, the High Court made a declaration that the county council was acting unlawfully in breach of its statutory duties by failing to accommodate all unaccompanied children in its area. The Home Secretary had also acted unlawfully by agreeing to the Kent Protocol. The High Court additionally quashed the Kent Protocol, but suspended the quashing order for three weeks to enable the county council and Home Secretary to make alternative arrangements.

A situation where a prospective only order might be appropriate is where a public body has set up a scheme pursuant to which it has made thousands of small payments to individuals. If a court were to find the scheme unlawful, it would cause considerable administrative inconvenience if the public body had to re-open all the payments it had made pursuant to the scheme. As the amount paid to each individual concerned was modest, this would cause a considerable burden with little corresponding benefit.

7.8.1.2 Prohibiting order

A prohibiting order will order a public body to refrain from acting beyond its powers. Such orders are comparatively rare as claimants often prefer to apply for injunctions (see **7.8.2.2** below). The case of *R v Liverpool Corporation, ex p Liverpool Taxi Fleet Operators' Association* (see **Chapter 6**) provides a good example of a prohibiting order. The council had decided to issue new taxi licences, breaching an assurance that existing licence holders would first be consulted. The court granted a prohibiting order preventing the council from implementing its decision pending consultation with existing licence holders.

7.8.1.3 Mandatory order

A mandatory order is designed to enforce the performance by public bodies of the duties they are by law required to carry out. For example, if a public body has even refused to consider an application for a benefit or licence, a mandatory order would compel the body to consider the application.

### 7.8.2 Private law remedies – the 'non-prerogative orders'

Although prerogative orders are the main orders used in judicial review proceedings, it is also possible to apply for the following private law remedies in judicial review proceedings.

7.8.2.1 Declaration

A declaration is a court order confirming, but not changing, the legal position or rights of the parties. It is a non-coercive remedy so can be ignored without any legal sanctions. Nonetheless, declarations do perform a useful function. For example, in *Royal College of Nursing v Department of Health and Social Security* [1981] AC 800 a government circular asserted that nurses could lawfully undertake part of a procedure for terminating a pregnancy without a doctor's supervision. The claimants applied for a declaration that the government circular was wrong in law, as its own guidance had pointed in the opposite direction. A quashing order would not have been appropriate as there was no act or decision that could be quashed; however, it was desirable in the interests of nurses and the public for the correct legal position to be established. This was the case even though, in the absence of any prosecutions of nurses, it was an abstract point of law. The Government in turn counterclaimed for a declaration that its guidance was not wrong in law and in fact was granted a declaration in those terms.

7.8.2.2 Injunction

An injunction is a court order performing essentially the same function as a prohibiting order (see **7.8.1.2**), namely, to restrain a person or body from illegal action; eg a tort or breach of contract. One of their main benefits is that it is possible to obtain an interim, as well as a final, injunction. Temporary injunctions, for example preventing a decision from being implemented pending the court's final ruling on the decision's lawfulness, can be very useful. For example, a court may grant an interim injunction preventing an asylum seeker's deportation pending judicial review of the lawfulness of the decision to deport them. This may be essential to guarantee that the person concerned has not been deported by the time the court determines the lawfulness of the decision.

7.8.2.3 Damages

Under s 31(4) of the Senior Courts Act 1981, the Administrative Court can award damages on a claim for judicial review where the claimant is seeking other relief (eg a quashing order) and damages could have been awarded in a civil claim. This means that the claimant must have a private law cause of action (eg in tort or contract) or a claim for breach of a Convention right (see **Chapter 9**). Damages cannot be awarded just because the claimant has a ground of challenge. This was confirmed in *R v Knowsley MBC, ex p Maguire* (1992) 142 NLJ 1375.

In the *Maguire* case, the claimant was a taxi driver who had been refused a taxi licence by his local council. He sought judicial review of this and the court found in his favour, quashing the decision. He also sought damages, claiming he had suffered losses as a result of the unlawful refusal of the licence. The court ruled that no damages were available.

The court found that Parliament had not intended an individual to have a private right of action in respect of a failure by a licensing authority properly to exercise its powers under the Act governing the granting of taxi licences. In the absence of any negligence or breach of contract, there was therefore no right to damages.

So there is no general right in law to damages for maladministration.

The next example exercise will enable you to check your understanding of this area.

***Example***

*A market is held each week in Porchester. Stallholders are licensed annually by Porchester Borough Council. Stefan was awarded a licence in March. In June, following allegations made to the Council's trading standards department that Stefan was selling fake 'Rolex' watches, the Council revoked Stefan's licence with immediate effect, without giving him any opportunity to respond to the allegations (which he denies). Stefan says he has incurred significant losses through being unable to trade.*

*Consider what remedies (if any) may be available to Stefan on a successful claim for judicial review, and whether he would be likely to obtain damages for his losses.*

***Answer***

*Assuming Stefan makes a successful claim for judicial review (on the basis of procedural impropriety), he would seek a quashing order. This would quash the revocation and allow him to continue trading under the licence.*

*Stefan is unlikely to obtain damages. Because of s 31(4) of the Senior Courts Act 1981, damages are in effect available in a claim for judicial review only where the claimant is seeking another remedy (as here) and, in addition to breach of public law rights or legitimate expectations, the claimant can establish that their private law rights have been infringed. However, damages are not available purely for the infringement of a public law right (*R v Knowsley MBC, ex p Maguire *(above)).*

## Summary

In this chapter you have considered the procedure and remedies in a judicial review claim, and how they affect whether a claim is successful.

You have considered in particular the following:

- The decision-maker must be a public law body to be amenable to judicial review.
- Claimants must have 'sufficient interest' to have the standing to bring claims.

- Claimants who are directly affected by a decision have little difficulty in showing this.
- Pressure groups need to show they have a genuine interest in the proceedings and are not 'busy-bodies'.

- Claimants should apply for permission for judicial review promptly, without undue delay and within three months of the date of the decisions affecting them. A claimant who waits until the end of the three months before lodging a claim runs the risk of undue delay. Courts have the discretion to extend the time limit of three months where good reasons exist.
- Ouster clauses sometimes purport to preclude challenges to the decisions of a decision-maker.
  - The courts have found ways of circumventing legislative attempts to exclude their judicial review jurisdiction and have held that complete ouster clauses will not protect decisions that were never valid ('nullities').
  - The courts are willing to uphold partial ouster clauses that do not attempt to exclude judicial review, but merely shorten the time limit for bringing claims.
- There are two stages to judicial review claims:
  - The permission stage
  - Full hearing
- The following remedies are available:
  - Prerogative remedies: Quashing, mandatory and prohibitory orders
  - Non-prerogative remedies: Declarations, injunctions and damages.

See also the summary flowchart in **Figure 7.3** that consolidates the issues you have studied in **Chapters 6** and **7**. It also refers to judicial review claims based on Convention rights, which you will study in **Chapter 8**.

Even litigation lawyers who do not specialise in public law will occasionally have to deal with a judicial review claim. You should now be aware that making such a claim requires prompt action and involves very different principles from an ordinary civil claim.

**Figure 7.3** Chapters 6 and 7 – summary flowchart

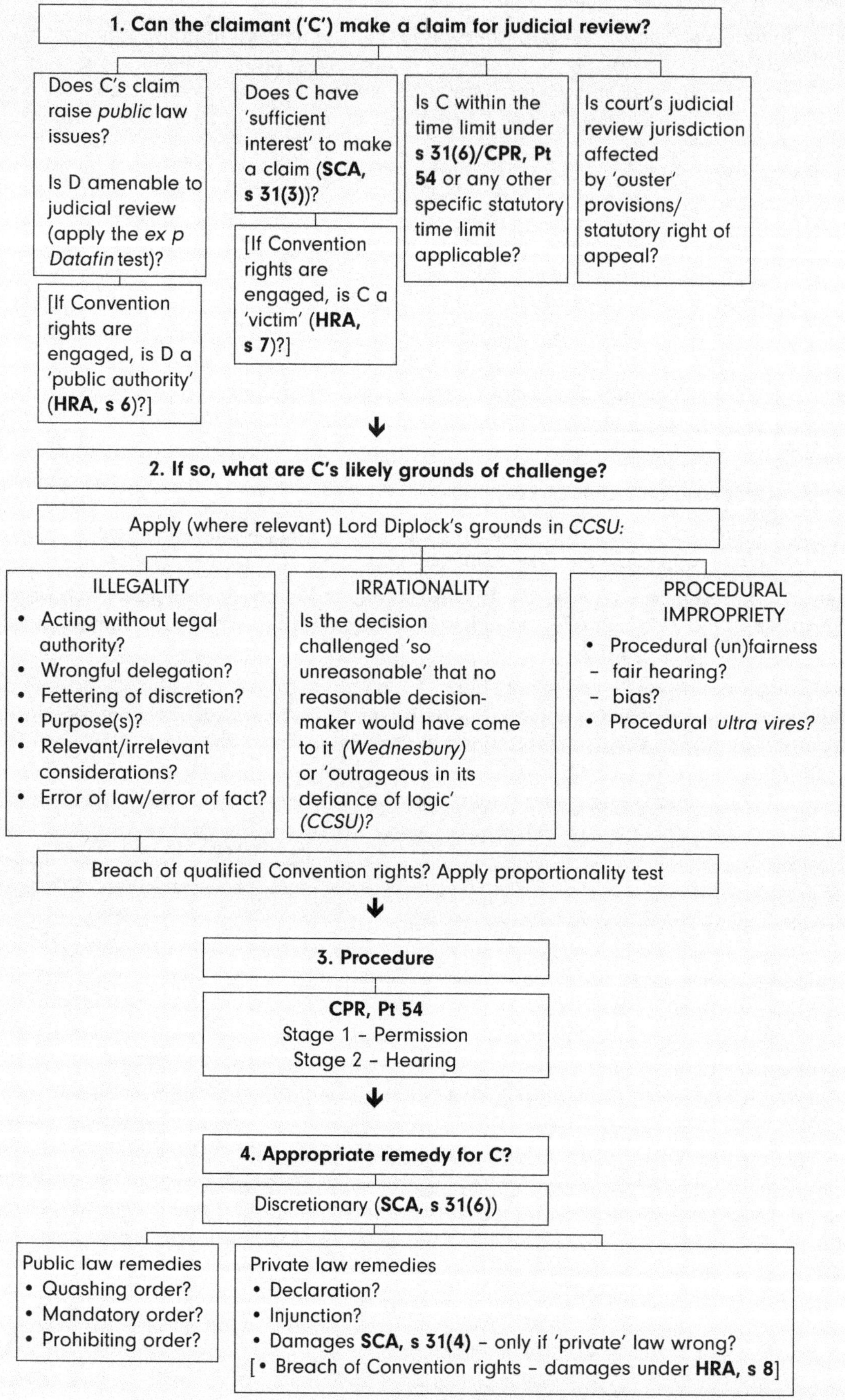

## Sample questions

**Question 1**

In order to address concerns about the behaviour of nightclub door supervisors in controlling patrons, Parliament passed the (fictitious) Regulation of Nightclubs Act 2016 ('the Act'). The Act creates the Entertainment Conduct Authority (the Authority) to regulate the nightclub industry and to grant licences to individuals. Every door supervisor must hold a licence from the Authority to work in the industry.

The Nightclub Workers' Federation (NWF) is concerned about the fee that the Authority is asking its members to pay on applying for their licences, believing it has exceeded its statutory powers and has acted in a biased manner. The NWF wishes to challenge this on their behalf.

**Can the NWF seek judicial review of the licence fee?**

A No, because the Authority is not amenable to judicial review claims, nor does the NWF have sufficient interest to apply for judicial review.

B No, because although the NWF does have sufficient interest to apply for judicial review, the Authority is not amenable to judicial review claims.

C No, because although the Authority is amenable to judicial review claims, the NWF does not have sufficient interest to apply for judicial review.

D Yes, because the Authority is amenable to judicial review claims, and the NWF does have sufficient interest to apply for judicial review.

E Yes, because as the NWF has sufficient interest to apply for judicial review, the Authority will be deemed to be amenable to judicial review claims.

**Answer**

Option D is correct. In order to seek judicial review of a decision, there must be a public body carrying out a public function. Here, the Authority is empowered to grant licences, so both elements are satisfied (*ex p Datafin*). The Authority is therefore amenable to judicial review.

As regards standing, the NWF is a body representing a number of members but, not being able to apply for a licence, is not itself directly affected by the decision. As such, it will have to show that it has 'sufficient interest' to challenge the decision relating to application fees, and the factors from the *World Development Movement* case will assist. The court will consider the need to uphold the rule of law, which here involves what may be an arbitrary attempt to impose a fee and a biased decision by a public body. The importance of the issue, which in this instance is whether or not power is given in the statute to charge a fee, and the facts of the case, which suggest that the challenge by the NWF would decide a point of interest to a number of different applicants, would also be relevant. It is also unlikely that its members would themselves have the resources to mount an individual challenge. As such, the NWF may be permitted to seek judicial review.

Option A is wrong because it incorrectly states the position regarding both amenability and standing. Although option B correctly states the position regarding standing, it is wrong regarding amenability. Option C is correct regarding amenability, but wrong regarding standing.

Option E is wrong. Although it correctly states that the NWF has standing, it does not therefore follow that the decision-maker is amenable to judicial review claims.

**Question 2**

A statute provides that all decisions by a particular public body 'shall not be called into question in any legal proceedings whatsoever'. A company now wants to challenge a decision that adversely affects its interests two months after the decision was made. The reason the company waited for two months before deciding to challenge the decision was that its board of directors was unsure whether or not it was in the company's interests to bring a challenge. However, last week it obtained counsel's opinion that there were valid grounds for challenge.

**Can the company seek judicial review of the decision?**

A Yes, because the ouster clause will not protect decisions of the public body from challenge and the claim will be lodged within the time limit of three months.

B Yes, because the ouster clause will not protect decisions of the public body from challenge and the claim will be lodged without undue delay on the part of the company.

C No, because even though the ouster clause will not protect decisions of the public body from challenge, there has been undue delay on the part of the company in lodging the claim.

D No, because the ouster clause will protect decisions of the public body from challenge even though the claim will be lodged within the time limit of three months.

E No, because the ouster clause will protect decisions of the public body from challenge and there has been undue delay on the part of the company in lodging the claim.

**Answer**

Option C is correct. The ouster clause is unlikely to protect the decision from challenge as in *Anisminic* (above) the House of Lords held that ouster clauses would not protect decisions that were 'nullities'. Assuming that the counsel's opinion correctly indicates there are valid grounds for challenge, the ouster clause will not protect the decision from challenge. However, the company must comply with the time limits and must seek permission promptly and without undue delay (SCA 1981, s 31) and in any event within three months of the date of the decision (CPR, Part 54). As the company has waited for two months without good reason, it is probably guilty of undue delay so will not be granted permission to bring a claim.

Option A is wrong; although it correctly sets out the position regarding the ouster clause, it is wrong regarding the time limit; there has been undue delay on the part of the company and so it probably cannot bring a claim even though it is still within three months of the date of the decision. Option B is wrong as there has been undue delay on the company's part.

Options D and E are wrong because the ouster clause will not protect decisions of the public body, even though option E does correctly state there has been undue delay.

**Question 3**

A local authority has the statutory power to license ice cream vans to sell ice cream within its boundaries. A woman has applied to the local authority for a licence to operate an ice cream van. The local authority has refused to consider her application. She has lost money as a result of being unable to trade.

**What remedy or remedies should the woman apply for?**

A A quashing order.

B A quashing order and damages.

C Damages.

D A mandatory order and damages.

E A mandatory order.

**Answer**

Option E is correct. The purpose of quashing orders is to set aside unlawful decisions, but the local authority has refused even to consider the application. A mandatory order will force the local authority to consider the woman's application lawfully.

Although the woman has lost money due to the refusal to consider the application, she is unlikely to obtain damages. In a claim for judicial review, a claimant can only be awarded damages if they can establish that their private law rights have been infringed. However, damages are not available purely for the infringement of a public law right *(ex p Maguire* (above)).

Options A and B are therefore wrong because there is not a decision to quash, and additionally option B refers to damages. Options C and D are wrong because they refer to damages, even though option D does correctly refer to a mandatory order.

# 8 The European Convention on Human Rights



## SQE1 syllabus

This chapter will enable you to achieve the SQE1 assessment specification in relation to functioning legal knowledge concerned with core constitutional and administrative law principles, including:

- HRA 1998 and the ECHR; and
- Schedule 1 of HRA 1998: the 'Convention Rights'

Note that for SQE1, candidates are not usually required to recall specific case names or cite statutory or regulatory authorities. Cases are provided for illustrative purposes only.

## Learning outcomes

By the end of this chapter you will be able to apply relevant core legal principles and rules appropriately and effectively, at the level of a competent newly qualified solicitor in practice, to realistic client-based and ethical problems and situations in the following areas, including the ability to:

- identify the rights and freedoms set out in the ECHR;
- understand the procedure for bringing claims before the European Court of Human Rights (ECtHR); and
- identify where a breach of a right granted by the ECHR occurs.

## 8.1 Introduction to the ECHR and the HRA

This chapter will introduce you to the main articles that make up the ECHR. However, before we look at the articles themselves, it is necessary for you to understand the background to the Convention and the Human Rights Act 1998, both of which you looked at in outline in Chapter 2.

## 8.2 Background to the ECHR

The ECHR is distinct from EU law, with its own institutions and procedures. The ECHR was adopted in 1950 and was drafted by the Council of Europe, an international organisation that was formed after World War II, in an attempt to establish a common European heritage.

In adopting the ECHR the member states of the Council accepted an obligation to 'accept the principles of the rule of law and of the enjoyment by all persons within its jurisdiction of human rights and fundamental freedoms'. The ECHR was a response to the Holocaust and other atrocities and egregious human rights violations that Europe had witnessed during and before the War, and also to the spread of Communism into Central and Eastern Europe after the War. The idea was that the ECHR would be a statement of the fundamental principles of liberty accepted by the countries of Western Europe, and would prevent future violations of human rights.

The ECHR is an international treaty, which has now been signed by 47 European states; indeed Belarus is the only European state that has not signed it. However, as a result of the war in Ukraine, Russia was expelled from the Council of Europe on 16 March 2022 and so ceased to be a party to the ECHR on 16 September 2022. Accordingly, the Council now has only 46 member states.

The UK ratified the Treaty in 1951. The effect of this is that the UK is bound as a matter of international law to comply with the ECHR, by ensuring that UK law gives effect to a list of rights set out in the ECHR. If the UK breaches the ECHR, it is possible for other states who are parties to bring proceedings before the European Court of Human Rights (ECtHR) in Strasbourg, in addition to individual applications to enforce rights under the ECHR. Judgments of the ECtHR are binding on the UK as a matter of international law. Article 1 of the ECHR requires the signatories to the ECHR, including the UK, to secure the rights conferred by the ECHR in their own jurisdiction.

It was not until the enactment of the HRA 1998 that rights under the ECHR were incorporated into UK law. Section 1 and Schedule 1 of the HRA 1998 incorporated most ECHR rights into UK law as 'Convention rights'. The HRA 1998 is covered in more detail is **Chapters 2** and **9**.

## 8.3 Procedure

### 8.3.1 Types of proceedings

There are two ways in which proceedings may commence:

(a) *State applications.* If a state is in violation of the ECHR, proceedings may be brought against it by another signatory state.

For example, Georgia lodged during Russia's membership two separate inter-state applications against Russia. The first was filed in 2007 and related to the deportation of hundreds of ethnic Georgians by Russia following a row about spying (*Georgia v Russia I* (Application No 13255/07)). The second was in connection with the conduct of the Russian military forces in the 2008 war between the two countries (*Georgia v Russia II* (Application No 38263/08)).

A recent example of a state application is the one lodged by the Republic of Ireland against the UK regarding the Northern Ireland Troubles (Legacy and Reconciliation) Act 2023, discussed further at **8.8.3** below (*Ireland v United Kingdom*, Application No 1859/24).

(b) *Individual petitions to the ECtHR.* Individuals who allege that their Convention rights have been breached as a result of domestic law may start their own proceedings against the state before the ECtHR in Strasbourg. However, it must be shown that any domestic remedies that exist have first been exhausted. Furthermore, there is a time limit, requiring the petition to be made within four months of the final decision (in the UK this will usually be the decision of the highest UK court having jurisdiction).

Applicants must, personally and directly, be victims of violations of the ECHR, and must have suffered a significant disadvantage.

In 2023, 38,260 cases were disposed of judicially by the ECtHR, a 3% decrease on the previous year. Judgments were delivered in respect of 6,931 applications (compared with 4,168 in 2022, an increase of 66%, though this was mainly attributable to a large number of applications being joined), while 31,329 applications were declared inadmissible or struck out. Most cases therefore do not proceed to a full hearing but, of those that have done so since 1959, state violations have been found in 84% of cases.

Possible remedies include the court awarding compensation or requiring the state to change its law. However, individual decisions are only binding as a matter of international law under the ECHR and have no direct binding force in domestic law. The ECtHR relies on the willingness of states to abide by the ECHR and accept its judgments.

It is also important to appreciate that the ECHR is a 'living instrument' in the sense that it has to be generously interpreted in the light of its aim of protecting human rights, the understanding of which may change with evolving social conditions. Thus the content of the rights may change over time as the ECtHR reinterprets the ECHR to keep it attuned to changing values.

### 8.3.2 Two-stage process

There are two main stages in cases brought before the Court: the admissibility stage and the merits stage.

A single-judge formation will declare an application inadmissible should inadmissibility be obvious from the outset; there is no right to appeal against its decisions.

Cases that are covered by well-established case law of the court will be allocated to a three-member Committee, which will give a final decision or judgment.

Other cases will be heard by a Chamber of judges, which will give judgment by a majority. The Chamber's judgment will become final only after three months, during which the applicant or state party may ask for the case to be referred to the Grand Chamber for fresh consideration. If the request for referral is accepted by the panel of the Grand Chamber, the Grand Chamber will reconsider the case and hold a public hearing if necessary. The Grand Chamber judgment will be final.

The Committee of Ministers of the Council of Europe is responsible for ensuring that states comply with judgments of the ECtHR.

## 8.4 Absolute, limited and qualified rights

You will have noticed in looking through the ECHR that not all Convention rights are absolute. Sometimes a public authority may be able to show that its action is within one of the limitations or qualifications permitted by the Article in question, and is therefore lawful. You will be looking at some of the limitations and qualifications in more detail later, but it is important at this stage to understand the general concepts. These are derived from the case law of the ECtHR in Strasbourg.

Convention rights are normally divided into three types:

(i) Absolute rights: These rights can never be interfered with in any circumstances whatsoever. States must uphold them at all times.

(ii) Limited rights: These rights can only be limited in clearly defined and finite situations.

(iii) Qualified rights: These rights require a balance between the rights of the individual and the wider public interest, and so may be interfered with to protect an important general interest or the rights of others.

Before you look at the general concepts, it is important to establish which rights are absolute, which are limited and which are qualified.

**Table 8.1** below indicates whether each right is absolute, limited or qualified. The distinction between absolute and limited rights can sometimes be a difficult one to draw. In this regard you should distinguish between:

- rights that list exceptions that help to define the rights; these are absolute rights as any conduct that falls within an exception does not constitute an interference with the right in question; and
- rights that list specific and finite situations in which they can be interfered with; these are limited rights as there are set circumstances where an interference is permissible.

You should note that there is scope for disagreement with some of the categorisations made in the table below. The distinction between absolute and limited rights is not made in the ECHR itself, and there is no authoritative list. For example, whilst there is universal agreement that Article 3 is an absolute right, some sources agree with the above categorisations of Articles 2 and 6, but others regard them as limited.

Generally speaking, Articles 2–7 (absolute and limited rights) cover the most fundamental human rights and contain either no exceptions whatsoever or narrow express exceptions or limitations, and Articles 8–11 and Article 1 of Protocol 1 cover qualified rights, which can be overridden in the public interest.

**Table 8.1** Absolute, limited and qualified rights

| Convention right | Absolute | Limited | Qualified |
|---|---|---|---|
| Article 2 (right to life) | Absolute. Note that deprivation of life resulting from the use of no more force than is absolutely necessary in narrowly defined circumstances does not constitute an interference with this right. | | |
| Article 3 (freedom from torture, inhuman and degrading treatment) | Absolute. | | |
| Article 4 (freedom from slavery, etc) | Absolute. Note that certain activities are excluded from the scope of compulsory labour and so do not constitute an interference with this right. | | |
| Article 5 (liberty and security of the person) | | Limited – contains exceptions in relation to lawful arrest and detention. | |
| Article 6 (fair trial) | Absolute as to a fair trial. | Limited in relation to the trial being in public. | |
| Article 7 (punishment according to existing law) | Absolute. Note that Article 7 does not preclude the trial and punishment of acts that are criminal according to general principles recognised by civilised nations. | | |
| Article 8 (respect for private and family life) | | | Qualified. |

(*continued*)

**Table 8.1** *(continued)*

| Convention right | Absolute | Limited | Qualified |
|---|---|---|---|
| Article 9 (freedom of thought, etc) | Absolute in relation to freedom of thought, etc. | | Qualified in relation to manifestation of freedom in worship, teaching, practice or observation. |
| Article 10 (freedom of expression) | | | Qualified. |
| Article 11 (freedom of assembly and association) | | | Qualified. |
| Article 12 (right to marry) | Absolute, but according to national law governing the exercise of the right. | | |
| Article 1 of Protocol 1 (right to peaceful enjoyment of possessions) | | | Qualified |

## 8.5 Qualified rights

We shall now look in more detail at how the courts determine whether the interference with a qualified right can be justified.

### 8.5.1 Qualifications must be express

Only restrictions on qualified rights that are expressed in the ECHR are recognised, and these must be used for the purpose for which they have been prescribed (Article 18).

In addition, a restriction may only be relied upon if it is prescribed by law, has a legitimate aim and is necessary in a democratic society. It must not be applied in a discriminatory fashion (Article 14). We will now look in more detail at each of these requirements.

### 8.5.2 Qualifications must be prescribed by law (or be 'in accordance with the law')

A government can rely on a Convention qualification to justify a restriction on a Convention right only if provisions of that state's law actually take advantage of the qualification. So, for example, it would not be possible for the UK Government to justify infringement of the right to respect for private life (eg by telephone tapping) on the basis that it was needed for the prevention of crime (Article 8), unless UK law clearly permitted the infringement. The law giving effect to the qualification may be written or unwritten, but the qualification must be embodied in law.

Moreover, the law must be accessible (in published form) and sufficiently precise to enable the citizen to regulate his or her conduct. So in *Malone v UK* (1984) 7 EHRR 14, the ECtHR held that English law on telephone tapping was not clear enough at that time to provide a sufficient legal basis for a restriction on the right to respect for private life.

In the case of multiple sclerosis sufferer Debbie Purdy, the absence of a crime-specific policy relating to assisted suicide, identifying the facts and circumstances that the Director of Public Prosecutions (DPP) would take into account when deciding whether to prosecute an individual for assisting another person to commit suicide, meant that the statutory offence of assisted suicide was not *in accordance with the law* for the purposes of Article 8(2); accordingly it amounted to a violation of her right to lead a private life (*R (Purdy) v DPP* [2009] UKHL 45). The existing law was insufficiently clear about the factors the DPP would take into account, and therefore a person could not accurately predict if they were likely to be prosecuted with assisting another's suicide.

### 8.5.3 Legitimate aims

Qualifications must be *justified* by reference to the aims specified for each right. The principle is that the interests of society may justify restrictions on the rights of individuals.

The following are frequently specified in the Convention as legitimate state aims:

(a) The interests of national security, public safety or the economic well-being of the country (eg Article 8)

(b) The prevention of disorder or crime (eg Articles 8 and 10)

(c) The protection of health or morals (eg Articles 8 and 10)

(d) The protection of the rights or freedoms of others (eg Article 8)

(e) The prevention or disclosure of information received in confidence (eg Article 10)

(f) Maintaining the authority and impartiality of the judiciary (eg Article 10)

### 8.5.4 Necessary in a democratic society

Qualifications are usually required to be 'necessary in a democratic society' (eg Articles 8 and 10). This means the following:

(a) There must be a 'pressing social need' (rather than an absolute necessity for any restriction imposed).

(b) The interference with the ECHR right must be proportionate. This means that in order to justify the restriction, public authorities may have to show that they have chosen methods of achieving legitimate aims that do not go further than is necessary. Thus, for example, any restriction imposed upon freedom of expression based on concerns for public order must be shown to be a proportionate response to the fears. You will consider the 'proportionality test' in more detail at **8.14.2** below.

However, the state is allowed a 'margin of appreciation' in judging necessity (*R v Handyside* (1976) 1 EHRR 737). This means that where member states may legitimately reach different conclusions on a particular issue, the ECtHR will respect the judgment of a member state as to what the public interest requires.

The qualities of a 'democratic society' include tolerance of minority opinions and lifestyles. So the fact that a majority in a state opposes homosexuality does not excuse a law that criminalises homosexual conduct in private contrary to Art 8 (*R v Dudgeon* (1982) 4 EHRR 149).

## 8.6 Derogations

Under Article 15 of the ECHR, a state may derogate from part of the ECHR 'in time of war or other public emergency threatening the life of the nation'. This means that for the period of the derogation the state is not bound to apply the specified provisions. There are, however, conditions that limit the power to derogate, and no derogation is possible in respect of Articles 3 (torture, etc), 4(1) (slavery), or 7 (retrospective criminal offences), or from Article 2 (right to life) except in respect of deaths resulting from lawful acts of war. The principle is clearly that some violations of human rights are so wrong that no state should countenance them, even in wartime.

Section 14 of the HRA 1998 creates a statutory procedure for enacting a derogation as part of UK law, and s 1 states that Convention rights are to be read subject to any such derogation. As a result, a UK court will not be able to enforce Convention rights where a derogation is in operation.

The UK has issued derogations from Article 5 of the ECHR (personal liberty) in respect of the prevention of terrorism legislation in Northern Ireland (now expired) and the Anti-terrorism, Crime and Security Act 2001. The delegated legislation implementing the latter derogation was quashed by the House of Lords in *A v Secretary of State for the Home Department*, and the Government subsequently removed the derogation on the enactment of the Prevention of Terrorism Act 2005.

## 8.7 Rights under the European Convention on Human Rights

We will now look in greater detail at some absolute and limited rights and cases associated with them. It is important for you to understand the scope of these absolute rights and how they have been interpreted by the courts.

### 8.7.1 Article 2 – Right to life

Article 2 is an absolute right, but with exceptions that define its scope. It:

(a) prohibits the state from taking life; and

(b) places on the state a positive duty to protect life (see *Osman v United Kingdom* [1997] 1 FLR 193).

Article 2 does not prohibit the use of the death penalty, but Protocol 6 (which the UK ratified in 1999) does. The death penalty cannot be reintroduced except for acts committed in time of war/imminent threat of war.

No derogation from Article 2 is possible, except in respect of deaths resulting from lawful acts of war.

Article 2(2) permits the use of force that results in the deprivation of life, but only if certain conditions are met. The first condition is that the use of force must be no more than absolutely necessary.

The second condition is that the use of force must be in pursuit of one or more of three objectives.

- the force is used in defence of any person from unlawful violence.
- the force is used to effect a lawful arrest or to prevent the escape of a person lawfully detained
- the force is used in action lawfully taken for the purpose of lawfully quelling a riot or insurrection

The leading case in this area is *McCann v United Kingdom* (1996) 21 EHRR 97 (the 'death on the rock' case), which involved a challenge by the relatives of three Provisional IRA members who were shot dead by SAS soldiers in Gibraltar in 1988. The relatives won by a slim majority

(10:9) on the basis that the force used was more than absolutely necessary. Whilst the actions of the SAS soldiers who had killed the terrorists did not violate Article 2, the control and planning of the operation lacked sufficient regard for the protection of the lives of the suspects, so Article 2 had been violated.

### 8.7.2 Scope of Article 2

Case law has helped to define the scope of Article 2.

#### 8.7.2.1 Embryos/foetuses

Article 2 has been held not to protect embryos by preventing their destruction when one party withdraws his or her consent to implantation (*Evans v UK* (2006) 4 EHRLR 485–88). In this case, the ECtHR dismissed an appeal by the applicant under Article 2 and accepted the decision of the domestic courts that the embryos had no right to life under Article 2. The Court said this decision was within the margin of appreciation allowed to member states. In the cases of *Re F (In Utero) (Wardship)* [1988] 2 FLR 307 and *Re MB (Medical Treatment)* [1997] 2 FLR 426, it had already been established that a foetus has no such right to life, so the right could clearly not apply to an embryo.

#### 8.7.2.2 The right to die

There is also case law regarding whether the right to life also encompasses the right to die in the context of litigation regarding whether laws banning assisted suicide breach Article 2. In *Pretty v UK* (2002) 35 EHRR 1, Diane Pretty suffered from motor neurone disease. Both the Divisional Court and the House of Lords held that the DPP had no power to give an undertaking that her husband would not be prosecuted if he assisted her to commit suicide as s 2(1) of the Suicide Act 1961 makes it an offence to encourage or assist suicide. The ECtHR held that the right to die could not be read into the right to life protected by Article 2.

Whilst a right to die cannot be read into Article 2, there has been litigation regarding whether laws banning assisted suicide breach Article 8, the right to respect for one's private life, most recently the case of *R (Conway) v Secretary of State for Justice* [2018] EWCA Civ 1431. The appellant was terminally ill with motor neurone disease and applied for a declaration of incompatibility of s 2(1) of the Suicide Act under the s 4 of the HRA 1998, arguing that the blanket ban on assisted suicide in s 2(1) was a disproportionate interference with his Article 8 rights.

Although the Court of Appeal accepted that Article 8 was engaged, it nonetheless held the blanket ban on assisted suicide in the Suicide Act 1961, s 2(1) was a necessary and proportionate interference with the appellant's Article 8 rights.

#### 8.7.2.3 The duty to investigate

Article 2 also has a procedural element. This requires the state to carry out a full and thorough investigation where an allegation has been made that there has been a breach of Article 2. One of the most controversial cases regarding the duty to investigate followed the death of Jean Charles de Menezes.

On 22 July 2005 (shortly after the attacks of 7 July 2005 when suicide bombers had murdered 52 people in London), Mr Menezes was wrongly identified as a suspected suicide bomber. He was followed to an underground station and shot dead by armed officers while on board a stationary train. In 2007, the Office of the Commissioner of the Police of the Metropolis was found guilty of breaches of the Health and Safety at Work Act of 1974 in connection with Mr Menezes's death, but no individual police officers were prosecuted.

In *Da Silva v United Kingdom* (2016) 63 EHRR 12, the ECtHR found that there had been no breach of the duty under Article 2 to conduct an effective investigation into the death. As soon as it was confirmed that Mr Menezes was not a suspected suicide bomber, the Metropolitan Police Service publicly accepted that he had been killed in error by special firearms officers. A representative of the Metropolitan Police Service flew to Brazil to apologise to his family face to face and to make a payment to cover their financial needs. They were further advised to seek independent legal advice and assured that any legal costs would be met by the Metropolitan Police Service.

The decision not to prosecute any individual officer was not due to any failings in the investigation or the state's tolerance of or collusion in unlawful acts. Rather, it was due to the fact that, following a thorough investigation, a prosecutor considered all the facts of the case and concluded that there was insufficient evidence against any individual officer to meet the threshold evidential test in respect of any criminal offence.

8.7.2.4 Environmental litigation

The ECHR is increasingly being invoked in environmental litigation. For example, in *Cannavacciuolo v Italy*, Application No 51767/14, [2025] 1 WLUK 487, local residents complained about long-term illegal waste disposal and burning. They argued that the Italian authorities had not taken adequate measures to protect their lives contrary to Article 2.

The ECtHR noted that this case involved a particularly complex and widespread form of pollution which occurred primarily on private land. It did not concern properly regulated industrial activities, but instead concerned activities carried out by organised criminal groups, businesses and individuals. However, the national authorities had known about the existence of these dangerous activities for many years. Given the seriousness of the circumstances, the Italian state had not done enough to protect the applicants' lives, and so had violated Article 2.

See also **8.15.3** below for an example of the use of Article 8 in climate change litigation.

## 8.8 Article 3 – Torture, inhuman or degrading treatment or punishment

Article 3 of the ECHR provides very simply that 'No one shall be subjected to torture or to inhuman or degrading treatment or punishment'. It is an absolute right and there are no limitations or exceptions to this. Any treatment of an individual that falls within the scope of Article 3 violates the Convention. The importance of Article 3 is also reflected in that it is one of those articles from which the state is not permitted to derogate under Article 15.

### 8.8.1 Scope of Article 3

The leading case on what amounts to torture and inhuman treatment is *Ireland v United Kingdom* (1979–1980) 2 EHRR 25. This case concerned the ill-treatment of suspected Irish Republican Army terrorists in Northern Ireland in 1971. As part of the interrogation techniques adopted by the police and security services, the suspects were made to stand against a wall in an unnatural position for long periods of time, and were also placed in hoods and deprived of sleep and food.

The ECtHR defined 'torture' as being 'deliberate inhuman treatment causing very serious and cruel suffering' whilst it defined 'inhuman treatment' as treatment or punishment likely to cause actual bodily injury or intense physical and mental suffering'. The ECtHR found that the conduct in this case constituted inhuman or degrading treatment, albeit it was not severe enough to be torture.

In *Tyrer v United Kingdom* (1979–80) 2 EHRR 1 a court in the Isle of Man sentenced the applicant to three strokes of the birch for the offence of assault occasioning actual bodily harm against another pupil at his school. A policeman administered the birch to the applicant's naked buttocks while he was being held down by two other policemen. The ECtHR held that the punishment did not amount to torture or inhuman treatment within the meaning of Article 3, as it did not meet the test set out in the *UK v Ireland* case. The ECtHR did, however, find that Tyrer was subjected to degrading punishment under Article 3, as judicial corporal punishment constituted an assault on an individual's dignity and physical integrity.

Following a series of cases that came before the ECtHR in the late 1970s and 1980, Parliament enacted legislation to outlaw corporal punishment in both state and – later – private schools.

The ECtHR has also held that the state has an obligation to ensure that non-state actors such as parents or guardians do not punish children to a level at which Article 3 will be engaged. In *A v United Kingdom* (1999) 27 EHRR 611, between the ages of 6 and 9 A had been frequently beaten with a garden cane by his stepfather. These beatings had left significant bruising. The stepfather was subsequently charged with assault occasioning actual bodily harm. At trial, he raised the defence available under English law that the beatings represented reasonable chastisement, which he was entitled to inflict. The stepfather was acquitted and A applied to the ECtHR, arguing that his treatment constituted a violation of his rights under Article 3.

The Court found that the injuries inflicted on A were sufficient to engage Article 3, and that the state had failed to put in place laws that would satisfactorily protect the rights of children such as A. The Court found in particular that the law was deficient in leaving it up to a jury to decide whether the treatment received by A amounted to reasonable chastisement. Parliament subsequently amended the law in this area.

### 8.8.2 Deportation cases

A controversial area in which Article 3 has been applied involves cases where those who are not British citizens are required to leave the UK. These cases usually involve people who are being deported under the Immigration Act 1971. This Act allows the Government to deport those who are lawfully in the UK but are not UK citizens if either they have been convicted of a serious offence or their presence in the UK is not conducive to the public good. This latter reason would cover those who are viewed as a risk to national security.

Other situations in which individuals may be required to leave the UK are removal and extradition cases. Removal is where those who are not in the UK lawfully are removed. This would, for example, include illegal immigrants. Extradition cases involve anyone living in the UK being sent to another country in order to be tried for a criminal offence allegedly committed in that country. The UK has an extradition treaty with many countries.

The ECtHR has held that it would be a violation of Articles 2 and/or 3 of the Convention if an individual were to be deported to, removed to or extradited to a country where there was a real risk that they might be killed, tortured or treated in any other way that would violate one or both of these articles. The Court outlined this principle in *Soering v United Kingdom* (1999) 11 EHRR 439. In this case, the United States had applied to the UK for the extradition of Soering, who was alleged to have committed two murders while in the US.

The Court found that the proposed extradition of Soering to the United States would breach his rights under Article 3. This was because, were Soering to be convicted of murder and sentenced to death, the time he would spend on death row while awaiting execution would cause him to suffer intense psychological suffering that would fall within the scope of Article 3.

The *Soering* case was decided before Article 1 of the Thirteenth Protocol came into force (see **8.25** below). This Article bans the imposition of the death penalty. As a result, it would now also violate Article 2 for an individual to be deported, removed or extradited to a state if there are substantial grounds to believe that there is a real risk of that individual facing the death penalty.

What is the position if the deportation of an individual to another country will not result in his death but may lead to him suffering other forms of ill-treatment?

This was considered by the ECtHR in *Chahal v United Kingdom* (1997) 23 EHRR 413. In 1990, the Secretary of State decided to deport Chahal, an Indian citizen lawfully resident in the UK, in the interests of national security. In 1984, on a visit to India, he had been detained and tortured by the Punjabi police due to his participation in a campaign for a Sikh homeland.

The Court found that Article 3 contained an absolute prohibition on the use of torture or inhuman or degrading treatment, regardless of the circumstances of the case. There was substantial evidence of serious human rights abuses by the Indian authorities and promises that they had given as to Chahal's safety were unreliable. The Court concluded that, where there was a real risk that the receiving country would treat an individual in such a way as to breach his Article 3 rights, any deportation would be unlawful.

*R (AAA (Syria)) v Secretary of State for the Home Department* [2023] UKSC 42 concerned a challenge to the Secretary of State's policy of relocating asylum seekers to Rwanda for determination of their asylum claims, on the basis that Rwanda was not a safe third country. The Supreme Court affirmed the decision of the Court of Appeal. It stated that Article 3 would be breached, not only where there was a real risk of ill-treatment in Rwanda itself, but also if an inadequate system of asylum in Rwanda meant that there was a real risk of asylum seekers being returned, directly or indirectly, to their country of origin and there was a real risk that their Article 3 rights would be breached in that country. It decided that Rwanda was not a safe country due to the inadequacy of its asylum system, and therefore relocation to Rwanda would constitute a breach of Article 3.

### 8.8.3 Northern Ireland

In *Re Dillon (Northern Ireland Troubles (Legacy and Reconciliation) Act 2023)* [2024] NICA 59, the Northern Ireland Court of Appeal ruled that provisions in the Northern Ireland Troubles (Legacy and Reconciliation) 2023 Act ('the Legacy Act') which granted immunity from prosecution breached both Article 2 and Article 3 of the Convention. While wide-ranging amnesties might be justifiable where they represented the only way out of a violent dictatorship or interminable conflict, this was not the case in Northern Ireland as the relevant conflict had ended over 20 years before.

Furthermore, the Legacy Act provided that the Independent Commission for Reconciliation and Information Recovery (which was set up under the Legacy Act) *must* grant immunity to an applicant if certain conditions were met and did not provide for any exceptions for grave breaches of fundamental rights, including allegations of torture.

The Labour Government has drafted a proposed remedial order pursuant to s 10 of the HRA 1998 which will remove the incompatible provisions from the Legacy Act. In the longer term, the Government intends to repeal and replace the Legacy Act following a consultation process.

---

## 8.9 Article 4 – Slavery

### 8.9.1 Introduction

Article 4 of the ECHR prohibits slavery and forced labour. Article 4(1) provides that 'No one shall be held in slavery or servitude' and Article 4(2) provides that 'No one shall be required to perform forced or compulsory labour'.

Article 4(3) states that certain forms of work do not constitute forced or compulsory labour. These are:

- work ordinarily done by convicted prisoners as part of their sentence;
- compulsory military service in those European countries that still have this;
- work required in an emergency or calamity threatening the life or well-being of the community; and
- any work or service that forms part of normal civic obligations.

Although slavery was abolished in most parts of the world in the 19th century, Article 4 is a response to what happened during World War II, between 1939 and 1945. During the War, Nazi Germany used millions of people from across the continent of Europe to carry out forced labour in support of the Nazi war machine.

We shall now consider the meaning of some of the terms used in Article 4.

### 8.9.2 Slavery

The internationally accepted definition of slavery was set out in Article 1 of the 1926 Slavery Convention. This defined slavery as 'the status or condition of a person over whom any or all of the powers attaching to the right of ownership are exercised'. The ECtHR has accepted this definition.

### 8.9.3 Servitude

Someone in a position of servitude is not owned by another, and so is not a slave. The ECtHR has found that servitude includes an obligation on the part of the person who is the 'serf' to live on the property of another, and an inability for that person to change that condition.

### 8.9.4 Forced or compulsory labour

The meaning of the term 'forced or compulsory labour' was considered by the ECtHR in *Van der Mussele v Belgium* (1984) 6 EHRR 163. Belgian law required trainee lawyers - as part of their qualification process - to carry out legal work for poor clients without receiving any payment. The trainees argued that this constituted a violation of Article 4(2), but the Court disagreed. The Court said that the requirement to do this work had to be seen in its proper context, which was that the trainees were gaining valuable experience, they were in the process of qualifying into a profession, and doing this work did not prevent them from also doing paid work for other clients.

The Court said that forced labour was work or service that an individual was forced to do against their will. Although there is no easy test to work out when this will be met, the Court said that a range of circumstances needed to be considered. These included the type of work involved, the 'penalty' or burden to be imposed if the work was not carried out, and the level of hardship or oppression to which the individual was subjected.

The Supreme Court considered the interpretation of forced labour in *Reilly v Secretary of State for Work and Pensions* [2013] UKSC 68. This case involved a challenge to the requirement that a person in receipt of the state benefit called Job Seeker's Allowance had to carry out unpaid work experience as a condition of continuing to receive this benefit. The Supreme Court found that this requirement did not breach of Article 4. The Court said that an essential element of forced labour was that the individual had to be exploited, and that requirement was not met here.

---

## 8.10 Article 5 – Right to liberty and security

### 8.10.1 Introduction

The overall purpose of Article 5 of the ECHR has been described as ensuring that no one is deprived of their liberty in an 'arbitrary fashion'. In particular, it lays down procedural standards that must be followed before a person is deprived of their liberty.

Article 5(1) begins, 'Everyone has the right to liberty and security of person. No one shall be deprived of his liberty save in the following cases and in accordance with a procedure prescribed by law'.

From this, you can see that Article 5 is a limited Article - it creates a right to liberty, but that right is subject to several specific limitations set out in the rest of the Article. Also, even if one of those limited situations exists, the deprivation of an individual's liberty must still be carried out through due process of law. An example of this would be if the police were to detain an individual whom they reasonably suspect to have committed a crime, but fail to carry out the arrest in the correct manner by not telling the individual that they are under arrest or the reason for the arrest.

Article 5(1)(a)-(f) lists six ways in which an individual's right to liberty may lawfully be interfered with by the state. The most significant ways in which the state may lawfully restrict the liberty of an individual are arrest and detention by the police, imprisonment after conviction of a criminal offence, detention of the mentally ill in hospitals, and detention of foreigners in the context of asylum and deportation cases.

In relation to arrest and detention, Article 5 requires:

(a) breach, or reasonable suspicion of breach, of some known law (Article 5(1)(a) and (c));

(b) the giving of reasons for arrest and charge (Article 5(2));

(c) a prompt and fair trial (Article 5(3) and (6));

(d) the availability of judicial review of the legality of detention (Article 5(4)); and

(e) the right to compensation for breach of Article 5 (Art 5(5)).

### 8.10.2 The meaning of deprivation of liberty

When a person is locked up in prison, they have clearly been deprived of their liberty, so Article 5 will be engaged. However, there are situations that are less clear-cut so it is essential to consider what the phrase 'deprivation of liberty' means to ascertain when Article 5 is engaged.

There may be situations when an individual has their right of free movement restricted but is otherwise free to carry on with their life. An example of this is an Anti-Social Behaviour Order that prohibits an individual from entering a specific area, or a Football Banning Order that prohibits an individual from attending football matches. These restrictions on movement do not engage Art 5, because they do not deprive an individual of their liberty.

Although the above examples to do not engage Article 5, the ECtHR has said that the term deprivation of liberty has a wider meaning than simply detaining someone in a cell. The Court has held that what constitutes a deprivation of liberty is a matter of judgment based upon all the circumstances.

*The leading case in this area is* Guzzardi v Italy *(1980) 3 EHRR 333. In 1975, an Italian court ordered that Guzzardi, a suspected Mafia leader, should be placed under special supervision for three years with an obligation to reside on a small Italian island. The island measured some 50 square kilometres but the area for Guzzardi's compulsory residence was limited to some 2.5 square kilometres.*

*A majority of the ECtHR held that these limitations amounted to a deprivation of liberty. In its judgment, the Court said that: 'The difference between deprivation of and restriction upon liberty is one of degree or intensity, and not one of nature or substance.'*

*What the Court meant by this was that, in any given situation, it was necessary to look at the level of the restrictions placed on an applicant, rather than their specific nature. The Court held that deprivation of liberty may take many forms, going beyond what it referred to as 'classic detention in prison'.*

*In Guzzardi's case, the Court found that, whilst the area around which Guzzardi could move far exceeded the dimensions of a cell and was not bounded by any physical barrier, it covered a tiny fraction of an island to which access was difficult and about nine-tenths of which was occupied by a prison. Also, Guzzardi was housed in a tiny village, living in the company of other persons subjected to the same measure. He was not permitted to visit the main settlement on the island, and his social contacts were limited to his near family, his fellow 'residents' and the supervisory staff. In addition, Guzzardi was not able to leave his dwelling between 10pm and 7am without giving prior notification to the authorities. He had to report to the authorities twice a day and inform them of the name and number of his correspondent whenever he wished to use the telephone. In conclusion, the Court said:*

> *It is admittedly not possible to speak of 'deprivation of liberty' on the strength of any one of these factors taken individually, but cumulatively and in combination they certainly raise an issue of categorisation from the viewpoint of Article 5. In certain respects the treatment complained of resembles detention in an 'open prison' or committal to a disciplinary unit.*

*In a UK context, the definition of the term 'deprivation of liberty' was considered by the House of Lords in* Secretary of State for the Home Department v JJ *[2007] UKHL 45. In this case, the Secretary of State used statutory powers to make what were called control orders over six people of Iranian or Iraqi nationality. The orders were made because the Secretary of State had reasonable grounds for suspecting them of involvement in terrorist-related activity and he considered the orders to be necessary to protect members of the public from a risk of terrorism.*

*The orders required each controlled person at all times to wear an electronic tagging device, to remain within his specified residence, a one-bedroom flat, except between 10am and 4pm, and to permit police searches of the premises at any time. Visitors to the premises were permitted only where prior Home Office permission had been given. During the six hours when the controlled persons were permitted to leave their residences they were confined to restricted urban areas, which deliberately did not extend, except in one case, to any area where they had previously lived. Each area contained a mosque, health care facilities, shops and entertainment and sporting facilities. Each controlled person was prohibited from meeting anyone by pre-arrangement without prior Home Office approval.*

*Adopting the approach taken by the ECtHR in the* Guzzardi *case, the House of Lords held that the right to individual liberty in Article 5 connoted the physical liberty of the person and, in cases of dispute, it was for the court to assess into which category a particular case fell. In order to do this, the court needed to consider the situation of the particular individual and, taking account of a whole range of criteria including the type, duration, effects and manner of implementation of the measures in question, to assess their impact on them in the context of the life they might otherwise have been living. Applying those factors, a majority of the House of Lords held that the right to liberty of the six individuals had been violated.*

*The cases of* Guzzardi *and* JJ *make it clear that a person may be deprived of their liberty under Article 5 without being detained in prison. However, in such cases there would need to be a significant element of physical confinement together with significant restrictions on the life that can be lived when not so confined.*

*In recent years, the ECtHR has had to determine whether the 'kettling' of protesters falls within the scope of Article 5. Kettling is the practice of containing a group of people in a particular area for a limited period of time in the interests of public order.*

*In* Austin v UK *(2012) 55 EHRR 14, four people had been contained within a police cordon for several hours during an anti-capitalism demonstration in central London. One had been taking part in the demonstration, but the others were simply passers-by. Police intelligence indicated that the demonstration presented a serious threat to public order, and a risk of damage to property and serious injury or death.*

*As in* Guzzardi*, the Court stressed that Article 5 was not concerned with mere restrictions on liberty of movement. The difference between a deprivation of liberty and a restriction upon it was one of degree, and therefore the type, duration, effects and manner of implementation of the measure used had to be considered.*

*The Court found that whilst the coercive nature, duration and effect of the containment suggested a deprivation of liberty, the context was significant. The police had had no alternative but to establish the cordon to isolate and contain a large crowd and to avert a real risk of injury or damage. The applicants did not argue that they had been deprived of their liberty as soon as the cordon was imposed, and the Court was unable to identify a point at which a restriction on their freedom of movement became a deprivation of their liberty. The police had made attempts at dispersal and had kept the situation under review, but the dangerous conditions that had necessitated the imposition of the cordon existed until early evening. Therefore, those within the cordon could not be said to have been deprived of their liberty within the meaning of Article 5.*

### 8.10.3 When may the state lawfully deprive an individual of their liberty?

Article 5(1)(a)–(f) lists six situations in which an individual may lawfully be deprived of their liberty without a violation of the basic right contained in Article 5. In summary, these limitations are:

(a) when an individual is sent to prison after being convicted of a criminal offence;

(b) when an individual is arrested or detained in order to ensure that the individual complies with a court order;

(c) when an individual is arrested on reasonable suspicion of having committed a criminal offence, to prevent them from committing an offence or to prevent them from fleeing after having committed an offence;

(d) when a minor is detained for the purposes of educational supervision;

(e) when someone who is mentally ill is detained for their own protection or the protection of others; and

(f) the detention of individuals in connection with asylum, deportation or extradition.

Even if one of the limitations exists, any deprivation of liberty will only be within the requirements of Article 5 if it takes place in accordance with a procedure prescribed by law.

This means that, if the state deprives an individual of his liberty, that detention must not be carried out in an arbitrary manner - proper legal procedures must exist and must be followed if a deprivation of liberty is to be lawful. In *Saadi v United Kingdom* (2008) 47 EHRR 17, the ECtHR stated that a number of requirements need to be met in order to prevent a deprivation of liberty being arbitrary.

- Firstly, the detention has to be carried out in good faith. This means that it has to be closely connected to one of the purposes listed in Article 5(1)(a)–(f).
- Secondly, the detention must be necessary. This means that it can only be justified when less severe measures have been considered and rejected.
- Thirdly, the length of the detention should not exceed that reasonably required for the purpose pursued.
- Fourthly, proper records of the reason for the detention must be kept.
- Finally, the detention must be lawful within the terms of the national law of the state concerned.

For example, Article 5(1)(a) permits the lawful detention of a person after conviction by a competent court. Detention under this sub-paragraph will only be lawful if the term of imprisonment imposed is proportionate to the crime committed, and there is a clear link between the offence, the crime committed and the purpose for which the convicted person is detained in prison.

## 8.11 Article 6 – Right to a fair trial

### 8.11.1 Introduction

Article 6 has three sections, Article 6(1), Article 6(2) and Article 6(3).

Article 6(1) provides:

> In the determination of his civil rights and obligations or of any criminal charge against him, everyone is entitled to a fair and public hearing within a reasonable time by an independent and impartial tribunal established by law. Judgment shall be pronounced publicly but the press and public may be excluded from all or part of the trial in the interest of morals, public order or national security in a democratic society, where the interests of juveniles or the protection of the private life of the parties so require, or to the extent strictly necessary in the opinion of the court in special circumstances where publicity would prejudice the interests of justice.

Article 6(1) applies both to civil and criminal cases. We shall examine each type of case in turn.

### 8.11.2 Civil rights and obligations

Article 6 does not provide a definition of what is meant by the term 'civil rights and obligations'. Rather it is a term to which the ECtHR has given its own particular meaning, and that meaning goes beyond whether the national law of a particular state views a matter as being civil in nature.

As a starting point, the Court has said that Article 6 will only be invoked where a case concerns an individual attempting to assert a substantive legal right that is recognised in national law. Typical cases that are clearly civil in nature are when an individual seeks to enforce their private law rights in contract, tort or property. To take an example, the right to a fair trial under Article 6 would apply in a trial involving an alleged breach of contract by the supplier of goods, or a trial where an individual claims damages for personal injuries sustained in a road traffic accident caused by the negligence of another driver.

The Court has also recognised that employment law cases and the decisions of disciplinary bodies that have the effect of preventing an individual pursuing their chosen profession also fall with Article 6.

Article 6 can also apply to the administrative decisions taken by local authorities and other public authorities, such as the determination of an application for a licence to carry out a particular activity or decisions on the grant or refusal of planning permission. If a public authority fails to provide an applicant in such cases with a fair trial, the applicant will have recourse to judicial review proceedings to challenge the decision made.

### 8.11.3 Criminal charges

The definition of what amounts to a 'criminal charge' is again something that the ECtHR has determined. The leading case on this point *is Engel v The Netherlands* (1979–80) 1 EHRR 647, where the Court needed to determine whether penalties imposed on conscripted soldiers for breaching military discipline amounted to criminal charges within the meaning of Article 6. The Court found that the disciplinary measures did fall within the definition of criminal charges. The Court set out a number of criteria that had to be applied by a court when deciding whether a legal process constitutes the determination of a criminal charge.

The starting point for a court is to determine whether the national law of a state classifies a matter as being 'criminal' as opposed to disciplinary or administrative. If it is so classified, Article 6 will apply.

If, however, the matter is not viewed by national law as being criminal in nature, a court must then determine whether the proceedings against an individual are similar to a criminal trial. For example, do the proceedings require a finding of guilt or innocence to be made? The court should also consider what the purpose behind the proceedings is. If the purpose is to impose some form of punishment on an individual, it is likely that the proceedings will be seen as involving the determination of a criminal charge.

Following the principles outlined in *Engel*, the ECtHR has found that cases involving prison discipline and administrative offences concerning road traffic or environmental matters constitute the determination of a criminal charge.

### 8.11.4 Articles 6(2) and 6(3)

The provisions set out in Article 6(1) apply in both civil and criminal cases. Articles 6(2) and 6(3), however, apply only to criminal matters.

Article 6(2) provides that everyone charged with a criminal offence shall be presumed innocent until proven guilty according to law. The presumption of innocence is also a longstanding part of English criminal law.

Article 6(3) sets out a series of minimum rights that apply to those charged with a criminal offence. These rights are:

- to be told promptly and fully the detail of the case against them;
- to have sufficient time and facilities to prepare their defence;
- to defend themselves either personally or with the assistance of a lawyer, who should be provided by the state where necessary;
- to call witnesses in their defence and to cross-examine witnesses who have given evidence against them; and
- to have an interpreter provided free where necessary.

### 8.11.5 Article 6(1) and criminal cases

Article 6(1) sets out the elements that need to be met when the civil rights and obligations of an individual, or criminal charges against an individual, are being determined. This paragraph will concentrate on how these elements apply in a criminal context.

The elements are:

- an individual should have access to the court;
- that court should be independent and impartial;
- the trial should be in public and the decision of the court pronounced publicly;
- the trial should take place within a reasonable time; and
- the trial itself should be conducted in a fair way.

We shall consider these elements in turn.

#### 8.11.5.1 Access to the court

The right of access to the court is unlikely to cause problems in a criminal case as the defendant will be on the receiving end of proceedings brought against him by the state.

#### 8.11.5.2 Independent and impartial tribunal

It is a fundamental requirement of a criminal case that the court is independent of the state and does not exhibit bias towards the prosecution.

The case of *R (Anderson) v Secretary of State for the Home Department* was covered in **Chapter 4**. Anderson was convicted of murder and received a mandatory sentence of life imprisonment. He was, however, eligible for release on licence after he had served a minimum term of imprisonment, known as a tariff. Although the trial judge could recommend how long the tariff should be, the ultimate decision belonged with the Home Secretary, a member of the executive. The Home Secretary gave Anderson a tariff longer than that recommended by the trial judge. The House of Lords found that this violated Anderson's rights under Article 6(1) because, as a member of the executive with a political motive for wanting to be seen to be tough on crime, the Home Secretary was not an independent tribunal.

In terms of the impartiality of the court, the rules of natural justice remain relevant. If a judge or magistrate has a personal interest in the outcome of a case, they should automatically remove themselves - or be removed - from the case. If not, bias will be presumed. To take an example, a magistrate should not hear a case involving an alleged theft, if the magistrate was the actual victim of the theft.

If a judge or magistrate has an indirect interest in a case, there is no automatic presumption of bias, and any appellate court would need to apply the test in *Porter v Magill* (covered in **Chapter 6**), namely whether a fair-minded and informed observer would conclude there was a real possibility that the court was biased. This situation might arise, for example, if a magistrate was hearing a case involving an alleged theft from that magistrate's next door neighbour.

#### 8.11.5.3 Public trial

There is an expectation that a criminal trial will take place in public. The idea that the state should be able to routinely conduct secret trials behind closed doors is anathema to the ECHR. Trials that are open to the press and public deter courts from acting inappropriately and help to maintain public confidence in the criminal justice system.

Article 6(1) does, however, permit the press and public to be excluded from all or part of a trial in a limited number of situations. These situations are:

- where the exclusion is required in the interests of morality, public order or national security;
- where the exclusion is required in the interests of juveniles or the protection of the private life of the parties; or
- where there are special circumstances that, in the opinion of the court, would prejudice the interests of justice.

#### 8.11.5.4 Trial within a reasonable time

Article 6(1) requires criminal trials to be held within a reasonable time. This may be particularly important for a defendant who has been refused bail by the court, and who is remanded in custody until their trial date. In the United Kingdom, rules that are known as custody time limits ensure that defendants who are remanded in custody have their trials heard within a reasonable time. Briefly, these rules say that defendants should not be held in custody for longer than 182 days prior to their trial, although the limit was temporarily extended to eight months due to the backlog of cases caused by COVID-19.

#### 8.11.5.5 Effective participation

A defendant should be able to participate effectively in their trial. At its most basic, this means that the trial should take place in the defendant's presence. It also means that the defendant should be able to follow and understand the proceedings. This can be a particular issue where the defendant is a child.

In *T v United Kingdom* (2000) 30 EHRR 121, two 11-year-old boys were charged with the horrific murder of a toddler. The case attracted enormous media attention, and was heard in the adult Crown Court, following the rules and procedure of that court. Normally children and juveniles are tried before the Youth Court, which operates on a more informal basis. Although some steps were taken to enable the boys to understand the proceedings - such as the advocates removing their wigs and gowns - the ECtHR found that these measures were insufficient to ensure their effective participation in the trial.

#### 8.11.5.6 Exclusion of evidence

Another crucial area to consider when looking at the fairness of a criminal trial is how the court deals with prosecution evidence that has been obtained in an illegal or improper manner. The ECtHR has made it clear that detailed rules of criminal procedure and rules on the admissibility of evidence are matters for the national law of states who are signatories to the Convention.

Article 6(1) does not require a court to exclude evidence that has been obtained illegally or improperly. The Court has accepted that national laws may allow for the use of such evidence, and the Court will only involve itself where the overall circumstances of a case make a trial unfair within the meaning of Article 6.

In the UK, s 78 Police and Criminal Evidence Act 1984 (PACE) provides a trial court with a discretionary power to exclude any prosecution evidence. Section 78(1) provides:

> In any proceedings the court may refuse to allow evidence on which the prosecution proposes to rely to be given if it appears to the court that, having regard to all the circumstances, including the circumstances in which the evidence was obtained, the admission of the evidence would have such an adverse effect on the fairness of the proceedings that the court ought not to admit it.

The ECtHR considered the use of section 78 in the case *Khan v United Kingdom* (2000) 31 EHRR 45. Khan was convicted of drugs offences, largely on the basis of admissions he had made that were recorded on a bugging device that had been placed at premises Khan was visiting. The trial judge declined to exclude this evidence under s 78. Khan argued that this violated his right to a fair trial under Article 6 and also his right to privacy under Article 8.

The ECtHR found that the installation of the bugging device had violated Khan's right to privacy, as the law in England concerning the use by the police of a covert listening device was not sufficiently clear, and the installation of the bug was therefore unlawful. Despite this, the Court held that there had been no violation of Khan's right to a fair trial. The Court said that the key question for the purposes of Article 6 was whether the trial as a whole was fair. Khan had ample opportunity to challenge both the authenticity and the use of the recording, and had the domestic courts been of the view that the admission of the evidence would have given rise to substantive unfairness, they would have had a discretion to exclude it under s 78 PACE.

The approach that UK courts now take to evidence that the police have obtained improperly or unlawfully is to allow the prosecution to use this evidence if it is relevant to an issue in the case. The courts will only exclude this evidence if there is something unreliable about it.

There are, however, some circumstances in which the courts must exclude prosecution evidence. The courts will refuse to allow the use of evidence in criminal proceedings if that evidence has been obtained through torture or inhuman treatment. To allow such evidence to be used at trial would be in breach of Article 3 of the Convention. Also, under s 76 PACE courts must exclude evidence of any confession given by a defendant in criminal proceedings if that evidence has been obtained either through oppressive behaviour by the police, or if there are any other circumstances that make it unreliable.

### 8.11.6 Article 6(2) – The presumption of innocence

A requirement of a fair trial at common law is that a defendant charged with an offence is presumed to be innocent until such time as they are convicted. If the state chooses to bring criminal proceedings against one of its citizens, it is for the state to prove the guilt of that citizen, rather than the citizen needing to prove their innocence. The citizen is not required to give evidence at their trial, to call witnesses in support of their case or to provide evidence to the prosecution that might serve to incriminate them.

Article 6(2) repeats this rule. It states that 'Everyone charged with a criminal offence shall be presumed innocent until proved guilty according to law'.

8.11.6.1 Strict liability offences

The criminal law of the United Kingdom, like many other countries, contains a number of offences of strict liability. A strict liability offence is an offence of which a defendant is guilty if the prosecution can prove the existence of certain facts. It is not necessary for the prosecution to also show that the defendant had any form of guilty mind.

The ECtHR considered whether such offences breach the requirements of Article 6(2) in *Salabiaku v France* (1991) 13 EHRR 379. In this case, the defendant was charged with an offence of smuggling prohibited goods. Under French law, there was a presumption of guilt if anyone was found in possession of prohibited goods. The ECtHR found that this provision did not violate Article 6(2). The Court said that such laws are permissible provided that they are reasonable.

8.11.6.2 Right to silence

Article 6(2) does not state explicitly that a defendant has a right to remain silent when questioned about their involvement in an offence. This right can, however, be read into the presumption of innocence in Article 6(2), as this requires the prosecution to prove its case against the defendant.

8.11.6.3 Inferences from silence

Of far greater significance is whether provisions in the criminal law that allow courts to draw negative conclusions - or adverse inferences as they are usually called - from a defendant's refusal to answer questions are compatible with the presumption of innocence in Article 6(2).

The Criminal Justice and Public Order Act 1994 contains provisions that permit a court to draw adverse inferences if a defendant does not answer questions from the police, but at their trial puts forward a defence that they could have raised when questioned at the police station. The inference that the court may draw is that the defendant made up or fabricated their defence after leaving the police station.

Similar provisions allow a court to draw an adverse inference from a defendant's failure to account for an object or substance in their possession if asked to do so by the police, or if the defendant fails to account for the fact that they are arrested at the place where an offence has been committed shortly after the offence has occurred. The inference that the court may draw in these cases is that the defendant remained silent because they had no innocent explanation to give.

In *Murray v United Kingdom* (1996) 22 EHRR 29, Murray was charged with the offence of aiding and abetting the false imprisonment of a police informer, after being arrested in a property where Irish terrorists had been holding captive a police informer. Murray refused to answer any questions put to him at the police station, and was convicted at trial after the judge drew adverse inferences from that silence.

The ECtHR found that this did not violate his rights under Article 6 as, in the circumstances, his presence at the property clearly required an explanation and, in the absence of such an explanation, it was reasonable for adverse inferences to be drawn. However, although the Court said that there was no rule to prevent adverse inferences being drawn, it would be in breach of Article 6 were a defendant to be convicted on the basis of their silence alone.

### 8.11.7 Additional rights of the defendant in criminal proceedings

Article 6(3) of the ECHR provides some additional rights to anyone charged with a criminal offence. Although set out separately, these rights are really part of the overall right to a fair trial in Article 6(1).

We shall consider each right in turn.

#### 8.11.7.1 The right to be informed

Anyone charged with a criminal offence has the right to be told the nature and cause of the accusation against them. This information must be given promptly and in detail, so that the defendant can prepare any defence they may wish to raise. The information must be given in a language that the defendant understands. This requirement means that the police must tell an individual the detail of any offence for which that individual has been arrested and charged. It also obliges the prosecuting authorities to supply details of their case to the defendant, so that they know what evidence will be used against them at trial.

#### 8.11.7.2 The right to have adequate time and facilities to prepare the defence

A defendant must also be given adequate time and facilities for the preparation of their defence. A defendant may, for example, require time to contact witnesses who may assist their defence or to obtain documents relevant to their defence.

#### 8.11.7.3 The right to defend themselves or have legal representation

A further right that the defendant has is to defend themselves in person or with legal assistance. If a defendant is unable to pay for that assistance, it should be provided free of charge when the interests of justice so require.

#### 8.11.7.4 The right to call and cross-examine witnesses

In a criminal trial, evidence will be called. This may be in the form of documents or other exhibits, but usually the evidence comes from witnesses who give oral evidence. A defendant has the right to have examined witnesses against them and to obtain the attendance and examination of witnesses on their own behalf.

There are circumstances when a defendant may be unable to cross-examine a witness, if, for example, that witness has died or is overseas. In such cases, the written statement of the absent witness may be read out to the court. This will not breach Article 6, although the judge will direct the jury to treat such evidence with caution as it cannot be tested by the defendant. Occasionally, the identity of a witness may be withheld by the prosecution. This might, for example, occur in a case involving matters of national security. The giving of evidence in this way will not breach Article 6, but again the trial judge must give appropriate directions to the jury.

#### 8.11.7.5 The right to have the free assistance of an interpreter if required

The final right set out in Article 6(3) requires the court to ensure that an interpreter is available if a defendant is unable to understand the language of the court.

## 8.12 Retrospective crimes

Article 7 provides that a person cannot be charged with a criminal offence for conduct that was not a crime when they committed it. This means that the state must clearly define what constitutes a criminal offence so people know when they are breaking the law. It is also a violation of Article 7 for the courts to impose a heavier penalty than was applicable at the time the offence was committed.

In *SW v United Kingdom; CR v United Kingdom* (1995) 21 EHRR 363 the applicants had been convicted of raping their wives. They complained that they had been made retrospectively criminally liable for rape within marriage, since at the time they committed their offences, an exception in the criminal law for intercourse in marriage still existed. Accordingly, they claimed that their actions were not criminal at the time they had been committed, and so there was a violation of Article 7. The ECtHR rejected the argument, as Article 7 did not preclude the gradual clarification of the principles of criminal liability on a case-by-case basis provided the development could reasonably be foreseen.

Article 7(2) ECHR contains an exception, which is that people can still be prosecuted retrospectively for conduct that was 'criminal according to the general principles of law recognised by civilised nations', even if the conduct was not criminal at the time it was carried out. This was included to ensure that after World War II Article 7(1) did not prevent individuals from being prosecuted for war crimes that did not constitute criminal offences in Nazi Germany and other relevant states at the time of their commission.

## 8.13 Absolute and limited rights: conclusion

This completes our consideration of some of the absolute and limited rights under the ECHR. As you have seen, absolute rights cannot be interfered with at all, whilst limited rights can be curtailed only in very specific circumstances. It is a case of judicial interpretation of the scope of each right and how widely the courts are prepared to apply it and (where applicable) any exceptions and limitations.

## 8.14 Qualified rights

### 8.14.1 Introduction

We are now going to move on to consider some of the qualified rights under the Convention in more detail. As we have already seen, these qualified rights have much wider qualifications written into them (see **8.5** above). A Government can only lawfully interfere with a qualified right if the interference is prescribed by law, has a legitimate aim and is necessary in a democratic society. You will now consider the 'proportionality test' in more detail, which is the test the courts apply when deciding whether interference with a qualified right is 'necessary in a democratic society'.

### 8.14.2 The proportionality test

The 'proportionality test' is used by the courts when states are seeking to justify interfering with a qualified Convention right. The doctrine of proportionality ensures that there is a fair balance between pursuing a legitimate aim and the protection of Convention rights. The test was originally set out in the case of *R (Daly) v Secretary of State for the Home Department* [2001] 2 AC 532. It was then built on in *Huang v Secretary of State for the Home Department* [2007] UKHL 11. The two tests were then combined in the case of *Bank Mellat v HM Treasury (No 2)* [2013] UKSC 39. In the *Bank Mellat* case the Supreme Court set out the following four-part test:

(i) whether the objective of the measure complained of is sufficiently important to justify the limitation of a fundamental right;

(ii) whether the measure is rationally connected to the objective;

(iii) whether a less intrusive measure could have been used; and

(iv) whether, having regard to these matters and to the severity of the consequences, a fair balance has been struck between the rights of the individual and the interests of the community.

*The case of* R (Swami Suryananda) v Welsh Ministers *[2007] EWCA Civ 893 shows how this test works in practice. Following the increased incidence of bovine tuberculosis amongst cattle, the Welsh Government adopted a policy of slaughtering all positively tested cattle to reduce the spread of the disease. A Hindu community's temple bullock tested positive. Its slaughter would have been a particularly sacrilegious act to the community, so they sought to have it excepted from the policy of automatic slaughter, suggesting instead a regime of isolation and testing. The ministers entered into a dialogue with the community, and took account of expert evidence before making the decision to slaughter the bullock.*

*The community applied for judicial review of the decision but, after success at first instance, lost in the Court of Appeal, which approached the case in the following way.*

*The Court asked if the slaughter of the bullock engaged the rights of the Hindu community under Article 9. The Court accepted that this was the case because the slaughter of the bullock was a violation of the community's religious beliefs.*

*The Court of Appeal then applied the test set out in Article 9(2).*

*Firstly, the slaughter of the bullock had to be prescribed by law. This requirement was satisfied because the ministers were using powers given to them in the Animal Health Act 1981.*

*Secondly, the slaughter of the bullock had to be in pursuit of a legitimate aim. One of the legitimate aims contained in Article 9(2) is the protection of health. As the slaughter of the bullock was intended to prevent the spread of bovine tuberculosis, this requirement was met. The Court also said that another legitimate aim - the economic well-being of the country - was also relevant as the spread of bovine tuberculosis was having a devastating effect upon the rural economy in Wales.*

*Finally, the Court of Appeal considered whether the decision to slaughter the bullock was proportionate. The Court said that it was. Stopping the spread of bovine tuberculosis in Wales was an objective that was sufficiently important to limit the rights of the Hindu community. As the temple bullock had tested positive for this disease, its slaughter was a rational way to stop the spread of the disease. The Welsh ministers had considered alternatives, such as quarantining the animal, but had obtained expert evidence to suggest that this would not prevent the spread of this highly contagious disease. The Court found ultimately that an appropriate balance had been struck between the rights of the Hindu community and the rights of the wider Welsh community - whilst the slaughter of the bullock was a significant interference with the community's religious beliefs, it was justified given the catastrophic consequences the disease could have were it not controlled.*

## 8.15 Article 8 – Right to respect for private and family life

### 8.15.1 Introduction

Article 8 guarantees respect for four things: a person's private life, family life, home and correspondence.

A lot of issues have been held to come within the scope of a person's private life, including:

(a) bodily integrity (eg being forced to have medical treatment);

(b) personal autonomy (the right to make decisions about how you live your life);

(c) sexuality; and

(d) personal information (its holding, use or disclosure).

*A case concerning an individual's Article 8 rights is* Peck v United Kingdom *(2003) 36 EHRR 41. Mr Peck (P) was standing in the street, attempting suicide by cutting his wrists.*

*He was captured on CCTV and, although the CCTV images did not show the attempted suicide, they clearly identified P brandishing a knife in a public place. The police attended the scene. P was not charged with any criminal offence, but the CCTV images were later used in a campaign by the authorities to reflect the effectiveness of CCTV in combatting crime. There was no attempt to mask P's identity. P complained to the relevant media commissions about the disclosures and unsuccessfully sought judicial review of the disclosure.*

*The ECtHR found that the disclosure by the local council of the relevant footage constituted serious interference with P's right to respect for his private life. Although disclosure pursued the legitimate aim of prevention of disorder and crime, it was disproportionate (no attempt was made to conceal P's identity or obtain his consent). The Court acknowledged that P was in a public street when he was filmed, but stated that 'he was not there for the purpose of participating in any public event and he was not a public figure'.*

In the case of *S and Marper v the United Kingdom* (2008) (Grand Chamber), (2009) 48 EHRR 50, the ECtHR held that the retention of fingerprints and DNA, as permitted by certain of the UK's statutory provisions, clearly both invoked Article 8 and breached the applicants' rights under that Article. The relevant statutory provisions were contained in PACE. They provided for the indefinite retention of fingerprints and DNA samples obtained as a result of being investigated, even where the person was subsequently acquitted of the offence being investigated or the proceedings against them were discontinued.

The ECtHR concluded that the retention constituted 'a disproportionate interference with the applicants' right to respect for private life and cannot be regarded as necessary in a democratic society'. This conflicted with a previous decision of the House of Lords in *R (S) v Chief Constable of South Yorkshire* [2004] UKHL 39. In this case their Lordships had held by majority that Article 8(1) was not engaged and held unanimously that the retention was justified under Article 8(2).

To comply with the ECtHR's judgment, Parliament enacted the Protection of Freedoms Act 2012, which includes provisions requiring the deletion of some DNA profiles from the DNA database; these provisions came into force on 31 October 2013.

#### 8.15.1.1 Family life

Family life covers one's relationship with one's close family, and includes a man and a woman who are not married but who live in a stable relationship.

#### 8.15.1.2 Home

This means the right to respect for one's home and where one currently lives.

#### 8.15.1.3 Correspondence

This includes phone calls, letters and e-mails.

### 8.15.2 Article 8 and deportation, removal and extradition

You have seen earlier on in the chapter (**8.8.2** above) that the provisions of the ECHR have had a significant impact in cases where the Government seeks to deport, remove or extradite an individual from the United Kingdom. Deportation, extradition and removal cases may also engage Article 8, particularly the right to respect for family life.

Some of these cases concern the conditions an individual will face in the country to which they are being sent. In *R (Razgar) v Secretary of State for the Home Department* [2004] UKHL 27, Razgar was a failed asylum seeker who was due to be removed back to Germany – from where he had come to the UK – or Iraq, his country of origin. Razgar was receiving psychiatric treatment for depression and post-traumatic stress disorder arising from his alleged ill-treatment in Iraq, and his fear of ill-treatment in Germany. He argued that the foreseeable consequences for his mental health were he to be removed from the UK would engage his rights under Article 8, and that his removal could not be justified under Article 8(2).

Although Razgar's particular claim was dismissed, the House of Lords held that Article 8 could be engaged where the main issue was not the severance of the family and social ties that the applicant had enjoyed in the expelling country, but was rather the consequence for their mental or physical health of removal to the receiving country. Their Lordships did, however, say that the threshold for establishing this was high, and would require an applicant to show that the violation of their rights would be flagrant. This would need to be something very much more extreme than showing that healthcare standards in the receiving country were not as good as those in the expelling country.

The much more usual situation in which those required to leave the UK raise arguments under Article 8 is when an individual argues that their deportation, removal or extradition will disproportionately damage family ties and relationships that they have established while in the UK.

This was considered by the European Court of Human Rights in *Uner v The Netherlands* (2007) 45 EHRR 14. Uner was born in Turkey, but had moved to the Netherlands with his mother and two brothers in 1981, when he was 12 years old. In 1988 he obtained a permanent residence permit. In 1991, Uner entered into a relationship with a Dutch national. They started living together shortly afterwards and had a son in 1992. They lived together for some 16 months before Uner moved out. In 1994, Uner was convicted of manslaughter and assault. He had two previous convictions in the Netherlands for violent offences. He was sentenced to seven years' imprisonment.

Uner continued to see his partner while he was in prison and a second child was born to the couple in 1996. In 1997, Uner's permanent residence permit was withdrawn and a 10-year exclusion order imposed on him in view of his conviction and sentence. This meant that he could not live in the Netherlands for a 10-year period.

The Dutch authorities considered that the general interest in ensuring public safety outweighed Uner's interest in being able to continue his family life in the Netherlands. Uner argued that the authorities had violated his rights under Article 8 by failing to strike a fair balance between those competing interests.

The ECtHR held that the deportation, removal or extradition of an individual could engage the right to respect for his family life under Article 8(1) and, if it did, there were several factors that the court needed to apply to determine if that deportation, removal or extradition was proportionate. These were:

1. The length of time the individual has been in the country;
2. The seriousness of the offences that the individual has committed;
3. Details of the particular family circumstances of the individual, such as the age of their children or the length of any relationship;
4. The interests of the children;
5. The seriousness of the difficulties that the family may experience in the receiving country; and
6. The nature of the ties that the individual has with both the expelling and the receiving country.

In Uner's case, the Court found that there had been no violation of Article 8. Whilst Uner had strong ties to the Netherlands, he had only lived with his partner and first-born son for a short period. He had then put an end to the cohabitation and had never lived with the second child. Whilst Uner had arrived in the Netherlands at a young age, he still had social and cultural ties with Turkey. The offences of manslaughter and assault committed by Uner were of a very serious nature. Taking his previous convictions into account, Uner had criminal propensities. Also, Uner's children were still very young and thus of an adaptable age. The Court said that given the nature and seriousness of Uner's offences, the Netherlands had struck a fair balance between its own interests and those of Uner.

We will be analysing Article 8 further in the next chapter, which looks at conflicting Convention rights.

### 8.15.3 Climate change litigation

Climate change litigation is becoming a significant feature of environmental law, as illustrated by the ECtHR's landmark judgment in Verein *KlimaSeniorinnen Schweiz v Switzerland*, Application No 53600/20, unreported 9 April 2024 (ECHR (Grand Chamber)). The applicants, including the Swiss association Verein KlimaSeniorinnen Schweiz (established to campaign for climate protection on behalf of its members), argued that the Swiss authorities were not taking adequate measures to mitigate the effects of climate change in violation of Convention rights. The ECtHR declared that the individual applicants' complaints were inadmissible, but the association had the requisite standing to lodge a claim as it represented those subject to threats or adverse effects of climate change.

On the substance of the claim, the ECtHR held that there had been a violation of Article 8 as it encompassed a right for individuals to effective protection by State authorities from serious adverse effects of climate change on their life, health, well-being, and quality of life. While the ECtHR recognised that national authorities enjoy wide discretion regarding the choice of means to pursue objectives, the Swiss authorities had breached their obligations as they had failed to establish a domestic regulatory framework for limiting greenhouse gas emissions and had previously missed emission reduction targets.

---

## 8.16 Article 9 – Freedom of thought, conscience and religion

### 8.16.1 Introduction

Article 9(1) provides: 'Everyone has the right to freedom of thought, conscience and religion; this right includes freedom to change his religion or belief and freedom, either alone or in community with others and in public or private, to manifest his religion or belief, in worship, teaching, practice and observance.'

So far as freedom of thought, conscience and religion are concerned, it is an absolute right. However, the right to manifest religion or belief is a qualified right and may therefore be subject to restrictions that are prescribed by law, in pursuit of a legitimate aim and are proportionate.

### 8.16.2 Restrictions

An issue that has arisen in recent years is the extent to which individuals may be prevented from manifesting their religious beliefs either through not being permitted to wear particular items of clothing or by being required to carry out certain tasks. This has arisen in the context of what an individual may not wear or may be required to do at work, and the restrictions that a school may impose on items of clothing worn by its pupils.

*The leading case on restrictions that may lawfully be imposed in the workplace is* Eweida and others v United Kingdom *(2013) 57 EHRR 8. In this case, four separate applicants argued that their respective employers had either imposed restrictions on dress or dismissed them in violation of their rights under Article 9. They had been unsuccessful before the domestic UK courts.*

(a) *Eweida*

*Eweida had been employed by British Airways. She wanted to wear a cross as a sign of her commitment to the Christian faith. Between September 2006 and February 2007, she was not allowed to remain in her post whilst visibly wearing the cross.*

(b) *Chaplin*

*Chaplin was a Christian who had worn a cross since 1971. She had been employed as a nurse by an NHS trust. Her employer's uniform policy prohibited the wearing of necklaces to reduce the risk of injury when handling patients. When she refused to remove the cross and chain she was wearing, she was moved to a non-nursing post, which shortly thereafter ceased to exist.*

(c) *Lavelle*

*Lavelle had been employed by a local authority as a registrar of births, deaths and marriages. She was a Christian and believed that same-sex civil partnerships were contrary to God's law. She refused to be designated as a registrar of civil partnerships, which resulted in disciplinary proceedings and the loss of her job.*

(d) *MacFarlane*

*MacFarlane, a Christian, had been employed by Relate - a marriage guidance organisation - which had a policy of requiring staff to provide services equally to heterosexual and homosexual couples. He refused to commit himself to providing psycho-sexual counselling to same-sex couples, which resulted in disciplinary proceedings being brought against him.*

*The ECtHR considered each application in turn.*

(a) *Eweida - outcome*

*The Court found that a fair balance had not been struck. On one side of the argument was Eweida's desire to manifest her religious belief. On the other was the employer's wish to project a certain corporate image. Whilst the Court accepted that this aim was legitimate, it said that the domestic courts had accorded it too much weight. Eweida's cross was discreet and could not have detracted from her professional appearance, and there was no evidence that the wearing of other, previously authorised, items of religious clothing by other employees had had any negative impact on British Airways' brand or image. The Court found that the domestic authorities had failed sufficiently to protect Eweida's right to manifest her religion, in breach of their positive obligation under Article 9.*

(b) *Chaplin - outcome*

*The Court found that the reason for asking Chaplin to remove her cross - namely the protection of health and safety on a hospital ward - was much more important than the reason given to Eweida. The Court also said that hospital managers were better placed to make decisions about clinical safety than a court. The measures were therefore not disproportionate. It followed that the relevant interference with her freedom to manifest her religion was necessary in a democratic society and that there had been no breach of Article 9.*

(c) *Lavelle - outcome*

*The Court accepted that, given the strength of Lavelle's religious conviction, she considered that she had no choice but to face disciplinary action and ultimately lose her job, rather than be designated a civil partnership registrar. On the other hand, the local authority's policy aimed to secure the rights of others, which were also protected under the Convention. The Court said that national authorities should be given a wide margin of appreciation when it came to striking a balance between competing Convention rights. Therefore, the local authority that brought the disciplinary proceedings and the domestic courts that had rejected Lavelle's claim had not violated Article 9.*

(d) *MacFarlane - outcome*

*The Court accepted that the loss of his job was a severe sanction with grave consequences for MacFarlane. However, the most important factor was that the employer's action was intended to secure the implementation of its policy of providing a service without discrimination. The state authorities should be given a wide margin of appreciation in deciding where to strike the balance between MacFarlane's right to manifest his religious belief and the employer's interest in securing the rights of others. The refusal by the domestic courts to uphold MacFarlane's complaints therefore did not give rise to a breach of Article 9.*

The leading case concerning the restrictions that a school may impose on the items of clothing worn by its pupils is *R (Begum) v Governors of Denbigh High School* [2006] UKHL 15. In this case, a schoolgirl called Shabina Begum had been excluded from her school for failure to comply with her school's dress code. Begum was Muslim and wished to wear a jilbab to school, rather than a shalwar kameez as required by the school's uniform policy. A jilbab is a more concealing form of dress than a shalwar kameez. She argued that her expulsion was a violation of her rights under Article 9, because the shalwar kameez did not comply with the requirements of her religion.

The House of Lords found that there had been no violation of Shabina Begum's right to manifest her religious beliefs under Article 9. The Lords said that what constituted interference depended on all the circumstances of the case, including the extent to which an individual could reasonably expect to be at liberty to manifest their beliefs in practice.

In this case, Begum's family had chosen for her a school outside their own catchment area. There was no evidence to show that there was any difficulty in her attending one of the three schools in her catchment area that permitted the wearing of the jilbab. Also, Shabina Begum had worn the shalwar kameez during her first two years at the school without objection. In addition, the school had taken pains to devise a uniform policy that respected Muslim beliefs but did so in an inclusive, unthreatening and uncompetitive way. The school had enjoyed a period of harmony and success to which the uniform policy was thought to contribute, and the rules were acceptable to mainstream Muslim opinion.

For all these reasons, the House of Lords found that the school had acted in a proportionate manner, and there had been no unlawful interference with Shabina Begum's rights.

## 8.17 Article 10 – Freedom of expression

### 8.17.1 Introduction

Article 10(1) of the ECHR gives an individual the right to freedom of expression, which includes 'freedom to hold opinions and to receive and impart information and ideas without interference by public authority'. But, just as with Article 9, Article 10 is a qualified right, and may therefore be subject to restrictions that are prescribed by law, in pursuit of a legitimate aim and are proportionate to that aim.

There are several forms that freedom of expression may take. It may, for example, be artistic in nature, such as the publication of a book that has graphic sexual content, or it may be a newspaper printing a story about the private life of a celebrity. However, the most important form of freedom of expression is the expression of views that are political in nature. For the state to attempt to suppress the expression of political views to which it objects would be a restriction on a fundamental right. It is no coincidence that one of the hallmarks of a dictatorial or oppressive state is the crushing of any political dissent.

### 8.17.2 Qualifications

Although the ECtHR has repeatedly stressed the importance of protecting political free speech, there are circumstances in which a state may lawfully interfere with the exercise of this right, particularly where matters of national security are concerned. An example of this is *Observer and The Guardian v United Kingdom* (1992) 14 EHRR 153. In this case, various newspapers complained that the granting of interim injunctions restraining them from publishing extracts from a book called 'Spycatcher' contravened their right to freedom of expression. The book was written by a former member of the security services, and contained allegations of unlawful behaviour by the British security service.

The Court was satisfied that the interim injunctions were lawful and in pursuit of the legitimate aim of national security. In addition, the injunctions were proportionate as they were only obtained on an interim basis, pending a final hearing to determine whether publication of the book should be allowed.

### 8.17.3 Ban on political advertising

A further issue concerning political free speech and Article 10 is the ban on broadcast political advertising in the UK, as set out in the Communications Act 2003. The compatibility of this ban with the rights set out in Article 10 was considered by the ECtHR in *Animal Defenders v United Kingdom* [2013] ECHR 362.

Animal Defenders campaigned against the use of animals in commerce, science and leisure. It had wished to broadcast a television advertisement, but the UK's relevant broadcasting authority refused to clear it for broadcast as its objectives were political as defined in the Communications Act. The House of Lords rejected Animal Defender's argument that this prohibition breached its Article 10 rights.

It was agreed that the prohibition was an interference with Animal Defender's Article 10 rights, but that it pursued the legitimate aim of preserving the impartiality of broadcasting and therefore protected the democratic process. The issue was the measure's proportionality.

The House of Lords found that the ban on broadcast political advertising had been the culmination of an extensive consideration by Parliament, having been reported on and commented on by specialist bodies, and having been enacted with support from all political parties. Further, a range of alternative media were available to Animal Defenders to disseminate their views. The ECtHR also found that the ban was a proportionate means of ensuring that the facts about the perceived exploitation of animals were not distorted. The Court's conclusion was that, for all these reasons, the ban was proportionate and did not violate Article 10.

### 8.17.4 Hate speech

Political free speech is given a high degree of protection by the courts. Free speech that is offensive, shocking or disturbing is also protected by Article 10 and should not be restricted by the state. But what is the position with speech that goes beyond this and, for example, expresses racial or religious intolerance?

In *Jersild v Denmark* (1995) 19 EHRR 1, a Danish journalist conducted a television interview with some young people, known as 'green jackets', who made racist remarks in the course of the interview. The ECtHR ruled that the expression of outright racist views would not be protected by Article 10 because such views went beyond what was offensive, shocking or disturbing.

In the United Kingdom, the Public Order Act of 1986 creates several criminal offences in connection with racial, religious and sexual hatred. However, criticism of religions is permitted to a certain extent, because there are wider ethical and moral considerations that might lead someone to criticise particular religious beliefs.

A particular provision of the Public Order Act has given rise to concern due to its implications for freedom of expression. This is s 5, which provides that it is a criminal offence for someone to use threatening or abusive words or behaviour, or to display any writing, sign or other visible representation that is threatening or abusive, within the hearing or sight of a person likely to be caused harassment, alarm or distress by such actions. A defendant does have a defence if they can show that their conduct was reasonable.

Arguments involving whether a conviction for an offence under s 5 may be in violation of the right to freedom of expression have come before domestic courts on several occasions.

In *Percy v DPP* [2001] EWHC Admin 1125, Percy – who was a protester against American military policy – appealed against her conviction for an offence under s 5. Percy had defaced an American flag, putting a stripe across the stars and writing the words 'Stop Star Wars' across the stripes. Then, while outside an American airbase, she stepped in front of a vehicle containing American service personnel, put the flag on the road and trod upon it. At her trial, the judge found that the restrictions on Percy's freedom of expression resulting from her conviction were necessary and proportionate.

The Divisional Court found, however, that her conviction had not been compatible with her right to freedom of expression. The fact that Percy could have demonstrated her message by means other than defacing the flag was a factor to be taken into account but only one of a number of factors. The Court said that other relevant considerations in similar cases included:

- whether the behaviour had gone beyond legitimate protest;
- whether the behaviour had been part of an open expression on an issue of public interest but had been disproportionate and unreasonable;
- whether the individual could have expressed their views in another way;
- the knowledge of the individual of the likely effect of their conduct upon those who witnessed it; and
- whether the use of any object – in this instance a flag – had no relevance to the conveying of the message of protest and had been used as a gratuitous and calculated insult.

The case of *Norwood v United Kingdom (Admissibility)* (23131/03) (2005) 40 EHRR SE11 is a good illustration of the ECtHR's approach to hate speech. Norwood was convicted for an offence of causing alarm or distress under s 5. Norwood was a regional organiser of the British National Party who had had visibly displayed a poster on the window of his flat bearing the words 'Islam out of Britain', with graphic references to the attacks on the World Trade Centre on 11 September 2001.

After being convicted in the UK, Norwood applied to the ECtHR, but his application was rejected because the views he sought to express were aimed at undermining others and were therefore incompatible with the values that underpinned the ECHR, such as tolerance, respect and non-discrimination.

## 8.18 Article 11 – Freedom of assembly and association

Article 11 of the ECHR gives a right of peaceful assembly, and the separate right of freedom of association. The effective exercise of these freedoms is of crucial importance for free expression and for protection of groups of a social, cultural, political and economic nature.

Conduct will fall within scope of Article 11 provided two conditions are satisfied. Firstly, the conduct must constitute 'peaceful assembly'. This covers 'both private meetings, meetings on public highways, as well as static meetings and public processions'. Article 11 does not, however, afford protection to violent behaviour.

### 8.18.1 Freedom of assembly

In *Tabernacle v Secretary of State for Defence* [2009] EWCA Civ 23, the appellant (Tabernacle) appealed against a decision refusing to quash a byelaw that prevented Tabernacle from camping in the vicinity of the Atomic Weapons Establishment at Aldermaston. The camp had been going for 23 years, with the women assembling on the land for the second weekend of every month. They held vigils, meetings and demonstrations and the protest was always peaceful. The Secretary of State passed byelaws in 2007 that prohibited camping in the 'Controlled Areas', which included the area where the peace camp had always been held.

The Court of Appeal held that the byelaw's interference with Tabernacle's rights was far from being weak or insubstantial and the Secretary of State had to demonstrate under Article 10(2) a substantial objective justification for the particular byelaw, amounting to a pressing social need. In the circumstances, the effect of the 2007 Byelaws was to violate Tabernacle's rights of free expression and association guaranteed by Articles 10 and 11.

Often, as in this case, the two rights are interlinked. The judge regarded Article 11 not as an autonomous claim in its own right, but as underlining the mode of free expression relied on – a communal protest in a camp.

Article 11 does create a positive right to freedom of assembly, and this might suggest that the police should protect those trying to hold a lawful meeting. The ECtHR has said that the state may infringe freedom of assembly if it does not take positive measures to protect the exercise of the right and to protect protesters from those wishing to stop their protest or attack them (*Plattform 'Artze fur das Leben' v Austria* (1991) 13 EHRR 204). However, the state is not subject to an absolute obligation to facilitate peaceful protest, so it may be lawful for the authorities to restrict a protest if it is provoking, or is likely to provoke, others to respond violently.

### 8.18.2 Freedom of association

Article 11 does not merely contain the right to freedom of assembly. It also covers the right to freedom of association. Article 11(1) provides that 'Everyone has the right to ... freedom of association with others'. What does this mean?

The right to freedom of association is designed to protect an individual's right to participate with other people in an organised way in pursuit of a common aim. It applies to a wide variety of bodies, including pressure groups, political parties and religious organisations. In the absence of the right to freedom of association, the state could ban those groups of which it does not approve, such as opposition political parties or movements.

Article 11 is, however, qualified. As with the other qualified rights you have considered, the state may lawfully limit the exercise of the right to freedom of association provided that limitation is prescribed by law, is in pursuit of a legitimate aim, and is proportionate to that aim.

There are occasions on which a state has sought to proscribe particular political parties or associations. Proscription means simply that a party or association is banned.

The ECtHR first considered the proscription of political parties in the *United Communist Party of Turkey v Turkey* (1998) 26 EHRR 121. The United Communist Party of Turkey was formed in 1990. Turkish law required that all new political parties had to have rules, aims and a political programme that was compatible with the country's constitution. The authorities in Turkey applied to the country's constitutional court to have the United Communist Party dissolved. It was alleged that the Party had violated the Turkish constitution by having incorporated the word 'communist' into its name, and by having carried on activities likely to undermine the territorial integrity of the state, through advocating the establishment of a separate Kurdish nation. In July 1991, the constitutional court made an order dissolving the Party, based on the inclusion in its name of the constitutionally prohibited word 'communist' and the alleged encouragement of Kurdish separatism. The Party and its leaders applied to the ECtHR, complaining that the dissolution of the party infringed their right to freedom of association as guaranteed by Article 11.

The Court found that the dissolution of the Party was permitted under Turkish law and arguably had a legitimate aim - national security. However the Court found the ban to be disproportionate. The Court said that political parties had an essential role in ensuring pluralism and the proper functioning of democracy, and Article 11 therefore had to be viewed in the light of the protection of freedom of expression as guaranteed by Article 10.

The Court held that a political party's choice of name could not justify its dissolution in the absence of other relevant and sufficient circumstances, and there was no evidence that the United Communist Party represented a real threat to Turkish society or to the Turkish state. Also, a detailed reading of the Party's programme showed that it intended to resolve the Kurdish issue through dialogue, not violence.

The Court accordingly concluded that the drastic measure of dissolving the Party breached Article 11.

In 2003, the European Court considered another Turkish case that involved freedom of association. The case, *Refah Partisi (the Welfare Party) v Turkey* (2003) 37 EHRR 1, was very controversial.

Refah Partisi was a political party set up in 1983. By 1996, it was able to form a government in coalition with another party and its leader was Prime Minister. In 1997, Turkey's state counsel successfully applied to the country's constitutional court for the dissolution of Refah Partisi, on the ground that its activities were contrary to the principle of the separation of the state from religious institutions as set out in the Turkish constitution, and also because some of its members had called for the establishment of an Islamic state and the imposition of sharia law in Turkey. Refah Partisi applied to the European Court of Human Rights, arguing that the interference with its rights under Article 11 had been violated.

The Court found that the dissolution of the Refah Partisi did not violate Article 11. Although there had been an interference with the party members' rights under Article 11, this was justified as it met the urgent need to protect democracy, for which purpose the state could take pre-emptive steps where necessary. Refah Partisi's commitment to implement the strict requirements of Muslim sharia law was not compatible with Turkey's secular democracy. The Court said that the model of society and government that Refah Partisi wished to introduce would undermine the very basis on which the ECHR rested.

The fact that Refah Partisi could have gone on to implement those policies in government meant that it posed an immediate danger to Turkish democracy. Given the nature and immediacy of the threat, the actions of the Turkish Constitutional Court in dissolving the Party were proportionate.

## 8.19 Article 12 – The right to marry

Article 12 protects the right of men and women of marriageable age to marry and to start a family.

### 8.19.1 Scope

The ECtHR ruled in 2002 that the right extends to transsexual people (*Goodwin v United Kingdom* (2002) 35 EHRR 18). The ECtHR has, however, held that Article 12 does not require the state to recognise same-sex marriages (*Chapin and Charpentier v France* [2016] ECHR 504).

### 8.19.2 Restrictions to this right

The right to marry is subject to national laws on marriage, including those that make marriage illegal between certain types of people (for example, close relatives).

Although the Government is able to restrict the right to marry, any restrictions must not be arbitrary and not interfere with the essential principle of the right. Thus, The ECtHR held in

*B v United Kingdom* (2004) 39 EHRR SE19 that, in prohibiting the marriage of a father-in-law to a daughter-in-law, the Marriage Act 1949 violated Article 12. The Marriage Act was accordingly amended.

## 8.20 Article 13 – The right to an effective remedy

Article 13 provides for the right for an effective remedy before national authorities for violations of rights under the Convention.

## 8.21 Article 14 – Protection from discrimination

Article 14 requires that all of the rights and freedoms set out in the ECHR must be protected and applied without discrimination on any ground such as sex, race, colour, language, religion, political or other opinion, national or social origin, association with a national minority, property, birth or other status.

The protection against discrimination in the ECHR is not 'free-standing'. To rely on this right, a victim must show that the discrimination has affected their enjoyment of one or more of the other rights in the Convention.

Article 14 covers both direct and indirect discrimination.

## 8.22 Article 1 of the First Protocol – Protection of property

### 8.22.1 Introduction

This Article guarantees the right to peaceful enjoyment of possessions (both land (realty) and personal property).

'Peaceful enjoyment' of property would, on its face, suggest that it covers a wide range of situations. However, only interference that affects the financial value of property or possessions will engage the right to 'peaceful enjoyment' of them. Thus, for example, noise nuisance will only interfere with peaceful enjoyment to the extent that it reduces the value of that property.

### 8.22.2 Restrictions

There are some situations in which public authorities can deprive people of their property or restrict the way they can use them. This is only possible where the authority can show that its action is lawful and necessary for the public interest. Generally speaking, a 'deprivation of property' under this Article will not be considered to be in the public interest unless the owner receives compensation. The state must strike a fair balance between the interests of a property owner and the general interests of society as a whole.

Accordingly, a public authority wanting to use a compulsory purchase order to acquire property for public purposes must strike a fair balance between the rights of the individual property owners and the rights of the community. While a crucial factor in any such balance will be the availability of compensation reflecting the value of the property being compulsorily purchased, it is not necessarily decisive, as *R (L1T FM Holdings UK Ltd) v Chancellor of the Duchy of Lancaster* [2024] EWHC 2963 (Admin) shows.

In this case, the claimant challenged a government order to divest its shares in a broadband company over national security concerns, arguing a breach of Article 1 of Protocol 1 due to lack of compensation. The court held that full compensation is not guaranteed in all cases, and, here, a fair balance meant that the national security interest outweighed the claimant's financial interests. The claimant would still receive the proceeds of sale of its shares, and it was not disproportionate for the claimant, rather than the public, to bear the financial loss arising from the forced sale, especially given the risks inherent to large-scale investors in sensitive sectors.

This right does not affect the ability of public authorities to enforce taxes or fines.

## 8.23 Article 2 of the First Protocol – The right to education

### 8.23.1 Introduction

Article 2 of Protocol 1 provides: 'No person shall be denied the right to education. In the exercise of any functions which it assumes in relation to education and teaching, the state shall respect the rights of parents to ensure such education and teaching in conformity with their own religious and philosophical convictions. '

The leading case on the right to education is *Belgian Linguistic* (1968) 1 EHRR 252 in which the ECtHR stated that the rights protected in Article 2 of Protocol 1 are:

- a right to access to educational institutions existing at a given time. It does not require the Government to provide or subsidise any particular type of education.
- a right to official recognition of the studies a student has successfully completed;

Schools are allowed to use admission policies so long as they are objective and reasonable.

As the Article itself indicates, parents have a right to ensure their religious or philosophical beliefs are respected during their children's education. However, this is not an absolute guarantee and states may determine the content of their school curriculums, provided they are consistent with requirements of objectivity and pluralism and respect the parents' different religious and philosophical convictions.

### 8.22.2 Exclusions

Pupils who have been excluded from schools for disruptive behaviour have invoked this right, but usually without success, as the right is subject to limitations. In *Ali v United Kingdom* (2011) ECHR 17 the ECtHR held that the right did not preclude disciplinary measures such as expulsion or temporary exclusion, though to be lawful any such measures had to be foreseeable, had to pursue a legitimate aim and had to be proportionate to that aim. In determining whether an exclusion resulted in a denial of the right to education, the court would have to consider whether a fair balance had been struck between the exclusion and the justification for it. However, where an exclusion from a school is permanent, it is likely that states should ensure that pupils of school-going age receive education at another school.

## 8.24 Article 3 of the First Protocol – The right to free elections

Article 3 of Protocol 1 requires states to hold free elections at reasonable intervals by way of secret ballot.

The right to free elections is absolute, so it cannot be restricted in any way. However, governments have a wide margin of appreciation, and can decide what kind of electoral system to adopt – such as 'first past the post', as in UK general elections, or proportional representation.

Prisoners serving a custodial sentence in the UK do not have the right to vote. The ECtHR ruled in *Hirst v United Kingdom (No 2) (*2005) ECHR 681 that a blanket ban on all serving prisoners was not compatible with Article 3 of Protocol 1. Eventually, the UK Government agreed to allow prisoners who are released on temporary licence or on home detention curfew to vote (this did not require a change in legislation). The Council of Europe in December 2018 accepted that this is sufficient to comply with the ECtHR's judgment.

## 8.25 Article 1 of Protocol 13 – Abolition of the death penalty

This provides that the death penalty shall be abolished. This includes crimes committed during a war or when the threat of war is imminent. The UK ratified this Protocol in 2002.

## Summary

In this chapter you have examined the rights and freedoms guaranteed by the ECHR and how individuals can rely on them in practice.

- You examined how cases can reach the European Court of Human Rights, either through state action or individual petition.
- You then considered absolute, limited and qualified rights.
- Absolute rights are rights that cannot be limited or interfered with under any circumstances, even if strong public interest arguments were to exist. Article 2, the right to life, is an absolute right. However, there are exceptions that define its scope and if one of the exceptions exists, then there is no interference with this right. For example, if the police kill an armed person to prevent the murder of innocent people, then Article 2 is not engaged provided the police have used no more force than absolutely necessary.
- Limited rights can be restricted in certain circumstances as specified in the relevant Article of the ECHR. For example, Article 5, the right to liberty and security of the person, can be limited if a person is convicted and sentenced to prison. They are similar to absolute rights in the sense that, unlike qualified rights, they cannot be 'balanced' against the rights of other individuals or the public interest.
- Qualified rights may be interfered with in order to protect the rights of another or the wider public interest, eg Article 8, the right to private and family life. For example the state can interfere with a person's private life on grounds of national security provided the interference is prescribed by law, necessary in a democratic society and proportionate. UK courts use the text in the *Bank Mellat* case to evaluate proportionality.

## Sample questions

**Question 1**

The Waste Management Act 2015 (fictitious) established the Waste Disposal Commission to decide where incinerators to dispose of household waste shall be built in England and Wales. A woman has objected to a decision made by the Commission approving the building of an incinerator 200 metres from her home. Her main ground of objection is that emissions will harm her and other people living nearby. Experts had produced evidence to the Commission that there were other suitable sites in the locality further away from people's houses.

**Which of the following best describes whether the building of the incinerator breaches any of the woman's Convention rights?**

A The building of the incinerator does not engage any Convention rights as it is in the public interest.

B Although the building of the incinerator engages the woman's right to a private life, it is a proportionate interference in the public interest.

C Although the building of the incinerator engages the woman's right to a private life, it is prescribed by law and so cannot be challenged.

D Although the building of the incinerator is in the public interest, it is a disproportionate interference with the woman's right to a private life.

E The building of the incinerator is not prescribed by law and is a disproportionate interference with the woman's right to a private life.

**Answer**

Option D is correct. The woman may be able to argue that her Article 8 right (right to a private life) is being breached; accordingly option A is wrong as Article 8 is engaged. However, Article 8 is a qualified right. The qualification has a legal basis here – the Waste Management Act 2015; hence option E is wrong. The legitimate aim(s) being pursued by the Act are likely to be the 'economic well-being of the country'. However, the qualification must also be 'necessary in a democratic society'. Option C is therefore wrong because it incorrectly suggests that it is sufficient if the interference is prescribed by law.

As the qualification has a legal basis and the 2015 Act is pursuing a legitimate aim, it is necessary to apply the proportionality test. In other words, is the interference with the woman's rights proportionate to the objective being achieved, or would any lesser interference be possible? In this case, it seems likely that there are more suitable sites for the incinerator, away from residential areas. Option B is therefore wrong because it states the interference is proportionate.

**Question 2**

A country that is not a signatory to the European Convention on Human Rights ('the Convention') has asked the UK Government to extradite a woman living in the UK to stand trial for murder in that country. The woman holds the nationality of the country requesting her extradition, but not of any other country. The Secretary of State has ordered the woman's extradition and the woman has appealed to the High Court against the extradition order. During the hearing she produces evidence that she could face the death penalty if extradited and the High Court accepts the woman's evidence.

**Which of the following best explains whether the High Court would uphold the extradition order?**

A It would not uphold the order because the Convention prohibits extradition to non-signatory countries.

B It would not uphold the order because extraditing a person to stand trial for an offence that could result in the imposition of the death penalty would violate that person's Convention rights.

C It would not uphold the order because extraditing a person to stand trial for an offence that could result in the imposition of the death penalty fails to strike a fair balance between the rights of the individual and the interests of the community.

D It would uphold the order because it is not certain that the death penalty would be imposed on the woman if she was extradited.

E It would uphold the order because the Convention only protects the rights of people who hold the nationality of a state that has signed the Convention.

**Answer**

Option B is correct. Extraditing a person to a country where they could face the penalty would breach Article 2 (right to life) and probably also of Article 3 of the Convention (prohibition of torture) (*Soering* **(8.8.2** above) and Article 1 of the Thirteenth Protocol (abolition of the death penalty) (**8.25** above)). Option A is wrong because the Convention does not prohibit extradition to non-signatory countries, whilst option C is wrong as the right to life and prohibition of torture are absolute rights and, unlike qualified rights, do not involve a balancing act between the rights of the individual and the interest of the community. Option D is wrong as it is sufficient to engage Articles 2 and 3 if there is a possibility of the death penalty being imposed, whilst option E is wrong as the Convention covers nationals of non-signatory states resident in signatory states.

**Question 3**

A man employed as a shop assistant in a clothing shop has a small fish symbol tattooed on to his hand. The fish symbol is a Christian symbol. The clothing shop's employment policy permits shop assistants to have small tattoos that are visible to customers, but prohibits tattoos that have religious significance as it wants to adopt a secular image. The shop has taken disciplinary action against the man. The UK courts have upheld the lawfulness of the disciplinary action, so the man now wants to take action against the UK Government before the European Court of Human Rights.

**Can the man argue that the disciplinary action breaches his Convention rights?**

A Yes, because the shop's refusal to allow him to display a small tattoo means that the state has permitted a disproportionate interference with his right to manifest his religion.

B Yes, because the shop's refusal to allow him to display a small tattoo means that the state has permitted an interference with his absolute right to manifest his religion.

C Yes, because the shop's refusal to allow him to display a small tattoo means that the state has permitted an interference with his absolute right to freedom of religion.

D No, because the shop has treated all religious symbols equally, so there is no interference with the man's freedom to manifest his religion.

E No, because the shop's refusal to allow him to display a small tattoo is a proportionate interference with the man's freedom to manifest his religion.

**Answer**

Option A is correct. Based on the case of *Eweida* (**8.16.2**), it seems improbable that a small discreet religious symbol would detract from the image that the shop wants to project. It is therefore a disproportionate interference with the man's qualified right to manifest his religious belief. Option B is wrong because the right to manifest a religious belief is a qualified right, not an absolute right. Option C is wrong because having a tattoo comes within the scope of manifesting religious belief, a qualified right, rather than holding a religious belief, an absolute right.

Option D is wrong because treating all religions the same does not mean that the right to manifest one's religion fails to be engaged. Option E is wrong as the interference with the man's right to manifest his religion seems to go further than necessary to maintain the shop's image.

# 9 Human Rights Act 1998: European Convention on Human Rights in the UK



## SQE1 syllabus

This chapter will enable you to achieve the SQE1 assessment specification in relation to functioning legal knowledge concerned with core constitutional and administrative law principles, including:

- the HRA 1998 and the ECHR;
- Schedule 1 of the HRA 1998: the 'Convention Rights'; and
- sections 2, 3, 4, 6, 7, 8 and 10 of the HRA 1998.

Note that for SQE1, candidates are not usually required to recall specific case names or cite statutory or regulatory authorities. Cases are provided for illustrative purposes only.

## Learning outcomes

By the end of this chapter you will be able to apply relevant core legal principles and rules appropriately and effectively, at the level of a competent newly qualified solicitor in practice, to realistic client-based and ethical problems and situations in the following areas, including the ability to:

- appreciate the pervasive nature of the key provisions of the ECHR through its incorporation into UK law by the HRA 1998;
- understand how the HRA 1998 has incorporated the ECHR into UK law;
- understand the inter-relationship between different rights and freedoms, in particular Articles 8 and 10 of the ECHR;
- understand how to strike an appropriate balance in the legal protection when the different rights and freedoms conflict with each other; and
- apply case law pertaining to the HRA 1998 to the facts of a scenario.

# 9.1 The Human Rights Act 1998

In **Chapter 2** you read about the Human Rights Act (HRA) 1998 from the perspective of its effect on the doctrine of parliamentary sovereignty. In this chapter, we look at a different issue - how incorporation has altered the way in which English law deals with disputes between the individual and the state.

## 9.1.1 An overview of the act

The main sections of the HRA 1998 (many of which have been discussed in **Chapter 2**) are as follows:

- Section 1 - incorporates and gives effect to the Convention rights that are set out in Schedule 1 of the HRA 1998. These are rights contained in the ECHR save for Article 1 (states must secure the rights granted by the ECHR within their own jurisdiction) and Article 13 (the right to an effective remedy) on the basis that the HRA 1998 itself secures those rights and provides an effective remedy for their breach.
- Section 2 - domestic courts must 'take into account' judgments of the ECtHR but are not bound to follow them.
- Section 3 - 'So far as it is possible to do so, primary and subordinate legislation must be read and given effect in a way that is compatible with the Convention rights.' This applies to past and future legislation.
- Section 4 - the High Court and higher courts may declare an Act of Parliament to be incompatible with Convention rights.
- Section 6 - it is unlawful for a public authority (including a 'court') to act in a way that is incompatible with Convention rights (unless giving effect to an incompatible statute). This affects grounds of challenge in judicial review of administrative acts.
- Section 7 - a person who claims that a public authority acted contrary to s 6 may 'bring proceedings against the authority' or 'rely on the Convention right ... in any legal proceedings'. The person must be a 'victim of the unlawful act'.
- Section 8 - that a court in civil proceedings may award damages where a public authority unlawfully infringes a Convention right, if it is necessary 'to afford just satisfaction' to the injured party.
- Section 10 - creates a 'fast-track' procedure for changing legislation. Where a UK court or the ECtHR has found UK legislation to be in breach of the Convention, the Government may, if there are 'compelling reasons' to do so, make a 'remedial order' changing UK law. This is delegated legislation that has to be approved by Parliament under the 'affirmative procedure'.
- Section 19 - a minister introducing future legislation must make a written statement stating that the bill is compatible with Convention rights (a 'statement of compatibility') or that, although they are unable to make a statement of compatibility, the Government wishes to proceed with the bill.

## 9.1.2 Method of incorporation of Convention rights and interpretation of domestic legislation

In **Chapter 2** you were introduced to ss 2 and 3 of the HRA 1998, which deal with how the courts must interpret Convention rights and domestic legislation. Please refer back to **Chapter 2** for more detail on this topic.

### 9.1.3 Declaration of incompatibility

As we have noted above, s 3 of the HRA 1998 requires UK courts to interpret UK legislation consistently with the Convention only 'so far as it is possible to do so'. Section 4(2) gives the High Court and higher courts the power to declare legislation to be incompatible with Convention rights. Such a declaration does not affect the validity, continuing operation or enforcement of the provision in question, and does not bind the parties to the proceedings (s 4(6)). However, it does put political pressure on the Government to change the law.

### 9.1.4 Remedial orders

The Government is under no obligation to act upon a declaration of incompatibility. However, if it chooses to act upon it, the HRA 1998, s 10 and Sch 2 enable it to make delegated legislation to remedy the breach of the ECHR identified by the declaration (or a finding of the ECtHR). It may make 'remedial orders', which amend or repeal the offending legislation. However, remedial orders cannot be used to change the common law. Alternatively, the Government may submit a bill to Parliament to amend or repeal the offending legislation.

### 9.1.5 Acts of public authorities

As well as making the ECHR a yardstick against which to measure UK legislation, the HRA 1998 also makes Convention rights a standard with which the actions of public authorities must comply. Section 6(1) of the HRA 1998 provides that it is unlawful for a public authority to act in a way that is incompatible with Convention rights. However, this does not apply if, as a result of an Act of Parliament, the authority could not have acted differently, or the authority is giving effect to, or enforcing, provisions of an Act that are incompatible with the Convention (s 6(2)).

Therefore, s 6 is particularly relevant in judicial review cases, as in effect it adds a ground of challenge in judicial review of administrative acts - breach of a Convention right.

The Court of Appeal, in the case of *R (Beer) v Hampshire Farmers Market Ltd* [2004] 1 WLR 233, held that the two terms, 'public body' and 'public authority' are synonymous. In other words, if a decision-maker is a public body under the traditional principles of judicial review then it will also be a 'public authority' for the purposes of a decision that breaches a Convention right. This, of course, is extremely helpful to the claimant who wishes to raise traditional grounds for review alongside an allegation of breach of a Convention right.

You examined some judicial review cases involving Convention rights in earlier chapters. For example, the case of *R (Anderson) v Secretary of State for the Home Department* was covered in both **Chapters 4** and **8**. Anderson applied for judicial review of the Home Secretary's decision to increase the judicially recommended tariff setting the minimum period he would serve in prison after his conviction for murder. The House of Lords issued a declaration of incompatibility pursuant to s 4 of the HRA 1998 that the legislation authorising the Home Secretary was incompatible.

The case of *R (Swami Suryananda) v Welsh Ministers* (**8.14.2**) is also an example of a judicial review case, albeit an unsuccessful one. The Hindu community had applied for judicial review of the decision by Welsh ministers to slaughter a bullock belonging to the community to stop the spread of bovine tuberculosis. Although the court accepted the community's Article 9 rights (freedom of religion) were engaged, the slaughter was a proportionate response to a serious situation.

### 9.1.6 Enforcement against private individuals

Notice that the HRA 1998 only makes it unlawful for public authorities to infringe Convention rights. It does not expressly make it unlawful for private individuals to infringe the rights of other individuals. Does this mean that cases between individuals are unaffected by the ECHR? For example, can the right to respect for private life given by Article 8 be used only against public authorities? What about cases where the press intrudes on the private life of celebrities? Later in this chapter, you will consider these issues further. However, you should note that the court is a public authority within the meaning of s 6 of the HRA 1998 (see **9.1.5. above**). It therefore has a duty to apply the Convention. The effect is referred to as 'horizontality', as it means that Convention rights can affect relations between private citizens (or companies) and not merely relations between state and citizen ('vertical effect').

### 9.1.7 Section 6 and delegated legislation

Although courts are bound to apply Acts of Parliament that are incompatible with Convention rights, judicial review may be available under s 6 of the HRA 1998 to set aside incompatible delegated legislation. For example, as you saw in **Chapter 2**, in *A v Secretary of State for the Home Department*, the House of Lords quashed delegated legislation made under s 14 of the HRA 1998.

### 9.1.8 Standing

Section 7 of the HRA 1998 states that a claimant can bring proceedings for breach of a Convention right only if they are a 'victim' of the breach. This means that an individual or organisation must be directly and personally affected. Pressure groups will not be victims under s 7 and therefore cannot bring claims for breach of Convention rights (*R (Adath Yisroel Burial Society) v HM Coroner for Inner North London* [2018] EWHC 969 (Admin)), though the ECtHR showed a more flexible approach to standing in *Verein KlimaSeniorinnen Schweiz v Switzerland* in the context of climate change litigation (**8.15.3** above).

### 9.1.9 Damages for breach of Convention rights

Under s 8 of the HRA 1998, a court can award damages for breach of Convention rights where it is 'necessary to afford just satisfaction', taking into account principles laid down by the ECtHR. In many cases there will be no need to do so, as there will be a common law cause of action (eg misuse of private information) under which damages can be awarded. Moreover, in judicial review proceedings the courts will often regard a quashing order and/or one or more of the other available remedies as just satisfaction.

---

## 9.2 Convention rights in the UK

**Chapter 8** covered the rights and freedoms granted by the ECHR. You looked at the approach of the ECtHR and UK courts in cases involving alleged breaches of these rights, including the application of the 'proportionality' test by UK courts. Most of the examples you considered in **Chapter 8** involved interferences by the state with individuals' Convention rights. In this part of the chapter, you will be looking at situations where conflict can arise between different Convention rights, focusing in particular on Articles 8 and 10. However, before you do so, we shall analyse how Convention rights can be used in judicial review proceedings against public bodies.

### 9.2.1 Enforcement against public bodies

The following example exercise illustrates how Convention rights and the traditional judicial review grounds can be used to challenge a decision of a public body.

***Example***

*Assume that, owing to concerns regarding misleading information and the leaking of confidential statistical information on Internet sites about school performance league tables, Parliament passed the Electronic Communications Act 2018 ('the Act') (fictitious), which empowers the Government, by way of order (a 'restriction order'), to restrict the dissemination on Internet sites of any matters that may be specified in such an order.*

*A series of recent Internet articles has also alleged that the poor performance in the Government's league tables of inner-city schools is due to weak leadership by the relevant head teachers. In response to this, the Home Secretary issues a restriction order banning publication on the Internet of any information relating to the performance of schools. The Home Secretary believes that the widespread publication of information may embarrass the Secretary of State for Education and may undermine the confidence of the public in its local head teachers.*

*The Parent and Teachers Forum (PTF) represents a large number of interested parents. The PTF is prepared to fund a test case brought by Janice, an aggrieved parent, to challenge the new restriction order on the basis that it unduly restricts parents' rights of access to information of genuine public interest.*

*Consider whether Janice may bring a judicial review claim based on:*

*(i) breach of her Convention rights, and (ii) any traditional grounds of review.*

***Answer***

*1. Is the issue a public matter?*

*Yes, performance of schools is a public matter.*

*2. Who is the decision-maker?*

*The Home Secretary.*

*3. Is the Home Secretary amenable to judicial review?*

*Apply the two-part* Datafin *test: if the source of power is statute or a prerogative power, the decision-maker is amenable to judicial review. Here, the source of power is the Electronic Communications Act 2018, so there is no need to go on to consider the second part of the test.*

*The Home Secretary is also a 'public authority' for the purposes of s 6 of the HRA 1998.*

*4. Are there any ouster clauses, either complete or partial?*

*No, neither.*

*5. Does Janice have standing?*

*Yes, because she is an aggrieved parent who fears that her child(ren)'s education might suffer as a result of the restriction order. She therefore qualifies as a victim as required by s 7 of the HRA 1998, and clearly has 'sufficient interest' (the test for the domestic grounds).*

*6. ECHR grounds:*

*(a) Janice's challenge is likely to involve human rights issues (see below). As already stated, Janice will satisfy the victim test under s 7 of the HRA 1998.*

*(b) Janice may argue that her Convention rights have been infringed by the Home Secretary's order. Under s 6 of the HRA 1998, she may raise a human rights issue as part of her claim for judicial review on the basis that it is unlawful for a public authority to act in a way that is incompatible with Convention rights.*

*(c) The most relevant article here is Article 10 (freedom of expression). Article 10(1) includes 'the right to receive ... information ... without interference by public authority ...'.*

*Article 10(2) permits restrictions that are 'prescribed by law', pursue a legitimate aim and are 'necessary in a democratic society'. This is where proportionality becomes relevant: following Bank Mellat, the court would apply the four-stage approach outlined below, asking:*

(i) *whether the objective of the restriction order is sufficiently important to justify limiting a fundamental right;*

*(ii) whether the restriction order is rationally connected to this objective;*

*(iii) whether a less intrusive measure than the restriction order could have been used; and*

*(iv) whether, having regard to these matters and to the severity of the consequences, a fair balance has been struck between the rights of the individual and the interests of the community.*

*The measures taken by the Home Secretary, ie the restriction order, are prescribed by law '(the Act') and are in pursuit of the legitimate aims listed in Article 10(2) – the protection of the reputation or rights of others and the prevention of disclosure of information received in confidence.*

*Are the measures 'necessary in a democratic society' (ie proportionate)? At first sight, they derive from Parliament's legislative objective as expressed in the parent Act. That objective is arguably sufficiently important (ie protecting the public from misinformation) to justify the interference with a fundamental right, and the measures taken (the making of the restriction order) are rationally connected to this objective if the Home Secretary believes that he is acting in the interests of regulating publication on the Internet.*

*However, the order itself extends beyond these issues. Making the order (even partly) to prevent embarrassment to another minister is, Janice would argue, not rationally connected with the objective ('protection of the reputation of others' seems very tenuous when just talking about embarrassment!).*

*In any event, the means used appear to be more intrusive than necessary (ie disproportionate), banning all information relating to the performance of schools.*

*Given the above and the fact that the ban will mean parents have no access to any information on the performance of schools, the rights of the parents may well outweigh the interests of the community in such a ban.*

*Anther ground on which Janice would be able to base her claim is:*

***Illegality***

*All statutory powers must be exercised in accordance with the correct statutory purpose. Here the legislation has been passed due to a need to regulate publication of material on the Internet.*

*The Home Secretary has used the power in order to limit publication of material that may undermine public confidence in head teachers, and also to prevent embarrassment to a government minister. If the latter is actually the real reason for exercise of the statutory power, it might be possible to argue that it has been exercised for an improper purpose (*Congreve v Home Office*).*

*However, it seems more likely that the Home Secretary has in fact sought to achieve two purposes. Where there is a duality of purpose behind the order, the court would need to apply the primary (or 'true and dominant') purpose test to evaluate which was the main objective, ie the one authorised by statute or not (*Westminster Corp v LNWR*). Alternatively, the court may adopt the more 'modern' approach in* R v ILEA, ex p Westminster City Council*: if the unauthorised purpose 'materially influenced' the creation of the order then the order itself would be ultra vires. It seems that if the Home Secretary's concerns are to prevent embarrassment to the Secretary of State for Education, the unauthorised purpose may well have materially influenced his decision to make the order. Further, this concern is also an irrelevant consideration (*Padfield v Minister of Agriculture*).*

### 9.2.2 Private enforcement

The rise of the 'celebrity culture' has led to the ability of a newspaper or magazine to achieve a wide circulation through use of an exclusive photograph of a celebrity on its front page, often taken by a member of the paparazzi. As a result, the courts have had to consider the extent to which an individual's right under Article 8 of the ECHR, to respect for their private life, should be protected. This is particularly so where that right conflicts with another's (eg a newspaper's) right to freedom of expression under Article 10.

By analysing the approach taken by the UK courts in these cases, you should be able to assess how the courts will strike a balance when different individuals' rights compete with each other.

## 9.3 'Horizontal effect' of Convention rights

In the English cases you will study in the rest of this chapter, the defendants will be private bodies, often a newspaper, and not 'public authorities' for the purposes of s 6 of the HRA 1998. However, individuals have nevertheless been able to bring a claim against such bodies under the 'horizontal effect' principle as developed in cases such as *Thompson and Venables v MGN* and *Douglas v Hello! Ltd* (see below). Courts themselves are public authorities within the scope of s 6(3) HRA 1998 and so must act compatibly with Convention rights (s 6(1) HRA 1998). This principle allows individuals to bring a case based on an existing cause of action, which the courts will develop compatibly with Convention rights. In particular, the courts have developed the law on confidential information to give effect to Convention rights in horizontal claims.

## 9.4 Conflict between different rights and freedoms

One difficulty in setting out a list of fundamental rights is that sometimes rights can conflict with each other. The ECHR does not lay down any strict hierarchy of rights, and therefore the courts have to determine priority on a case-by-case basis. The case of *Venables and Thompson v News Group Newspapers Ltd* [2001] 2 WLR 1038 involved the right to life (Article 2), the right to respect for private life (Article 8) and also the right to freedom of expression (Article 10) of newspaper publishers.

The claimants, Venables and Thompson who at the age of 11 had been convicted of the murder of toddler James Bulger, applied for permanent injunctions protecting them from being identified upon their release from detention as there was a genuine risk that they would be subjected to revenge attacks. They relied on Articles 2 (right to life), 3 (prohibition of torture) and 8 (right to a private life) of the ECHR to claim that their identities should be kept confidential. For their part, various newspapers contended that such restrictions would interfere with their Article 10 rights (freedom of expression).

Article 2 is an absolute right, whereas Articles 8 and 10 are qualified rights. Subject to context, one would expect the absolute right to life to prevail; however, there was argument over the scope of the right to life. The court held that it was under a positive duty to operate to protect individuals from the criminal acts of others. In exceptional cases, such as this, the court had jurisdiction to widen the scope of the protection of confidentiality of information, even to the extent of placing restrictions on the press, where in the absence of restrictions it was likely that the person seeking confidentiality would suffer serious physical injury or even death and no other means of protection was available. The court acknowledged that restrictions on the right of the media to publish had to fall within the exceptions contained in Article 10(2), and those exceptions had to be given a narrow interpretation. Whilst the court was not convinced that it was necessary to override the press's Article 10 rights by keeping details of the claimants' identities secret in order to protect their Article 8 rights, there was a real and serious risk to their rights under Articles 2 and 3. The court therefore granted permanent injunctions against the whole world.

Contrast this with the case of Mary Bell (*X (A Woman formerly known as Mary Bell) and Y v Stephen O'Brien and News Group Newspapers and MGN Limited* [2003] EWHC 1101 (QB)). In 1968, when she was 11 years old, Mary Bell was convicted of the manslaughter of two children and sentenced to detention for life. During the trial, her name was made public. On her release in 1980 she was given a new identity, which had subsequently been discovered five times. She had a daughter, Y, who was 19 at the time of this hearing. This case concerned X and Y seeking lifetime injunctions to protect their identities. Here it was held that, in contrast to the *Venables* case, the risk of harm to X (formerly known as Mary Bell) did not reach the standard required to come within Article 2 of the Convention. The case therefore came down to a balance between the competing interests of X and Y under Article 8 and the press under Article 10, which is discussed at **9.4.1.3** below.

In 2005, Maxine Carr, the former girlfriend of Soham murderer Ian Huntley, was granted an indefinite order protecting her new identity by the High Court (*Carr v News Group Newspapers Ltd* [2005] EWHC 971 (QB)), as it was necessary to protect 'life and limb' as well as Carr's psychological health. Carr's lawyer had argued that such an order was justified on the grounds laid down in the *Venables and Thompson* and *Mary Bell* cases, where similar permanent injunctions were granted. The *Carr* case is significant because it is the first such order granted to an adult who has not committed a serious offence (she was convicted of perverting the course of justice with Huntley, but was not involved in the murder of the schoolgirls Holly Wells and Jessica Chapman in August 2002).

However, the threshold for an anonymity order is high. In *Tickle v BBC* [2025] EWCA Civ 42, the Court of Appeal considered a reporting restrictions order that anonymised judges involved in historic family proceedings related to Sara Sharif, who was brutally murdered by her father and step-mother in 2023. The court found no evidence that Articles 2, 3 or 8 were engaged, noting that any threats to the judges were typical, generic social media threats. Anonymisation would only be justified if risks were so serious that security measures would be insufficient, and, given judges' special role in upholding open justice, only exceptionally grave risks could override the principle of open justice.

## 9.4.1 Balancing freedom of expression with right to respect for private life

### 9.4.1.1 Human Rights Act 1998, s 12(4)

Section 12(4) of the 1998 Act is drafted so as to prevent claims of breach of privacy from unduly restricting the freedom of the press. It states that the courts must have particular regard to the right to the freedom of expression. Where proceedings relate to journalistic, literary or artistic material, the court must consider the extent to which the material is already in the public domain, whether publication would be in the public interest and any relevant privacy code.

### 9.4.1.2 Relative status of Articles 8 and 10

The rights people enjoy in Article 8 may affect another person's freedom of expression. A balance must be struck between the right to respect for one's private life and the right of others to their freedom of expression. There is therefore a challenge to the courts here. We know from **Chapter 8** that where qualified human rights are engaged, the court must apply the test of proportionality. When a claimant brings a case against the state for breach of human rights, the test used is the *Bank Mellat* test. However, where two Convention rights conflict, such as Arts 8 and 10, the correct approach is more complex, as discussed at **9.4.1.3** and **9.4.1.4** below

### 9.4.1.3 Protection of identity

In the *Mary Bell* case, Dame Elizabeth Butler-Sloss accepted that Article 8 had a meaning covering the physical and psychological integrity of a person, and a right to personal development and to establish and develop relationships with other human beings and the outside world. She accepted that not granting the injunction was likely to lead to an infringement of X and Y's Article 8 rights. There had been consistent press reporting of and articles about Mary Bell for many years. Her case aroused considerable media interest and remained of interest to the reading public'.

Dame Elizabeth also acknowledged that an injunction would interfere with the freedom of expression of the press. She also stressed that the existence of a free press was in itself desirable and so any interference with it could only be justified if exceptional circumstances existed. Dame Elizabeth took into account the following:

(a) X's fragile mental health;

(b) the young age at which she committed the offences;

(c) the length of time that had expired since offences were committed; and

(d) the serious risk of potential harassment and possible physical harm.

As a result of these exceptional circumstances, lifetime injunctions against the whole world were granted to X and Y.

It is important to note that Dame Elizabeth placed great emphasis on evidence of X's fragile mental health, a fact that may limit the potential wider effects of this case.

#### 9.4.1.4 Misuse of private information

The House of Lords case of *Campbell v Mirror Group Newspapers Ltd* [2004] UKHL 22 is the leading English authority on the misuse of private information.

The Daily Mirror had published the following regarding the supermodel Naomi Campbell:

(a) That she was addicted to drugs.

(b) That she was receiving treatment for her addiction.

(c) A photograph of her leaving a Narcotics Anonymous meeting.

Their Lordships acknowledged that the court, as a public authority itself, must act compatibly with both parties' Convention rights. This meant that Articles 8 and 10 were just as applicable in a case between two individuals as they were in disputes between an individual and a public authority. The courts have also debated whether a new cause of action relating to privacy should be developed, sometimes referred to as 'misuse of personal information'.

In *Campbell* itself, the House of Lords said that the appropriate test was whether the claimant (Ms Campbell) had a reasonable expectation of respect for her private life in the particular circumstances. This is an objective question and takes account of all the circumstances of the case, including the attributes of the claimant, the nature of the activity being engaged in, the place at which it happened, the nature and purpose of the intrusion, the absence of consent, the effect on the claimant and the circumstances in which, and purposes for which, the information reached the hands of the publisher. If the claimant has a reasonable expectation of privacy, then Article 8 will be engaged and the court must carry out a balancing exercise between the conflicting claims of Articles 8 and 10 to decide if there has been a breach of Article 8.

All the information that the newspaper had published regarding Campbell was private, as it related to a medical condition, something that attracts a high degree of protection. However, the newspaper in turn argued that in publishing the article and/or photographs, it was exercising its right to freedom of expression (Article 10), and further that under Article 10 the public had a legitimate right to read about the matter.

When balancing the two conflicting rights, courts must take account of s 12(4) of the HRA 1998, which provides that the court must have 'particular regard' to the importance of freedom of expression and, where material is journalistic, whether it would be in the 'public interest' for the material to be published. This does not, however, give Article 10 priority over Article 8, as neither right takes precedence over the other.

Where human rights are engaged, the court must apply the 'proportionality' test (*Bank Mellat* - see **8.14.2**). Where two qualified Convention rights (Articles 8 and 10) are engaged the position is more complex than when considering an interference with a single right. As Baroness Hale commented in *Campbell*, the court looks at the comparative importance of the actual rights being claimed in the individual case, and then at the justifications for interfering with or restricting each of those rights; and then it applies the proportionality test to each.

Baroness Hale suggested that there are different types of freedom of speech, some of which are more deserving of protection than others. Political speech is particularly deserving of protection, as is artistic speech or impression. Conversely stories about the intimate details of a celebrity's private life attract less protection.

However, the court accepted that the newspaper was entitled to publish the story that Campbell had been addicted to drugs to 'set the record straight', ie to correct her prior assertion that she was not addicted. The court then had to consider publication of the details of the Narcotics Anonymous meeting and the photographs of Campbell leaving the meeting.

The crucial factor in *Campbell* was that the model was photographed and the text identified her as leaving Narcotics Anonymous meetings, which, being a medical matter, made the issue particularly private and might even deter someone in these circumstances from having further treatment. Baroness Hale distinguished the subject matter of the photograph in this case from a photograph of Campbell simply walking down the street to go shopping. As a model who made her living out of modelling designer clothes, there would have been no objection to a photograph of her going about her daily business as readers of the newspaper would have been interested in how she looked.

It is important to note that had it not been for the publication of the photographs, the majority of the House of Lords would have been inclined to regard the balance between Articles 8 and 10 as about even.

It is also clear from *Campbell*, therefore, that it is not whether the individual action occurred in the public or private domain that is the determining factor as to whether the individual has a reasonable expectation of respect for their private life.

#### 9.4.1.5 Photographs

A year after *Campbe*ll, the ECtHR considered the position of photographs in the case of *Von Hannover v Germany (No 1)* (2005) 40 EHRR 1, which the domestic courts must take into account as persuasive authority. The *Von Hannover* case involved a successful claim brought by Princess Caroline of Monaco that a variety of photographs taken of her by the paparazzi breached her Article 8 right to respect for her private and family life. The Princess' claim was successful, despite the fact that the photographs showed her shopping and skiing, and riding with her children in a public place. In striking the balance between privacy and the freedom of expression, the ECtHR ruled that the decisive factor was the contribution that the published photos and articles made to a debate of general interest. As the applicant exercised no official function and the photos and articles related exclusively to details of her private life, they made no such contribution.

It is therefore clear from *Von Hannover (No 1)* that the fact that someone is a public figure does not mean that they have no right of respect for their private life when in a public place.

However, in *Von Hannover v Germany (No 2)* (2012) 55 EHRR 15, the ECtHR may have retreated slightly from the stringent approach to photographs that it took *in Von Hannover (No 1)*. *Von Hannover (No 2)* concerned the publication in a German magazine of a photograph showing Princess Caroline and her husband on a skiing holiday in Switzerland. Accompanying the photograph was an article about the health of Prince Rainier, Princess Caroline's father and then reigning prince of Monaco. The information about Prince Rainier's health was a matter of public interest due to his status, and the public were legitimately interested in how his children 'reconciled their obligations of family solidarity with the legitimate needs of their private life'. Moreover, even if Princess Caroline did not perform any official functions, she and her husband were not ordinary private individuals, but were public figures.

The link between the photograph and accompanying article was close enough to justify its publication, particularly as there was no evidence that the photographs were taken in either a covert or intrusive manner. The judgment in *Von Hannover (No 2)* indicates that the ECtHR may be allowing states a greater margin of appreciation in this type of case. Nonetheless the judgment does not clear the way for the press to publish photographs of celebrities carrying out everyday activities; the photographs must contribute to a genuine debate of general interest.

The case of *Murray (by his Litigation Friends) v Express Newspapers plc and another* [2008] EWCA Civ 446, [2009] Ch 48 concerned the publication in the Daily Express of a photograph of M, the infant son of the author JK Rowling, being pushed by his father down an Edinburgh street in a buggy with his mother walking alongside. The court, following *Campbell*, confirmed that the test of whether Article 8 has been engaged at all has to be answered first, before any balancing exercise between Articles 8 and 10 is carried out, or issues of proportionality discussed.

If there was a reasonable expectation of privacy, then the second question was how to strike the balance between the claimant's right to privacy and the publisher's right to publish. At that stage, the question of whether the publication of those private facts would be considered highly offensive to an objective, reasonable person might be relevant.

Due to the nature of the case, the Court of Appeal did not need to reach a definitive decision but concluded that it was at least arguable that M had a reasonable expectation of privacy and that Article 8 was engaged. The court also thought M had an arguable case that the balance between Articles 8 and 10 should be struck in his favour and against publication.

The court nonetheless thought there might well be circumstances, even after *Hannover*, in which there would be no reasonable expectation of privacy. However, it all depended on the circumstances of the case. Routine activities such as a walk down the street or a trip to the grocer to buy milk would not necessarily give rise to a reasonable expectation of privacy; everything depended on the circumstances. However, the court put particular weight on the need to protect children of parents who were in the public eye from intrusive media attention, at least to the extent of holding that the child had a reasonable expectation that they would not be targeted in order to obtain photographs in a public place for publication, where the taking of such photographs would be objected to on the child's behalf. Accordingly, the Court of Appeal's decision in *Murray* appears to have dramatically expanded privacy protection for children.

In the case of *RocknRoll v News Group Newspapers Ltd* [2013] EWHC 24 (Ch), the judge granted an injunction to the new husband of the actor, Kate Winslet, preventing publication by a newspaper of photographs that had been posted on Facebook by a friend of his.

### 9.4.1.6 Other case law since *Campbell*

Another case, this time involving a newspaper article, is *Mosley v News Group Newspapers* [2008] EWHC 1777 (QB). Max Mosley, the head of Formula 1 motor racing, claimed that his right to privacy under Article 8 had been infringed after the News of the World published a story alleging that he had engaged in a Nazi-themed sado-masochistic orgy with a group of prostitutes. The court found that Mosley's rights under Article 8 were clearly engaged – the activities had taken place in private and only come to light because one of the prostitutes sold her story. The real issue in the case was whether there was sufficient public interest so as to justify the publication of the story. The High Court found that there was not, because the newspaper failed to demonstrate that the activities did actually have a Nazi theme. The trial judge did suggest that, had the activities had a Nazi theme, there may have been a public interest in allowing publication. This was because of Mr Mosley's position as President of the FIA (the governing body of Formula 1) and son of the wartime fascist Oswald Mosley. Although the case essentially involved the court applying the test set out in *Campbell*, it does suggest that the courts may be more willing than previously to protect the sex lives of those in the public eye.

In *LNS v Persons Unknown* [2010] EWHC 119 (QB), the High Court overturned a so-called 'super-injunction' that had prevented a newspaper from reporting on an alleged extra-marital affair of John Terry, the England football team captain. 'Super-injunctions' not only prevent the publication of the story in question, but also forbid any reference that the injunction itself exists, and they have been criticised as a significant block to freedom of speech. The court thought that Terry's main concern was protecting his financial arrangements (eg sponsorship deals), rather than the protection of his private life. An injunction was not necessary or proportionate having regard to the level of gravity of the interference with the footballer's private life in the event of publication.

In *Ferdinand v MGN Ltd* [2011] EWHC 2454 (QB), another case involving an England football team captain, Rio Ferdinand claimed that a newspaper article about his relationship with a woman, which allegedly continued even once he had become engaged, breached his privacy. The court found that since Ferdinand had stated that he was a family man, there was a public interest in demonstrating that this image was false, particularly since he was by then captain of the England football team.

In *PJS v News Group Newspapers Ltd* [2016] UKSC 26, *The Sun on Sunday* proposed to publish the story of PJS's sexual encounters with AB, including a three-way sexual encounter involving PJS, AB and AB's partner. PJS sued for breach of confidence and breach of privacy and asked for an injunction to prevent publication. The story had already been published in the USA (and some other places) and on numerous websites. PJS argued that an injunction was necessary to protect himself, his partner and their young children.

The majority of the Supreme Court was of the view that, should the injunction be refused, there would be a 'media storm' in England and that an injunction was necessary to protect PJS, his partner and especially their children.

This case has proved controversial. Details of the story had been published in the USA but, as the celebrities involved were not so well known there, had not been widely taken up. There were further articles in Canada and a Scottish newspaper and the details then started to appear on numerous websites.

In *Bloomberg v ZXC* [2022] UKSC 5 the issue was whether individuals under investigation for a criminal offence who have not been charged with an offence may have a reasonable expectation of privacy. The Supreme Court found in favour of the claimant, ZXC, stating that, in general, individuals being investigated for a criminal offence do have a reasonable expectation of privacy. Accordingly, publishing details of the investigation was the misuse of private information, even though the information related to ZXC's business activities rather than personal activities.

9.4.1.7 Is there a new tort of invasion of privacy?

In *Wainwright and another v Home Office* [2003] UKHL 53 the House of Lords stated that there was no tort of invasion of privacy. However, the jurisprudence of the higher courts has developed since then as there has clearly been some judicial dissatisfaction with the need to 'squeeze' breach of privacy claims within the cause of action of common law breach of confidence.

The Court of Appeal in *Vidal-Hall v Google Inc* [2015] EWCA Civ 311 held that there was now a tort of misuse of private information, distinct from the equitable claim for breach of confidence. Moreover, in *PJS v News Group Newspapers Ltd* [2016] UKSC 26 the majority of the Supreme Court held that publication of private sexual encounters 'will on the face of it constitute the tort of invasion of privacy' and that 'repetition ... on further occasions is capable of constituting a further tort of invasion of privacy'. Thus it seems that a tort of invasion of privacy may now have been developed by the courts.

## Summary

- In this chapter, you have looked at how the HRA 1998 has incorporated rights conferred by the ECHR into UK law. **Figure 9.1** sets out how the HRA 1998 gives effect to the ECHR.
- You then considered how individuals can rely on Convention rights against public bodies, in particular by way of judicial review.
- You have looked at where conflict can arise between different Convention rights, with particular emphasis on Articles 8 and 10.
- You have examined situations that have involved the courts having to balance one person's right to respect for their private life with another's right to freedom of expression.

**Figure 9.1** Convention rights and the HRA 1998

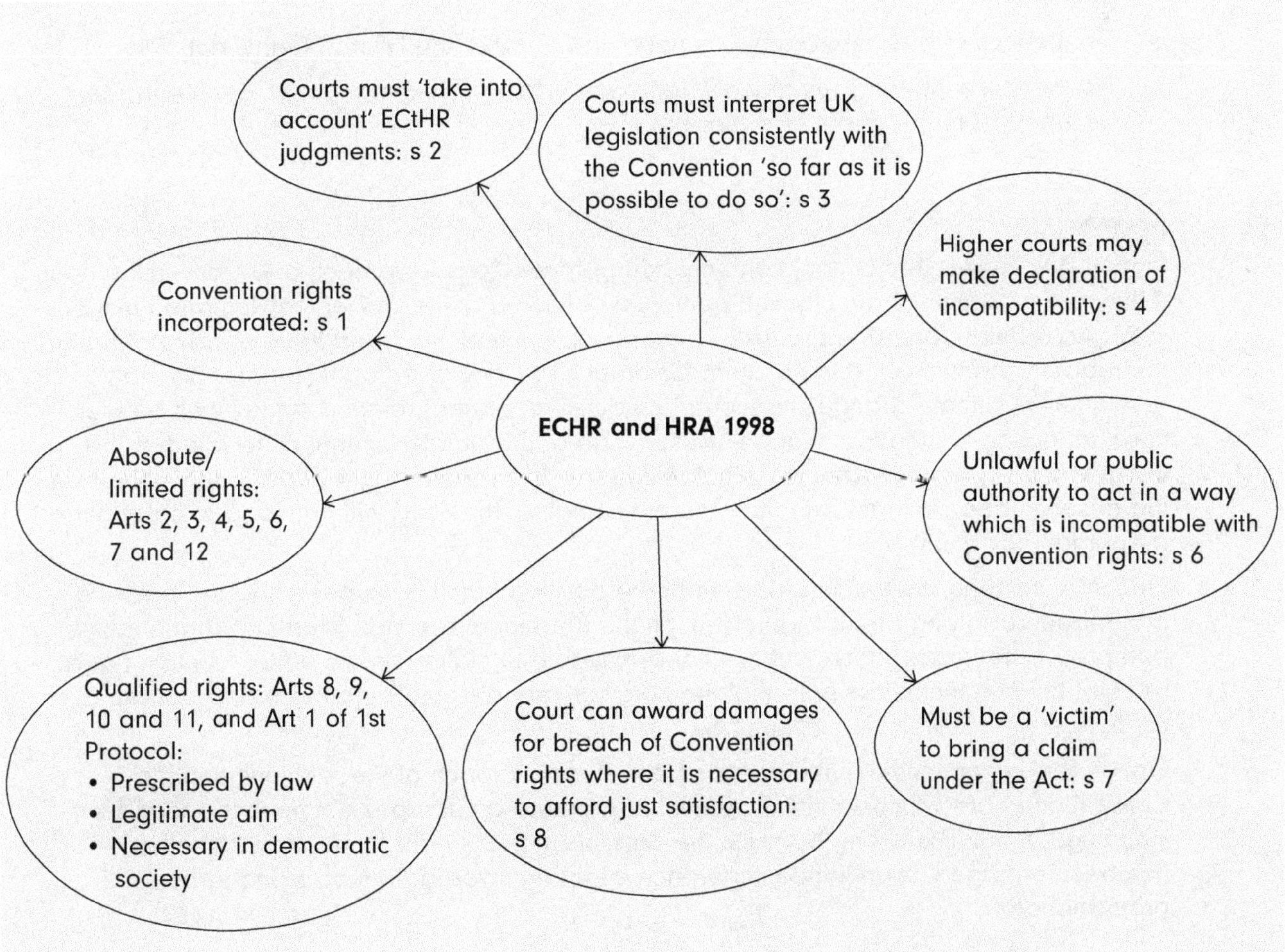

## Sample questions

**Question 1**

A religious group applied for planning permission to build a temple. Last week the local planning authority refused the group planning permission because one of its core beliefs is that women should have a subordinate role in society and be subject to the headship of men. As the religious group has already secured alternative premises, it does not want to challenge the refusal. However, a pressure group that campaigns for religious freedom wants to apply for judicial review of the decision. (Note that this question includes topics covered in **Chapters 7** and **8**).

**Can the pressure group challenge the decision of the local planning authority by way of judicial review on the grounds that it infringes the religious group's freedom of religion?**

A Yes, because of the importance of the matter (the Convention right of freedom of religion) and its role as a campaigner for freedom of religion.

B Yes, because there has been a clear breach of the Convention right of freedom of religion.

C No, because freedom of religion is a qualified right and the interference with it is proportionate.

D No, because the pressure group is not a victim under the Human Rights Act 1998.

E No, because the religious group's right to freedom of religion has not been engaged as it has found premises elsewhere.

**Answer**

Option D is correct. A claimant can only bring proceedings for breach of a Convention right if they are a 'victim'; ie directly and personally affected as per s 7 of the Human Rights Act 1998. Accordingly, pressure groups will not be victims under s 7 and therefore do not have the requisite standing to bring a claim for breach of Convention rights (except possibly in relation to climate change litigation), including freedom of religion. It may well be the case, as option C suggests, that an investigation of the situation might conclude that the interference is proportionate. Nonetheless, option D is a better answer than option C as, in the absence of a claimant with the requisite standing, the court will not need to carry out a proportionality analysis.

Option A is wrong, as it summarises what the position might have been had the pressure group been applying for judicial review on the traditional grounds (illegality, irrationality and procedural impropriety), but it is not applicable to claims based on Convention rights. (A court might nonetheless hold that the religious group would be a more appropriate challenger.)

Option B is wrong as, even if there has been a clear breach of the religious group's Convention rights (which seems unlikely), the pressure group does not have the requisite standing. Option E is wrong because the pressure group's right to manifest its beliefs has been engaged, even if the interference might on investigation be found to be proportionate.

**Question 2**

A man convicted of murder committed when he was an adult is released after serving his sentence. He changes his name and goes to live in a part of the country where he will not be recognised, as he does not want the community in which he is living to know about his past. Some newspapers have found out where he lives and want to publish the details.

**Will the man be able to obtain an injunction stopping the newspapers from disclosing his identity and where he lives?**

A Yes, because publication of the information will violate his right to life and right to privacy.

B Yes, because although publication of his details will not violate his right to life, it will be a disproportionate interference of his right to privacy.

C Yes, because although publication of his details will not violate his right to privacy, it will be an interference with his absolute right to life.

D No, because as he committed the murder as an adult, he has forfeited his right to privacy and there is no interference with his right to life.

E No, because publication of the information will not violate his right to life nor be a disproportionate interference with his right to privacy.

**Answer**

Option E is correct. Based on the *Mary Bell* case, it seems unlikely that the risk of harm to the man will reach the threshold to engage Article 2 (the right to life). As regards privacy (Article 8), freedom of expression of the press is highly important and can only be interfered with in exceptional circumstances, such as existed in the *Mary Bell* case. No such circumstances seem to exist here.

Options A, B and C are therefore wrong because they suggest either that there has been an interference with both Articles 2 and 8 (option A) or that one of them (options B and C) have been interfered with; as explained above it is unlikely that either has been interfered with. Option D is wrong as individuals do not forfeit their rights because of criminal conduct.

**Question 3**

A well-known actor was photographed leaving a walk-in HIV testing clinic in Birmingham. A newspaper has published the photograph. During her career the actor has disclosed very little about her private life.

**Which of the following best describes whether the actor can bring a claim in the High Court for breach of her Convention rights?**

A She cannot do so. Although the newspaper has interfered with her right to privacy, she can only bring a claim against it before the European Court of Human Rights.

B She cannot do so because freedom of expression is a more important right than the right to a private life.

C She cannot do so because English law does not recognise a tort of privacy.

D She can do so because the right to a private life is entitled to greater protection than freedom of expression.

E She can do so because the newspaper has disproportionately interfered with her right to a private life.

**Answer**

Option E is correct. The photograph, relating to a health condition, clearly engages Article 8, the right to a private life, whilst in publishing the photograph the newspaper will be exercising its Article 10 right of freedom of expression. Neither right has precedence over the other, hence options B and D are wrong. Instead, the court will balance the actor's Article 8 right with the newspaper's Article 10 right. In this instance, following the House of Lords' judgment in *Campbell*, the balance is likely to fall in favour of the actor's Article 8 right as the newspaper does not seem to have a legitimate reason for disclosing her medical condition.

Option A is wrong as the actor will be able to bring a claim in an English court under the horizontal effect principle.

Option C is wrong. Following the Supreme Court judgment in in *PJS v News Group Newspapers*, it is arguable that English law does recognise a tort of privacy. In any event, under the horizontal effect principle the courts will give effect to Convention rights through developing existing causes of action compatibly with the ECHR.

# 10 Retained EU Law/ Assimilated Law



## SQE1 syllabus

This chapter will enable you to achieve the SQE1 assessment specification in relation to functioning legal knowledge concerned with the status of EU law in the UK following the UK's exit from the EU, including:

- the place of EU law in the UK constitution

Note that for SQE1, candidates are not usually required to recall specific case names or cite statutory or regulatory authorities. Cases are provided for illustrative purposes only.

## Learning outcomes

By the end of this chapter you will be able to apply relevant core legal principles and rules appropriately and effectively, at the level of a competent newly qualified solicitor in practice, to realistic client-based and ethical problems and situations in the following areas, including the ability to:

- explain the meaning of retained EU law/assimilated law and its sources;
- understand the different categories of EU law;
- understand how retained EU law/assimilated law may be amended or repealed;
- interpret and apply retained EU law/assimilated law in practice;
- understand the categories and status of retained EU law/assimilated law; and
- understand how the Withdrawal Agreement agreed between the UK and EU may give rise to enforceable rights.

## 10.1 Introduction to retained EU law/assimilated law

The UK joined the European Communities on 1 January 1973. Over time the European Communities became the European Union (EU) and EU law became an ever more pervasive part of the UK legal system. Substantial parts of English law are based on or are profoundly influenced by EU law, in particular large swathes of commercial law, employment law (including laws prohibiting discrimination), environmental law, mergers and acquisitions and trade law. EU and English law are also very much intertwined in fields such as agriculture, consumer protection, public health and tourism. As you saw in **Chapter 2**, in many instances EU law had supremacy over UK law should there have been a conflict between the two. This was in accordance with the provisions of the European Communities Act (ECA) 1972, which was repealed by the European Union (Withdrawal) Act 2018 (EUWA 2018).

In a referendum held on 23 June 2016 the UK voted by 52% to 48% to leave the EU and subsequently the UK's exit took place on 31 January 2020 pursuant to a Withdrawal Agreement agreed between the UK and EU in October 2019, which entered into force on 1 February 2020. The Withdrawal Agreement provided for a transition period lasting until 31 December 2020 during which for many purposes the UK was treated as a Member State. During the transition period EU law remained in full force in the UK, and so there was little change in the UK legal system until 31 December 2020. However, the end of the transition period signalled a profound change in the UK legal system.

### 10.1.1 Retained EU law and the Withdrawal Agreement

If on the UK's exit from the EU all EU law had ceased to apply, there would have been massive gaps in the UK's statute book and regulatory systems. The UK Parliament therefore enacted the EUWA 2018, which aimed to provide legal continuity by creating the concept of 'retained EU law'. EU law as it existed at the date of the UK's exit from the EU would be preserved as a new category of English law with its own distinctive features. The original version of the EUWA 2018 was designed to cater for the possibility of the UK leaving the EU without agreement (a 'no-deal Brexit'); however, the UK did ultimately leave the EU on the basis of the Withdrawal Agreement. As the Withdrawal Agreement is an international treaty, the UK Government needed to ensure that its provisions were implemented into UK domestic law. Parliament therefore enacted the European Union (Withdrawal Agreement) Act 2020 (the Withdrawal Agreement Act 2020) in order to do this.

The Withdrawal Agreement Act 2020 gave effect to the Withdrawal Agreement in part by amending the EUWA 2018 and in part through its own self-standing provisions. Accordingly, to understand how the Withdrawal Agreement has been implemented into UK law, it is necessary to consider the EUWA 2018 as amended and the free-standing provisions of the Withdrawal Agreement Act 2020.

### 10.1.2 The Retained EU Law (Revocation and Reform Act) 2023

The previous Conservative Government believed that a gradualist approach towards the review, amendment or repeal of retained EU law was insufficient to allow the UK to take advantage of the benefits of Brexit. Parliament therefore passed the Retained EU Law (Revocation and Reform) Act 2023 (REULA 2023) which received royal assent on 29 June 2023 and made significant changes to the status, interpretation and application of retained EU law with effect from 1 January 2024. According to the Conservative Government, the aim of REULA 2023 was to enable it to amend retained EU law more easily and to remove its special features from the UK legal system. The Conservative Government believed REULA 2023 put the UK statute book on a more sustainable footing. By ending the special status of retained EU law, REULA 2023 reclaimed the sovereignty of Parliament and restored primacy to Acts of Parliament. It also enabled the Government to update outmoded legislation in response to various reviews it conducted.

The original Bill provided for the revocation of all retained EU law with effect from 31 December 2023, unless specifically retained or preserved, or contained in EU derived primary legislation. Following widespread criticism highlighting the risk of inadvertent omission, namely that some instruments of retained EU law might lapse on 31 December 2023 without anyone's knowledge because government departments had failed to identify them, these extensive sun-setting provisions were dropped from the Bill. Instead, REULA 2023 provided for a more limited sunset.

Section 1 of REULA 2023 provided for the revocation at the end of 31 December 2023 ('the sunset') of 587 instruments of retained EU law listed in Sch 1 to REULA 2023. However, this list was not completely reliable, as subsequently the Government removed a few of these instruments of retained EU law from the sunset by way of statutory instrument. Conversely, other legislation also contained sunsetting provisions. For example, the Procurement Act 2023 revoked some instruments of retained EU law relating to public procurement - that is the process by which public bodies acquire goods, services and construction works from external providers.

Notwithstanding REULA 2023, retained EU law (renamed assimilated law by REULA 2023) remains a significant source of law. As of March 2025, the dashboard maintained by the UK Government held a total of 6,901 individual pieces of retained EU law/assimilated law, covering around 400 policy areas. 4,417 pieces of this law remain unchanged, 806 amended, 1,484 repealed, 43 replaced and 62 expired, with the status of 89 to be confirmed.

REULA 2023 gives considerable powers to both UK ministers and the devolved administrations, but in this context the powers of the devolved administration are outside the scope of this book. While the previous Conservative Government was keen to eliminate all vestiges of EU law from the UK legal system as quickly as reasonably possible, the current Labour Government does not share this aim and hopes to reset relations with the EU. The rate of change in this area of law is therefore likely to slow down.

Since 1 January 2024 it is accordingly assimilated law that applies in the UK. However, to understand the concept of assimilated law, it is vital to grasp what retained EU law was, as all assimilated law was previously retained EU law.

### 10.1.3 Other instruments

It is also essential in considering the continuing impact of EU law in the UK to take account of

- the Trade and Cooperation Agreement between the UK and EU (TCA) (Trade and Cooperation Agreement between the European Union and the European Atomic Energy Community, of the one part, and the United Kingdom of Great Britain and Northern Ireland, of the other part [2020] OJ L444/14);
- the European Union (Future Relationship) Act 2020 (EU(FR)A 2020); and
- the Product Regulation and Metrology Bill.

The TCA governs the relationship between the UK and EU following the UK's exit from the EU and covers a wide range of issues. The TCA is a free trade agreement and provides for quota and tariff free trade in goods between the UK and EU. It also covers areas such as the movement of services, competition, state subsidies, air and road transport, energy and sustainability, fisheries, data protection, and social security. However, it falls considerably short of the arrangements that the UK had as a Member State and there are more barriers to trade than previously existed.

The EU(FR)A 2020 implements the TCA into domestic UK law. While it and other legislation expressly amends or repeals some domestic law, s 29 of the EU(FR)A 2020 is an extremely unusual provision which has an impact on the application of retained EU law/assimilated law. It is a 'sweeping-up' mechanism and provides that any modification (eg amendment) that is required to be made in existing UK domestic law (statute or common law) in order to implement the provisions of the TCA is deemed by s 29 to have been made. It only applies to provisions of the TCA which are not implemented by another mechanism and aims to ensure that all aspects of the TCA are implemented to the extent necessary to comply with the UK's international obligations.

The Product Regulation and Metrology Bill aims to ensure product safety and quality before products reach consumers. It sets requirements for product design, manufacturing and distribution to protect consumers from harm.

When enacted, the Bill will grant UK ministers the authority to align domestic regulations with EU product standards, particularly for the purpose of environmental impact mitigation. Clause 1(2) in particular allows the Secretary of State to implement domestic provisions resembling relevant EU laws. The Labour Government supports this alignment to reduce business costs and maintain regulatory stability, with decisions being made case by case in the UK's sovereign interest.

## 10.2 What is retained EU law/assimilated law?

Originally, retained EU law was intended to come into force on the day the UK left the EU (exit day). However, in order to give effect to the transitional arrangements provided for in the Withdrawal Agreement, the Withdrawal Agreement Act 2020 amended the EUWA 2018 so that retained EU law came into effect at the end of the transition period. Somewhat confusingly, the EUWA 2018 as amended refers to the end of the transition period as 'IP completion day', with 'IP' standing for 'implementation period', the UK Government's preferred description of the transition period. The Withdrawal Agreement Act 2020 defines IP completion day as 11.00pm on 31 December 2020. Retained EU law was therefore effectively a snapshot of EU law that was in force in the UK immediately before IP completion day, and that law continues in force despite the UK's exit from the EU. However, some key aspects of EU law were repealed with effect from IP completion day. For example, as the UK Government decided that the UK should leave the customs union and single market, UK legislation repealed the bulk of EU law on free movement, which was therefore not retained. Nonetheless, there remained a huge body of retained EU law, which the UK and devolved governments could decide over time whether to keep or replace with their own laws.

It is important to understand the different types of EU legislation that can be converted into retained EU law, and **2.5.3.2** above provides a summary of this. Please ensure in particular that you understand the following types of EU legislation:

- Treaty articles
- Regulations
- Directives
- Decisions.

Section **2.5.3.11** also gives a summary of the three main categories of retained EU law, and whether REULA 2023 converted it into assimilated law namely:

- EU-derived domestic legislation
- direct EU legislation
- rights etc arising under s 2(1) of the ECA 1972.

However, the following paragraphs cover these in more depth.

### 10.2.1 EU-derived domestic legislation

Section 2 of the EUWA 2018 preserved certain 'EU-derived domestic legislation' made under the ECA 1972. It includes secondary legislation enacted by the UK Government, often in the form of regulations (not to be confused with EU Regulations), to implement EU obligations, for example those contained in EU Directives. Under s 2(2) of the ECA 1972, ministers had the power to implement EU Directives into UK law through secondary legislation. For example, the EU adopted Council Directive 93/104/EC ([2003] OJ L299/9) concerning working time, which, subject to certain exemptions, provides for a maximum average working week of 48 hours.

The UK Government then enacted the Working Time Regulations 1998/1833 to implement the Working Time Directive.

If secondary legislation implementing EU obligations had not been converted into retained EU law, it would have fallen away at the end of transition period, leaving huge gaps in UK law. However, secondary legislation such as the Working Time Regulations is preserved to ensure continuity.

Whilst the bulk of EU-derived domestic legislation consists of secondary legislation, it also includes some Acts of Parliament. For example, parts of the Equality Act 2010 were enacted to implement EU anti-discrimination Directives, so falls within the scope of EU-derived domestic legislation. Whilst these Acts would have remained in force despite the end of the transition period, their status as retained EU law was significant, as it was subject to ministers' powers to correct deficiencies (**10.8** below) and benefited from a limited degree of supremacy (**10.9** below). REULA 2023 converted EU-derived domestic legislation into assimilated law and so has changed its status within the UK legal system. However, the impact of REULA 2013 is not as great on this category of retained EU law as on the other categories.

### 10.2.2 Direct EU legislation

Section 3 of the EUWA 2018 converted certain 'direct EU legislation' into UK law so far as 'operative' immediately before 'IP completion day'.

During the UK's membership of the EU, some EU legislation applied directly in the UK legal system without the need for any implementing UK legislation, in particular EU Regulations and certain decisions of the EU. EU Regulations are directly applicable and fully binding in all Member States. Decisions are binding on those to whom they are addressed (eg an EU Member State or an individual company) and are directly applicable. UK courts gave effect to rights and obligations arising under Regulations and decisions under s 2(1) of the ECA 1972.

Following the end of the transition period, EU legislation could no longer directly apply in the UK. Section 3 of the EUWA 2018 ensured that, where appropriate, EU legislation continued to have effect in the UK legal system by converting 'direct EU legislation' into domestic legislation at IP completion day. Where legislation was converted under this section, it was the English language text that existed on IP completion day that was converted.

EU decisions that were addressed only to a Member State other than the UK were not converted into domestic law. Additionally, if EU-derived domestic legislation under s 2 reproduced the effect of an EU Regulation or decision, then it was not converted under s 3. This was to avoid unnecessary duplication.

An example of an EU Regulation that became direct EU legislation is Regulation (EC) 261/2004 ([2004] OJ L46/1) protecting air passenger rights. This Regulation requires airlines to pay compensation to passengers (eg €250 for a flight of less than 1,500 km) if a flight is significantly delayed or cancelled unless due to circumstances beyond the airline's control and in any event to provide assistance (meals, accommodation and phone calls). Passengers in the UK, backed up by judgments in English courts, have claimed millions of pounds in compensation from airlines under this Regulation. Section 3 ensured that airline passengers in the UK continued to benefit from it after IP completion day, though as explained at **10.8** below it was amended slightly.

REULA 2023 converted direct EU legislation into direct assimilated legislation. However, as explained at **10.9** below, it made significant changes to its status.

### 10.2.3 Rights etc arising under s 2(1) of the ECA 1972

Section 4(1) preserved certain rights, powers, liabilities, obligations, restrictions, remedies and procedures recognised and available in UK law immediately before IP completion day under the ECA 1972. It aimed to ensure that any remaining EU rights and obligations that did not fall within the scope of ss 2 and 3 become part of retained EU law.

One of the main types of rights covered by s 4 was directly effective rights contained within EU treaties, ie those provisions of EU treaties that are sufficiently clear, precise and unconditional to confer rights directly on individuals, which they can enforce before national courts without the need for national implementing measures. It is, however, the right that was retained, not the text of the article itself.

The most important directly effective treaty right that became retained EU law in this way was the right for men and women to receive equal pay under Article 157 of the Treaty on the Functioning of the European Union (TFEU). The Equality Act 2010 prohibits sex discrimination in the workplace, so in practice most victims of discrimination would have relied on the Equality Act 2010 rather than the retained rights granted by Article 157. However, should for any reason the right to equal pay under the Equality Act 2010 have fallen short of the rights conferred by Article 157, then a victim of discrimination could have relied on their retained Article 157 rights against their employer to the extent of the shortfall.

Whilst many other treaty articles have direct effect, for example those relating to the free movement of goods, people and services, they did not form part of retained EU law as the UK repealed them due to the Government's decision to leave the single market and customs union.

Directives themselves were as a general rule excluded from the scope of retained EU law (EUWA 2018, s 4(1)) as they were implemented into national law by domestic legislation, which is preserved as EU-derived domestic legislation. However, they are also capable of having direct effect if they have not been implemented or have been implemented incorrectly, although only vertically against the state or state bodies. Where rights arising under directly effective provisions of Directives were of a kind that had been recognised by a UK or EU court or tribunal before IP completion day, rights of that kind became retained EU law. If, however, the right was of a kind that had not been recognised by a court, then it was excluded from retained EU law (EUWA 2018, s 4(2)).

EU Directives did not themselves become part of retained EU law, so any retention of rights and obligations in them depended on their implementation through EU-derived domestic legislation and/or s 4 of the EUWA 2018.

However, s 2 of REULA 2023 repealed s 4 of the European Union (Withdrawal) Act (EUWA) 2018 with effect from the end of 2023, so that no rights retained as a result of that section are enforceable in UK law from that date. This means that individuals (including businesses) can no longer rely on directly effective rights arising under Treaty articles or directives before UK courts. Nevertheless, under powers discussed at **10.9** below, it is possible for the Government to enact statutory instruments to codify rights that had been retained on IP completion day pursuant to s 4. The Government has done this with Article 157 TFEU which provides that men and women should receive equal pay for equal work or work of equal value. The rights granted by Article 157 go beyond those granted by the Equality Act 2010, and so the Government has issued a statutory instrument preserving the directly effective rights granted by Article 157 and codifying case law of the Court of Justice of the European Union (CJEU) to ensure that employees do not lose those rights.

The Finance Act 2024 also provides that s 4 of the EUWA 2018 continues to have effect for the purpose of interpreting VAT and excise law. This means that the principle of consistent interpretation (the *Marleasing* principle (discussed at **2.5.3.6**)) continues to apply to VAT and excise law. However, the principle of direct effect has been abolished, so it is no longer possible for any UK VAT or excise legislation to be quashed or disapplied on the grounds that it is incompatible with EU law.

## 10.3 Status of retained EU law/assimilated law

Section 7 of the EUWA 2018 (as amended by REULA 2023) defines the status of assimilated law. Section 7(1) provides that EU law assimilated under s 2 of the EUWA 2018 (EU-derived domestic legislation) has the same status as it had pre-IP completion day either as primary or secondary legislation.

EU law assimilated under s 3 of the EUWA 2018 (as amended by REULA 2023), however, does not fall into the existing categories as it is neither primary nor secondary legislation; instead it constitutes a new category of domestic law – assimilated direct legislation (previously retained direct EU legislation). Section 7 of the EUWA 2018 subdivides assimilated direct legislation (ie legislation retained under s 3) into two categories:

- assimilated direct 'principal' legislation; and
- assimilated direct 'minor' legislation.

The distinction is very technical. However, assimilated direct principal legislation includes most EU Regulations such as Regulation (EC) 261/2004 governing compensation for flight delays and cancellations. Assimilated direct minor legislation is defined as any assimilated direct legislation that is not assimilated direct principal legislation. This broadly covers EU tertiary legislation (acts adopted by the EU institutions pursuant to powers granted to them by a Regulation or Directive) and EU decisions.

The key difference between 'minor' and 'principal' assimilated direct legislation is that the EUWA 2018 treats the latter as if it were 'primary' legislation for the purposes of the Human Rights Act (HRA) 1998. This prevents it from being declared invalid for incompatibility with the Convention rights. A declaration of incompatibility pursuant to s 4 of the 1998 Act is possible, but this would not invalidate the legislation.

Before REULA 2023 came into force on 1 January 2024, it was easier to amend minor legislation than principal legislation, but both can now be amended in the same way.

## 10.4 Interpretation of retained EU law/assimilated law

Section 6(3) of the EUWA 2018 (as amended by REULA 2023) provides that questions on the meaning of assimilated law that remains 'unmodified' on or after IP completion day by UK law will be determined by UK courts in accordance with relevant 'retained case law'; see **10.5** below for an explanation of this concept.

Section 6(6) provides that questions on the meaning of assimilated law that has been modified, eg amended, on or after IP completion day by UK law can be determined in accordance with relevant retained case law if doing so is consistent with the intention of the modifications.

## 10.5 Retained EU case law/assimilated case law

As stated at **10.4** above, assimilated law is normally to be interpreted in line with assimilated case law. Assimilated case law consists of retained domestic case law and retained EU case law.

Assimilated domestic case law means the principles and decisions laid down by UK courts and tribunals before the end of IP completion day in relation to assimilated law (subject to certain exceptions).

Assimilated EU case law means the principles and decisions laid down by the Court of Justice of the European Union (CJEU) before IP completion day in relation to assimilated law (subject to certain exceptions).

Accordingly, although it is no longer be possible for UK courts to make references to the CJEU pursuant to Article 267 TFEU on questions of EU law, its judgments remain binding on all UK courts below the level of the Court of Appeal (or equivalent courts such as the Court Martial Appeal Court).

## 10.6 Retained general principles of EU law

General principles of EU law are an important source of EU Law, as explained at **2.5.3.3(b)** above. The EUWA 2018 as originally enacted provided for the retention of those general principles of EU law that had been recognised as such by EU case law before IP completion day. However, retained general principles could only be used to interpret retained EU law. Unlike the position before IP completion day, failure to comply with a general principle could not give rise to a right of action. This meant that UK courts could not disapply national legislation that breached a general principle.

However, s 4 of REULA 2023 abolished retained general principles of EU law from the end of 2023. Accordingly, they have not become assimilated law.

The consequence of abolishing them is illustrated by analysing *Kücükdeveci v Swedex GmbH & Co KG* (Case C-555/07) EU:C:2010:21, [2010] ECR I-00365, in which the CJEU stated that national courts had to set aside any provision of national law that breached the general principle of equality. In this case, an employee was suing his employer for age discrimination before a German court. The employer relied on German legislation that permitted employers to discriminate against employees aged under 25 years on the grounds of age. However, as the German law breached the principle of equality, the German court had to disapply the offending German law, enabling the employee to succeed in his claim.

During the UK's membership of the EU, UK courts would have been required to adopt the same approach and to disapply legislation, including primary legislation, that breached the principle of equality. However, after IP completion day this was no longer the case, although until the end of 2023 UK courts would have used the principle of equality to interpret retained EU law in the field of discrimination. Now they are not even an aid to interpretation of assimilated law, though remain relevant to the application of the Withdrawal Agreement between the EU and UK.

## 10.7 Exclusion of state liability

In addition to the exclusions referred to in **10.6** above, the EUWA 2018 also excluded the principle of state liability ('Francovich damages'). In certain circumstances, EU law gives individuals the right to claim damages from a Member State for its failure to implement a Directive at all or properly, or for other breaches of EU law. This was first recognised in the CJEU case of *Francovich v Italian Republic* (Joined Cases C-6/90 and 9/90) ECLI:EU:C:1991:428, [1991] ECR I-5357 so the principle of state liability has also been labelled the right to 'Francovich damages'.

There is a saving for claims for Francovich damages begun within the period of two years beginning with IP completion day so far as the proceedings relate to anything that occurred before IP completion day.

## 10.8 Correcting 'deficiencies' in retained EU law

Section 8 of the EUWA 2018 granted temporary powers for UK Government ministers, and devolved administrations in relation to domestic legislation within areas of devolved competence, to make secondary legislation that corrected 'deficiencies' in retained EU law.

Deficiencies were defined to include:

- provisions that have no practical application after the UK has left the EU;
- provisions on functions that during the UK's membership of the EU were carried out in the EU on the UK's behalf, for example by an EU agency;
- provisions on reciprocal arrangements or rights between the UK and other EU Member States that are no longer in place or are no longer appropriate;

- any other arrangements or rights, including through EU treaties, that are no longer in place or no longer appropriate; and
- EU references that are no longer appropriate.

Deficiencies not on the list but which were 'of a similar kind' to those listed also fell within the scope of the correcting power.

As this list indicates, deficiencies could have arisen for a number of reasons. For example, EU legislation would sometimes require governments of Member States to consult with the European Commission before taking certain action. Following IP completion day, it was no longer appropriate to require the UK Government to consult with the Commission. EU legislation might also contain references to the UK being a Member State. Where such legislation was converted into retained EU law, it would have contained inaccurate references or provided for arrangements that were no longer appropriate. Accordingly, it was possible to correct these deficiencies through secondary legislation.

The power could only be used to correct deficiencies arising from the UK's withdrawal from the EU; it was not a power to make changes of substance to retained EU law.

Regulation (EC) 261/2004 provided an example of where the UK Government corrected a deficiency. The Regulation states that it applies to passengers departing from, or arriving at, an airport in a Member State. The UK Government accordingly adopted a statutory instrument providing that the retained version of the Regulation applied to passengers departing from, or arriving at, an airport in the UK to ensure it made sense after the UK had ceased to be a Member State. Regulation 261/2004 as corrected now forms part of assimilated law.

The power granted to correct deficiencies expired two years from IP completion day, ie on 31 December 2022. However, REULA 2023 gives the Government extensive powers to amend and revoke retained EU law; see **10.11** below.

## 10.9 Supremacy of retained EU law/assimilated law

### 10.9.1 Position pre-REULA 2023

As explained at **2.5.3.11**, retained EU law kept a limited form of supremacy until the end of 2023 when REULA 2023 ended it. Although following IP completion day EU law itself no longer had supremacy over UK law, retained EU law would have had supremacy in limited circumstances. For this purpose there were three categories of law:

- retained EU law;
- UK legislation enacted pre-IP completion day that was not retained EU law; and
- all UK legislation enacted after IP completion day.

Should a conflict have occurred between a provision of retained EU law and a piece of pre-IP completion day legislation that was not retained law, then the former would have prevailed over the latter. For example, if there was a conflict between an EU Regulation adopted in 2010 that had become retained EU law under s 3 of EUWA 2018 and an Act of Parliament enacted in 2018, the regulation of 2010 would have had supremacy over the Act of 2018.

However, REULA 2023 ended the limited supremacy of retained EU law.

### 10.9.2 REULA 2023: abolition of supremacy

Section 3 of REULA 2023 provided for the abolition in the UK of the supremacy of retained EU law from 31 December 2023. Specifically, it ended the supremacy of EU law in relation to any enactment or rule of law whenever passed or made. It also explicitly sets out a new priority rule for assimilated direct legislation (previously retained direct EU legislation) which:

(a) must, so far as possible, be read and given effect in a way which is compatible with all domestic enactments, and

(b) is subject to all domestic enactments, so far as it is incompatible with them.

As explained in the example at **10.9.1** above, if there were a conflict between an EU regulation adopted in 2010 which had become retained EU law and an Act of Parliament enacted in 2018, the EU regulation would have prevailed until 31 December 2023. Now it appears the Act of 2018 will have priority. REULA 2023 has accordingly reversed the priorities that had previously applied in relation to direct legislation.

The Bar Council has criticised abolishing supremacy on the grounds that it creates legal uncertainty. For example, it would retrospectively alter the effect of domestic legislation in a way that the domestic legislator could not have foreseen at the time. The example above illustrates this. When Parliament passed the Act in 2018, the Act would not have overridden the EU Regulation adopted in 2010. Altering the effect of the Act of 2018 several years after it was passed to override the EU Regulation could lead to unpredictable and unforeseen consequences. Moreover, when Parliament passed the Act of 2018, it did so in the knowledge that it would take effect subject to any previously enacted EU legislation. To change the effect of the Act is arguably to contradict Parliament's intention.

REULA 2023 also removed the principle of consistent interpretation (the *Marleasing* principle) in relation to all domestic legislation. This means that UK courts are no longer required to interpret UK regulations enacted to implement an EU Directive consistently with that Directive. This does not necessarily mean that UK courts will disregard the existence of the relevant Directive. Under national principles of statutory interpretation, UK courts are likely to take the Directive into account as an extrinsic aid to interpretation.

Although the principle of supremacy and general principles have been abolished, ministers may by statutory instrument 'recreate' their effect, albeit in a limited form. Thus, a minister can specify that a provision of direct assimilated legislation will prevail over another specific enactment, but not all enactments in general. So, in the above example, a minister could specify that the EU Regulation of 2010 should have priority over the Act of 2018 or any other piece of domestic legislation, though not over domestic legislation in general.

Moreover, the Finance Act 2024 referred to at **10.2** above provides that the supremacy principle will be retained for certain purposes in relation to VAT and excise law, and, likewise, retained general principles will remain relevant to the interpretation of VAT and excise law.

**Table 10.1** below traces how the main categories of EU law were converted into retained EU law and then into assimilated law, and summarises the effect of REULA 2023 on the principle of supremacy.

**Table 10.1** REULA 2023 and the principle of supremacy

| During EU membership | IP completion day | 1 January 2024 | Status under REULA 2023 |
|---|---|---|---|
| Directive implemented by UK statutory instrument or Act | EU-derived domestic legislation (s 2 EUWA) | EU-derived domestic legislation (label unchanged) | Supremacy removed* |
| EU Regulation | Direct EU legislation (s 3 EUWA) | Direct assimilated legislation | Priorities reversed* |
| Directly effective rights under Treaty articles and directives | Saving for rights etc under s 2(1) of the ECA (s 4 EUWA) | Sun-setted unless specifically retained | Supremacy removed* |

*subject to power to grant effect similar to supremacy over specified enactments (**10.12.1** below)

The Government did not analyse the actual impact of ending the principle of supremacy of retained EU law so that it does not apply to assimilated law. Accordingly, the extent to which ending supremacy affects the rights of individuals and businesses in particular cases is unclear. Assimilated law remains an important source of the rules governing consumer rights, data protection, employment law and health and safety, so it was risky to make a change when the impact of that change was unknown. Time will tell whether there will be any adverse consequences for ending supremacy.

### 10.9.3 Incompatibility orders

If a court finds that there is a conflict between a piece of retained direct EU legislation and domestic legislation, then it must issue an incompatibility order (s 8). The Act gives the courts considerable discretion in setting out the legal consequences of the incompatibility in the incompatibility order. The incompatibility order may:

- set out the effect in the case concerned of one provision taking priority over another;
- delay the order coming into force; or
- remove or limit the effect of the operation of the relevant provision in any other way before the coming into force of the order, eg where this might give rise to unfairness to individuals or other effects contrary to the public interest.

However, courts cannot change the order of priority of the conflicting pieces of law. Incompatibility orders are a novelty in the UK's legal system, and it remains to be seen how the courts will use them in practice.

## 10.10 Challenges to retained EU law/assimilated law

As explained at **10.3** above, domestic law that has become assimilated law by virtue of s 2 of the EUWA 2018, as amended by REULA 2023 (EU-derived domestic legislation) continues to be classed as primary or secondary legislation as applicable. EU-derived domestic legislation that is primary legislation will be treated in the same way as any other Act of Parliament.

Secondary legislation that falls within s 2 of the EUWA 2018 can be challenged on the same public law grounds that apply to any other secondary legislation, as covered in ***Administrative Law and Human Rights***.

The EUWA 2018 also provides that no provision of assimilated EU law can be challenged on or after IP completion day on the basis that an EU instrument, such as an EU regulation or decision, was invalid. For example, if an EU regulation had become retained EU law and subsequently assimilated law under s 3 of the EUWA 2018, it is not possible to challenge the validity of the assimilated regulation on the grounds that the original EU regulation was invalid. However, this exclusion does not apply where the CJEU has found the EU instrument to be invalid prior to IP completion day, or where regulations made by a UK minister permit the challenge. The Challenges to Validity of EU Instruments (EU Exit) Regulations 2019 (SI 2019/673) do, in fact, permit such a challenge as they allow the courts to decide challenges to the validity of EU instruments that started before IP completion day but concluded after it.

As explained at **10.3** above, assimilated direct principal legislation is treated as primary legislation for the purposes of challenges under the HRA 1998, ie it can be subject to a declaration of incompatibility, but that finding does not affect its continued validity. Conversely, assimilated direct minor legislation is treated as subordinate legislation for HRA 1998 purposes, so it can be declared invalid if held to be incompatible.

It is likely that a significant number of challenges will be in relation to modifications made to retained EU law by ministers using the powers to correct deficiencies. Although the EUWA 2018 defines deficiencies widely, challenges are probable on the basis that ministers have used them to make substantive policy changes rather than simply to correct deficiencies. There are also likely to be challenges to secondary legislation made by the Government to revoke retained EU law/assimilated law discussed further at **10.12** below.

## 10.11 UK courts and retained EU law/assimilated law

### 10.11.1 Applying retained EU law/assimilated law

The Court of Appeal judgment in *Lipton & Anor v BA City Flyer Ltd* [2021] EWCA Civ 454 provides helpful guidance in applying retained EU law. The case involved Regulation 261/2004 (discussed at **10.2.2** above); the claimants were relying on it to sue the defendant airline for compensation following the cancellation of their flight.

As the Court of Appeal was hearing the claim after IP completion day, it applied the retained version of Regulation 261/2004 even though the events leading to the case took place before IP completion day. However, the Supreme Court, when hearing the appeal from the Court of Appeal's judgment, ruled that the EU text of Regulation 261/2004 as it existed at the date of the claim should apply and not the retained version ([2024] UKSC 24). Although this did not change the outcome of the case, it was therefore unnecessary for the Supreme Court to analyse how to apply the retained version. Accordingly, subject to certain modifications discussed below, Green LJ's analysis remains the most authoritative.

In applying retained EU law, Green LJ set out the following approach:

- It was necessary to determine the status of any relevant EU regulation and whether it had become retained EU law.

  Green LJ found that Regulation 261/2004 was operative prior to IP completion day (11pm on 31 December 2020) and so continued in force as direct EU legislation, a category of retained EU law (EUWA 2018, s 3(1) and (2)).

  The principle of supremacy, albeit limited, applied to Regulation 261/04. It therefore took precedence over any other domestic law that pre-dated IP completion day which might be inconsistent with it (EUWA 2018, s 5(2)).

- It was then necessary to consider whether any domestic UK legislation had amended it.

  As explained at **10.8** above, the UK version of Regulation 261/2004 was amended to ensure that it applies to flights departing from or arriving at UK airports.

- Retained EU law should be given a purposive construction.
- UK courts should take into account pre-IP completion day case law of the CJEU.

  While the Court of Appeal had the power to depart from CJEU, Green LJ did not consider it necessary to do so (see further **10.11.2** below).

- UK courts should take into account general principles of EU law that had been recognised in case law before IP completion day.

  However, in *Lipton* there did not appear to be any relevant general principles.

- Finally, it was necessary to analyse whether retained EU law has been amended or superseded by the TCA and the EU(FR)A 2020.

  The TCA provides that the EU and UK must ensure there are effective remedies in the pursuit of consumer protection to protect air passengers whose flights are cancelled or delayed. As Regulation 261/2004 already provided effective procedures, there was no need to use s 29 of the EU(FR)A 2020 to amend it.

  Green LJ thought that s 29 of the EU(FR)A 2020 automatically repealed or rewrote any laws (statute or case law) existing on IP completion day that were inconsistent with the TCA. However, on appeal, the Supreme Court took the position that s 29 does not have the effect Green LJ suggested regarding provisions of the TCA 'which are expressed in ... general and aspirational terms', though it acknowledged that, if a future party were to submit an argument that the effect of s 29 is to modify the wording of some existing domestic law, then the court should consider the effect of s 29 afresh without regard to Green LJ's views.

There are as yet no reported judgments on how the courts will approach assimilated law. It is likely that they will adopt a similar approach to that in *Lipton* subject to the following:

- They will no longer consider if there are any relevant general principles of EU law following their abolition by REULA 2023.
- While it is probable that they will continue to adopt a purposive approach, they will no longer use the *Marleasing* principle of consistent interpretation.
- They will also need to consider any arguments based on s 29 of the EU(FR)A 2020 having regard to the Supreme Court's views of its effect.

### 10.11.2 Departing from retained/assimilated EU case law

Retained case law comprises both judgments of the CJEU handed down before IP completion day – retained/assimilated EU case law – and judgments handed down by domestic courts before IP completion day – retained/assimilated domestic case law. Both have precedential value, but there are differences between the two.

#### 10.11.2.1 Retained/assimilated EU case law

Originally, the EUWA 2018 only gave the power to depart from retained EU case law to the UK Supreme Court and the High Court of Justiciary as the final criminal court of appeal in Scotland in cases where there is no appeal to the UK Supreme Court. Section 6(6) provided that in deciding whether to depart from any retained EU case law, the Supreme Court or the High Court of Justiciary had to apply the same test as it would apply in deciding whether to depart from its own case law. Thus, the Supreme Court had to apply the principles contained in the *Practice Statement (Judicial Precedent)* [1966] 1 WLR 1234.

However, s 6(5A)–(5D) of the EUWA 2018 (inserted by the Withdrawal Agreement Act 2020) gave the Government the power to make regulations by extending the ability to depart from retained EU case law to additional courts and tribunals. The Government accordingly adopted the European Union (Withdrawal) Act 2018 (Relevant Court) (Retained EU Case Law) Regulations 2020 (SI 2020/1525) extending the power to depart from retained EU case law to the Court of Appeal and courts of equivalent status.

In deciding whether to depart from retained EU case law, these courts had to apply the same test as the Supreme Court would apply in deciding whether to depart its own case law (2020 Regulations, reg 5). Thus, they also had to apply the principles in the *Practice Statement*. REULA 2023 has renamed retained EU case law as 'assimilated EU case law' (s 5). REULA 2023 introduces a new test discussed at **10.11.4** below which courts should apply in deciding to depart from assimilated EU case law, but these provisions are not yet in force. Accordingly, the *Practice Statement* remains relevant, but there is little guidance on how the courts will exercise their power to depart from assimilated EU case law. However, it is likely that the courts will exercise their power sparingly, as a court will not overturn an earlier decision merely because it believes that decision is wrong. For example, if an earlier albeit wrong decision has been relied on by many people and businesses in arranging their affairs, it is unlikely that it will be overturned. Overturning the earlier decision could cause considerable difficulties for everyone who had relied on it in good faith, as judicial decisions apply retrospectively. The courts are likely to leave it to the legislature to make any changes, as statutes normally apply prospectively only and would not upset existing arrangements. The Court of Appeal judgment in *TuneIn Inc v Warner Music UK Ltd* [2021] EWCA Civ 441 confirms that the courts are likely to take a cautious approach.

TuneIn is an internet radio app which provided hyperlinks to various radio stations around the world. Some of these stations played music without obtaining the consent of the holders of the copyright in the works played. The holders of the copyright sued TuneIn for copyright infringement under the Copyright, Designs and Patents Act 1988. Section 20 of the 1988 Act prohibits a 'communication to the public' of a work protected by copyright without the requisite consents, and CJEU case law had held that providing hyperlinks was a communication to the public. TuneIn asked the Court of Appeal to depart from the CJEU's case law. The Court of Appeal declined to do so for various reasons, including the following:

- There had been no change in the domestic legislation (ie retained EU law). Parliament could amend it, but for the time being it was Parliament's will that the legislation should remain in its current form. It would therefore be inappropriate for the courts to change the law when Parliament had not yet chosen to do so.

- There had been no change in the international legislative framework, which was relevant in circumstances where the EU law in question gave effect to other international law obligations. Where an issue is regulated by international treaties, courts in the states that have signed the relevant treaty should seek consistency of interpretation, rather than unilaterally adopting their own interpretations.
- The interpretation of the relevant provision (whether hyperlinking amounted to 'communication to the public') was 'a difficult task' as the legislation contained no guidance and there was a conflict between copyrights which are exploited on a territorial basis and the global nature of the internet. According to Arnold LJ, the CJEU 'has unrivalled experience in confronting this issue in a variety of factual scenarios. Moreover, it has developed and refined its jurisprudence over time.'
- Although there was distinguished academic commentary criticising the CJEU's view, there was also considerable support for it. (This seems to imply that overwhelming academic criticism of a judgment might be grounds for departing from it.)
- Jurisprudence from other courts in countries such as Australia, Canada and the USA was materially irrelevant as the statutory framework differed in those countries and their case law did not offer helpful and settled guidance.
- Departing from the CJEU's case law would result in returning to the drawing board and starting all over again, creating considerable legal uncertainty for little purpose as it would not provide TuneIn with a clear defence to the infringement proceedings in any case.

While the judgment in *TuneIn* concerned retained EU law rather than assimilated law, it is unlikely that UK courts will change their approach unless the new test provided for by REULA 2023 comes into force. However, in *Industrial Cleaning v Intelligent Cleaning Equipment* [2023] EWCA Civ 1451, the Court of Appeal did depart from the CJEU's decision in *Budejovicky Budvararodni Podnik v Anheuser-Busch Inc* (Case C-482/09) EU:C:2011:605, a case involving trade marks.

The reason for doing so was that the CJEU's judgment in *Budvar* was simply a bald statement of its conclusions and did not contain any analysis of the issues. It was also an 'isolated judgment', not entirely consistent with other CJEU cases. In contrast the CJEU cases considered in *TuneIn* constituted well-reasoned and settled jurisprudence. While courts should be slow to depart from settled case law in the interests of legal certainty, that was not a factor in *Industrial Cleaning* as few trade mark owners would have based their strategies on the *Budvar* judgment.

### 10.11.3 Departing from retained/assimilated domestic case law

During the UK's membership of the EU, UK courts would sometimes interpret provisions of EU law without referring the question to the CJEU. Generally, these judgments have the same precedential value as any other judgment by a UK court. The approach of the Court of Appeal in *Merck Serono v Comptroller-General of Patents* [2025] EWCA Civ 45 illustrates this. A key issue considered by the Court of Appeal was whether it could depart from assimilated domestic case law. It decided that the usual domestic rules of precedent applied. This meant that the court could only depart from one of its previous decisions that formed part of assimilated case law if one of the exceptions in *Young v Bristol Aeroplane Co Ltd* [1944] KB 718 applied. (According to this case, the Court of Appeal is only able to depart from its own decisions in limited circumstances, eg if its own decisions conflict or its previous decision has been implicitly overruled by the Supreme Court.)

In accordance with the usual rules of precedent, it remains bound by judgments of the Supreme Court, but can depart from judgments of lower courts.

### 10.11.4 REULA 2023: departing from assimilated case law

#### (a) Assimilated EU case law

Section 6 of REULA 2023 sets out a new test for the Supreme Court and Court of Appeal to apply once its provisions come into force. It lists the following non-exhaustive factors they must take into account in deciding whether to depart from assimilated EU case law:

(a) the fact that decisions of a foreign court are not usually binding;

(b) any changes of circumstances which are relevant to the assimilated EU case law; and

(c) the extent to which the assimilated EU case law restricts the proper development of domestic law.

The intention may be to make it more likely for the courts to depart from assimilated EU case law, as the previous Conservative Government was keen for the UK's legal system and regulatory framework to develop according to common law principles which it believed were better suited to the UK than civil law principles. However, while the previous Government had issued a commencement order providing that the new test should come into force on 1 October 2024, the Labour Government revoked the commencement order. As the Labour Government hopes to reset relations with the EU, it is possible that the new test will never come into force.

While lower courts will not be able to depart from assimilated EU case law, REULA 2023 establishes a reference system whereby a lower court may refer a point of law to a higher court for its decision. The point of law must be relevant to the case the lower court is hearing and, if so, it may exercise its discretion to refer if it is bound by the assimilated case law and the issue is one of general public importance. The introduction of the reference system is, however, dependent on s 6 coming into force.

The law officers of the UK Government and devolved administrations are also given the power to make references regarding points of assimilated EU case law which arise in legal proceedings.

**(b) Assimilated domestic case law**

The higher courts will, if s 6 ever comes into force, apply a similar test in deciding whether to depart from assimilated domestic case law, only differing on the first factor which instead reads 'the extent to which the assimilated domestic case law is determined or influenced by assimilated EU case law from which the court has departed or would depart'.

### 10.11.5 Post IP-completion day

Section 6(1) of the EUWA 2018 provides that UK courts and tribunals cease to be bound by principles laid down by the CJEU, or any decisions made by that court, after IP completion day, though such judgments may have persuasive effect (s 6(2)). This means that assimilated EU case law comprises only those judgments of the CJEU that were handed down pre-IP completion day. UK courts may therefore have regard to post-IP completion day judgments of the CJEU, but will not be bound by them.

---

## 10.12 REULA 2023: ministerial powers

As part of the Government's wider ambitions for regulatory reform and to reduce the impact of EU law in the UK's legal system, REULA 2023 gives ministers extensive powers.

### 10.12.1 Power to restate or reproduce

These powers are set out in ss 11–16 of REULA 2023.

#### 10.12.1.1 Restating retained EU law

Ministers had the power to restate retained secondary EU law (all retained EU law that was not contained in primary legislation) up till 31 December 2023. The reason this power ended then is that retained EU law became assimilated law on 1 January 2024, and ministers have continuing equivalent powers regarding assimilated law.

#### 10.12.1.2 Power to restate assimilated law or reproduce retained EU rights, powers, liabilities etc

Ministers also have the power to restate secondary assimilated law.

Ministers may also reproduce directly effective rights that became retained EU law by virtue of s 4 of the EUWA 2018. See **10.2.3** above for an example of this in relation to Article 157 TFEU.

As part of any restatement, ministers cannot reproduce into domestic legislation the principle of supremacy or general principles, but ministers may reproduce an effect that is equivalent to them. This enables ministers to achieve the same policy outcome as the retained EU law/assimilated law being restated, where they consider it appropriate. In restating retained EU law/assimilated law, ministers may:

- resolve ambiguities;
- remove doubts or anomalies;
- facilitate improvement in the clarity or accessibility of the law.

The Aviation (Consumers) (Amendment) Regulations 2023 (SI 2023/1370) ('the Aviation Regulations 2023') provide an example of a restatement of retained EU law. EU Regulation 261/2004 provides that airlines must compensate passengers for flight cancellations and delays in certain circumstances. Regulation 261/2004 subsequently became retained EU law and is now assimilated law. There has been a considerable amount of litigation concerning the interpretation of Regulation 261/2004 leading to judgments by the CJEU clarifying ambiguities and uncertainties in the text. However, under REULA 2023, the supremacy of retained EU law ceased to have effect at the end of 2023 and assimilated law is now interpreted differently from retained EU law. The Aviation Regulations 2023 accordingly restate and codify certain key principles derived from CJEU case law by inserting them into Regulation 261/2004 to ensure that the changes to the status of retained EU law made by REULA 2023 do not create uncertainty regarding the interpretation and application of Regulation 261/2004.

#### 10.12.1.3 Power to revoke etc

Ministers also have the power as regard retained EU law/assimilated law to:

- revoke it without replacement;
- revoke and restate it, and
- revoke or replace it with an 'appropriate' provision that 'achieve[s] the same or similar objectives' as the provisions being revoked. In replacing retained EU law, ministers may not impose new regulatory burdens.

The powers listed at **10.12.1.2** and **10.12.1.3** expire on 23 June 2026.

#### 10.12.1.4 Status of restated or replaced retained EU law/assimilated law

Where ministers have used their powers to restate or replace retained EU law or assimilated law, the effect of the restatement or replacement is that the relevant law will be contained in a domestic statutory instrument and will not form part of retained EU law or assimilated law. Accordingly, the statutory instrument carrying out the restatement or replacement is domestic law and is subject to normal domestic principles of statutory interpretation and precedent, and not to the provisions governing assimilated law. This means that even where a piece of retained EU law has been restated verbatim, assimilated EU case law will merely be persuasive. Overall, there is the risk that issues that have been settled by judgments of the CJEU will be relitigated, causing uncertainty, expense and delay. However, as illustrated by the Aviation Regulations 2023 above, the restatement or replacement may codify relevant CJEU judgments.

#### 10.12.1.5 Extent of powers

The Secondary Legislation Scrutiny Committee of the House of Lords believes that the powers given to ministers are too wide-ranging due to the absence of consultation on the changes to retained EU law and the lack of effective parliamentary scrutiny. While Parliament will need to pass an Act to change primary assimilated law, much secondary assimilated law is of considerable importance.

For its part the previous Conservative Government claimed that the Act would make it easier to amend or remove outdated retained EU law and to get rid of burdensome 'red tape'. Many EU laws which were retained were originally agreed as a messy compromise between 28 different EU Member States and often did not reflect the UK's own priorities or objectives, nor did many receive sufficient scrutiny in the UK's democratic institutions.

## 10.13 EU law/retained EU law and assimilated law

Despite the UK's exit from the EU and the changes to retained EU law wrought by REULA 2023, EU law through the medium of assimilated law remains a significant source of UK law and is likely to remain so for the foreseeable future. **Table 10.2** below summarises how REULA 2023 has relabelled retained EU law. Despite the abolition of supremacy and the general principles of EU law, assimilated law retains significant characteristics derived from EU law.

**Table 10.2** Retained EU law and assimilated law

| *Name until 31 December 2023* | *Name since 1 January 2024* |
|---|---|
| Retained EU law | Assimilated law |
| Retained case law | Assimilated case law |
| Retained direct EU legislation | Assimilated direct legislation |
| Retained direct minor EU legislation | Assimilated direct minor legislation |
| Retained direct principal EU legislation | Assimilated direct principal legilation |
| Retained domestic case law | Assimilated domestic case law |
| Retained EU case law | Assimilated EU case law |

## 10.14 The Withdrawal Agreement

In October 2019 the UK Government and the EU reached agreement on a Withdrawal Agreement, which set out the terms for the UK's exit from the EU. It entered into force on 1 February 2020 together with the Political Declaration setting out the framework of the future EU-UK partnership. The Withdrawal Agreement is legally binding in international law, whereas the Political Declaration is not legally binding but aimed to set out the parameters of the negotiations for the future relationship between the UK and EU.

### 10.14.1 Scope of the Withdrawal Agreement

The Withdrawal Agreement covers a number of issues, including the following:

- **Citizens' rights**: The Withdrawal Agreement protects the rights of UK citizens living in the EU and EU citizens living in the UK at the end of the transition period, as well as their family members. They will have the right to continue to live and work in their host state. This also applies to citizens who moved to the UK or the EU during the transition period, ie after the UK's exit from the EU but before IP completion day.

  The Withdrawal Agreement states that citizens may need to apply for a residence status in their host state in accordance with the host state's law. EU citizens resident in the UK must apply using the EU Settlement Scheme. Citizens who have been living in the host state for five years continuously will be eligible for permanent residence (termed 'settled status' in the UK).

- **Financial settlement:** The UK agreed to abide by the financial commitments it made as a Member State, including its contributions to the EU budget.
- **The Northern Ireland Protocol**: This aims to avoid the introduction of a hard border on the island of Ireland between Northern Ireland and the Republic of Ireland should the UK and EU fail to agree a free trade agreement that deals satisfactorily with the border issues.
- **Governance and dispute resolution**: A joint committee oversees the Withdrawal Agreement. It comprises representatives from – and is co-chaired by – the EU and the UK. The UK and EU will first seek to resolve disputes through the joint committee where they will try to find a solution. If the committee cannot agree, then either the EU or the UK can request that the dispute be referred to an arbitration panel.

The provisions of the Withdrawal Agreement that lawyers practising in England and Wales are most likely to come across relate to citizens' rights. These are likely to remain relevant for many decades as not only EU citizens born in the UK before IP completion day will be able to rely on them, but also their children.

### 10.14.2 Application of the Withdrawal Agreement in the UK

Article 4 of the Withdrawal Agreement states that the provisions of the Withdrawal Agreement itself and the provisions of EU law that it incorporates shall have the same effect in UK law as they produce within the EU and EU Member States. This includes the ability of individuals (including businesses) to rely directly on provisions contained or referred to in the Agreement that meet the criteria for direct effect under EU law. One of the main practical effects of this is that EU citizens living in the UK at the end of the transition period should be able to rely on the direct effect of the citizens' rights provisions in the Withdrawal Agreement.

Section 7A of EUWA 2018 (inserted by the Withdrawal Agreement Act) provides for the enforcement of rights arising under the Withdrawal Agreement in very similar terms to those contained in the ECA 1972 regarding the EU Treaties. This gives supremacy to the Withdrawal Agreement in much the same way that the ECA 1972 gave supremacy to the EU Treaties. Direct effect will continue to play a role in UK law, albeit in a more limited field.

### 10.14.3 Citizens' rights

Even though most of the EU legislation regarding free movement of persons does not form part of retained EU law as the UK has repealed it, much of that legislation remains relevant after the UK's withdrawal from the EU under the Withdrawal Agreement. For example, whether UK citizens, EU27 citizens and their respective family members are eligible for permanent residence depends largely on whether they satisfy the criteria set in relevant EU legislation.

Additionally, UK courts are still be able to make Article 267 references concerning the citizens' rights provisions in the Withdrawal Agreement for a period of up to eight years after the end of the transition period. However, this is a discretionary power in that UK courts are not obliged to make a reference, unlike the position during the UK's membership of the EU when references were in certain circumstances mandatory. Nevertheless, if a UK court does make a reference, it will be bound by the CJEU's ruling.

As indicated above, the wording of the Withdrawal Agreement also suggests that the citizens' rights provisions have direct effect, so UK and EU27 citizens and their respective family members are able to rely on them even if national legislation implementing those provisions is defective. For example, suppose UK immigration legislation denies an EU citizen rights granted to them by the Withdrawal Agreement. The EU citizen will be able to enforce those rights in a UK court and possibly also claim damages under the *Francovich* principle for any loss suffered.

The case of *R (Independent Monitoring Authority for the Citizens' Rights Agreements) v Secretary of State for the Home Department* [2022] EWHC 3274 (Admin) provides a good example of the direct effect of the Withdrawal Agreement. Following the UK's exit from the EU, the UK Government introduced an EU Settlement Scheme enabling EU nationals resident in the UK on IP completion day to obtain residence rights in the UK. The Administrative Court issued a declaration that an aspect of the Settlement Scheme was unlawful, as it breached the Withdrawal Agreement by making it harder for EU nationals who had lived in the UK for less than five years to obtain permanent residence. The Administrative Court applied the direct effect of the Withdrawal Agreement in reaching this conclusion.

Subsequently, in *AT v Secretary of State for Work and Pensions* [2023] EWCA Civ 1307, the Court of Appeal held that the Charter of Fundamental Rights applied to EU citizens with pre-settled status. EU citizens who fall within the scope of the Withdrawal Agreement are therefore able to rely on its provisions. Accordingly, the Secretary of State was required to take into account the claimant's fundamental rights (and the rights of her child) when making his decision whether to refuse her universal credit.

The judgment of the Northern Ireland Court of Appeal in *Re Dillon (Northern Ireland Troubles (Legacy and Reconciliation) Act 2023)* [2024] NICA 59 is also significant. The Northern Ireland Troubles (Legacy and Reconciliation Act) 2023 ('the Legacy Act') provided that criminal and civil investigations and inquests into events arising out of the Troubles should cease and be replaced with investigations carried out by a new body, the Independent Commission for Reconciliation and Information Recovery ('ICRIC'), which had the power to grant conditional immunity for perpetrators who cooperate with it.

*Re Dillon* involved numerous grounds of challenge to the Legacy Act including some on human rights grounds discussed at **8.8.3** above. A further ground was that it breached the Victims' Directive (Directive 2012/29/EU of the European Parliament and of the Council of 25 October 2012 establishing minimum standards on the rights, support and protection of victims of crime, and replacing Council Framework Decision 2001/220/JHA). The Victims' Directive had been implemented into UK law, and hence Northern Ireland law. One of its key provisions is that victims must be able to review a decision not to prosecute, a right which would be infringed where the ICRIC granted immunity from prosecution under the Legacy Act. The Belfast/Good Friday Agreement of 1998 which ended the Troubles includes provisions protecting the rights of victims; the Victims' Directive gave effect to those provisions. The Northern Ireland Protocol (now known as the Windsor Framework), part of the Withdrawal Agreement agreed between the UK and the EU, provides that there will be no diminution of such protections as a result of Brexit. The Northern Ireland Court of Appeal, invoking s 7A of the EUWA 2018, accordingly disapplied those parts of the Legacy Act that breached the Victims' Directive.

## Summary

In this chapter you have examined the concept of retained EU law/assimilated law. EU law pervaded into large parts of the UK legal system and repealing and replacing it prior to the UK's exit from the EU would have been impossible. EUWA 2018 aimed to ensure legal continuity and a functioning statute post-exit by taking a snapshot of EU law as it existed in the UK at the end of the transition period (defined as IP completion day) and converting it into 'retained EU law', a novel type of law with its own characteristics.

REULA 2023 made some significant changes that came into effect on 1 January 2024. REULA 2023 renamed retained EU law as 'assimilated law' and made changes to its status.

### Assimilated law

The main categories of assimilated law are:

- EU-derived domestic legislation (secondary legislation and primary legislation enacted to implement the UK's EU obligations)
- Direct assimilated legislation (primarily EU Regulations and decisions).

Retained EU law kept a limited form of supremacy in that it prevailed over other legislation enacted pre-IP completion day. Conversely, legislation enacted after IP completion day prevailed over retained EU law. However, REULA 2023 abolished the principle of supremacy.

**Legislative powers**

REULA 2023 gives relevant national authorities such as the UK Government and the devolved governments the power to reform secondary retained EU law and assimilated law by introducing secondary legislation to amend, revoke, restate and/or replace retained EU law and assimilated law. Ministers can reproduce the legal effects associated with retained EU law/assimilated in restated EU law or assimilated law, including the effect of supremacy in relation to specific enactments. The restated law may include relevant case law from the CJEU.

**The Withdrawal Agreement**

Although the Withdrawal Agreement covers a range of issues relating to the UK's exit from the EU, it is the citizens' rights provisions that practising lawyers are most likely to encounter. The key point is that these provisions appear to have direct effect, and that means that EU citizens will be able to rely on them in national courts should domestic UK legislation fail to protect their rights adequately.

## Sample questions

**Question 1**

An EU Directive (fictitious) adopted in 2017 provides that Member States must ensure that the use of latex gloves is prohibited in restaurants, cafeterias and other places that serve hot food for consumption on the premises. The Directive was adopted due to medical evidence that latex gloves were causing an allergic reaction. The Directive further provides that Member States should implement it by 30 November 2019. The UK Government took no steps to implement it. In May 2020 the CJEU ruled that the provisions of the Directive have direct effect.

After IP completion day but before the end of 2023, a woman working in a cafeteria operated by a government department suffered an allergic reaction as a result of wearing latex gloves. Last month a man working in the cafeteria also suffered an allergic reaction as a result of wearing latex gloves.

**Which of the following best explains whether the woman and the man can make a claim against the government department based on the Directive?**

A The woman can bring a claim can bring a claim based on the rights arising under the Directive vertically against a state body, but not the man because the harm he suffered occurred after the end of 2023.

B Both the woman and the man can bring a claim based on the rights arising under the Directive vertically against a state body.

C Neither the woman nor the man can bring a claim as the harm they suffered occurred after IP completion day.

D Neither the woman nor the man can bring a claim as rights arising under directives ceased to be enforceable after the end of 2023.

E Neither the woman nor the man can bring a claim as the principle of supremacy of EU law was abolished with effect from the end of 2023.

**Answer**

Option A is correct. Directives are capable of having direct effect if they have not been implemented or implemented incorrectly, although only vertically against the state or state bodies. As the rights granted by the Directive in this question were of a kind that had been recognised by a UK or EU court or tribunal before IP completion day, the rights it granted became retained EU law under s 4 of EUWA 2018. However, s 2 of REULA 2023 repealed s 4 of EUWA 2018 with effect from the end of 2023, so rights arising under directives are no longer enforceable from that date and have accordingly not become assimilated law. The woman can therefore bring a claim because the harm she suffered occurred before the end of 2023, but not the man as s 4 of EUWA 2018 no longer applied when he suffered his harm.

Option B is wrong because only the woman can bring a claim, as explained above.

Option C is wrong as the woman can bring a claim for harm suffered after IP completion day but before the end of 2023.

Option D is wrong. Although rights arising under directives ceased to be enforceable from the end of 2023, the harm the woman suffered occurred before then so she can still bring an action based on the law that was in force at that time.

While it is true that REULA 2023 ended the supremacy of EU law from the end of 2023, Option E is wrong as the supremacy of EU law is not relevant to this scenario.

**Question 2**

A woman wants to pursue an equal pay claim based on the rights granted by Article 157 TFEU against her employer and on judgments of the Court of Justice of the European Union regarding the scope of Article 157 TFEU. The woman claims that the employer newspaper has infringed her right to equal pay for work of equal value under Art 157 TFEU.

**Which of the following options best represents the approach an English court is likely to adopt towards her claim?**

A The court will enforce her rights under Article 157 TFEU because directly effective rights arising under the TFEU have become assimilated law.

B The court will enforce her rights to equal pay as defined by Article 157 TFEU because the UK government has passed secondary legislation restating the effect of Article 157 TFEU and relevant CJEU judgments. This restatement forms part of normal domestic law.

C The court will enforce her rights to equal pay as defined by Article 157 TFEU because the UK government has passed secondary legislation converting the rights granted by Article 157 TFEU and relevant CJEU judgments into assimilated law.

D The court will not enforce her rights under Article 157 TFEU because the UK has left the EU so rights arising under the TFEU are irrelevant.

E The court will not enforce her rights to equal pay provided for in Article 157 because directly effective rights arising under treaty articles do not form part of assimilated law, despite being retained EU law.

**Answer**

Option B is the correct answer. Rights etc arising under s 2(1) of the ECA 1972 became retained EU law (s 4 EUWA 2018), and the right to equal pay was a prime example of such a right. However, s 2 of REULA 2023 abolished such rights at the end of 2023, but gave the government the power to restate them by way of statutory instrument (REULA 2023, s 12). The government accordingly adopted regulations restating the effect of Article 157 TFEU and associated CJEU case law (Equality Act 2010 (Amendment) Regulations 2023). The restatement, though, is not assimilated law but normal domestic law (REULA 2023, s 12(3)).

Option A is wrong because REULA 2023 abolished directly effective Treaty rights from the end of 2023, even though they had originally formed part of retained EU law.

Option C is wrong as the restatement of Article 157 TFEU and associated case law is not assimilated law.

Option D is wrong as it clear from the above explanation that Treaty rights remained relevant in the UK legal system after IP completion day.

Option E is wrong as it does not take into account the restatement of the rights granted by Article 157 TFEU.

**Question 3**

A man who is a Danish citizen has been resident in the UK for over five years and applies for settled status. Under the terms of the Withdrawal Agreement governing the UK's exit from the EU, he is entitled to permanent residence in the UK. The Home Office rejects his application on the grounds that a section in an Act (fictitious) of the UK Parliament excludes a person in his position from settled status. The Act does not, however, attempt to override the Withdrawal Agreement.

**Can the man challenge the Home Office's refusal to grant him settled status?**

A No, because an Act of Parliament will automatically override conflicting provisions in the Withdrawal Agreement.

B No, because the Withdrawal Agreement is an international treaty, which does not give rise to rights in UK law.

C Yes, because international treaties are automatically incorporated into UK law when ratified by the UK Government.

D Yes, because UK legislation has provided for the direct effect of the relevant provisions of the Withdrawal Agreement.

E Yes, because the UK Parliament cannot legislate contrary to international treaties.

**Answer**

Option D is correct. EUWA 2018 provides for the Withdrawal Agreement, including the citizens' rights provisions, to have direct effect, so its provisions will override the conflicting UK statute. If the UK statute had expressly and unequivocally overridden the relevant provisions of the Withdrawal Agreement, then UK courts would have applied the statute. However, the question indicates that is not the case, so option A is wrong. Option B is wrong; although international treaties do not in themselves give rise to rights in UK law, EUWA 2018 has incorporated the Withdrawal Agreement into UK law.

Option C is wrong because international treaties need to be incorporated into UK law to have direct effect. However, the Withdrawal Agreement Act 2020 did this. Option E is wrong because Parliament can legislate contrary to international treaties, as Parliament is sovereign. Nonetheless, any such legislation would breach international law.

# Index

## E

## I



## J

## Q



## R